T0327500

Early Stage Valuation

The Wiley Finance series contains books written specifically for finance and investment professionals as well as sophisticated individual investors and their financial advisors. Book topics range from portfolio management to e-commerce, risk management, financial engineering, valuation and financial instrument analysis, as well as much more. For a list of available titles, visit our Web site at www.WileyFinance.com.

Founded in 1807, John Wiley & Sons is the oldest independent publishing company in the United States. With offices in North America, Europe, Australia and Asia, Wiley is globally committed to developing and marketing print and electronic products and services for our customers' professional and personal knowledge and understanding.

Early Stage Valuation

A Fair Value Perspective

ANTONELLA PUCA

WILEY

Published by John Wiley & Sons, Inc., Hoboken, New Jersey.

Published simultaneously in Canada.

For general information on our other products and services or for technical support, please contact our Customer Care Department within the United States at (800) 762-2974, outside the United States at (317) 572-3993 or fax (317) 572-4002.

Wiley publishes in a variety of print and electronic formats and by print-on-demand. Some material included with standard print versions of this book may not be included in e-books or in print-on-demand. If this book refers to media such as a CD or DVD that is not included in the version you purchased, you may download this material at http://booksupport.wiley.com. For more information about Wiley products, visit www.wiley.com.

Library of Congress Cataloging-in-Publication Data:

Names: Puca, Antonella, author.
Title: Early stage valuation : a fair value perspective / author
   Antonella Puca.
Description: First Edition. | Hoboken : Wiley, 2020. | Series: Wiley
   finance series | Includes index.
Identifiers: LCCN 2020009976 (print) | LCCN 2020009977 (ebook) | ISBN
   9781119613633 (hardback) | ISBN 9781119613671 (adobe pdf) | ISBN
   9781119613619 (epub)
Subjects: LCSH: Business enterprises–Valuation. | Financial
   statements–Standards. | Fair value–Accounting. |
   Accounting–Standards.
Classification: LCC HG4028.V3 E364 2020 (print) | LCC HG4028.V3 (ebook) |
   DDC 658.15–dc23
LC record available at https://lccn.loc.gov/2020009976
LC ebook record available at https://lccn.loc.gov/2020009977

Cover Design: Wiley
Cover Image: The Lady and the Unicorn: Sight © RMN-Grand Palais /Art Resource, NY

Printed in the United States of America

10 9 8 7 6 5 4 3 2 1

Le Dor Va Dor
To Anna, Paola, and Anna

Contents

Acknowledgments

As I think of the individuals who participated in this book, I would like to recall three people who are not with us today, but who are present in its pages: my father, Carlo Puca, who introduced me to the world of finance on the floor of the stock exchange in Naples, Italy; Francesco Lucarelli, who helped me find my way as a student of Economics and Finance at the University Federico II of Naples; and Morton Kenner, who welcomed me in New York and introduced me to the world of private investment funds in the early 1990s. I would also like to thank the friends, mentors, and colleagues who have accompanied me in my professional journey and have helped shape the content of this book. I especially thank, in order of acquaintance, Maria Teresa Della Cioppa, Massimo Marrelli, Todd Goldman, David Sung, Jeffrey Schwartz, David Kaufman, Jacques Gagné, John Budzyna, and Jeff Yager for their guidance over the years.

In writing this book, it has been a privilege to collaborate with Neil Beaton, Alexander Davie, Andreas Dal Santo, John Jackman, and Mark Zyla as contributors and co-authors of some chapters. I wish to express my gratitude to the friends and colleagues who have read and shared their views on selected chapters, and whose perspectives helped inform my understanding of key issues around the topic of this book, including William Bareiss, Mark Bhasin, Keith Black, Melissa Brady, Rich Carson, Shilpa Chandra, Chandu Chilakapati, Raffaele Cicala, Athan Demakos, David Dufendach, Andy Dzamba, Erik Edson, Darrin Erickson, Davide Erro, Alfredo Gallone, Jonathan Grubbs, Maria Hall, Sidney Hardee, Brett Hickey, Tom Kehoe, Rahul Keshap, Gunes Kulaligil, Lorre Jay, Steve Jugan, Vincent LaRosa, Paul McCaffrey, Andrew Metrick, Elvira Passeggio, Bruno Pinto, Jerry Pinto, Ray Rath, Sindhu Rajesh, Lorenzo Restagno, Michael Rose, Todd Rosen, Enrico Rovere, John Sawyer, Greg Siegel, Paolo Siniscalco, Mark Smith, Christine Song, Kris Thiessen, Heidi Morrow, Bill Trent, Laura Yunger, Jared Waters, Michael Weinberg, and my husband, Alexander Gamburd. I also would like to thank Aswath Damodaran, whose published work has been especially influential in certain areas of my analysis and in that of many others. I thank Sheck Cho, Elisha Benjamin, Beula Jaculin and the production team at Wiley for their support during the production of this book.

This book is dedicated to my daughter, Anna Gamburd, my mother, Paola Leosini, and my grandmother, Anna Leosini, as everyday sources of wisdom, inspiration, and strength.

About the Author

Antonella Puca, CFA, CPA/ABV, CEIV, is a senior director with Alvarez & Marsal Valuation Services LLC in New York. She specializes in the valuation of private equity and venture-backed companies for financial and tax reporting, M&A transactions, buy-sell agreements, estate planning, and litigation purposes. Prior to that, Antonella has been part of the alternative investment group at KPMG/Rothstein Kass, where she helped launch RK's Bay area practice, the global investment fund practice of EY in San Francisco and New York, the financial services team at RSM US, and the valuation team at BlueVal Group in New York.

Antonella is currently serving on the Business Valuation Committee of the AICPA and as a consultant on the CFA certification team. She has served as a member of AIMA's research committee and as a director of the board and treasurer of the CFA Society of New York. She has served at CFA Institute as a consultant in the area of practice analysis and curriculum review, and as a director in the GIPS, ethics, and professional standards group. She is currently serving as a board member and treasurer of Snehacares Inc., a nonprofit organization that she co-founded in 2015 dedicated to assist children with HIV AIDS in Bangalore, India.

She is a frequent presenter and author on valuation and alternative investment topics. She holds the CFA charter and is licensed as a CPA in California and New York. Antonella holds the Certificate in Entity and Intangibles Valuation (CEIV) and is accredited in business valuation by the AICPA.

Antonella graduated in economics, with honors, at the University Federico II of Naples, Italy, with a thesis in public finance, and has a master of law studies from NYU School of Law. She has been a research fellow at the Hebrew University of Jerusalem and has held the Italian national title in the 420 sailing class for Circolo del Remo e della Vela Italia.

About the Contributors

Neil J. Beaton, CPA/ABV/CFF, CFA, ASA, is a managing director with Alvarez & Marsal Valuation Services, LLC. Mr. Beaton specializes in the valuation of public and privately held businesses and intangible assets for purposes of litigation, acquisitions, sales, buy-sell agreements, ESOPs, incentive stock options, and estate planning and taxation. He earned a bachelor's degree in economics from Stanford University and a master's degree in finance from National University. He is a certified public accountant (CPA), chartered financial analyst (CFA), and accredited senior appraiser (ASA). Additionally, he is accredited in business valuation (ABV) and certified in financial forensics (CFF). Mr. Beaton is a frequent lecturer at universities, is an instructor for various business valuation courses, and speaks nationally on business valuation with a special emphasis on early stage and high-technology companies. He has written two books on early stage company valuation, has contributed to chapters for a number of other books on valuation and damages issues, and has written numerous articles on these topics. He is a former co-chair of the AICPA's Valuation of Private Equity Securities Task Force, and a former member of the AICPA's ABV Exam Committee and the AICPA's Mergers & Acquisitions Disputes Task Force. He is currently a member of the *Business Valuation Update* editorial advisory board, a member of the board of experts for the publication *Financial Valuation and Litigation Expert*, and on the editorial board of the National Association of Certified Valuation Analysts' *Value Examiner*.

Andreas Dal Santo, CFA, is a managing director with BlueVal Group, LLC. Mr. Dal Santo specializes in the valuation of technology companies and diversified businesses for purposes of financial reporting, M&A transactions, and business sales, partnership buyouts and buy-sell agreements, IRC 409A, and estate and gift taxes. He earned a master's degree in economics and finance with distinction from Ca' Foscari University, Venice, Italy, and has taken coursework at the Massachusetts Institute of Technology Future of Commerce. He is a chartered financial analyst (CFA), accredited in business valuation (ABV) and holds an advanced risk and portfolio management (ARPM) certificate. Mr. Dal Santo has more than 20 years of experience in investments, business valuation, and management consulting. Prior to BlueVal, he has managed more than $1 billion in European, North American, and Emerging Market assets for Arca Fondi, a leading investment management firm based in Milan. As head of global emerging markets for Arca Fondi, he has gained experience in business modeling and valuation in a broad range of securities in a variety of sectors across different countries and markets. Prior to that he was a specialist in North American Tech, Media, and Telecom investments for Arca Fondi. He has served as a director on the boards of private companies and nonprofit organizations, including the CFA Society New York and the CFA Society Italy.

Alexander Davie is a member in the Nashville, Tennessee, law firm Riggs Davie PLC. He works extensively with technology companies, including startups and emerging growth companies, as well as businesses in other industries, providing legal counsel on company formation, business planning, mergers and acquisitions, technology transactions, corporate governance, debt and equity financings, and securities offerings. In addition, Mr. Davie represents investment advisors, securities brokers, hedge funds, private equity funds, and real estate partnership syndicators in numerous private offerings of securities and in ongoing compliance.

Mr. Davie has experience serving on the boards of a number of civic organizations, including the Nashville Business Incubation Center. He is also active in the Tennessee Bar Association, serving on the executive counsel of its business law section.

Mr. Davie received his bachelor of arts degree in economics from the University of Pennsylvania, graduating magna cum laude and his Juris Doctor degree from Duke University School of Law, graduating with high honors. While in law school, he served as the managing editor of the *Duke Law & Technology Review*. In addition, he received a master of education degree in organizational leadership from Peabody College at Vanderbilt University.

John Jackman, CFA, is the president and managing director of Cortland Valuation Group. He chairs Cortland's oversight committee for the firm's valuation technical standards and plays an active role in working closely with clients, providing authoritative oversight to the valuation engagement leaders.

He has 20 years of experience in the valuation industry, providing valuation and financial consulting services worldwide for the purposes of financial reporting, tax planning and compliance, financing, bankruptcy, litigation, mergers and acquisitions, restructuring and recapitalizations, leveraged buyouts, private equity and investment.

He is an expert in financial reporting requirements, including fresh start accounting, ASC 805, Business Combinations; ASC 350, Intangibles—Goodwill and Other; ASC 360, Property, Plant and Equipment; and ASC 718, Compensation—Stock Compensation. He has particular expertise in the valuation of intellectual property and intangible assets and regularly performs valuations and/or arm's-length royalty rate/transfer price analyses related to intangible assets. He has been a co-leader of a team hired as the designated expert on behalf of the United States Internal Revenue Service in the area of intellectual property valuation.

Mr. Jackman has in-depth experience with the valuation review process with national and regional accounting firms throughout the United States and has worked closely with international firms under the IFRS financial standards. He also performs in-depth audit reviews of third-party valuation work product on behalf of various accounting firms. Additionally, he remains current with industry standards and best practices by actively participating in conferences throughout the country. He has been a formal speaker and presenter to many organizations and professional groups on topics ranging from valuation in the context of licensing to intellectual property and economic lives, to enterprise value and steady-state analysis. He also develops and delivers in-house valuation training programs to select clients.

Prior to Cortland, he was chairman and managing director of the Windward Group, Inc., which merged with Cortland in January of 2014. Preceding TWG, he was the managing director-valuations of Cove Partners LLC, a boutique investment banking firm in San Diego, California; and the vice president of Caliber Advisors, Inc., where he was the head of the financial reporting group. He previously held positions with Navigant Capital Advisors and Kroll Zolfo Cooper.

Mark L. Zyla is a managing director of Zyla Valuation Advisors, LLC, an Atlanta, Georgia based valuation and litigation consultancy firm. He received a BBA degree in finance from the University of Texas at Austin and an MBA degree with a concentration in finance from Georgia State University. He also completed the Mergers and Acquisitions Program at the Aresty Institute of the Wharton School of the University of Pennsylvania and the

Valuation Program at the Graduate School of Business at Harvard University. He is a certified public accountant, accredited in business valuation (CPA/ABV), certified in financial forensics (CFF) by the American Institute of Certified Public Accountants (AICPA), a certified financial analyst (CFA), and an accredited senior appraiser with the American Society of Appraisers certified in Business Valuation (ASA).

Mr. Zyla is the chairman of the Standards Review Board of the International Valuation Standards Council (IVSC). He recently served on the AICPA's Forensic and Valuation Services Executive Committee. He is a member of the Business Valuations Committee of the ASA where he also serves as a member of the Business Valuation Standards and Technical Issues subcommittees. Mr. Zyla is on the Advisory Council of the Master of Science in finance program at the University of Texas at Austin. In 2013, he was inducted into the AICPA Business Valuation Hall of Fame.

He is a frequent presenter and author on valuation issues. He has served on the faculty of the Federal Judicial Center and the National Judicial College teaching business valuation concepts to judges. He is author of *Fair Value Measurement: Practical Guidance and Implementation*, 3rd ed., published by John Wiley & Sons (2019). Mr. Zyla is also the author of the course "Fair Value Accounting: A Critical New Skill for All CPAs" published by the AICPA. He is also co-author of several portfolios related to fair value measurement published by Bloomberg BNA.

Preface

Early stage valuation addresses the valuation of companies that are in the early years of their life cycle, are growing rapidly, and where most of the value is based on expectations about the future. Early stage enterprises (ESEs) include companies that may have an initial concept, design, or business plan, but not an actual product. They also include multibillion-dollar "unicorns" with significant revenue and operations that have yet to reach profitability. The valuation of an ESE that approaches an IPO or an M&A transaction is based on a mix of quantitative analysis, people insight, and intuition for the company's growth prospects.

In spite of their diversity, ESEs have unique characteristics as a group that warrant special consideration in valuation. An ESE valuation starts from a vision of the company's future. The valuation of an ESE requires a dynamic model that takes into account the change in the ESE's operations through a period of high revenue growth and up to a stage of long-term stable growth. At each stage of the company's development, the three key fundamental factors of value (the cash flows generated by the business), time (the time horizon of the projection), and risk (the cost of capital for the firm and the target return for the investors) are going to have a distinct relationship that needs to be captured in the valuation model. Many ESEs will not survive through an exit event such as an IPO or a business combination/sale. The assessment of the risk of failure is especially challenging in ESE valuation.

In this book, early stage valuation is presented under the fair value standard of Financial Accounting Standards Board, Accounting Standards Codification Topic 820, *Fair Value Measurement*, and International Accounting Standards Board, International Financial Reporting Standards 13, *Fair Value Measurement*. The fair value standard is used globally for financial reporting. It provides a common framework for the asset management industry to value investments, make asset allocation decisions, evaluate investment manager performance, and assess manager compensation. It drives the work of securities analysts in financial research organizations around the world. While the fair value standard continues to raise controversy in certain areas of implementation, particularly in the banking sector, it still represents the most comprehensive set of principles with global acceptance in valuation around the world today.

In presenting the "state of the art" in ESE valuation, this book intends to harmonize the views of venture capital investors, investment bankers, auditors, and valuation analysts. The book is conceived for a reader who is interested in a broad perspective on early stage valuation. It presents step-by-step examples that can help build fundamental analytic tools with basic algebra. Some of the methods discussed include:

- Venture capital method
- Scorecard methods for seed investing
- Backsolve with option pricing methods
- Asset accumulation method
- Various methods for valuing intangible assets

- Analysis using non-GAAP metrics, including ESG metrics
- Calibration under various methodologies
- Scenario analysis and Monte Carlo simulation
- Black-Scholes-Merton option pricing model
- Binomial option pricing model

There are chapters dedicated to the valuation of preferred stock, options and warrants, debt securities, and contingent consideration (earnouts and clawbacks).

In our presentation, we have considered current practice in early stage company investment, transactions, and financial reporting. We have looked at guidance from academic studies, as well as from the AICPA Accounting and Valuation Guide on the *Valuation of Portfolio Company Investments of Venture Capital and Private Equity Funds and Other Investment Companies*, the Appraisal Foundation, the International Private Equity and Venture Capital Valuation Guidelines, the International Valuation Standards and other sources that we list in our reference section. We have considered the documentation requirements under the Mandatory Performance Framework (MPF) for the Certified in Entity and Intangible Valuations (CEIV) Credential and the Application of the MPF for the CEIV credential. We have also considered the guidance on valuation processes and governance of the Alternative Investment Management Association.

The book provides a historical perspective on fair value and highlights how fair value principles are at the heart of our economy.

Enjoy your journey!

Introduction

Early Stage Valuation covers a broad range of valuation methods that reflect the variety of early stage enterprises (ESEs), from entities that may have just started operations to companies that have substantial revenue and have already gone through multiple rounds of venture capital financing. A recurring message throughout this book is that the approach to ESE valuation needs to follow the company's evolution and adapt to reflect the company's characteristics at each stage of development. The structure of this book consists of three parts:

Part One: Early Stage Valuation in Context lays the foundation for ESE valuation under the fair value standard and describes the main characteristics of ESEs, including their market and capital structure.

Chapter 1: Early Stage Enterprises and the Venture Capital Market introduces the definition of ESE and provides an overview of the capital markets in which ESEs operate. This chapter considers the objectives and target returns of venture capital investors and how they reconcile to the historical returns realized by ESE investments. We discuss how the venture capital market has evolved over the past decade. We identify recent trends in ESE exit strategies and valuation, considering data on M&A transactions, buyouts, and IPOs over the past decade.

Chapter 2: Fair Value Standard presents the fair value standard for financial reporting as defined in Financial Accounting Standards Board, Accounting Standards Codification 820, *Fair Value Measurement* (ASC 820) and International Accounting Standards Board, International Financial Reporting Standards 13, *Fair Value Measurement* (IFRS 13). We provide a historical overview on the development of the fair value concept, from the medieval debate on the "fair price" (*justum praetium*) in Franciscan and Scholastic theology through the writings of Alfred Marshall, the Railroad Rate regulation of the 1890s–1910s, and the interpretation of fair value in the wake of post–World War II economic liberalism.

We then examine the fair value definition for financial reporting under generally accepted accounting principles (GAAP) and illustrate the income, market, and asset-based valuation approaches under ASC 820/IFRS 13 as they apply to ESEs.

The last part of this chapter reviews some key reference material that we use in our analysis, with an emphasis on the most recent guidance on fair value implementation, including:

- American Institute of Certified Public Accountants Accounting and Valuation Guide on the *Valuation of Portfolio Company Investments of Venture Capital and Private Equity Funds and Other Investment Companies* (the "AICPA PE/VC Valuation Guide")
- International Valuation Standards (IVS) 210, *Intangible Assets* and IVS 500, *Financial Instruments*, latest edition.
- International Private Equity and Venture Capital Valuation Guidelines: latest edition (the "IPEV Guidelines")
- Appraisal Foundation: VFR Valuation Advisory #4, *Valuation of Contingent Consideration* ("VFR #4")

- Alternative Investment Management Association: *Guide to Sound Practices for the Valuation of Investments* (2018).
- Financial Instruments Performance Framework (FIFP) for the Certified in the Valuation of Financial Instruments (CVFI) Credential
- Mandatory Performance Framework for the Certified in Entity and Intangible Valuations (CEIV) Credential and Application of the Mandatory Performance Framework for the CEIV Credential (collectively the MPF)

We also include some less recent sources that are also relevant for ESE valuation and that we have used in various chapters of this book. More references can be found in our selected Reference section at the end of the book.

Chapter 3: Capital Structure discusses the capital structure of ESEs, which are often complex structures with multiple classes and series of securities. We consider the most common features of common stock, preferred stock, options, and option-like instruments, debt and hybrid instruments such as simple agreements for future equity (SAFE) and keep it simple securities (KISS). We discuss economic rights of preferred stock, including liquidation, antidilution, participation, conversion, dividend and redemption rights, as well as noneconomic rights such as registration, voting, board composition, drag along, preemptive, first refusal, tag-along, management and information rights. We provide practical examples of antidilution provisions and various types of liquidation preferences and insights into how these rights may play out in valuation depending on the company's exit strategy.

Part Two: Enterprise Valuation illustrates the valuation of an ESE at the level of the overall enterprise. Most ESEs do not have debt in their capital structure or have debt with equity features (convertible debt). In this context, the enterprise value of the firm will coincide with its equity value.

Chapter 4: Seed Stage Valuation and the Venture Capital Method presents an overview of valuation of ESEs in their initial stages up to their Series A funding with venture capital financing.

We review the market for seed investing and the role that angel investors play in providing seed capital. We introduce the concepts of premoney and postmoney valuation and provide examples of how postmoney valuation is affected by a company's capital structure. We illustrate how an "up" round where the postmoney valuation of a company increases may actually be a "down" round from the perspective of an individual investor whose interest has been diluted by the addition of new investors into the company.

We walk through some of the scorecard methodologies that are used in the earliest stages of seed investing, including the Payne Scorecard, the Risk Factor Summation Model, the Berkus method, and the Modified Berkus method. Most of the chapter is dedicated to the Venture Capital (VC) method, which is a common approach to valuation for negotiating new stakes in portfolio company deals. One of the challenges of the VC method is how to reconcile the "Target Returns" that VC investors aspire to in entering into a new deal (typically 30% or above), with the "Required Returns" that investors expect to achieve based on the historical evidence of venture capital fund returns (typically in the 15–25% range). In this chapter we show some practical examples of how, given the (1) time horizon, (2) projected exit value for the deal, (3) expected risk of failure, and (4) the expected dilution percentage over the term to exit, an investor can determine the ownership percentage that needs to be negotiated in order to achieve its Required Return in a specific deal.

We conclude the chapter with an illustration of the First Chicago Method by applying a simple scenario analysis to the valuation of a company in the seed stage.

Chapter 5: The Backsolve Method is a common method under the market approach to estimate enterprise value based on the price of a recent transaction in the company's own securities. Chapter 5 walks through a case study in the implementation of the Backsolve method based on Case Study 10 of the AICPA PE/VC Valuation Guide. The chapter explores how to apply the Backsolve method in combination with an option pricing model (the "OPM Backsolve Method") to a company with a complex capital structure.

We discuss how secondary transactions can be factored into the reference price that is used as the starting point of the valuation. Finally, we illustrate how to estimate the volatility of the company's equity, which is a key input in the OPM model.

Chapter 6: Discounted Cash Flow Method is dedicated to the Discounted Cash Flow method (the DCF Method or DCF), which is a cornerstone of the income-based approach. Of all the valuation techniques discussed in this book, the DCF method is the one that has the greatest variety of applications and is also the most controversial in terms of its ESE implementation. A DCF model can provide an appropriate methodology for ESE valuation for companies that already have an established revenue stream, especially when recent transactions in the company's securities are not available or the transaction prices that are available are not indicative of fair value (for instance, a related party transaction at other-than-market terms).

It is common practice in a DCF model to use a single discount rate throughout the projection period. In this chapter, we present a dynamic DCF model that includes three stages of development: a high growth period with revenue growth and discount rates significantly above industry average (Years 1–5 in our example), a stable growth phase (Years 10-plus) where revenue growth rates are in line with the risk-free rate and the discount rate is in line with industry averages, and an intermediate declining growth stage where revenue growth and the discount rate gradually converge to their stable growth values.

In our model, the high-growth stage is based on management's projections of revenue and cash flow amounts. The stable growth stage reflects the company's capital structure, revenue growth rate, operating margin, tax rate, depreciation, and reinvestment rate based on the analyst's long-term "vision" of the company. The intermediate or declining growth stage is formula-driven.

Most of the ESE value depends on the terminal value that results from the analyst's estimates and assumptions in the stable growth stage. The chapter uses the Gordon Growth Model to estimate the terminal value of the company at the end of the projection period. In practice, multiples of revenue or earnings are often used and are also consistent with the guidance in the AICPA PE/VC Valuation Guide and the IPEV Guidelines.

Other sections of the chapter discuss:

- How to estimate the cost of capital using the Build-Up method, the "pure" CAPM method, the diversification-adjusted CAPM, and the CAPM with additional risk premia
- How to treat the risk of failure in the context of DCF valuation
- How to incorporate changes in capital structure in three stages
- How to estimate the reinvestment rate that is needed to sustain growth
- How to reconcile the results of the DCF model with the postmoney valuation under the Venture Capital method
- Use of calibration at subsequent measurement
- Documentation best practices based on the guidance provided by the MPF.

Chapter 7: Asset Accumulation Method presents the Asset Accumulation Method (AAM) as an example of an asset-based approach in ESE valuation and highlights the relevance of intangible assets as drivers of valuation. In this chapter, we identify the most common categories of intangibles that can be found in ESEs, and discuss some of the more common methods for valuing intangible assets under ASC 820/IFRS 13, including:

- Multiperiod Excess Earning Method
- Royalty Relief Method
- Replacement Cost Method Less Obsolescence
- Real option pricing
- With and Without Method

We provide an example of implementation of the AAM for an ESE that emphasizes forward-looking information alongside historical, cost-based information in the valuation of intangible assets. We discuss the advantages and limitations of the AAM versus the methodologies under the market- and income approach.

Chapter 8: Non-GAAP Metrics in ESE Valuation provides an overview of non-GAAP metrics that can be used in valuation to assess the performance of an ESE relative to its targets, evaluate its prospects and trends toward profitability, and in some cases, build a more formal model for enterprise valuation. We break out non-GAAP metrics into two categories: non-GAAP financial measures, which are derived by adjusting GAAP financial statement accounts by adding or removing GAAP components, and "Other Metrics," which include elements that are outside the scope of the financial statements. Other metrics discussed in this chapter include:

- Number of customers
- Number of active users
- Bookings
- Revenue run rate
- Revenue per user
- Annual recurring revenue
- ESG metrics

The chapter includes a sample model for ESE valuation that uses the value of current users, new users, and general corporate expenses to estimate the value of the enterprise.

Part Three: Valuation of Financial Instruments focuses on the methodologies for allocating enterprise value to preferred and common stock in an ESE, and on the valuation of other interests in a company, such as options and warrants, convertible debt, and contingent consideration (earnouts and clawbacks).

Chapter 9: Allocation of Enterprise Value presents the methodologies for allocating enterprise value to preferred and common stock based on the guidance in the AICPA PE/VC Valuation Guide and in the IPEV guidelines. We illustrate the simplified bimodal scenario, full-scenario, and the relative-scenario approaches, as well as the hybrid approach and the current value method.

Chapter 10: Valuation of Options and Warrants presents the valuation of options and warrants in an ESE. We walk through the details of the Black Scholes-Merton (BSM) option model and show an example of how a call option can be valued using the BSM option model and the binomial lattice model. We discuss how to estimate the volatility of preferred and common stock using an OPM enterprise valuation model. Finally, we address the dilution effect that is typically associated with warrants and how it is reflected in warrant valuation.

Chapter 11: *Valuation of Debt Securities* is dedicated to the valuation of ESE convertible debt. After a review of the basic principles in debt valuation, we walk through an example of a convertible note that shows how to break out the valuation of the embedded option component from that of the "pure" debt component valued using the yield method. We also show how debt can be valued as if it were a special class of preferred stock with senior liquidation preferences relative to all other classes in an OPM model for the enterprise. We present an example of a convertible bond valuation using calibration and we provide a step-by-step example of the valuation of a convertible bond using a binomial lattice model. We then focus on bridge notes, which are a type of convertible debt that is common in ESE capital structures. We present an example of the valuation of bridge notes on an as-if converted basis (assuming the note gets converted into preferred stock at the next round), and of bridge notes with warrants attached. We add some considerations on the valuation of debt using broker quotes (an unusual circumstance in ESE valuation) and conclude with a discussion of how to treat debt in the context of equity valuation.

Chapter 12: *Valuation of Contingent Consideration* is dedicated to the valuation of earnouts and clawbacks that may result from M&A and buyout transactions. The purchase price of an ESE in an M&A or buyout transaction often includes a component that is dependent on the future performance of the company. A VC fund that sells an interest in an ESE, for instance, may have to recognize an earnout in its portfolio of assets with changes in fair value recorded as capital gains or losses until the contingency event is resolved. In this chapter, we address the valuation of contingent consideration based on the guidance provided by the Appraisal Foundation in VFR #4 as well as in the AICPA PE/VC Valuation Guide. We provide detailed examples of how contingent consideration in the form of earnouts (assets for the seller) and, less frequently, clawbacks (liabilities for the seller) can be valued using a probability-weighted discounted cash flows model, an option pricing model, and Monte Carlo simulation. In particular, we provide examples of the valuation of contingent consideration in the presence of:

- Technical milestones with binary outcomes
- Simple linear payoff structures
- Linear payoff structures with floor
- Linear payoff structures with floor and cap
- Systematic binary structures

References conclude the book with a selected list of references that identify the main sources that we have used in our analysis, including FASB and IASB provisions, guidance from the AICPA, the Appraisal Foundation, the International Valuation Standards Council and other professional organizations, SEC filings, reports from data service providers, and research literature in the field.

PART One

Early Stage Valuation in Context

Early Stage Enterprises and the Venture Capital Market

Early stage enterprises (ESEs) consist of private companies that are in the early years of their life cycles and have yet to reach profitability. ESEs include a broad range of entities, from companies that have an initial concept, design, or business plan but not necessarily an actual product, to multibillion-dollar enterprises with significant revenue and operations. Most recently, a surge of capital from investors and strategic partners has enabled some ESEs to reach unprecedented sizes and access the public markets while still in the process of developing sustainable commercial operations. The range of players in the venture capital (VC) markets has expanded to include a variety of institutional investors, high net worth individuals, foreign investors, and corporate players. According to a recent study, global VC assets under management (AUM) have passed the $850 billion mark, representing an estimated 14% of the global private capital industry.[1] The VC market involves a global community of players, with the United States leading the way in terms of investment activity (7 out of 10 VC investment firms are U.S.-based) and other regions expanding quickly, most notably China.[2] In a scenario of low interest rates, and with substantial cash at their disposal, investors are competing to enter into the high growth opportunities that ESEs can provide, pushing down the cost of capital and enhancing liquidity. In spite of their diversity, ESEs have unique characteristics as a group that warrant special consideration in valuation. In this chapter, we consider some of the characteristics that distinguish ESEs from other types of companies. We provide an overview of the VC market and ESE exit strategies, and we highlight some recent market trends that are of special relevance in ESE valuation.

---

[1]Preqin and Vertex, "Global Venture Capital Perspectives: A Preqin & Vertex Study," September 2019.
[2]On the growth of venture capital in China, see Alex Frederick and Jordan Beck, "Venture Capital in China," *PitchBook 1Q 2019 Analyst Note*, PitchBook Data Inc., March 18, 2019.

CHARACTERISTICS OF EARLY STAGE ENTERPRISES

Stage of Development

The early years in a company's life cycle are often broken out in three stages of development:

1. **Seed stage/angel stage:** Commercial operations are being established, there is little or no product revenue and little expense history. Seed capital is typically provided by friends and family or "angel" investors. Financing consists of relatively small investments (often less than $100,000) summing up to rounds that are generally in the $0.2 million–$3 million range.
2. **Early VC stage/start-up stage:** The company has started operations and is building up its management team. The ESE has revenues, but operating expenses are significantly higher than revenues. Losses are driven by research and development expenses and by product development costs. The company has its early VC rounds of Series A and Series B financing. It may also attract the attention of strategic investors that are interested in the synergies that the company may bring to their own operations. As the company develops, it may become a suitable candidate for a merger and acquisition (M&A) or buyout exit transaction.
3. **Later VC stage:** The company has high revenue growth and may have substantial revenue but continues to generate losses and has negative cash flows from operations. The investment in research and development is substantial; marketing expenses may also be significant and offset any incoming operating cash flows. The company engages in new rounds of financing (Series C, D, E, etc.). As it continues to grow, it may start looking at an IPO or M&A exit. As the company develops, revenue growth subsides, operating margins improve, and the company approaches self-sustaining operations.

As a company proceeds through its early-stage development, the risks associated to its future cash flow stream decrease, its likelihood of survival increases, and its valuation increases.[3] In the software sector, for instance, the median valuation of companies backed by VC investment was $8 million in the angel/seed stage, $29 million in the early VC stage, and $88 million in the later VC, respectively as of December 31, 2019.[4] Median valuations for software companies in the United States have increased over the past decade in all three stages, especially in the later VC stage.

Life science companies also represent a significant share of the VC market and have special operational features that need to be taken into account in developing an appropriate valuation approach.[5] In most countries, the development path of life science companies is

---

[3] Our definition of "early stage" includes companies that are in Stages 1 through 4 in the classification of stages of enterprise development of the American Institute of Certified Public Accountants (AICPA) as it applies to a generic company held as a portfolio investment (a "portfolio company"), as presented in the AICPA PE/VC Valuation Guide, I.15 Table 1.1.

[4] Exhibit 1.1, as all other exhibits with dollar references in this chapter, reflect nominal dollar amounts and are not adjusted for inflation. On U.S. VC median premoney valuations by stage for software companies as of December 31, 2019, see PitchBook Data Inc. and National Venture Capital Association, Q4 2019 PitchBook NVCA Venture Monitor Summary.

[5] The AICPA has published a separate classification for companies in the life science industry (e.g. biotech, pharma, medical devices) by stages of development, as illustrated in the AICPA PE/VC Valuation Guide I.15 Table 1.2.

strongly influenced by government regulation. In the United States, pharmaceutical and medical device companies must test their products through clinical trials under the supervision of the U.S. Food and Drug Administration (FDA). During clinical trials, medical devices or drugs are tested in four Phases to ensure that the product is safe and is working the way it was intended and designed.[6]

A comprehensive study of clinical drug development in the United States over the period 2006–2015 by the Biotechnology Innovation Organization has indicated that only 9.6% of the drugs that start the clinical trial actually obtain FDA approval to enter the postclinical marketing phase.[7]

As we further discuss in the next chapter, the stage of development has a significant impact on the methodologies that can be used in ESE valuation.

Expectation of High Growth in Revenue

The expectation of revenue growth significantly above industry average is a common feature of ESEs. In many cases, ESEs have ideas for innovative products and services that require research and development efforts as well as marketing support to become commercially viable. It is critical for the valuation analyst to consider the subject company's competitive environment and assess whether the company's products and competitive advantage are sustainable over time. Even if a company succeeds in developing a product that is commercially viable, the ability of the company to command significant revenue growth and eventually maintain market share may be limited if other companies are able to step into the same market with low barriers to entry.

Net Losses and Negative Cash Flows from Operations

By definition, ESEs have not yet reached profitability. ESE losses are typically driven by substantial investments in research and development, product development, sales and marketing, which flow through as expenses in the income statement. No income taxes are charged in the early years of an ESE's life and a potential tax benefit may have to be factored into the valuation to the extent early losses can be used to offset future taxable income in some jurisdictions. For a company that is incurring operating losses and negative cash flows from operations, an

---

[6]Critical trials are normally managed outside the organization by a contract research organization (CRO). The cost of CRO services can be substantial and extend over a long period of time. On the cost of new drug development, see especially Joseph A. Di Masi, Henry G. Grabowski, and Ronald W. Hansen, "Innovation in the Pharmaceutical Industry: New Estimates of R&D Costs," *Journal of Health Economics* 47 (2016): 20–33. The estimated average out-of-pocket cost per approved new drug compound is $1,395 million (2013 dollars). Capitalizing out-of-pocket costs to the point of marketing approval at a real discount rate of 10.5% yields a total preapproval cost estimate of $2,558 million (2013 dollars). Adding an estimate of post-approval R&D costs increases the cost estimate to $2,870 million (2013 dollars).

[7]Biotechnology Innovation Organization, Clinical Development Success Rate 2006–2015, BIO:2016. This study has indicated that the transition success rates in the FDA approval process of clinical testing are 63.2% from Phase 1 to Phase 2, 30.7% from Phase II to Phase III, 59.1% from Phase III to submission of the official New Drug Application (NDA) or Biologic License Application (BLA), and 85.3% for the final NDA/BLA approval.

assessment of working capital provides critical insight into the company's financial strength. The percentage of the company's cash balance that is consumed in one month of operations (the monthly "cash burn rate") is an important metric to assess the company's risk of failure. A company with a monthly cash burn rate of 5%, for instance, can only survive for 20 months without additional funding, asset sales, or an improvement in operating cash flows.

Risk of Failure

Many ESEs will never reach profitable operations. A company may end up being acquired while still in the process of product development. In other cases, a company may end up exhausting its cash resources and liquidate with little or no residual value for its investors. Exhibit 1.1 presents the survival statistics of new companies in the United States for the period 2000–2015. Based on data from the Bureau of Labor Statistics, of the companies founded in the year 2010, only 51.4% were still in operation as of YE 2015.[8] The survival rate is especially low for companies in the first three years of operations.

A study of Cambridge Associates that includes an analysis of 36,286 venture capital fund investments over the period 1990–2016 estimates that 51.1% of portfolio company investments turned into a full or partial loss for the funds and that investment losses were 32.7% of invested capital.[9] A recent study conducted by PitchBook on exits from VC-backed companies from January 1, 2013, through August 8, 2019, indicates that only 25% of deals return more than 1× and only one in every eight reaches a 5× return.[10] The PitchBook study points out that for companies that reach an exit, the earlier stage deals (Series A and B) provide significantly higher returns (27.7% on an annualized basis for Series A versus 7.5% for Series F). On the other hand, once failure rates are taken into account, the Series return ranking changes significantly, with Series A–C investments generating negative returns, and Series F returns posting the more favorable annualized returns. We look forward to more research that can help assess the risk of failure at various stages in an ESE development.

Intangible Assets and Off-Balance-Sheet Liabilities

In most ESEs, intangible assets represent a significant driver of value. The International Glossary of Business Valuation Terms (IGBVT) defines intangible assets as "non-physical assets such as franchises, trademarks, patents, copyrights, goodwill, equities, mineral rights,

---

[8]Frequently referenced studies by Amy Knaup and M.C. Piazza for the period 1998–2005 concluded that only 44% of all companies were still extant at the end of the seven-year period. See Amy E. Knaup, "Survival and Longevity in the Business Employment Dynamics Data," *Monthly Labor Review*, May 2005, pp. 50–56; Amy E. Knaup and M.C. Piazza, "Business Employment Dynamics Data: Survival and Longevity," *Monthly Labor Review*, September 2007, pp. 3–10. These studies are based on data from the Bureau of Labor Statistics Quarterly Census of Employment and Wages.

[9]Cambridge Associates LLC, "Growth Equity: Turns Out, It's All About the Growth," January 2019. The capital loss ratio is defined as the percentage of capital in deals realized below cost, net of any recovered proceeds, over total invested capital.

[10]Cameron Stanfill and Bryan Hanson, VC Returns by Series: Part I, *PitchBook 3Q 2019 Analyst Notes*, PitchBook Data Inc., September 27, 2019. The population of deals considered by PitchBook may also include companies that have already reached profitability. We thank Cameron Stanfill at PitchBook Data Inc. for providing some color on the deal dates covered by the report.

Number of years since starting	2000	2001	2002	2003	2004	2005	2006	2007	2008	2009	2010	2011	2012	2013	2014	2015
1	100	100	100	100	100	100	100	100	100	100	100	100	100	100	100	100
2	78.4	75.7	78.4	79.3	78.9	80.1	78.3	77.3	75.2	76.7	78.6	79.4	79.2	79.6	79.9	–
3	66	64.7	67.4	68.4	69.1	68.7	66.3	64	63.3	66.4	68.6	69.3	68.7	69.3	–	–
4	58.2	57.6	60	61.4	61.2	60.2	56.7	55.5	56.5	59.9	61.6	61.9	61.5	–	–	–
5	52.8	52.3	54.8	55.3	54.5	52.6	49.8	50.2	51.7	54.8	56	56.3	–	–	–	–
6	48.2	48.1	50.1	50	48.4	46.8	45.4	46.4	47.8	50.1	51.4	–	–	–	–	–
7	44.7	44.2	45.9	44.8	43.7	43.2	42.3	43.1	44.2	46.3	–	–	–	–	–	–
8	41.6	40.9	41.8	40.9	40.5	40.5	39.6	40.1	41.1	–	–	–	–	–	–	–
9	38.6	37.4	38.4	38.1	38.2	38.2	37.1	37.5	–	–	–	–	–	–	–	–
10	35.5	34.5	36.1	36	36.1	35.9	34.9	–	–	–	–	–	–	–	–	–
11	32.9	32.4	34.2	34.2	34	33.8	–	–	–	–	–	–	–	–	–	–
12	31.2	30.9	32.5	32.3	32.1	–	–	–	–	–	–	–	–	–	–	–
13	29.8	29.5	30.8	30.8	–	–	–	–	–	–	–	–	–	–	–	–
14	28.6	28.1	29.4	–	–	–	–	–	–	–	–	–	–	–	–	–
15	27.3	26.8	–	–	–	–	–	–	–	–	–	–	–	–	–	–
16	26.3	–	–	–	–	–	–	–	–	–	–	–	–	–	–	–
17	–	–	–	–	–	–	–	–	–	–	–	–	–	–	–	–
18	–	–	–	–	–	–	–	–	–	–	–	–	–	–	–	–
19	–	–	–	–	–	–	–	–	–	–	–	–	–	–	–	–
20	–	–	–	–	–	–	–	–	–	–	–	–	–	–	–	–
21	–	–	–	–	–	–	–	–	–	–	–	–	–	–	–	–
22	–	–	–	–	–	–	–	–	–	–	–	–	–	–	–	–

Note: Dashes indicate not applicable.

Source: Bureau of Labor Statistics.

EXHIBIT 1.1 U.S. Bureau of Labor Statistics: Survival Rate of New Companies Founded 2000–2015

securities and contracts (as distinguished from physical rights) that grant rights and privileges and have value for the owner."[11] U.S. GAAP defines them as assets (not including financial assets) that lack physical substance. Most intangible assets do not appear in the balance sheet, and the related costs are expensed as incurred. For many ESEs, intangible assets need to be identified and considered as part of the ESE valuation process.

A company may have off-balance-sheet liabilities that increase its risk of failure. Also, a company may have a high risk of patent infringement litigation that is not captured in the balance sheet. The risk of off-balance-sheet liabilities is not exclusive to ESEs, but is especially significant in an ESE context where a company may not have adequate funding to defend itself in litigation and be able to survive an unfavorable litigation outcome.

Size

For an ESE, it is common to define size in terms of its equity value based on the latest round of financing. The size of an ESE will typically vary significantly depending on the stage in the ESE life cycle. One of the most striking developments in ESE financing in recent years has been the increasing number of venture-backed companies in the private markets that have passed $1 billion in valuation. In November 2013, Aileen Lee, seed-stage investor and founder of Cowboy Ventures, coined the term "unicorn" to indicate these large ESEs, noting that unicorns were once an extremely rare occurrence.[12]

As of June 30, 2019, there were more than 300 unicorns in the world, including more than 60% in the United States, and a growing number in China, the EU, India, Singapore, Israel, Canada, Japan, with an aggregate valuation of approximately $602 billion, from $27.3 billion in 2009.[13] The year 2019 has also seen a record for unicorn exits in numbers and value in M&A and IPO transactions. The U.S. list of unicorns that have chosen the route of public listing includes high profile enterprises such as Lyft, Uber, Zoom, Slack, and Pinterest. The unicorn phenomenon is an attestation to the fact that more of the value is currently generated in the private markets, and that companies can develop to a very large size and stay private for a longer period of time before seeking public funding. In spite of their size and high valuations, many unicorns are ESEs that are still incurring net operating losses and negative cash flows from operations.[14]

Capital Structure

The capital structure of an early stage company typically consists of multiple classes and series of shares with different rights and privileges. Founders are typically granted common stock. The company's employees may also receive common stock or options on common stock as part of employee compensation. As the company enters into the early VC stage, it will start raising capital from VC investors in the form of preferred stock or bridge loans convertible

---

[11]International Glossary of Business Valuation Terms: Intangible Assets.

[12]Aileen Lee, "Welcome to the Unicorn Club: Learning from Billion Dollar Start-Ups," *TechCrunch*, November 2, 2013. We now also have decacorns ($10+ billion) and hectacorns ($100+ billion) galloping in the world markets.

[13]PitchBook 2019 Unicorn Report, PitchBook Data Inc., 2019.

[14]On the valuation of Unicorn IPOs, see also Antonella Puca, "Investing for Retirement: Beware the Unicorn IPO Stampede," *Enterprising Investor*, CFA Institute, March 26, 2019.

into preferred stock. In its later VC stage, the ESE will typically have built a complex capital structure with common stock, multiple series of preferred stock, and related instruments. We discuss the capital structure of ESEs in greater detail in Chapter 3.

Governance

In many ESEs, the founders have a controlling interest in the company and are actively involved in the company's management. As VC investors enter into the company's capital structure, they often demand a strategic role and one or more seats on the company's board of directors. Building a board, and managing it effectively, is a key task for an ESE CEO and a VC team. The board can provide guidance that may be critical for the company's survival and growth. Some of the most successful cases of VC investors/ESE founder partnerships involve a strategic collaboration where the VC investors combine financial expertise with a deep knowledge and experience in the area of the company's operations and provide assistance in areas such as:

- Strategic insight and advice on the company's market prospects
- Introductions for business development, financing, and recruitment
- Exit planning: identification of exit market and potential buyers, IPO assistance, adviser introduction and selection, advice on timing and type of exit.

In a market with significant amounts of liquidity available for investment, a board that has solid financial expertise may be able to negotiate a favorable exit deal even if there is still significant uncertainty concerning the company's prospects and business strategy.

Availability and Quality of Financial Information

For ESEs that are in the seed and early VC stage of financing, the availability of financial information is a primary challenge in most valuations. At the seed stage, the company may not yet have generated a full set of financial projections or may have projections for a single year. By the time the company engages in its first round of VC capital financing (a round of Series A preferred stock issuance, for instance), it will typically be asked to provide at least three to five years of projections to its prospective VC investors. At this stage, the company still has a very limited history of operations, and management's projections will be subject to high projection risk. As we move toward the later VC stage (Series C and above), the quality of the company's financial information is likely to improve. The analyst will be able to compare prior projections to actual results and get a better sense of the company's forecasting process.

THE VENTURE CAPITAL MARKET

For companies that are not yet profitable, it is critical to ensure that a consistent flow of capital can be accessed to sustain operations. Even if technical or economic product feasibility is achieved, it may still take years before an ESE achieves profitability. The company's ability to access the capital needed to support its growth and meet its expense obligations is a key factor for its survival and ultimate success.

Market Overview

ESEs have generally not been able to rely on bank lending as a primary source of financing. ESE bank lending often requires the guarantee of the founders or other related parties. Some companies obtain bank lending to finance an M&A transaction (leveraged buyout), with the expectations that the ESE will repay its loans once it becomes part of a larger profitable entity. Without the backing of the founder, the acquirer, or another party with tangible assets, banking institutions have been reluctant to loan funds to ESEs.[15]

The primary source of funding for ESEs has come from VC investors that buy shares of an ESE with the expectation of reselling them at a profit at a later stage. The VC market has grown significantly over the past decade. The number of VC-backed deals and the total VC deal value in the United States have increased at an annualized rate of 15.8% and 7.1%, respectively, over the period 2010–2019.[16]

Exhibit 1.2 shows the allocation of U.S. deals between the three stages of VC investing in terms of number of deals over the period 2010-2019. A striking feature of Exhibit 1.2 is the significant increase in the number of seed deals as a percentage of total (from 31.7% in 2010 to 42.3% in 2019). In terms of dollar value, companies in the later VC stage continue to attract the vast majority of capital (62.4% of total deal value versus 60.4% in 2010), with

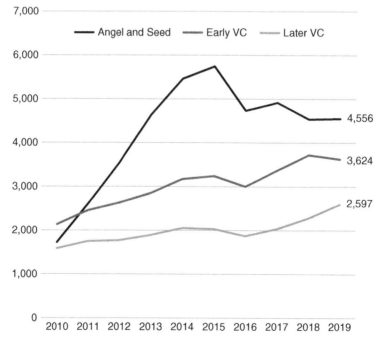

EXHIBIT 1.2 U.S. Number of VC Deals by Stage, by Year, 2010–2019

---

[15]Kyle Stanford and Darren Klees, "Venture Debt Overview," *PitchBook 4Q 2019 Analyst Note*, Pitch-Book Data Inc., October 11, 2019.
[16]PitchBook Data Inc. and National Venture Capital Association, Q4 2019 PitchBook NVCA Venture Monitor Summary. Data as of December 31, 2019.

fewer, but significantly larger deals are taking place in the later VC stage segment. The median deal size has also increased, reaching a peak of $1.1 million and $6.5 million for the seed and early VC stage, respectively, in 2019, and down slightly to $10.4 million in 2019 from a peak of $11.5 in 2018 for the later VC stage.[17]

Over the past decade, the average age that it takes for a company to reach Series A through D+ rounds of financing has also increased. With the exception of the late rounds (Series D+), which have remained at about 8.0 years from inception, the average time it takes to reach a financing round has increased for all rounds over the past decade. Most companies will take about four years to reach their Series A round.[18]

Financial Investors and the Mechanics of Financial Performance   The most significant share of capital provided to ESEs comes from financial investors, a category that includes VC funds, institutions, and individuals that have been willing to take on the risk of investing in new businesses with the expectation of obtaining enhanced financial returns, primarily in the form of capital gains upon the sale of their investments.

Most of the capital flowing into ESEs has traditionally come through the intermediation of VC funds.[19] In the United States, VC funds are closed-end private funds that typically have a term life of 8 to 12 years. The investors in a VC fund do not disburse their entire contribution at inception. Rather, they commit to a certain amount of capital (the "committed capital") and disburse a portion of it each time the fund manager issues a "capital call" or "draw down" to cover for the fund's expenses or to make a portfolio company investment. The fund manager is responsible for determining when it is appropriate to call capital and has no obligation to call the full amount of committed capital over the life of the fund. In fact, there is a growing amount of "dry powder" in markets, which is committed, but uncalled capital. The fund manager's decision affects the amount of time the investors' capital is effectively deployed and may have a significant effect on the investor's ultimate return over the time horizon of the investment. Once contributed, capital is locked into the fund until the fund's investments are liquidated and the proceeds from liquidation are distributed to the investors, generally starting four to six years after the initial contribution date.

The number of VC funds has increased consistently after reaching a bottom in 2011 in the aftermath of the 2007–2009 crisis. As of July 30, 2019, Preqin counts 1,004 U.S. funds that are actively raising capital in the United States, a growth of more than sixfold from the bottom in 2011.[20]

According to a recent PitchBook report, the median and the average VC fund size in the United States as of December 31, 2019, were $78 million and $182 million, respectively.[21]

---

[17]PitchBook Data Inc. and National Venture Capital Association, Q4 2019 PitchBook NVCA Venture Monitor Summary. Data as of December 31, 2019.

[18]PitchBook Data Inc. and National Venture Capital Association, Q3 2019 PitchBook NVCA Venture Monitor Summary. Data as of September 30, 2019.

[19]For an introduction to closed-end private funds, see Donald R. Chambers, Keith H. Black, and Nelson Lacey, *Alternative Investments: A Primer for Investment Professionals*, Chapter 9: "Private Equity," CFA Institute and CAIA Association, 2018. The considerations in this chapter in terms of fund structures, fees, and returns apply also to Venture Capital funds.

[20]Preqin, Preqin and First Republic Update: U.S. Venture Capital in 1H 2019.

[21]PitchBook Data Inc. and National Venture Capital Association, Q4 2019 PitchBook NVCA Venture Monitor. Data as of December 31, 2019.

VC funds typically invest in multiple deals, which helps to spread the risk of failure across a variety of ESEs and increases the probability that one or more of the portfolio investments will succeed. In some cases, investors prefer to have access to a single investment opportunity or to a subset of opportunities within a VC portfolio. A VC fund manager may allow its investors to participate in a single deal parallel to the fund ("co-investment"). Typically, the manager will do so by setting up an investment vehicle that is separate from the fund and that invests exclusively in a specified deal. Co-investment opportunities give investors the ability to control risk on a deal-by-deal basis and reduce investment management fees. They also reduce portfolio diversification as compared to a fund investment and may involve additional direct administrative costs for the investors.

Venture capital funds report to the investors their net asset value (NAV) at least on a quarterly basis. In addition, they report their total assets under management (AUM) as the sum of their NAV and the committed capital that has not yet been called by the fund manager (the "uncalled capital" or "dry powder"). For instance, a fund with a NAV of $200 million, and uncalled capital that has not yet contributed to the fund of $50 million, would report a total AUM of $250 million.

Institutions such as sovereign wealth funds, pension funds, endowments, foundations, insurance companies, and individuals with substantial assets have also been investing in ESEs directly by acquiring shares or convertible notes in an ESE round of financing. Some of the largest and most sophisticated players in the VC space have dedicated significant assets to develop internally managed programs of direct ESE investments, alongside their investments in VC funds.[22]

Investors may also be able to access VC investments in the secondary market, by purchasing VC fund shares or shares of an ESE from preexistent investors.[23] Secondary market transactions generally represent a small share of ESE transactions, but have increased in frequency in recent years, and often take place in proximity of an exit event. They may provide an important value indication especially ahead of IPO events.

The return expectations of VC fund investors have a significant influence on the cost of capital of an ESE. The historical returns of VC fund investors (net of fees and direct costs of management) may provide a framework to estimate the return that VC market participants would like to target in an ESE investment, and the cost of capital that an ESE is likely to incur in order to access VC financing. Most VC investors have now the option of investing in an ESE portfolio directly or through a VC fund vehicle. In our analysis, we assume that an investor will choose the alternative that maximizes its expected return, net of fees, and direct costs of management, for a given level of risk and over a specified time horizon.

The measurement of the performance of a VC fund presents some complexities that reflect the irregular nature of its cash flows and the illiquid character of its investments. There is no single metric that takes into account simultaneously the three key variables in investment

---

[22]See for instance the Alaska Permanent Fund, which takes direct positions in joint ventures with smaller to middle market VC managers. For an overview of the role of Sovereign Wealth Funds, see Wylie Fernyhough, Sovereign Wealth Funds Overview, *3Q 2019 PitchBook Analyst Note*, PitchBook Data Inc., August 9, 2019.

[23]For a perspective on secondary market investments of a leading private equity firm in this space, see the interview with Brett Hickey from Star Mountain Capital in Antonella Puca, "Growing Trends in Private Equity: Secondary Market Investing," *Enterprising Investor*, CFA Institute, May 10, 2018.

performance of time, value, and risk. To assess fund performance, we need to look at a variety of metrics and take into consideration the vintage year of the fund, which is the year in which the fund initiated its investment activity or effected its first capital call.

An important performance metric for VC funds is the total value to paid in capital (TVPI) or MOIC (multiple of invested capital), which is the ratio of (1) the total amount distributed to the investors plus the value of the investments that are still in the VC fund's portfolio (numerator) and (2) the total amount of invested capital (denominator). The TVPI can be calculated with reference to a single investment as well as with reference to the fund as a whole. For instance, a fund that received contributions from its investors of $100 million, made $30 million in distributions, and has a portfolio value of $80 million, has a TVPI of $(80 + 30)/100 = 110/100 = 1.1$. A TVPI that is greater than 1 indicates that the sum of the distributions to investors and the value of the investments that are still in the portfolio is in excess of the originally invested capital and that the fund has therefore generated capital gains for its investors. A TVPI of less than 1 indicates that the fund is in a cumulative loss position.

Exhibit 1.3 presents the TVPI of VC funds by vintage year for funds that started operations (vintage year) between 1994 and 2016 based on data as of September 30, 2019.[24] The average TVPI is 2.30× for funds with a vintage year between 1994 and 2016 and 2.02× for funds that launched in the period 2008–2016.[25]

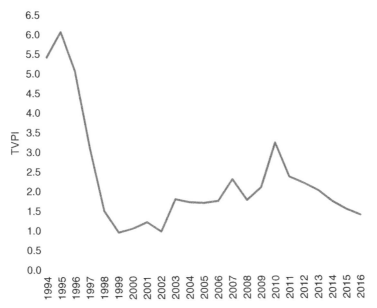

EXHIBIT 1.3 TVPI of Venture Capital Funds by Vintage Year, 1994–2016

---

[24]On the TVPI of VC funds by vintage year, see the series of Cambridge Associates LLC, US Venture Capital Index and Selected Benchmark Statistics.

[25]As we discuss in greater detail later in this chapter, the most recent vintages are not meaningful in terms of ultimate performance as the fund has not yet had a chance to fully deploy its capital, and the

The TVPI measures the value generated by a particular fund or investment, including the unrealized gains that are still embedded in the fund's current holdings. A limitation of the TVPI is that it does not take into account the time horizon of the investment or the risk component. For instance, a TVPI of 1.3 indicates that, based on the current value of the portfolio, the fund has generated 30 cents of gains on each invested dollar. We don't know when the investor contributed funding, how long the investment was outstanding and what was the investment's risk profile. To address the time component of performance, VC funds report also the fund's internal rate of return (IRR), a money-weighted rate that reflects the return of the fund over the period from the inception of the fund's activity through the current measurement date and that is typically presented on an annualized basis. An annualized IRR of 15%, for example, indicates that the investor has earned 15 cents on each dollar invested at the beginning of each annual period over the time horizon of the fund's life.

Exhibit 1.4 illustrates the relationship between the TVPI, the exit year of an investment and the IRR. For example, assuming an investment of $1 million and a TVPI of 2× ($2 million of distributions at exit, for a net gain of $1 million), the IRR will be 26% if the exit event occurs at the end of Year 3, but will drop to 15% if the distribution of $2 million is received at the end of year 5. The table in the exhibit is based on the assumption that all investments get liquidated at the same time at the end of the exit year and that proceeds are immediately distributed. Another way of looking at the Exit Year is to consider it as the weighted average year of exit of all the cash distributions made to the investors in the fund. Exhibit 1.4 points to the critical effect of extending the time horizon of an investment on the return metrics.

The annualized IRR of a fund is likely to change significantly over the life of the fund, and will only stabilize in most cases in six to eight years from the fund's inception date.

In a typical fund, the IRR declines in the first two to three years of the fund's life, as the fund gradually builds its investment portfolio while it incurs management fees, administrative costs, and transaction expenses to execute its investment deals. At first, the investments are

		Exit Year									
		1	2	3	4	5	6	7	8	9	10
Multiple on Invested Capital (TVPI)	1.0×	0%	0%	0%	0%	0%	0%	0%	0%	0%	0%
	2.0×	100%	41%	26%	19%	15%	12%	10%	9%	8%	7%
	3.0×	200%	73%	44%	32%	25%	20%	17%	15%	13%	12%
	4.0×	300%	100%	59%	41%	32%	26%	22%	19%	17%	15%
	5.0×	400%	124%	71%	50%	38%	31%	26%	22%	20%	17%
	6.0×	500%	145%	82%	57%	43%	35%	29%	25%	22%	20%
	7.0×	600%	165%	91%	63%	48%	38%	32%	28%	24%	21%
	8.0×	700%	183%	100%	68%	52%	41%	35%	30%	26%	23%
	9.0×	800%	200%	108%	73%	55%	44%	37%	32%	28%	25%
	10.0×	900%	216%	105%	78%	58%	47%	39%	33%	29%	26%

EXHIBIT 1.4   IRR Based on TVPI (MOIC) and Exit Year

---

investments have not yet realized their full potential. On the dynamics of VC fund returns, see especially Cambridge Associates, "Portfolio Benchmarking: Best Practices for Private Investments," Cambridge Associates, 2018.

likely to be valued at or close to the transaction price, no sales or write-offs have occurred, and the fund is experiencing negative cash flows related to its investment purchases and operational costs. As the fund moves forward in its active "investment" phase, net cash flows and IRR will turn positive. The fund will start recording gains and losses on its investments and liquidate some of its investment position. Eventually, the proceeds from investment sales will exceed the cash outflows related to the fund's expenses and new investment purchases, and the residual will be distributed to the fund's investors. Typically within four to six years from inception, the fund ceases to make new investments and enters into the "liquidation" phase. At this stage, the fund will focus exclusively on exiting from its current investment positions. The manager may still make add-on investments in existing portfolio companies, but overall, the active pursuit of new investment opportunities has effectively come to a halt. The liquidation phase may last several years for a VC fund, depending on market conditions and on the ability of the fund manager to identify suitable exit opportunities. It is not unusual for a VC fund to have a total life of more than 12 years, as the gains (or losses) that have accrued in the fund's portfolio are realized in an exit transaction. As the IRR of the fund stabilizes (six to eight years into the life of the fund), also the fund's risk/return profile becomes stable. Overall, the trajectory of the fund's IRR over the course of the fund's life is expected to follow a "J Curve": an initial decline (Years 1–2) followed by a steep increase as investments increase in value and distributions to investors take place (Years 3–6), and eventually a flattening toward the IRR limit (Years 6 to 12+).[26]

The IRR profile of a fund may be significantly affected by the extent to which the fund is using subscription lines of credit instead of capital calls from investors to finance its investment activity, which is becoming increasingly common.[27] A subscription line of credit is a revolving credit facility (a form of financing or "leverage") that is provided to a fund by one or more lenders and that is collateralized by a pledge of the right to call and receive capital contributions from the fund's investors. Subscription lines of credit have traditionally been used in VC funds as a form of short-term bridge financing to facilitate payments of expenses and make the capital call process more efficient. In recent years, subscription lines of credit have evolved beyond a short-term bridging function to serve as a broader tool used to manage the overall cash of the fund, with repayment terms often extending well beyond 90 days. These lines can be used with the intent to improve the fund's stated IRR due to the mechanics of the IRR calculation and offset the negative pressure on the IRR associated with the "J curve" effect.

Exhibit 1.5 shows an example of how a line of credit can impact the IRR of a fund. The first column presents the scenario of no line of credit (Scenario 1). The manager calls $100,000 in cash from investors in Year 1, pays annual management fees of 2% over six years, and then realizes a gross value of $170,000 at the end of Year 6, generating an annualized IRR of 7.51% for the fund over the period. TVPI in this case is 1.52×, calculated as the realized value of $170,000 divided by $112,000, the capital called from investors to cover purchases

[26]Antonella Puca, "Private Equity Funds: Leverage and Performance Evaluation," *Enterprising Investor*, CFA Institute, July 16, 2018.
[27]The Institutional Limited Partners Association (ILPA) has released a report to provide guidance on best practices in the use and reporting of subscription lines of credit, which highlights their effect on IRR calculations. See ILPA, Subscription Lines of Credit and Alignment of Interest, ILPA, June 2017.

		Scenario 1	Scenario 2	Scenario 3
Year	Transaction	Cash flows with no line of credit	Cash flows with one-year line of credit	Cash flows with two-year line of credit
1/1/2020	Investment	$ (100,000)		
1/1/2020	Management Fees	$ (2,000)	$ (2,000)	$ (2,000)
1/1/2021	Investment		$ (100,000)	
1/1/2021	Management Fees	$ (2,000)	$ (2,000)	$ (2,000)
1/1/2021	Interest		$ (4,000)	$ (4,000)
1/1/2022	Investment			$ (100,000)
1/1/2022	Management Fees	$ (2,000)	$ (2,000)	$ (2,000)
1/1/2022	Interest			$ (4,000)
1/1/2023	Management Fees	$ (2,000)	$ (2,000)	$ (2,000)
1/1/2024	Management Fees	$ (2,000)	$ (2,000)	$ (2,000)
1/1/2025	Management Fees	$ (2,000)	$ (2,000)	$ (2,000)
12/31/2025	Realization Event	$ 170,000	$ 170,000	$ 170,000
	IRR	7.51%	8.18%	9.10%
	TVPI	1.52	1.47	1.42

EXHIBIT 1.5   Effect of Subscription Line of Credit on IRR and TVPI – Example

of investments and management fees charged to the account.[28] The second column presents the scenario of a one-year line of credit at an interest rate of 4% per annum (Scenario 2). In this scenario, there is an improvement in the IRR since now the investors have to disburse $100,000 in cash at the beginning of year 2, but the TVPI is actually lower by the amount of the interest expense. Similarly, in the third column the IRR increases again while the TVPI decreases (Scenario 3). The IRR/TVPI effect for the non-managing investors is amplified in practice by the effect of performance-based compensation to the manager. Assuming a hurdle rate of 8%, the manager would not receive any performance-based compensation in Scenario 1, where no line of credit is used. However, the manager would receive performance-based compensation in Scenario 2 and Scenario 3, since the fund performance as measured by the IRR with the line of credit is above the hurdle rate of 8%.

Subscription lines of credit provide the advantage for investors of significantly improving the overall cash flow profile of the fund and allowing for investments without having to go through the negative IRR associated with the J curve effect in the early years. In some cases, investors may be able to redeploy some of the committed cash in other, more profitable ways, and enjoy the increase in reported return figures. The existence of longer-term subscription lines of credit, however, does create issues in performance comparability among managers that may be using such lines and managers that do not. It has become common practice for many investors, particularly on the institutional side, to ask for return figures both with and without the effect of the line of credit, or to ask for detailed cash flow information that can

---

[28]Cash disbursements by investors to cover investment purchases and management fees can also take place in response to a single capital call, rather than in multiple calls as in Scenario 1 in the example of Exhibit 1.13.

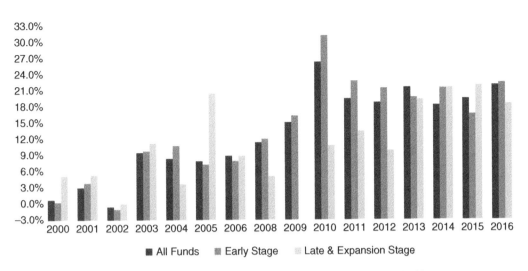

EXHIBIT 1.6   US Venture Capital Funds: Annualized IRR by Vintage Year, 2000–2016

be used to recalculate the returns. The risk of investors not responding to their capital call obligations should also be considered.

Exhibit 1.6 presents the annualized IRR for VC funds with an inception date between 2000 and 2016, by vintage year, as of September 30, 2019. The "All Funds" column represents the IRR for funds in different VC stages with all assets pooled together as if they were a single fund. The Early Stage and the Later & Expansion Stage columns represent only the subset of funds that invest exclusively in companies in the respective stages of development. A striking feature of the IRR by Vintage Year is the difference in results over time. In 1999–2002, the burst of the internet bubble has significantly affected VC returns, particularly for funds that had a focus on the early VC stage. Starting from 2003 vintages, returns have become positive again, and have stayed in the single digit realm through 2006. It is only at the inception of the financial crisis that we can find again funds that are able to generate double-digit growth over time. The period from 2010 onward has been characterized by IRRs of 15% or above. If we exclude the 2010 outlier, a net required return in the range 15–20% for VC investors is consistent with the industry benchmark returns of the past decade.

Exhibit 1.7 presents the pooled horizon IRRs for Indices of U.S. VC funds developed by Cambridge Associates LLC ("CA") as compared to representative equity market indices such as the Nasdaq Composite Index, the Russell 2000, and the S&P500, based on data for the periods ended September 30, 2019.[29] The horizon returns are calculated by pooling together the fund cash flows independently of vintage year and treating them as if they were taking place in a single pooled fund. Returns have generally been higher over the 5-year and 10-year time horizons than over the 15-year and 20-year horizons, which include the effect of the 2008 financial crisis. On the other hand, returns over the 5-year horizon have been lower than those over the 10-year horizon and, for the early stage index, substantially below the long-term 25-year horizon return. The lower returns in recent years may be an indication of

---

[29]The data in Exhibit 1.13 is compiled from 1,858 funds, including fully liquidated funds, formed between 1981 and 2018.

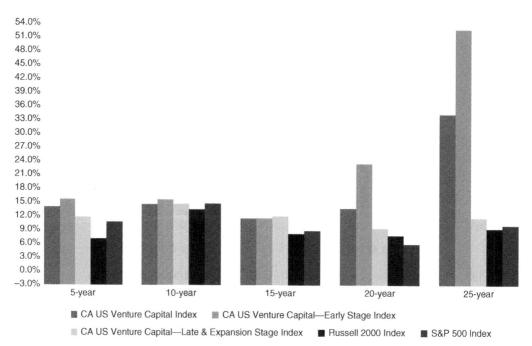

EXHIBIT 1.7   Fund Index Summary: Horizon Pooled Return, Net to Limited Partners – Periods ended September 30, 2019

greater "efficiency" in the VC market as of the end of 2019 and of a decade of economic growth, fostered by easier access to capital and private company information, and greater competition for deals. They also reflect a general decline in the level of real and nominal interest rates, which has contributed to lower the cost of capital for ESEs.

From another perspective, investors may want to consider the performance of a fund manager in comparison to the manager's peer group. For instance, an institutional investor may have received a mandate from its board of directors to allocate a certain percentage of assets to VC funds. The investor will strive to select managers that at a minimum can outperform their peer group, and possibly perform in the top quartile. The investor will review the performance of multiple managers and make comparisons between them to identify its preferred solution. The manager selection process will typically include a review of the historical series of the peer group quartile IRR returns. Most likely, the investor will focus on the 5- to 10-year performance of managers that have active funds and that are currently looking to raise capital, and that may provide suitable investment alternatives. As part of the process, the investor will develop expectations about a required rate of return based on the historical performance of the top quartile of managers, as well as by the investor's expectations on the future market environment for the peer group.

Exhibit 1.8 presents the top quartile net IRR boundary and the median net IRR for VC funds that started operations (vintage year) in the period 2006–2016 for the period from the inception of the life of the fund through September 30, 2019.

In reviewing the quartile returns of Exhibit 1.8, it is important to keep in mind that, similarly to the IRR, a fund position in the return quartiles will also change significantly over the course of the fund's life, depending on the stage of its life cycle (start-up, investment, or

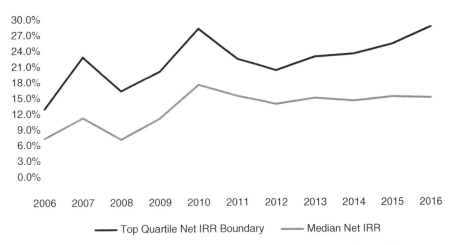

EXHIBIT 1.8 U.S.-Based Venture Capital Funds, Median Net IRR and Quartile Boundaries by Vintage Year

liquidation phase). A fund will typically find a stable spot in the return quartile within six to eight years from inception, as the IRR also settles toward its limit.

In Exhibit 1.8, the fund performance metrics for 2016 is likely to still be skewed by a combination of the J curve effect and the more frequent use of subscription lines of credit, which somewhat impair their use as an indicator of portfolio investment performance over time. For the 2006–2015 series, and if we exclude the 2006 and 2008 outliers, the net IRR for the top quartile falls in the 20.1–28.2% range (11.1–17.5% if the median net IRR is used).

Overall, from the earlier analysis, a required portfolio IRR in the 15–25% range for VC investors would be consistent with the VC performance record of the past 10–15 years and in the current low interest rate scenario. It is important to note that the 15–25% range is based on the performance of an investment after taking into account the effect of the probability of failure that some of the portfolio investment will experience over time.[30] In other words, the 15–25% range applies to investments that are included in a diversified portfolio (a fund with a diversified portfolio or a portfolio of direct deals). The risk of failure associated with individual ESE investments is significantly reduced at the portfolio level by portfolio diversification and, in our view, should be modeled separately from the discount rate used in the valuation of an individual ESE investment. As we discuss in greater detail in Chapter 4, assuming that an investor expects to write off 30% of its invested capital in nonperforming deals, and given a time horizon of five years, the investor will have to target a return at a minimum in the 24–34% range for individual deals in order to achieve its overall 15–25% portfolio return objective. Within these ranges for target and required returns, respectively, we would expect VC investments in seed and ESE to gravitate toward the high end of the range, and investments in later stage enterprises to gravitate toward the low end.

Also, neither the TVPI (value) nor the IRR (value and time) provide information on the risk component of investment performance. In a VC fund's performance report, the risk aspect

---

[30]The dilution effect from subsequent rounds of financing on the fund's equity interest in a portfolio company will also affect realized returns. See Chapter 4 for further discussion.

is typically addressed with qualitative disclosures that identify the fund's vintage year and its strategy (stage of portfolio companies, industry, leverage, etc.) and quantitative metrics that represent the variability of fund returns (the capital loss ratio, the since-inception annualized standard deviation of fund returns, or a metric that tracks the fund's performance relative to a benchmark).

In terms of benchmarks, VC funds present special challenges as well. Investors may want to compare the performance of VC funds to that of a public equity index as an investment alternative. The return of public equity indices is typically calculated by assuming that the invested capital is deployed in one spot at the beginning of the measurement period. Cash flows in VC funds, however, are irregular, which makes comparison to public equity indices difficult to implement in practice and requiring some adjustments to get to a "Public-market equivalent" (PME) return metric. Also, performance comparisons need to take into account the vintage year of the fund.

Strategic Investors

Strategic investors are typically larger operating companies or competitors that target an ESE primarily in view of the synergies that the ESE can provide to their own core operations and strategy. Strategic investors are a primary driver in M&A exit transactions, where control of the ESE is transferred to the acquirer. Companies that engage in significant VC activity, such as Intel, SoftBank, and Google, often find it suitable to establish a corporate venture capital (CVC) arm to invest in ESE minority positions, alongside their M&A transactions. In some cases, large ESEs have also engaged in CVC investing by setting up their own private VC fund.[31] CVC arms typically operate through investment funds that are similar to independent VC funds in terms of legal structure. A strategic CVC fund, however, will significantly differ from an independent VC fund in view of its objectives, which are tied to the mission of the parent company. For instance, a parent company may want to acquire an interest in an ESE to have access to a new geographical market or a new customer segment, or to access a new technology or a drug that an ESE has successfully developed and that it may take years for the parent to develop independently. The investment may be a first step toward the acquisition of the ESE at a later stage, or a step to access business intelligence that would otherwise not be available to the parent.

Over time, some CVCs have evolved to resemble VC funds more closely in targeting returns that are more financial than strategic in nature. The compensation structure of management in a CVC often provides a key to the true nature of these entities and on whether there is truly an incentive for management to execute on the parent's objective at a strategic level. For instance, for a parent company that has the expansion in a new geographical market as a strategic objective, a compensation structure that rewards CVC management based on the increase in revenue in that market as a result of CVC investing is likely to result in greater

---

[31]For instance, Slack Inc. has established the Slack Fund, a private investment fund run by Slack. The Slack Fund is similar to a traditional VC fund, with a 10-year lifespan and capital from outside the company's balance sheet (only existing company investors in this case). The fund focuses on investments in enterprise software companies that have potential for substantial contribution to the Slack's echosystem. For an overview of CVC arms based in the United States investing in deals globally, see Brendan Burke and Darren Klees, "The Golden Mean of Corporate Venture Capital," *PitchBook 2Q 2019 Analyst Note*, PitchBook Data Inc., May 16, 2019.

strategic alignment between the CVC and the parent than a bonus structure based purely on the CVC portfolio's IRR. Other factors that are indicative of a CVC's strategic focus may include:

- Investment staff includes a significant component of former parent employees.
- Base salary is a higher percentage of total compensation.
- Financial performance is not the main driver of compensation.
- The CVC has to report to the parent on the achievement of predefined objectives, expressed in terms of the parent's strategic goals and key performance indicators.
- The CVC has contributed to the parent company's M&A pipeline, by identifying and investing in companies that were eventually acquired by the parent.
- The CVC invests in sectors that are consistent with the parent company's operations and strategic goals.

Rather than using TVPI and IRR as primary measures of performance, a CVC fund may focus on key performance indicators such as the number of new products introduced to market, the amount of new revenue generated, the number of deals sourced and evaluated in a given sector, commercial pilot projects implemented, patents acquired, new users, clients or customers.

In 2018 and 2019, corporate investors participated in rounds contributing more than 50% of the total deal value for U.S.-based companies and have been especially active in the larger size deals.[32] CVC investors may be willing to pay higher valuations than a pure financial player and are often able to exercise an influence on the company's operations, even as a minority investor that may have a significant impact on the company's valuation. The presence and objectives of strategic investors may affect the price-setting mechanism of a transaction and result in transaction prices that include entity-specific synergies and that may need adjustments to reach a fair value conclusion.

Mission Investors

By "mission investors" we identify a class of investors that target an ESE primarily in view of the contribution that the ESE can provide in reaching their program objectives, above and beyond the expected financial return from the investment (and sometimes aside from them). Mission investors may include individuals, foundations, and other nonprofit organizations that have environmental, social, and governance (ESG) objectives in their mission statement, government-sponsored entities that are looking to have an impact on their local communities, infrastructure funds, and corporations that dedicate funding specifically for ESG and other "impact" investments. These investors typically fall under the "financial investor" label in commonly used databases, and most of them indeed operate under the assumption that it is possible to pursue a strategy with a primary program objective while maximizing financial returns.[33] Having said that, mission investors do have special characteristics that may affect their approach to valuation.[34] In some cases, these investors may be available to provide

---

[32] PitchBook Data Inc. and National Venture Capital Association, 4Q 2018 and 4Q 2019 PitchBook NVCA Venture Capital Monitor Summary.
[33] See, for instance, Andreas Dal Santo, Antonella Puca, and Greg Siegel, "Effective ESG Investing: An Interview with Andrew Parry,"*Enterprising Investor*, CFA Institute, June 15, 2018.
[34] I thank Paolo Siniscalco for highlighting the relevance of mission investors as a separate category of investors with their own set of objectives in the VC market.

funding to ESEs at a significantly lower cost of capital than otherwise available in the market, particularly if they are backed by community or governmental funding specifically dedicated to support their program objectives.

According to Milton Friedman in a 1970 article for the *New York Times Magazine*, the doctrine of "social responsibility" involves the acceptance of the view that "political mechanisms, not market mechanisms, are the appropriate way to determine the allocation of scarce resources to alternative uses."[35] The reconciliation of social responsibility with the principles of market economy on which the fair value standard is based is a challenge in our economy.

Cross-Border Investing

The past decade has seen an increase in cross-border investment transactions, with investors exploring opportunities outside of their home market, and additional funding from foreign investors, especially to companies in China and the U.S. market. SoftBank, a Japanese telecoms conglomerate, is a good example of this trend. In addition to making direct venture investments, SoftBank has served as the principal manager and the second-largest shareholder of the SoftBank Vision Fund, an investment vehicle with more than $100 billion in AUM that is administered by London-based SoftBank Investment Advisors. The Vision Fund has focused on ESEs in the later rounds of financing, generally seeking between 20% and 40% of ownership, including unicorns such as Uber, WeWork, Fanatics, and Flexport.[36]

Along similar lines, Temasek Fund, a Singapore-based investment company with $200-plus billion in AUM, has grown from a local fund investing mostly in Singapore-based companies to a large international player in Asia, Europe, and America. Temasek has established a number of U.S. offices that focus on investments in technology ESEs. Qatar, United Arab Emirates, and Saudi Arabia have each opened offices in Silicon Valley to facilitate U.S. investments.[37]

In the United States, foreign investment in U.S. companies and operations is subject to screening by the Committee of Foreign Investment in the United States (CFIUS), an interagency committee of the U.S. government, which was established in 1975 for national security purposes. In August 2018 the *Foreign Investment Risk Review Modernization Act* (FIRRMA) delivered enhanced power to the CFIUS. Under the FIRRMA, CFIUS has been moving from a world in which it mostly looked at situations where a foreign entity was buying an entire company to a new world that also includes minority, noncontrolling investments. In response to the new legislation of FIRRMA, NVCA updated its model VC Term Sheet to include several provisions regarding CFIUS review.[38]

---

[35] Milton Friedman, "The Social Responsibility of Business Is to Increase Its Profits," *New York Times Magazine*, September 13, 1970.

[36] On the Vision Fund, see Kyle Stanford and Van Le, "The Vision Fund's Only Competitor is Itself", *PirchBook Q2 2020 Analyst Note*, PitchBook Data Inc., April 6, 2020.

[37] On the role of non-U.S. investors in the U.S. venture capital industry, see also Kyle Stanford and Van Le, "Nontraditional Investors in VC Are Here to Stay," *PitchBook 4Q 2019 Analyst Note*, PitchBook Data Inc., December 6, 2019.

[38] For an overview of the NVCA changes to its term sheet related to CFIUS terms, see Dorsey & Withney LLC, "NVCA Includes Detailed CFIUS Terms in Its Model VC Term Sheet," April 29, 2019, https://www.dorsey.com/newsresources/publications/articles/2019/04/nvca-includes-detailed-cfius-terms.

EXIT STRATEGY

For many investors in ESEs, one of the conditions for entering into a new deal is to be able to envision a profitable path to exit. For a financial investor, identifying a potential exit strategy is part of the initial investment due diligence process that leads to the decision of whether to execute an investment transaction. From the point of view of the ESE, an exit event represents a change in ownership structure and typically results from one of the following:

- Going out of business
- Change of control: Buyout transaction
- Change of control: M&A transaction
- Initial public offering/direct listing

Going Out of Business – Dissolution

As previously noted, dissolution events are a frequent occurrence for ESEs. An ESE dissolution results in the partial or full write-off of the ESE investment. For an ESE investor, the valuation of the enterprise in a dissolution scenario depends on the proceeds that are expected to be available for distribution, the timing of the distribution, and how the proceeds will be allocated among different classes and series of shares in a complex capital structure. The investor in an enterprise that is going out of business may still be able to recover at least some proceeds from the sale of its assets. The liquidation preferences of preferred stockholders and other seniority rights are most valuable in a distressed scenario. Preferred stockholders may also benefit from an adverse redemption feature, which may grant them the right to demand a redemption of preferred stock at a purchase price equal to the original purchase price plus any declared and unpaid dividends. In the most severe cases, a full write-off will be necessary for all equity investors, independently of seniority rights.

Buyout Transaction

Buyout sales (or "trade sales") consist of sales of a control position in a business to a financial investor (another VC or private equity investor). The enterprise being sold will generally continue to operate as an independent entity under this scenario. GAAP metrics that reflect the company's operations and projects as a stand-alone entity are likely to drive a buyout valuation. Exhibit 1.9 illustrates the trend in the value and number of buyout transactions for U.S. VC-backed companies in the period 2010–2019.[39] Buyout transactions represented 19.8% of VC exits in 2019 (in number, excluding write-offs), a significant increase from the period 2006–2011 where they had been below 10%.

NVCA's legal agreements, including the Model VC Term Sheet, are available at https://nvca.org/model-legal-documents/.

[39] On buyout transaction activity for U.S. VC-backed companies, see PitchBook Data Inc and National Venture Capital Association 4Q 2019 PitchBook NVCA Venture Capital Monitory Summary as of December 31, 2019.

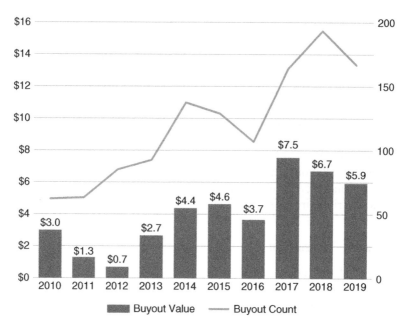

EXHIBIT 1.9 U.S. VC Buyout Exits, Years 2010–2019 (Value in $billion)

M&A Transactions

M&A transactions consist of sales that transfer the control of a company to a strategic buyer that is attracted by the contribution that the target can make to the combined entity. In order to be a successful target for an acquisition, an ESE does not necessarily have to demonstrate the capacity to generate revenue as a stand-alone entity. Rather, a strategic buyer will look at how the company can enhance the revenue potential and growth for the combined entity and help the acquirer meet its own corporate objectives.

The AICPA PE/VC Valuation Guide recommends that when evaluating an exit with a strategic buyer, the valuation analyst consider among others:

- The number of larger companies for which the portfolio company's products or services would be complementary to their existing business.
- The extent that the portfolio company's products or services are a "need to have" or a "nice to have" either to the end user or to the potential acquirer, to round out their product portfolio.
- The strategic positioning of potential buyers and their perception of the need to diversify in one direction or another.
- The regulatory impediments to a strategic buyer's ability to acquire portfolio company (e.g. antitrust/anticompetition concerns).
- The strategic buyer's financial condition and its ability to finance an acquisition of the portfolio company.[40]

---

[40] AICPA PE/VC Valuation Guide 1.50.

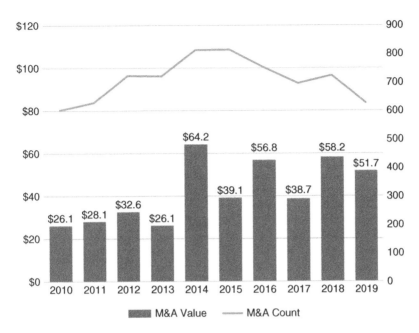

EXHIBIT 1.10 U.S. VC M&A Exits – Years 2010–2019 (Value in $billion)

M&A transactions represent the most common VC exit type. Exhibit 1.10 shows the data related to U.S. M&A transactions for VC-backed enterprises in terms of value and number of deals over the period 2010–2019.[41] In 2019, there were 627 VC M&A transactions, aggregating to $51.7 billion and representing approximately 71% of the total number of VC exit transactions (excluding write-offs). The percentage of total exits represented by M&A transactions has declined recently from a high of 85% in 2010.

A change of control in an M&A transaction will typically trigger a number of special provisions included in the company's certificate of incorporation and securities agreements. For instance, a convertible bond outstanding at the time of the acquisition may have to mandatorily convert into preferred stock of the acquiring company. Alternatively, the acquiring company may have to pay off the target company's convertible bonds, sometimes at a multiple of invested capital.

It is also common for the target company's warrants to expire in a merger, unless they are exercised just prior to the transaction. Also, the vesting of options granted under a target company stock option plan is often accelerated in the event of an M&A transaction. A single-trigger acceleration refers to an automatic acceleration of vesting upon the occurrence of the merger event. A double-trigger acceleration refers to an accelerated vesting that takes place upon the occurrence of two events, typically the acquisition of the target company combined with an employee being dismissed by the acquiring company. Acceleration on change of control is often a contentious point of negotiation between founders and VC investors.

---

[41]On acquisition activity for U.S. VC-backed companies, see PitchBook Data Inc. and National Venture Capital Association 4Q 2019 PitchBook NVCA Venture Monitor Summary as of December 31, 2019.

A question that may arise ahead of an M&A transaction as well as in a financial sale is how much relevance to place on a nonbinding offer of intent in an estimate of the company's fair value. The AICPA PE/VC Valuation Guide recommends considering whether the offer is realistic, and if indeed it is likely that it will result in an actual transaction at the stated price.[42] The offer price has to be weighted alongside the value that is expected to be realized if the transaction does not take place.

There are many circumstances in which a transaction that involves a change of control for the target company may indeed fall through. The closing of an M&A transaction may be subject to regulatory approval, which eventually is not obtained. Also, the buyer may conclude, at the end of the due diligence process, that the target company does not satisfy its due diligence requirements. Market conditions may change, which may make the transaction no longer appealing to either or both parties. The valuation analyst may want to be especially weary of nonbinding offers at a price that is significantly higher than the price of the target company's latest round. The adjustments and weighting applied to a nonbinding offer price should be a function of financing contingencies, and the timing of the due diligence and regulatory approval process, among other factors.

Initial Public Offering

In an IPO, a company goes through the process of offering its shares to the general public for the first time, typically by listing them on an established stock exchange such as the New York Stock Exchange or the NASDAQ in the United States. An IPO represents a financing event for the company, as new shares are issued as part of the public offering process.

IPOs help establish a trading market for a company's shares and generally result in the highest valuation multiples for early investors in an exit scenario. The IPO price is supported by the underwriting syndicate, a team of investment banks that may engage in price stabilization activities in order to decrease volatility and support the price of the stock. Underwriters typically have Greenshoe options that allow them to purchase up to an additional 15% of shares from the company if demand exceeds supply. Alternatively, underwriters can repurchase shares on the market if supply exceeds demand. Both actions help decrease the volatility of the stock price in the days and weeks after the IPO.

IPOs come with high implementation costs due to extensive regulatory and compliance requirements. Under the federal securities laws of the United States, a company may not lawfully offer or sell shares unless the transaction has been registered with the SEC or an exemption applies. To register an offering, a company files a registration statement with the SEC (Form S-1). Any planned exchange listing will be disclosed in the prospectus for the IPO. Once the company has been listed, it will also be required on a going-forward basis to disclose certain information to the public, including its quarterly and annual financial statements on Forms 10-Q and 10-K. These regulatory and compliance requirements result in significant fees. An IPO may also expose the company's management to significant pressure to meet investors' expectations in the public market and pursue short-term financial objectives, which may distract management from the company's strategic objectives.

---

[42] AICPE PE/VC Valuation Guide Q&A 14.42 Offers to Purchase, Q: "Does an offer or a nonbinding letter of intent constitute fair value?"

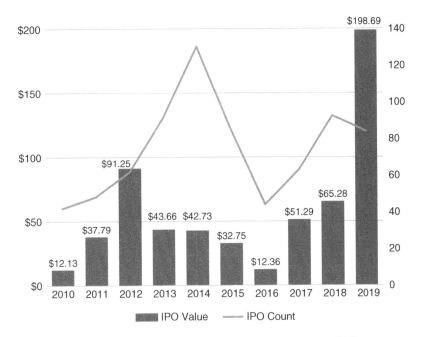

EXHIBIT 1.11 U.S. VC-backed IPO Deals 2010–2019 (Value in $billion)

The year 2019 has been a record year in IPO activity for VC-backed companies in the United States, with very large unicorn deals that have pushed volumes to a record high, as shown in Exhibit 1.11.[43]

Historically, the number of IPOs has been highly dependent on general market conditions. In the period 2017–2019 IPOs have represented less than 10% of total exits in number of deals in a given year (excluding write-offs), but more than 50% of total exits in dollar value.

The IPO market has evolved significantly over the past two decades, as technology companies have come to represent an increasing share of the overall listed markets. In the late 1990s, a company with $30–$60 million in revenue, recent profitability, and a sound management team could look at the opportunity of an IPO as a realistic exit target. After the internet bubble crash of 2000–2001, and through most of the following decade, the IPO venue was accessible primarily to the largest and most profitable VC-backed enterprises, typically mature companies with revenue in excess of $150 million. Starting in 2011, the IPO market has witnessed an increase in the number of unicorns. Many of these companies are ESEs in that they are still experiencing losses at the time of the IPO. Still, they have been able to command valuations at multiples of invested capital. Over the decade 2010–2019, the median valuation of VC-backed companies at the time of the IPO ranged between a low of $178.3 million in 2016 and a high of $377.6 million in 2019. Median trailing enterprise

---

[43] On IPO activity of U.S. VC-backed companies, see PitchBook Data Inc. and National Venture Capital Association 4Q 2019 PitchBook NVCA Venture Monitor Summary as of December 31, 2019.

value/revenue multiples have shown a strong upward trend, from a low of 3.6× in 2009 to multiples in excess of 10× in 2018–2019.[44]

Although VC investors consider an IPO of a portfolio company as an "exit," it is perhaps more appropriate to view it as a financing event for the company, which may provide little, if any, proceeds to the VC fund itself. Typically, upon completion of the IPO, all of the existing equity capital of the portfolio company is converted into a single class of common equity (mandatory conversion). The IPO is also typically subject to a minimum price per share (for instance, no less than two times the original issue price as of the latest round of preferred stock, adjusted for stock splits, dividends) and needs to generate a minimum amount of proceeds from the offering to be finalized (a "Qualified IPO"). In some cases, the IPO may result in a dual share system, with control rights assigned only to one class. Dual-class structures have become more frequent in recent years, particularly in the technology sector following the example of Alphabet Inc. (Google's parent), Facebook, Alibaba, and others. The dual-class structure may help founders preserve control of a company after the IPO, but may also lead to a misalignment of interest between the controlling shareholders that are making decisions for the firm and shareholders that have limited voting rights which are most exposed to the risk of the company's strategy. In modeling an IPO scenario as an ESE potential exit event, the valuation analyst will typically adjust the company's capitalization structure to reflect the risks associated with the single- or dual-class post-IPO structure.

After the company has become public, the shares held by the pre-IPO shareholders are typically subject to a lock-up period, whereby shares cannot be sold in the public markets for a period of up to 12 months from the IPO date. A valuation analyst will generally reflect the lock-up provision by adjusting the traded stock price with a discount that takes into account the period remaining from the measurement date through the lock-up expiration date.

Even after the portfolio company has gone public, a shareholder may still find challenges in liquidating its position, particularly if the shares are thinly traded and if the shareholder has a significant position to sell. To the extent a market price is available coming from orderly transactions on a public exchange, the market price will not be subject to any illiquidity discount that reflects the size of the shareholder's holding. The valuation analyst may want to consider in its ESE valuation the significant costs that are involved in an IPO transaction, and any additional pre-IPO financing that may be needed to cover such costs.

Most recently, some companies have elected to pursue a direct listing as an alternative path to access the public markets for their shares, in the attempt to control costs and also avoid the dilution of ownership that an IPO typically involves.[45] In a direct listing, a company is granted access to a public offering for its securities without issuing additional stock. The company's shareholders are able to offer their shares for sale on a public exchange while the capital structure of the company remains substantially intact. The company forgoes the

---

[44]Data on median valuation and EV/revenue of VC-backed technology companies is from Asad Hussain and Jordan Beck, "Ridesharing Gears Up to Go Public", *PitchBook 1Q 2019 Analyst Note*, PitchBook Data Inc., February 25, 2019.

[45]In April 2018, Spotify Inc. started trading its shares on the New York Stock Exchange in a high-profile direct listing. Prior to Spotify, direct listings had been a rare occurrence in the venture capital world. In June 2019, Slack, an ESE unicorn, followed suit with an offering where the direct listing price was established by the New York Stock Exchange without underwriters. For an analysis of Slack's direct listing, see Cameron Stanfill, "The Only Time Slacking Off Could Pay Off," *PitchBook 2Q 2019 Analyst Note*, PitchBook Data Inc., April 30, 2019.

assistance of the investment banks, which can help stabilize the price of the security in the aftermath of the offering. The post-listing price is exposed to the ordinary market dynamics of the exchange in which the securities are listed and may be subject to considerable volatility. Unlike the IPO, a direct listing is not a fundraising event as only preexistent stock can be sold on the exchange.

A direct listing is generally significantly less expensive than a traditional IPO and subject to a lighter regulatory regime. It can be executed more quickly and allows preexistent shareholders to immediately sell their shares without the restriction of an IPO lock-up period. A direct listing provides a way to access the public markets and obtain liquidity for investors without having a dilution effect on those shareholders that elect to hold on to their shares. This can be a very attractive proposition for founders and shareholders that don't want radical changes in the company's ownership structure.

From a valuation perspective, the IPO price and the direct listing price are likely to represent a significant step-up in valuation versus the pre-IPO value of the company's equity. Access to the public markets has generally the immediate benefit of increasing the value of the enterprise and reducing its cost of capital. The long-term effect of an IPO on the equity value of the enterprise is more controversial.[46]

Exits in Summary Exhibit 1.12 summarizes the U.S. VC exit activity over the period 2010–2019.[47] Since 2015, the U.S. VC market has experienced a decline in the number of

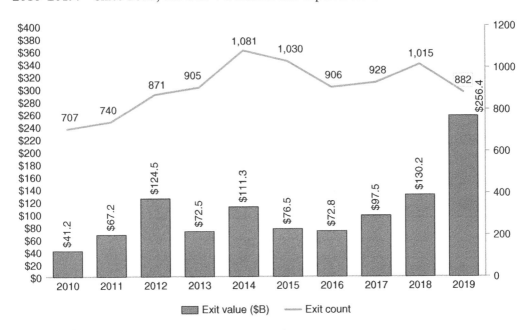

EXHIBIT 1.12 U.S. VC Exit Activity, Years 2010–2019

[46]For an analysis of valuation performance for VC-backed unicorn exits, see Cameron Stanfill and Jordan Beck, "Searching for Validation," *PitchBook 1Q 2019 Analyst Note*, PitchBook Data Inc., March 21, 2019.
[47]On U.S. exit activity, see PitchBook Data Inc. and National Venture Capital Association, 4Q 2019 PitchBook NVCA Venture Monitor Summary.

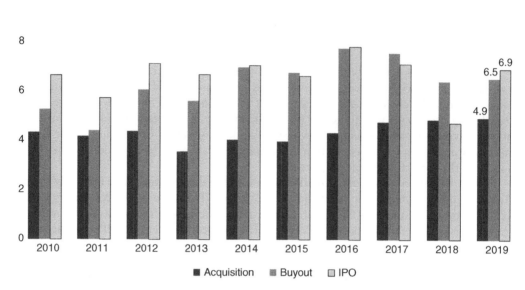

EXHIBIT 1.13   Median Time to Exit (in Years) by Exit Type, 2010–2019

deals, but has significantly increased in dollar value. The average size of an exit increased significantly for all exit types.

Exhibit 1.13 shows the median time to exit in years by type of exit. Based on a given value at exit, the time to exit has a significant impact on the ultimate return earned by a VC investor.[48] For acquisitions, the median time to exit has increased from a low of 3.6 years in 2013, to 4.9 years in 2019. Acquisitions tend to occur earlier in the life of a company than buyouts and IPOs, with IPOs having the longest time to exit (in a range of 4.7 to 7.8 years over the period).

CONCLUSION

Early stage enterprises include a broad range of entities that, in some cases, have been able to command multibillion-dollar valuations in the VC market. ESEs share the expectation of high growth, lack of current profitability, reliance on external financing for survival, and a number of other characteristics. A fair value perspective on ESE valuation brings forth the key role that investors in the VC markets play for their survival and ultimate success. The return expectation of VC investors, their risk preferences, time horizon, available capital, behavioral biases, and nonfinancial objectives, are all part of the framework that a valuation analyst needs to consider to establish suitable financial projections for an ESE, estimate the company's cost of capital, identify and assign probabilities of occurrence to exit scenarios,

---

[48] On median time to exit for U.S. VC-backed companies, see PitchBook Data Inc. and National Venture Capital Association, 4Q 2019 PitchBook NVCA Venture Monitor Summary.

and ultimately come to a valuation conclusion that is realistic and consistent with fair value principles. The analysis in this chapter indicates that:

- Companies tend to be further along in their business operations at each round of financing than under the traditional AICPA classification. Most companies that are raising Series A funding already need to have revenue in order to be able to attract VC investors. While there is a significant amount of capital available for new deals, the total number of VC deals has actually been falling for the past several years and companies are taking longer to achieve each round of funding than in the pre-2009 decade. ESEs that had developed in the private markets to reach a multibillion-dollar valuation used to be a rare occurrence (hence the "unicorn" name) and have now significantly grown in number across the world.

- The VC markets have expanded to include categories of investors that have strategic or mission-oriented goals and that are willing in some cases to provide capital at a lower cost of capital than otherwise available in the market. Together with historically low interest rates, this increased availability of capital has contributed to push down the cost of capital and increase valuations at all stages in ESE development.

- The valuation of ESEs needs to take into account the risk of failure. Many ESEs will never reach an exit transaction or profitable operations. More research in this area is desirable to help assess these probabilities with reasonable accuracy. ESE investors need to target returns for individual deals that are significantly higher than the return they ultimately expect to realize to reflect the reality that only a few of their deals are likely to turn out to be successful. Overall, the target returns that investors would like to see in a deal negotiation have declined over the past decade relative to long-term historical averages.

- In evaluating investment returns, it is important to be aware of the interaction of the three key factors of value, risk, and time. The performance evaluation of an ESE investment needs to take into account, in addition to return metrics, also a multiple of invested capital (TVPI), the time to exit and of risk considerations to provide an adequate picture of an investment's results.

- The IPO environment for ESE exits is highly dependent on general market conditions. The 2018–2019 period has seen very high IPO volumes in historical terms. The valuation of a pre-IPO company should take into account the possibility of a post-IPO dual share class and the additional risk that such structure may involve for ordinary shareholders. Also, the potential effect on market prices of the expiration of the lockout periods for owners and underwriters should be considered.

CHAPTER 2

Fair Value Standard

The fair value standard is the standard of value that is used in business valuation for financial reporting under generally accepted accounting principles (GAAP) globally. It is also commonly used in the valuation of investments to make asset allocation decisions, evaluate investment manager performance, and assess manager compensation. It is used in the valuation of business and intangible assets in M&A transactions and in other types of business combinations. It drives the work of securities analysts and creates a global benchmark to compare company performance results. In an economy where prices are determined by the competitive action of market forces, the fair value standard points to the importance of looking at the "exit" price in an orderly transaction between market participants as a reference for valuation. The fair value standard is inspired by the idea that "fairness" can find an expression in the pricing mechanism of a market economy. At the inception of the 2008 economic crisis, it was described as "a cornerstone to building the infrastructure needed for a more broadly effective risk management system."[1]

In this chapter, we present the fair value standard as it applies to early stage enterprise (ESE) valuation. We highlight some points in the history of the fair value concept, illustrate the key features of the current fair value standard in financial reporting, distinguish it from other valuation standards, and identify resources that help implement fair value measurement in the practice of ESE valuation.

Most recently, there has been a significant volume of guidance on the fair value standard in business valuation. Some of this guidance has explicitly targeted venture capital valuation and issues that are of special relevance for ESEs. The Financial Accounting Standards Board (FASB) Accounting Standard Codification (ASC) 820, *Fair Value Measurement* and the International Accounting Standards Board (IASB) International Financial Reporting Standard (IFRS) 13, *Fair Value Measurement* provide authoritative guidance for the fair value standard

---

[1]Kurt Schacht, CFA Institute Center for Market Integrity, Statement in support of FASB and IASB fair value measurement for financial instruments released April 17, 2008. The statement was released shortly after the Bear Stearns debacle of March 2008, which is at the outset of the 2008 financial crisis. In the April 2008 Statement, the CFA Institute supports the position that "the widespread use of fair value measurement will ultimately play an important role in improving market discipline and transparency, as well as assist in making more informed risk management decisions."

in financial reporting. The latest edition of the International Private Equity Valuation Guidelines (2018) (the IPEV Guidelines) and the Accounting and Valuation Guide on the *Valuation of Portfolio Company Investments of Private Equity and Venture Capital Funds and Other Investment Companies* by the American Institute of Certified Public Accountants (the AICPA PE/VC Valuation Guide) (2019), together with a number of other recent releases, have given a significant contribution to expand the breadth and depth of guidance on the implementation of ASC 820/IFRS 13 in the valuation of ESEs. The standard of fair value under ASC 820 is substantially identical to the standard under IFRS 13. In the discussion that follows, we refer to ASC 820 principles that can also apply to valuations under IFRS 13.

HISTORICAL NOTES ON THE FAIR VALUE STANDARD

Medieval Theory of "Just Price"

The idea of a standard of value that could provide a basis for "fairness" (*aequitas*) in the practice of business transactions can be traced back in Western thought to medieval philosophy and canon law. In the twelfth century, Gratian's Decretum opened the door for a system of positive law distinct from theology and from the secular system of Roman Law. In matters of commercial transactions, Roman Law, as handed down in Giustinian's Corpus of Civil Law, had given utmost freedom to the counterparties to negotiate the terms of their contracts, limiting the judge's intervention to exceptional circumstances such as fraud or to cases where a very significant discrepancy between the transaction price and the "true value" was deemed to exist. In Gratian's Decretum, a legitimate transaction had to meet the ethical principle of "equity" (*aequitas*) or "equality" (*aequalitas*). A legitimate transaction settles at a "just price" (*justum praetium*), which is equitable for both parties.

The theory of just price was further developed by Thomas Aquinas (1225–1274) in his Summa Theologiae.[2] As a university professor of theology in the rapidly growing urban centers of thirteenth-century Paris, Naples, and Rome, Thomas Aquinas had witnessed the rise of a new class of merchants, traveling to remote locations, using money as a means of exchange and rapidly accumulating significant amounts of wealth. In a section on "fraud that is committed in buying and selling," Aquinas asks the question: "Is it right to sell a thing for more than its value?"[3]

In scholastic fashion, Aquinas starts his debate by presenting the arguments that he intends to rebut. One may argue that selling something at a price that is higher than its value is permissible under common law (*licitum*) and is a common practice (*ab omnibus acceptatum*). One may also argue that a price is "just" to the extent it has been agreed upon by willing parties (*ex conventione agatur*). For Aquinas, however, justice cannot be identified with legality, customs, or even convention between a willing buyer and a willing seller.

---

[2]On the medieval theories of the just price, see J. W. Baldwin, "The Medieval Theories of the Just Price: Romanists, Canonists and Theologians in the Twelfth and Thirteenth Centuries," *Transactions of the American Philosophical Society* 49 (1959): 8–40; Raymond De Roover, "The Concept of Just Price: Theory and Economic Policy," *Journal of Economic History* 18 (1958): 418–438.

[3]Thomas Aquinas, Summa Theologiae IIa, IIe, quaest. 77, art. 1. Queastio: "De fraudulentia quae committitur in emptionibus et venditionibus." "Utrum liceat aliquid vendere plus quam valeat."

Human laws and customs do not necessarily stem from virtue and the individual parties in a transaction come to the negotiating table with different bargaining powers, which don't always result in a "just price" being settled. In Aquinas's view, justice in commerce must rather find its root in the evangelical principle of Matthew VII, "Do for others what you wish others would do for you."[4] For Aquinas, in the practice of commerce, this principle translates into a practical mandate: the prohibition from selling an item at a price that is higher than its value in terms of damage to the seller.[5]

In his question, Aquinas identifies the damage (loss of utility) for the seller as the basis for setting a just price in monetary terms. While he acknowledges that objects have a "value" per se, in order to establish the just price of an object in a specific transaction, one should look not only at the thing that is sold, but at the damage (*damnum*) that the seller experiences from the sale. In a system where sellers are often in a position of strength, the "equity" in the transaction ultimately depends on the seller's individual moral choice. With bargaining powers on their side, sellers should be willing to contain their profit margin at an equitable level, even when a higher price could be negotiated from the buyer.

For Aquinas, a competitive marketplace in which the parties are free to negotiate their own contractual terms is in itself neither more nor less equitable than any other market system. The responsibility of implementing justice in human affairs relies on each individual, independently of the system in which the individual operates. Merchants have an important function in society which is accompanied by enhanced responsibilities. Merchants facilitate exchanges and make goods available where they are most needed and deserve to be compensated for their labor and for the risks involved in their activity. However, they also have the responsibility of establishing just prices, and ensuring that exchanges are equitable for all parties. In this context, merchants are especially exposed to the moral risk of using their eloquence for fraudulent purposes (*peccata labiorum*) and of engaging in the pursuit of wealth accumulation beyond their needs and honest desires.[6] For Aquinas, in view of their enhanced responsibilities and moral risk exposures, merchants have an especially arduous path to salvation.

Writing a generation later than Aquinas, the Franciscan friar Pietro di Giovanni Olivi (1248–1298) presents a theory of the just price in the first part of his treatise "On buying and selling, on usury and on restitutions" that elaborates on some of Aquinas' principles but also departs from them in significant ways.[7] One of the most interesting aspects of Olivi's treatise for our purposes is that he shifts the focus from the moral perspective of the individual

---

[4]Thomas Aquinas, Summa Theologiae, IIa, IIe, quaest. 77, art. 1, co. Matthew VII, "omnia quaecumque vultis ut faciant vobis homines, et vos facite illis."

[5]Thomas Aquinas, Summa Theologiae, IIa, IIe, quaest. 77 art.1 co.: "Iustum pretium erit ut non solum respiciatur ad rem quae venditur, sed ad damnum quod venditor ex venditione incurrit."

[6]Thomas Aquinas, Summa Theologiae IIa, IIae, quaest. 77, art 4 co: "Et ideo negotiatio, secundum se considerata, quandam turpitudinem habet, inquantum non importat de sui ratione finem honestum vel necessarium."

[7]The treatise of Pietro Giovanni degli Olivi is available in Giacomo Todeschini, Un trattato di economia politica Francescana. Il "De emptionibus et venditionibus, de usuris, de restitutionibus" di Pietro di Giovanni Olivi. Roma: Istituto Storico Italiano per il Medioevo, 1980. On Olivi's treatise see also J. Kirshner, and K. Lo Prete, "Olivi's Treatise on Contracts of Sale, Usury and Restitution. Minorite Economies or Minor Works?," *Quaderni fiorentini per la storia del pensiero giuridico moderno*, 1984 n. 13, pp. 233–286.

participant in a transaction, to the idea that equity in transactions has to be assessed in view of the "common good" (the *bonum commune*). For Olivi, who was well versed in the small city life of central Italy, life within a political community is essential not only for human survival, but for the perfection of human virtue. The concept of a market where multiple participants need to be active in order for the exchange mechanism to lead to the assessment of a just price in a state of "equilibrium" finds an early expression in the work of Olivi.

"Normal Value" in Marshall's Equilibrium Theory

In the mid-nineteenth century, at the dawn of modern economic theory, the doctrine of the medieval theologians, after a period of eclipse during the Age of Enlightenment, was returning to occupy a very prominent place in European culture. In 1879, Pope Leo XIII's encyclical Aeterni Patris called for a restoration of the Christian philosophy of the medieval church. The works of Aquinas, and in particular the Summa Theologiae, had a special place in the Church's late 19th century revival of medieval thought. Aquinas' search for justice in the practice of trade and in the nascent banking industry was of special resonance in a world where the industrial revolution had brought about extraordinary progress in many areas of daily life, but also striking inequality of opportunity and material conditions.

In the late 1860s, Alfred Marshall (1842–1924), one of the founders of neoclassical economics and one of the most influential economists of his age, turned from the study of theology in view of a career as an evangelical minister, to ethics and economics. John Maynard Keynes, who was Marshall's student, recalls Marshall saying:

In my vacations, I visited the poorest quarters of several cities and walked through one street after another, looking at the faces of the poorest people. Next I resolved to make as thorough a study as I could of Political Economy.[8]

Similarly to Aquinas, Marshall's interest in economics was spurred by ethical consideration. According to Marshall, the possibility of progress "depends in a great measure upon facts and inferences, which are within the province of economics; and this it is which gives to economic studies their chief and their highest interest." In order to be able to pursue the liberal studies, which may lead to salvation, men need to be driven out of poverty and be able to satisfy their minimum needs for material welfare. Keynes recalls Marshall saying:

About the time that I first resolved to make as thorough a study as I could of Political Economy I saw in a shop-window a small oil painting of a man's face with a strikingly gaunt and wistful expression, as of one "down and out" and bought it for a few shillings. I set it up above the chimney-piece in my room in college and thenceforward called it my patron saint, and devoted myself to trying how to fit men like that for heaven.[9]

---

[8]John Maynard Keynes, "Alfred Marshall 1842–1924," *The Economic Journal* 34, no. 135 (September 1924): p. 319.
[9]John Maynard Keynes, "Alfred Marshall 1842–1924," *The Economic Journal* 34, no. 135 (September 1924): p. 346.

Marshall's concern for the needs of the poor could have brought him to sympathize with socialist ideology. Instead, he makes it clear that "no socialist scheme, yet advanced seems to make adequate provision for the maintenance of high enterprise and individual strength of character nor to promise a sufficiently rapid increase in the business plant and other material implements of production."[10] In "Principles of Political Economy," Marshall develops a general theory of economic equilibrium where free enterprise, supported by government intervention in social welfare, is meant to lead over the long term to an allocation of resources that maximizes social prosperity. From a static, long-term perspective, the equilibrium is reached at the point of intersection of long-term demand and supply, where the natural value of products and factors of production is determined.

As noted by Keynes, for Marshall, the idea that "value is determined at the equilibrium point of Demand and Supply was extended so as to discover a whole Copernican system, by which all the elements of the economic universe are kept in their places by mutual counterpose and interaction."[11] By letting free enterprise play out in the economy, a kind of universal harmony is restored. "Just as the motion of every body in the solar system affects and is affected by the motion of every other," Marshall wrote, "so it is with the elements of the problem of political economy."[12]

Central to Marshall's theory of equilibrium is the concept of normal value. As Marshall explains,

The "Normal" or "Natural" value of a commodity is that which economic forces tend to bring about in the long run. It is the average value that economic forces would bring about if the general conditions of life were stationary for a run of time long enough to enable them all to work out to their full effect.[13]

In discussing the drivers of value, Marshall adds a temporal dimension to the approach of previous economists such as Jevons and Walras. In the short term, equilibrium prices are driven by demand, which in turn is driven by utility considerations. Over the long period, the normal value will converge to the cost of production (normal cost). Paraphrasing Jevons, Marshall explains that in a long-term equilibrium state,

Utility determines the amount that has to be supplied

The amount that has to be supplied determines cost of production

The cost of production determines value, because it determines the supply price which is required to make the producers keep to do their work.[14]

---

[10] Alfred Marshall, *Preface to Industry and Trade*, 1919 (1st ed.).

[11] John Maynard Keynes, "Alfred Marshall 1842–1924," *The Economic Journal* 34, no. 135 (September 1924): 311–372.

[12] Alfred Marshall, "Mr. Jevons' Theory of Political Economy," in *Memorials of Alfred Marshall*, edited by A.C. Pigou (Macmillan: London, 1925) (reprint), pp. 94–95. Marshall's Review of Jevons's theory of political economy was first released in *Academy*, April 1, 1872.

[13] Alfred Marshall, *Principles of Economics*, Digireads.com: 2012, Book VI, Ch. 3 para. 11, p. 421.

[14] Alfred Marshall, *Principles of Economics*, Digireads.com, Appendix I, Ricardo's Theory of Value, p. 498.

The normal cost of a product must include, in addition to the direct expenses of production, also a component of entrepreneurial profit and for the use of capital and any additional costs related to the aggregate process of production and marketing (for instance, an allocation of insurance expenses and other charges).

Marshall was keen to point out that free enterprise does not always imply free competition. He is one of the first economists, for instance, to build a quantitative model of monopoly theory. Still, the belief in free enterprise as a force to maximize social welfare is a fundamental tenet of his model. In a chapter dedicated to progress in the standards of life, he emphasizes that, in spite of the social and economic challenges of his times, "the social and economic forces already at work are changing the distribution of wealth for the better. [...] The assumption and ownership by government of all the means of production, even if brought about gradually and slowly, as the more responsible "collectivists" propose, might cut deeper into the roots of social prosperity than appears at first sight."[15] In his view:

> *The chief cause of the evil is want of confidence. The greater part of it could be removed almost in an instant if confidence could return, touch all industries with her magic wand, and make them continue their production and their demand for the wares of others.*[16]

Debate on Fair Value in Railroad Rate Regulation

Marshall's theory of value in a long-term equilibrium state as the normal cost of production finds a practical application in the controversies on the regulation of the price of railroad services at the turn of the 20th century. As public utilities with a critical role for the welfare of the community, railroad companies were subject to governmental oversight in their operations. In the absence of a free market for railroad services, prices for transportation had to be set at an amount deemed "fair" both for the private companies running those services as well as for the service users.

In 1893, Nebraska had passed a law (the "Maximum Rate Bill"), which had established maximum rates for freight transportation within the State. The Maximum Rate Bill was contested by a number of private railroad companies that would have seen their profitability significantly reduced by the implementation of the bill. In 1898, the case was adjudicated by the U.S. Supreme Court in *Smyth v. Ames*.[17] The U.S. Supreme court found the Maximum Rate Bill in violation of the Fourteenth Amendment to the U.S. Constitution. The Court considered the limitation on prices at a level that would not allow for a "fair return" for the service provider as analogous to the taking of property without the due process of law. The Court maintained that, while the State has the power to establish maximum rates for the transportation of passengers and freight on railroads, the State must also ensure that those maximum rates are reasonable:

---

[15]Alfred Marshall, *Principles of Economics*, Digireads.com: 2012, Ch. 3, p. 212.

[16]Alfred Marshall, *Principles of Economics*, Digireads.com, Book VI, Ch. 3 para. 11, p. 421.

[17]For a summary of the *Smyth v. Ames* case and its implication for railroad rate regulation, see Harleigh Hartman, *Fair Value: The Meaning and Application of the Term "Fair Valuation" as Used by Utility Commissions* (Boston: Houghton Mifflin Company, 1920), pp. 59–63.

The general question argued before us on the original hearing was whether the rates established by the Nebraska statute, looking at them as an entirety, were so unreasonably low as to prevent the railroad companies from earning such compensation as would be just, having due regard to the rights both of the public and of the companies. […] Under pretense of regulating fares and freights, the State cannot require a railroad corporation to carry persons or property without reward, neither can it do that which in law amounts to the taking of private property for public use without just compensation, or without due process of law.

The U.S. Supreme Court concludes that the value of the transportation services should be determined at fair value. At a minimum the rate should cover the cost of producing the service, inclusive of a fair return on the capital invested:

The basis of all calculations as to the reasonableness of rates to be charged by a corporation maintaining a highway under legislative sanction must be the **fair value** *of the property being used by it for the convenience of the public. And in order to ascertain that value, the original cost of construction, the amount expended in permanent improvements, the amount and market value of its bonds and stock, the present as compared with the original cost of construction, the probable earning capacity of the property under particular rates prescribed by statute, and the sum required to meet operating expenses, are all matters for consideration, and are to be given such weight as may be just and right in each case. What the company is entitled to ask is a* **fair return** *upon the value of that which it employs for the public convenience, and on the other hand, what the public is entitled to demand is that no more be exacted from it for the use of a public highway than the services rendered by it are reasonably worth.*[18]

In 1920, Harleigh H. Hartman published a treatise that provides a comprehensive overview of the theory and application of fair value in rate setting by public utilities.[19] Harleigh notes that the term fair value has been used as a scapegoat of the cost theory coined by the courts and adopted by the public utility commissions. It has been employed in many phases of regulation, including rate making, purchases and sales, security issues, reorganization, tax and government ownership cases, without a systematic definition or approach to valuation.

Accordingly to Harleigh, "Valuation in public utility regulation is a legal question, but the principles applied are economic."[20] The mechanism for establishing prices of public utilities cannot rely on the free exchange between transaction parties. Rather, it has to be controlled so that the common good is protected even at the expense of private rights.

Harleigh's book is divided into two parts. First, he considers fair value as the valuation standard that is best suited to public service regulation and to existing legal rules. In his

---

[18] *Smyth v. Ames*, 169 U.S. 466, 468 (1898).
[19] Harleigh Hartman, *Fair Value: The Meaning and Application of the Term "Fair Valuation" as Used by Utility Commissions* (Boston: Houghton Mifflin Company), 1920.
[20] Harleigh Hartman, *Fair Value: The Meaning and Application of the Term "Fair Valuation" as Used by Utility Commissions* (Boston: Houghton Mifflin Company, 1920), p. 77.

arguments, fair value is identified with the cost of service along the lines of Marshall's Normal Cost, and is urged as a proper basis for rates. The second part of the book applies the general principles formulated in the first part to the actual practice in commission valuation cases.[21]

For Harleigh, as in Marshall, the cost of service must include an adequate return on investment. The proper basis for the assessment of the investment return is the actual, unimpaired investment in property after deduction for depreciation. Reproduction cost can only be used as a check upon the proper valuation and does not by itself constitute fair value.

In Part II, Harleigh goes through the valuation at fair value of tangible property (land, buildings, water rights), intangible property (overhead charges, entrepreneur's profits, franchise value, goodwill, going-concern value), and discusses in detail how to estimate depreciation and return of capital. The presentation has a technical tone that combines economic, accounting, and legal considerations. Overall, this book still provides valuable insights into fair value as applied to situations that fall outside the dynamic of free market exchanges.

Development of the Fair Value Standard in U.S. GAAP

The modern theory of fair value is born in the spirit of post–World War II economic liberalism that inspired Milton Friedman's *Capitalism and Freedom* (1962) and the development of the capital asset pricing model (CAPM) in the early 1960s, based on the foundation of Harry Markowitz's modern portfolio theory (MPT). In a CAPM/MPT framework, the pursuit of self-interest by the individual players in the market leads to a situation that maximizes the efficiency in the use of available resources and to a point of equilibrium on the "efficient frontier." In an efficient market, the most reliable evidence of value comes from market prices that incorporate all available information and that reflect market participants' expectations on the risk-return profile of each asset/liability. Only when quoted prices in active markets are not available, alternative valuation inputs become relevant.

The central role assigned to market prices in the assessment of fair value is a notable feature of the fair value standard under U.S. GAAP and IFRS, and one that distinguishes it from the fair value approach developed in early railroad rate regulation. In fact, it is interesting to note that in the United States the idea of a comprehensive program to measure all financial instruments at fair value, which first led to the issuance of Statement of Financial Accounting Standards (FAS) No. 107, *Disclosures About Fair Value of Financial Instruments* in 1991 and eventually to the issuance of FAS No. 133, *Accounting for Derivate Instruments and Hedging Activities* in 1998, takes place in the 1980s around the time when the system of fixed prices for utilities was lifted, and when it became possible to trade energy on the open market as if it were a commodity like any other.[22] One of the immediate effects of deregulation

---

[21]Harleigh Hartman, *Fair Value: The Meaning and Application of the Term "Fair Valuation" as Used by Utility Commissions* (Boston: Houghton Mifflin Company, 1920).
[22]For an overview of the fair value standard and its historical development, see Neil Beaton, "Fair Value in Financial Reporting," Chapter 6 in *Standards of Value: Theory and Applications*, edited by Jay E. Fishman (Wiley, 2013), pp. 323–346; Mark Zyla, "Fair Value Measurement Standards and Concepts," Chapter 2 in *Fair Value Measurement*, 2nd ed. (Wiley: 2013), pp. 37–78. In 1986 the FASB added a project to its agenda on financial instruments and off balance-sheet financing which eventually led to the issuance of FAS 107 and FAS 133 (see Neil Beaton, "Fair Value in Financial Reporting," p. 329).

combined with the new fair value or "mark-to-market" accounting rules, was to allow energy companies that used to work in a system of fixed prices to be able to book unrealized profits in their income statement, which has been seen as having unintendedly contributed to the Enron debacle.[23]

The period 1995–2000 in the United States saw the rapid growth of the internet sector as a share of overall market value on U.S. stock exchanges. The "internet bubble" came to a sudden crash in 2001–2002. By the end of 2001, the Nasdaq had fallen more than 70% from its peak, and even the share price of well-established technology stocks like Cisco had lost in some cases more than 50% of their value.

In May 2003, the FASB initiated a project with the aim of developing fair value guidance that could help more accurately reflect the value of financial assets and liabilities in the current market. In 2006, the project resulted in the issuance of FAS No. 157, *Fair Value Measurements*, a significant milestone in the application of the fair value standard to public and private companies.

In 2009, the FASB's Accounting Standard Codification (ASC) became effective as the single authoritative source for U.S. GAAP, replacing previous accounting guidance. Within the Codification, ASC 820 *Fair Value Measurement* superseded FAS 157. ASC 820, defines fair value, establishes a framework for measuring fair value, and provides guidance on the disclosures that are needed about fair value measurement.

After more than 10 years since the issuance of ASC 820, the use of fair value/ mark-to-market accounting is still subject to controversy. In his 2017 letter to Berkshire Hathaway's shareholders, Warren Buffett warned that mandatory implementation of fair value accounting for certain investment securities previously carried at amortized cost under Accounting Standards Update (ASU) No. 2016-01, *Financial Instruments – Overall (Subtopic 825-10), Recognition and Measurement of Financial Assets and Financial Liabilities* will "severely distort Berkshire's net income figures and very often mislead commentators and investors." Buffett continues:

> *The new rule says that the net change in* unrealized *investment gains and losses in stocks we hold must be included in all net income figures we report to you. That requirement will produce some truly wild and capricious swings in our GAAP bottom-line. [. . .] The new rule compounds the communication problems we have long had in dealing with the* realized *gains (or losses) that accounting rules compel us to include in our net income.*

Most recently, as part of its *Action Plan on Sustainable Finance*, the European Commission (EC) has asked the European Financial Reporting Advisory Group to explore potential alternative accounting treatments to fair value measurement for long-term investment portfolios of equity and equity-type instruments. In the investment industry, the CFA Institute, among others, has been a strong promoter of the fair value standards as a way to provide investors with a better understanding of the risk, volatility, and valuation of companies in the current markets for public and private companies, and of providing analysts with the most

---

[23] Mary Poovey, "Can Numbers Ensure Honesty? Unrealistic Expectations and the U.S. Accounting Scandal," *Notices of the American Mathematical Society*, January 2003, pp. 27–35.

up-to-date information on asset and liability values.[24] The AICPA has also promoted the use of fair value standards in its own comment letter to the IVSC Standards Review Board's proposal of a revised statement IVS 500 – Financial Instruments on the valuation of financial instruments.[25] The fair value standard is especially suitable for the valuation of investments by investment companies, including venture capital and private equity funds. Aside from being the mandatory standard for financial reporting, investors and other industry participants in the venture capital and private equity industry have broadly adopted the fair value standard as the most suitable approach for making investment and portfolio allocation decisions based on and understanding of the current exit value of each portfolio component.[26]

THE FAIR VALUE STANDARD UNDER CURRENT U.S. GAAP

Under ASC 820, fair value is defined as:

> *the price that would be received to sell an asset or paid to transfer a liability in an orderly transaction between market participants at the measurement date.*[27]

From the perspective of a venture capital or private equity fund, fair value may apply to the valuation of the portfolio company as a whole, or to the valuation of a business interest in a portfolio company, as represented by an equity or debt security, or by a derivative instrument (option, contingent consideration). In this latter case, the valuation of the enterprise is a step in the valuation of the investor's business interest.

It's important to note that the definition of fair value under ASC 820/IFRS 13 places an emphasis on the "exit" value of an asset or liability as the price that can be obtained to "transfer" the asset/liability rather than on its initial acquisition cost. Also, in order to provide a suitable fair value indication, a transaction needs to be "orderly," and such as to allow for a period before the measurement date for marketing activities that are usual and customary for the transaction. The transaction, in other words, should not be a forced transaction such as a forced liquidation or a distress sale.

---

[24] Sandy Peters, "Berkshire's Bottom Line: More Relevant than Even Before." See also the CFA Institute's comment letter to the EFRSG "Equity-Instruments – Research on Measurement " questionnaire and discussion on background paper, dated July 29, 2019: "Fair values are the premise of all asset and liability exchanges, and, as such, should be represented in the financial statements. [. . .] As such, to gain our support financial instruments accounting must advance wide use of fair value for the recognition and measurement of such instruments.

[25] AICPA, "Forensic and Valuation Services Letter to the International Valuation Standards Council" dated September 27, 2019, in response to IVSC Financial Instruments invitation to comment issued in August 2019 (IVS Financial Instruments Agenda Consultation 2019).

[26] AICPA PE/VC Valuation Guide, 2.07.

[27] ASC 820-20 Glossary, "Fair Value."

Market Participants

The ASC 820 Glossary provides a definition of "Market Participants" as the buyers and sellers in the principal (or most advantageous) market for the asset or liability that have all of the following characteristics:

- They are independent of each other, that is, they are not related parties, although the price in a related party transaction may be used as an input to a fair value measurement if the reporting entity has evidence that the transaction was entered into at market terms.
- They are knowledgeable, having a reasonable understanding about the asset or liability and the transaction using all available information, including information that might be obtained through due diligence efforts that are usual and customary.
- They are able to enter into a transaction for the asset or liability.
- They are willing to enter into a transaction for the asset or liability, that is, they are motivated but not forced or otherwise compelled to do so.

Fair Value Hierarchy ASC 820 establishes a fair value hierarchy that categorizes into three levels the inputs to valuation techniques used to measure fair value as follows:

Level 1 inputs are defined as "quoted prices (unadjusted) in active markets for identical assets and liabilities that the reporting entity can access at the measurement date."[28] An active market is a market in which transactions occur with sufficient frequency and volume to provide pricing information on an ongoing basis.

Level 2 inputs are "inputs other than quoted prices included within Level 1 that are observable for the asset or liability, either directly or indirectly."[29] Level 2 inputs include:

- Quoted prices for similar assets and liabilities in active markets.
- Quoted prices for identical or similar assets or liabilities in markets that are not active or that are not the principal market for the subject interest.
- Inputs other than quoted prices that are observable. For an ESE these may include the risk-free rate, yield curves that are observable at commonly quoted intervals, default rates, credit spreads, implied volatilities, publicly available data on guideline comparable companies such as EPS, financial ratios, market capitalization, market transaction multiples.
- Inputs that are derived from or corroborated by observable market data by correlation or other means (market-corroborated inputs).

Level 3 inputs are unobservable inputs for which market data are not available and that are developed using the best information available about the assumptions that market participants would use when pricing the asset or liability. Examples of unobservable inputs for an ESE typically include managements' financial projections, the company-specific risk premium

---

[28] ASC 820 Glossary Level 1 Inputs.
[29] ASC 820 Glossary Level 2 Inputs.

in the estimate of the weighted-average cost of capital, the asset and equity volatility in an option pricing model, the component that represents counterparty risk in a discount rate, the probability assigned to various scenarios in scenario analysis, and others.

The fair value hierarchy gives highest priority to quoted prices (unadjusted) in active markets for identical assets and liabilities (Level 1 inputs) and the lowest priority to unobservable inputs (Level 3 inputs). A quoted price in an active market provides the most reliable evidence of fair value and should be used without adjustment to measure fair value whenever available. Level 3 unobservable inputs should only be used to the extent that relevant observable inputs are not available, thereby allowing for situations in which there is little, if any, market activity for the asset or liability at the measurement date.

The distinction between Level 3 and Level 1 inputs does not typically present special issues in practice. In some cases, it may be more difficult to distinguish a Level 2 from a Level 3 input. For instance, a VC or PE fund may be able to obtain an indicative broker quote for a debt security of a portfolio company. To the extent the broker quote does not represent an actual transaction or the availability of the broker to act upon it as a counterparty in a transaction, the quote would qualify as a Level 3 unobservable input.

The input classification ultimately determines the "bucket" in which the investment will fall for purposes of financial statement reporting, and the disclosures that will be required.

Overview of Valuation Approaches

ASC 820 identifies three main approaches to valuation.

Market Approach As defined by FASB, the market approach "uses prices and other relevant information generated by market transactions involving identical or comparable (that is similar) assets, liabilities or a group of assets and liabilities such as a business." In the absence of an active exchange with market prices, a typical example of a market approach for an ESE consists of using the price of the latest round of financing as the basis for valuation. Under the "Backsolve method," the price of the latest round is used to backsolve into the value of the enterprise, which is then allocated to all business interests in a hypothetical waterfall. We discuss this methodology in some detail in Chapter 5. Alternatively, evidence of market prices can be obtained from secondary transactions between investors.

Other common methodologies under the market approach can be applied also in the lack of actual transaction prices in ESE interests and include the Guideline Public Company (GPC) method and the Guideline Transactions (GT) method. Under the GPC method, fair value is estimated by comparing financial metrics of the subject company such as revenue, earnings, and cash flows to those of publicly traded companies that are deemed to be reasonably comparable to the subject company. Under the GT method, an indication of value is developed based on the prices paid to purchase an interest in comparable companies that have been acquired within a reasonable time period prior to the valuation date.

Exhibit 2.1 lists some common factors of comparability that can be of assistance in the identification of guideline public companies.

Exhibit 2.2 shows some of the common key multiples that are used to estimate enterprise value using the GPC and GT methods.

The GPC and the GT methods are commonly used in the valuation of developed enterprises but are typically of less relevance for an ESE due to the challenge of finding companies

Identification of Guideline Public Companies

Operational characteristics	Industry or sector (North American Industry Classification System or Standard Industrial Classification Code)
	Line of business
	Geographical reach
	Customers and distribution channels
	Contractual versus noncontractual sales
	Seasonality of business
	Business cycle (short cycle characterized by ever-changing technology vs. long cycle driven by changes in commodity pricing)
	Stage of business life cycle
	Operating constraints
Financial characteristics	Size
	Profitability (EBITDA, operating margin, contribution margin)
	Anticipated future growth in revenues and profits
	Asset base (e.g., manufacturing vs. service business)
	Patterns of owning versus leasing properties, machinery, and equipment

EXHIBIT 2.1   Identification of Guideline Public Companies

GPB and GT: Multiples to Use

Financial metrics	Market value of equity to net income
	MVE to book value of equity
	Enterprise value (excluding cash) to EBIT
	EV (excluding cash) to EBITDA
	EV (excluding cash) to Revenue
	EV (excluding cash) to Debt-free Cash Flows
	EV (excluding cash) to Book Value of Assets
Nonfinancial metrics	Price per subscriber
	Price per bed (hospital industry)
	EV (excluding cash) to research and development investment (pharmaceutical industry)
	Levels of probability-weighted reserves (oil and gas exploration company)
	Page views (internet company)
	Other industry-specific metrics

EXHIBIT 2.2   GPC and GT: Multiples to Use

and transactions that are similar enough to support a comparison. The availability of transaction and financial data on private companies and private deals is rapidly expanding, which is making the Guideline Company and Guideline Transactions methods more useful also in ESE valuation, especially for companies in sectors such as health care and technology where there has been a significant volume of private transaction activity.

The use of selected information from comparable companies can also help in some area of the market and income approach, for instance, in the estimate of volatility of returns for the subject company as used in the option pricing method, in the estimate of terminal value (when presumably the subject company will be indeed comparable to other companies in the same industry), or to establish a suitable industry risk premium in the cost of capital.

Income Approach   According to the FASB Glossary, the income approach includes "valuation techniques that convert future amounts (for example cash flows or income and expenses) into a single current (that is, discounted) amount." FASB notes that fair value should adjust the data to the extent that other market participants would use different data or there is something peculiar to the reporting entity that is not available to other market participants. In other words, the effect of synergies that are specific to an individual market participant (for instance, a strategic buyer that includes in the estimate a consideration of some additional benefits from an acquisition that other participants would not be able to take advantage of) should be excluded from fair value.

The income approach is typically based on unobservable inputs, which include management's projections and inputs that affect the cost of capital, among others. The Discounted Cash Flow method (DCF) can be used under the income approach in the valuation of ESEs that already have an established revenue stream or for which a revenue stream can be projected with a reasonable basis. The DCF method requires estimation of future economic benefits and the application of an appropriate discount rate to equate them to a single present value. The DCF method is illustrated in Chapter 6.

Alternatively, the Expected Present Value (EPV) method estimates a set of future cash flows and assigns to each cash flow a probability of occurrence. The expected value of the enterprise is then determined as the probability-weighted average of the cash flow associated with each scenario, discounted to present value. The EPV method is discussed in relation to scenario analysis (Chapter 4 with the First Chicago Method and Chapter 9), and in Chapter 12 with reference to the valuation of contingent consideration. It is also at the basis of the Option Pricing method as discussed in Chapter 5.

The income approach is forward looking, in that it reflects projections and expectations about the future value of most of the key inputs that factor into the valuation model. It also involves significant assumptions and estimates for most of the key inputs, which makes it generally more prone to subjective judgment than the market approach.

Asset-Based Approach   The asset-based approach estimates the value of an entity's equity by reference to the value of the entity's assets minus the value of the entity's liabilities. When using the asset-based approach, it is important to consider not only those assets and liabilities that are recognized in the entity's financial statements, but also assets and liabilities that are not recognized. For instance, a company may have intangible assets that are internally developed that are typically not recognized but that are an important component of enterprise value for many ESEs. From a fair value perspective, it is critical that the intangible assets that drive an ESE valuation are identified and factored into valuation. For a company where most of the value lies in its intangible assets, as it is often the case in a technology-intensive ESE or a research pharma company, the asset-based approach will result in a value that may be significantly different from the company's book value in the reported financial statements. This approach may require a forward-looking analysis of the revenue stream that is expected to be generated by intangible assets such as patents, licenses, and copyrights, alongside cost-based methodologies in the estimate of other components of the balance sheet. The asset-based approach is discussed in Chapter 7 with reference to the asset accumulation method, and may provide an appropriate indication of value particularly in the seed or early VC stage.

Use of Multiple Valuation Techniques   In some cases, a single valuation technique will be appropriate in valuation. For instance, for an ESE that recently underwent a new round of financing, the unit price of the latest round (a market-based input) will often be used to estimate the value of the enterprise and of the other equity interests in the firm. In other cases, multiple valuation techniques will be appropriate. The analyst should consider the range of values obtained from the use of the various methodologies, in determining the point within the range that is deemed most suitable to represent fair value.[30]

In the chapters that follow, you will notice that it is common to combine multiple techniques also within a single valuation model. For instance, elements of the expected present value method and of the guideline public company method are used in the market approach that we discuss in Chapter 5. The DCF model that we present in Chapter 6 relies on a comparison with guideline companies to assess terminal value. In the asset-based method that we discuss in Chapter 7, the income method is used to estimate the value of certain intangible assets.

In the practice of valuation, the analyst has discretion to select the most suitable technique under each valuation approach as is most fitting for the purpose of the valuation. Once a technique or a set of techniques has been chosen, however, it is important that it continues to be applied consistently. A change in a valuation technique or its application for an investment that represents a material share of a fund portfolio is a significant occurrence that may need financial statement disclosure. A change in methodology may be appropriate if it results in a measurement that is equally or more representative of fair value. The development of new markets, the availability of new information, and a significant change in market conditions, for instance, can all be reasonable causes for changing valuation methodology to one that is more representative of fair value under the circumstances.[31]

Calibration   The AICPA PE/VC Valuation Guide places a renewed emphasis on calibration as a technique that can help support a valuation with market-based information.[32] For instance, let's assume that a company issues a bridge loan to an investor with a par value of $1 million at a price of 90 cents per unit of principal. If the issue price is deemed to be at fair value at initial recognition, the analyst can "calibrate" to the 90 cents price per unit to estimate, for instance, the discount rate of expected cash flows that is embedded in that price. At subsequent measurement dates, the discount rate can be adjusted to estimate a new value for the bridge loan to reflect current market conditions.

Use of Statistical Techniques   Another significant development that has taken place in recent years is the more pervasive use of statistical techniques such as option pricing models and Monte Carlo simulation in the valuation of privately held companies, and particularly in the

---

[30] ASC 820-10-35-24B.
[31] ASC 820-10-35-25.
[32] AICPA PE/VC Valuation Guide: Q&A 14.33: "Calibration is the best approach for estimating the assumptions to be used in valuing portfolio company investments."

Common Milestones	
Financial measures	Revenue growth
	Profitability expectations
	Cash burn rate
	Covenant compliance
Technical measures	Phases of development
	Testing cycles
	Patent approvals
	Regulatory approvals
Marketing and sales measures	Customer surverys
	Testing phases
	Market introduction
	Market share

Source: Based on the IPEV Valuation Guidelines 2018.

EXHIBIT 2.3 Common Milestones

valuation of ESEs. This was driven not only by an easier access to computational power and software that facilitates the use of such techniques, but also and most importantly by the awareness that an increasingly significant share of value is generated today by factors that are subject to considerable estimation uncertainty. As you read through this book, you will notice that option pricing models in particular are used extensively in almost all the chapters, sometimes in a context that is far removed from that in which the models were originally developed and with very different assumptions and implications.

Milestone Analysis For an ESE, the performance of the company in relation to a set of milestones that may pertain to various aspects of the company's operations is often a key factor in valuation.[33] Exhibit 2.3 illustrates some of the most common milestone measures related to the company's operations identified in the IPEV Guidelines. These include financial metrics such as revenue growth and profitability, technical targets such as patent and regulatory approvals, and marketing and sales-related measures, such as market share.

Internal milestones for ESEs may also include the assembly of key members of the management team, delivering a proof of concept, establishing ongoing relationships with strategic partners, and executing contracts with key customers. The achievement of a significant milestone will typically involve a revaluation and also, in some cases, a change in valuation methodology.

Premia and Discounts

Control Premia and Minority Discounts The value of an ESE may be measured from the perspective of a party that holds a controlling interest in the enterprise (controlling interest basis) or from the perspective of a party that holds a minority interest (minority interest basis).

---

[33] AICPA PE/VC Valuation Guide: Q&A 14.34: "For pre-revenue companies, the key factors to consider in the valuation are what progress the company has made toward achieving its milestones." See also 13.42.c: "Have any significant value events (internal or external) occurred since the previous financing round?"

Shareholders that have control over the enterprise may direct the company's strategy in a way that is most beneficial for their interests, including altering the company's capital structure and its operations. A minority shareholder, on the other hand, has little influence on the company's strategy and operations. Valuation practitioners have often concluded that, to the extent a controlling shareholder is able to extract additional value from a company relative to the return that a minority shareholder could achieve, having a control position may warrant a valuation premium (or, in the case of a minority shareholder, a minority discount).

In venture capital and private equity valuation, the fair value standard rarely justifies the application of control premiums and minority discounts to a portfolio company. As noted in the AICPA PE/VC Valuation Guide: "It would not be appropriate to apply an inadequately supported control premium or acquisition premium in the enterprise value used in valuing the fund's interest in the portfolio company."[34] Instead, funds should "evaluate the instruments in each portfolio company considering the improvements to the business that an investor would expect under current ownership, as modified given by the degree of influence that the buyer would have over those plans."[35] In an exit event, all shareholders, whether controlling or not controlling, will be able to participate at conditions that depend on the liquidity preferences and other contractual features of their interests and on the type of exit (IPO, sale, etc.) rather than on whether the interest is a controlling or minority interest.

Discounts for Lack of Marketability A portfolio company investment is deemed marketable when it can be readily sold at a price that reflects current market conditions. Marketability is different from "liquidity" in that the investment sale of a marketable investment may also take place in a market where trading is not active or where there are trading restrictions. For example, a portfolio investment in an ESE is "marketable" as there are potential investors willing to participate in the investment's market, but is also "illiquid" as transactions are sporadic and there is no active market.

Valuation practitioners have often concluded that an interest in a company that may not be readily sold may indeed warrant a lower valuation than if the interest would be readily convertible into cash. In the context of VC portfolio investments, however, discounts for lack of marketability under the fair value standard are rarely used. In a portfolio company valuation, it is generally assumed that, in most situations, the investment is marketable when looked at from the perspective of the current investors as a whole, and that any lack of marketability consideration is already factored in the valuation.

---

[34] AICPA PE/VC Valuation Guide, 9.13.
[35] AICPA PE/VC Valuation Guide, 9.13. See also Q&A 14.33: Question: "Should I be applying discounts or premia when estimating the fair value of the enterprise for the purpose of valuing investments?" Answer: Generally, no. The value of the enterprise used for valuing the instruments in the enterprise should reflect the cash flows under current ownership, as modified given the degree of influence that the buyer would have over those plans considering the nature of the interest acquired, discounted at the required rate of return for the investors who in aggregate have control of the business.[...] In many cases, a portfolio company's multiples might be higher than the peers relative to historical performance and lower than the peers relative to projected performance, reflecting the high risk in the projections." See also 9.04–9.23.

Still, there are a few circumstances in which a discount for lack of marketability may be warranted also for portfolio company investments. For instance, a VC fund may hold shares in a public company, which are restricted subject SEC rule 144A, or to contractual vesting requirements. A discount for lack of marketability may also apply to shares that lack information rights or certain noneconomic rights that a market participant would expect to be embedded in the transferred interest.[36]

The spare use of premia and discounts, including discounts for lack of marketability and control, distinguishes the fair value standard under ASC 820 from other standards of value, such as the fair value-based standard of ASC 718/ASC 505, the fair market value standard for U.S. tax reporting, and the fair value standard in shareholders' dissent cases.

FAIR VALUE AND OTHER STANDARDS OF VALUE

This section highlights the difference between fair value under ASC 820/IFRS 13 and other standards of value that are used in business valuation outside of the ASC 820 framework.[37]

Fair Value–Based Standard of ASC 718 and ASC 504-50

Under U.S. GAAP, a fair value–based standard applies to equity-based compensation (stock options, stock appreciation rights) under ASC 718, *Compensation – Stock Compensation* and ASC 505-50, *Equity-based payments to non-employees*.[38]

Under the fair value–based standard of ASC 718/ASC 505-50, fair value is defined as:

> *the amount at which an asset (or liability) could be bought (or incurred) or sold (or settled) in a current transaction between willing parties, that is, other than in a forced liquidation or sale.*

This definition refers explicitly only to assets or liabilities, but the concept of value in a current exchange embodied in that definition applies equally to equity instruments subject to ASC 718 and 505-50. One of the main differences with the fair value standard of ASC 820 pertains to the use of control and marketability discounts. The fair value–based standard of ASC 718/ASC 505-50 applies to a minority position and reflects the perspective of a willing buyer (the party that issued stock compensation) for a minority interest in an enterprise, not for the entire enterprise. Accordingly, a minority interest discount is typically granted.

Also, under the fair value–based standard, the value of a non-vested share granted to the employee of a public company would not be discounted due solely to the fact that the share could be transferred only to a limited population of investors, while under ASC 820, shares of public companies that are restricted under SEC 144A are typically granted a marketability discount through the end of their restriction term.

---

[36]AICPA PE/VC Valuation Guide 9.32 Note 25.

[37]On the standards of value in valuation practice, see Jay E. Fishman, *Standards of Value: Theory and Applications* (Wiley, 2013).

[38]ASC 718 applies to transactions in which an entity exchanges its equity instruments for good or services provided by its employees as share-based compensation. ASC 540-50 pertains to share-based payments provided in exchange for goods or services provided by nonemployees.

Fair Market Value for the Internal Revenue Service

Fair market value is defined under IRS Revenue Ruling 59-60, para 2.02 as the "price at which the property would change hands between a willing buyer and a willing seller when the former is not under any compulsion to buy and the latter is not under any compulsion to sell, both parties having a reasonable knowledge of relevant facts."[39]

In an IRS fair market value context, the valuation of an equity interest often concludes on a minority interest which may warrant a discount for lack of control. The IRS fair market value standard brings with it a large body of IRS regulation and interpretative case law that was developed in the context of tax regulation and that is outside the scope of an ASC 820/IFRS 13 valuation.

Fair Value in Statutory Appraisals

Fair value for U.S. GAAP is distinct from fair value as employed by state courts to determine the value of minority shares in appraisal (dissent) cases.[40] Shareholders customarily have appraisal rights when they are involuntarily cashed out in a merger or consolidation.[41] In dissent cases, fair value is used in a situation where the seller is not a willing seller, is compelled to sell, and has less knowledge of the relevant facts than does the buyer.

The American Bar Association (ABA) and the American Law Institute (ALI), together with Delaware corporate laws on appraisals, have developed approaches to fair value that have influenced a majority of state statutes. Under the Delaware's appraisal statute, fair value entitles the shareholder to be paid a pro rata share of the value of the company as a going concern.[42]

In Delaware, the fair value standard does not permit the benefits of synergies resulting from a transaction to be included in a going concern valuation.[43] Also, statutes and judicial interpretations in most states now reject minority or marketability discounts in the determination of fair value. Dissenting shareholders have been awarded amounts lower than the transaction price when the court determined that the transaction price included synergies and/or a control premium that should not have been included in fair value under Delaware Law.

---

[39] The IRS definition is consistent with the definition of the International Glossary of Business Valuation Terms, which defines "fair market value" as "the price, expressed in terms of cash equivalents, at which property would change hands between a hypothetical willing and able buyer and a hypothetical willing and able seller, acting at arm's length in an open and unrestricted market, when neither is under compulsion to buy or sell and when both have reasonable knowledge of the relevant facts."

[40] Gilbert E. Matthews, "Statutory Fair Value in Dissenting Shareholder Cases: Part I," *Business Valuation Review*, Spring 2017, pp. 15–31. The basic concept of value under the appraisal statute is that the stockholder is entitled to be paid for that which has been taken from him, namely, his proportionate interest in a going concern. See also Brett A. Margolin and Samuel J. Kursh, "The Economics of Delaware Fair Value," *Delaware Journal of Corporate Law* 30 (2005): 413, 435.

[41] Some states also permit dissenters to seek appraisal in other circumstances, such as a sale of assets, recapitalization, stock-for-stock merger, amendments to articles of incorporation or other major changes in the nature of their investments.

[42] Delaware Supreme Court clarified its meaning in Tr-Continental in 1950.

[43] *Gearreald v. Just Care Inc.*, 2012 Del.Ch. LEXIS 91 (April 30, 2012).

GUIDANCE ON THE FAIR VALUE STANDARD IN ESE VALUATION

ASC 820 and IFRS 13 provide a theoretical, principles-based framework for the fair value standard in financial reporting. Most of the guidance on the practical implementation of the fair value standard has come from the work of professional associations such as the American Institute of Certified Public Accountants, the American Society of Appraisers, the Royal Institution of Chartered Surveyors, the Appraisal Foundation, the International Valuation Standards Council. At the international level, and the International Private Equity and Venture Capital Valuation Board has been especially active in promoting fair value implementation by releasing valuation guidelines that specifically target the needs of private equity and venture capital funds. The IPEV Board was created as an independent body in 2005 and is responsible for maintaining, promoting, monitoring, and updating the IPEV Valuation Guidelines. The board has an advisory role and gives guidance on the application of the guidelines to all stakeholders in the private equity and venture capital industry, including practitioners, investors, regulators, and auditors.

The guidance on the practical implementation of the fair value standard has been significantly expanded in recent years, providing a wealth of new insight and case study applications. The paragraphs below discuss some of the guidance that is most relevant for the valuation of ESEs as presented in this book.

Most recent guidance (this list is not all-inclusive):

- American Institute of Certified Public Accountants (2019): Accounting and Valuation Guide on the Valuation of Portfolio Company Investments of Venture Capital and Private Equity Funds and Other Investment Companies. The AICPA PE/VC Valuation Guide, released in the summer of 2019, targets the PE/VC industry, and includes a wealth of examples and case studies that are relevant for the implementation of ASC 820 by PE and VC funds. The guide dedicates a section to the valuation of ESEs, and includes a number of case studies that feature ESEs, including, among others, a case on how to value interests in a complex capital structure for a biotech company (Case 10) and a case on scenario analysis in the context of an early stage company (Case 11). The guide provides examples of the valuation of convertible bridge notes, options, warrants, and earnouts in an ESE context. It also provides and extensive discussion of the rights and privileges of preferred stock and how they affect valuation in a complex capital structure.
- Public Company Accounting Oversight Board (PCAOB), Auditing Accounting Estimates, including Fair Value Measurements (2019): The PCAOB was created by the Sarbanes-Oxley Act of 2002, to oversee the accounting profession. In July 2019, the PCAOB issued a new standard on Auditing Accounting Estimates that replaces three preexistent standards by establishing a uniform, risk-based approach in fair value measurement. The new standard provides guidance, among others, on the use of pricing information from third parties such as pricing services and brokers or dealers (see our discussion of broker quotes in Chapter 11), and on how to evaluate evidence from transactions that take place after the measurement date (see our discussion in Chapter 5 of subsequent rounds of financing). PCAOB's attention to the challenges faced by auditors in fair value estimates is likely to ripple down through the industry and affect the valuation practices of venture capital and private equity funds.
- International Valuation Standards Council - International Valuation Standards (IVS) (2019): These standards are meant to promote transparency and consistency in valuation

practice using generally recognized concepts and principles. While they are not specific to Fair Value, the IVS provide useful guidance for the implementation of the market, income and asset-based approaches to businesses and business interests, and have dedicated sections on the valuation of Intangible Assets (IVS 210) and on the valuation of Financial Instruments (IVS 500) that are of special relevance for ESEs.

■ Appraisal Foundation – VFR Valuation Advisory #4: Valuation of Contingent Consideration (2019): Contingent consideration represents the portion of the transaction price in an acquisition that is contingent upon the occurrence of a future event (earnouts, clawbacks). Contingent consideration is especially relevant in ESE transactions, whose value is to a significant extent dependent on future performance. VFR #4 is written primarily from the perspective of a buyer which needs to value contingent consideration as part of its purchase price in an M&A transaction. The guidance in VFR #4, however, is also applicable to the seller, such as a venture capital fund that receives contingent consideration as part of an investment divestiture. In Chapter 12, we develop a number of examples based on VFR #4, including an example of how Monte Carlo simulation can be applied in the valuation of contingent consideration and several examples of option pricing models.

■ International Private Equity and Venture Capital Valuation Guidelines (latest edition: 2018): The guidelines reflect the experience of industry practitioners in applying IFRS 13 and ASC 820 in the context of PE/VC valuation. The definition of fair value is consistent with ASC 820/IFRS 13. The Guidelines are broadly used by managers globally and are required by numerous fund formation or limited partner agreements, especially outside the United States. The Guidelines include a section on valuing seed, start-up, and early-stage (pre-revenue)/(pre-earnings) investments, which emphasizes the relevance of the transaction prices from recent rounds as indications of fair value, and calibration in subsequent measurement. The guidelines also discuss the use of milestone analysis to identify situations that warrant a change in fair value.

■ Alternative Investment Management Association, Guide to Sound Practices for the Valuation of Investments, latest edition (2018): The AIMA Guide provides an indication of sound practices for establishing appropriate controls and procedures around the valuation of investments by alternative investment funds, including private funds that invest in illiquid securities, consistently with ASC 820/IFRS 13 and with the Alternative Investment Fund Managers Directive. The Guide provides governance recommendations for the valuation process. Compared to prior editions, the Guide has an expanded section on the valuation of illiquid instruments and the due diligence on valuation service providers and independent valuation experts.

■ Financial Instruments Performance Framework (FIPF) for the Certified in the Valuation of Financial Instruments Credential (2018): The FIPF sets forth the common concepts regarding the scope of work and extent of documentation that valuation professionals can apply to the valuation of financial instruments, including equity and debt securities issued by ESEs. The framework is the result of the Certified in the Valuation of Financial Instruments (CVFI) task force formed by the AICPA and is mandatory for professionals who hold the CVFI credential. Among others, the FIPF requires that regardless of which valuation technique is used, all valuation models that can be calibrated should be calibrated to current markets to ensure the accuracy of the inputs, assumptions, and calculations.

- Mandatory Performance Framework for the Certified in Entity and Intangible Valuations (CEIV) Credential and Application of the Mandatory Performance Framework for the CEIV Credential (collectively the "MPF") (2017): The MPF is designed to support the analysis performed by a valuation professional in a business valuation and in the valuation of intangible assets. The framework reflects the combined efforts of the American Institute of Certified Public Accountants, the American Society of Appraisers, and the Royal Institute of Chartered Surveyors and is mandatory for analysts that hold the CEIV credential. More broadly, the MPF represents a set of sound practices on the procedures to perform and the documentation to gather to support valuations for financial reporting. The MPF guidance can also be useful as a set of sound practices to meet regulatory and board due diligence requirements related to valuation. In an ESE valuation, it provides useful guidance, among others, on estimating cost of capital, the valuation of intangible assets, and the implementation of various aspects of the asset-accumulation method.

Other guidance (this list is not all-inclusive):

- Appraisal Foundation – VFR Valuation Advisory #2 (2016): The Valuation of Customer-Related Assets. This document provides helpful guidance to prepare fair value measurements of customer-related intangible assets, which may be included in the balance sheet under the asset-accumulation method.
- AICPA – Accounting and Valuation Guide – Valuation of Privately-Held Company Securities Issued as Compensation (2013). This guide addresses the valuation of equity securities issued as compensation in private enterprises at all stages of development. The guide refers to ASC 718 and can best be interpreted under the fair value–based standard. For instance, it allows for discounts related to lack of control, which would most likely not be appropriate in an ASC 820 context. Having said that, the guide is still useful in PE/VC valuation, especially in view of its discussion of the option pricing method and the probability-weighted expected return method (PWERM) as tools to allocate enterprise value to the various classes/series of shares in a complex capital structure.
- AICPA Accounting and Valuation Guide *Assets, Acquired to Be Used in Research and Development Activities* (2013): This publication provides nonauthoritative guidance on the valuation and disclosure requirements for financial reporting pertaining to intangible assets that are acquired in an asset acquisition or business combination and that are used in R&D activities. These assets would have to be considered in a valuation conducted under the asset-accumulation method.
- Appraisal Foundation – VFR Valuation Advisory #1: Identification of Contributory Assets and Calculation of Economic Rent (with Toolkit) (2010): The identification and allocation of contributory asset value is one of the most complex areas of intangible assets valuation. This VFR provides useful guidance and a wealth of implementation examples that can help in the application of the asset-accumulation method.

Please refer to the References section in this book for additional information on ESE valuation guidance and reference materials.

CONCLUSION

The fair value standard under ASC 820/IFRS 13 is a broadly recognized standard in business valuation that affects asset allocation decisions, investment selection, and financial reporting. The fair value standard has deep roots in the foundations of the modern market economy and has accompanied the growth of the asset management industry over the past decades. The standard reflects the basic principle that the value of a business interest should reflect an "exit" value, which is the result of the forces at play in an orderly market with participants that are ready to execute transactions at arm's length. In ESE valuation, the implementation of the fair value standard emphasizes the role of calibration in linking valuation projections and assumptions to market-based inputs coming primarily from transactions in the company's own shares. The fair value standard can help enhance comparability in investment and company performance and provide insight into the factors that drive financial results for ESEs.

CHAPTER 3

Capital Structure

Alexander Davie

Antonella Puca

The capital structure of an early stage enterprise (ESE) is typically the result of multiple layers of financing rounds, which are negotiated independently and may involve different investors. At the inception stage, financing is provided by the founders and their immediate personal circle of relationships in exchange for common stock in the company. As the company builds its operations, additional rounds of financing take place, which typically involve the issuance of multiple classes and series of preferred stock with different rights and preferences. For most ESEs, debt is not a significant part of capital structure. When present, debt financing tends to have equity features and be in the form of short-term bridge loans that are expected to convert into preferred stock or be repaid at the time of a forthcoming equity round. An ESE may also engage in the issuance of equity-like instruments such as stock options and warrants. Stock options can provide an effective way to reward employees and establish a competitive compensation system to attract and retain talent without deploying cash resources. Warrants may be used to enhance the value of a preferred stock issuance or as an add-on to attract convertible bond investors.

This chapter presents an overview of the financial instruments that can be found in the capital structure of an ESE, with a special focus on the rights and privileges that are associated with preferred stock as the most prevalent type of instrument in ESE financing.

COMMON STOCK

Common stock is the most basic form of equity in an ESE capital structure. Common stock has no seniority or liquidation rights and offers to its holders a full exposure to enterprise risk. It is also the type of equity that carries the strongest features in terms of control and ability to exercise an influence on the company's operations. In an ESE, common stock is typically held by founders, board directors, and management. Some companies have implemented a dual-class common stock structure, for instance, including Class A and Class B shares. The two classes typically have identical rights, except that one class has super-voting rights in favor of the founders and company's management. For most companies, common stock still consists of a single class of shares with equal rights.

PREFERRED STOCK

Preferred stock is a class of equity interests in a company that has special contractual rights and privileges relative to common stock. Preferred stock rights consist of economic rights and noneconomic rights. Economic rights have a direct impact on the return that an investor will ultimately get in a liquidity event and on the allocation of enterprise value among different classes and series of shares. Economic rights directly affect the timing, priority, and amounts of returns that an investor in that class/series may receive as compared to investors in other classes/series of stock. Noneconomic rights enhance the power of preferred shareholders to participate in the company's strategic oversight and key management decisions. Noneconomic rights may impact the valuation of an interest in the enterprise indirectly, in view of their impact on the expected exit scenario and time horizon of the investment and on the assessment of control.

Most preferred stock rights find their legal source in the company's certificate of incorporation and in certain ancillary agreements, such as stock purchase agreements, investor rights agreements, voting agreements, management rights letters, right of first refusal, and co-sale agreements between the company, existing shareholders, and new investors.[1] The certificate of incorporation of a company includes a description of the various classes and series of stock, and of the key economic and voting rights and privileges of each class/series of stock. The ancillary agreements include a description of certain other preferred stock rights, particularly noneconomic rights. The National Venture Capital Association provides a set of model legal documents that are intended to reflect current practices and that can be used as a starting point for establishing preferred stock rights in venture capital financing.[2]

The earliest rounds of a company's financing are a critical stage for defining the rights and privileges that are likely to affect those of all subsequent rounds. An early stage investor needs to balance the desire for adequate protection and control over the company's strategic decisions with the need to allow enough flexibility to the company to pursue its operations effectively and to adequately reward founders and key employees.

Economic Rights

Conversion Rights   Conversion rights give the preferred shareholders the right to convert their shares into shares of common stock at a contractually stated price (the "conversion price"). In a preferred stock purchase agreement, the "conversion ratio" indicates the number of shares of common stock that can be obtained by exercising the conversion right of a share of

---

[1]Depending on the jurisdiction, the certificate of incorporation may be called the "articles of incorporation," "articles or organization," or also "certificate of formation." On the capital structure of ESEs and preferred stock rights, see especially AICPA PE/VC Valuation Guide, 8.09–8.13, "Rights associated with Preferred Stock" and 13.44–49, "Rights and Privileges not Enforced"; Neil Beaton, Chapter 2, "Understanding Early Stage Preferred Stock Rights," *Valuing Early Stage and Venture-Backed Companies* (Wiley, 2010), pp. 17–33; Alexander J. Davie and Casey W. Riggs, *Guide to Negotiating a Venture Capital Round, 2014–2017*; Brad Feld and Jason Mendelson, *Venture Deals: Be Smarter Than Your Lawyer and Venture Capitalist* (Wiley, 2016), pp. 39–101.

[2]The model documents of the National Venture Capital Association can be accessed at www.nvca.org and include, among others, a Model Amended and Restated Certificate of Incorporation, Investor Rights Agreement, Voting Agreement, Stock Purchase Agreement, Management Rights Letter, Term Sheet, Right of First Refusal and Co-Sale Agreement.

preferred stock. For instance, a conversion ratio of 2 and a conversion price of $1 indicates that each share of preferred stock can be converted into two shares of common stock at a price of $0.50 each ($1 for the two shares).

The provisions relating to the conversion of preferred stock to common stock typically require that all outstanding preferred stock automatically convert to common stock in the event of a "Qualified IPO," as defined in the preferred stock agreement or certificate of incorporation. Such conversion is generally a prerequisite for an investment banker to market the IPO.

A mandatory preferred stock conversion may also result upon the consent of a majority of the preferred shareholders, cumulatively or per individual class or series of share. To the extent that different series of preferred stock have different economic rights or protective provisions, the requirement to have a majority by class/series of shares is critical to ensure that the rights of each class/series are adequately protected.

Liquidation Rights   Liquidation rights give preferred shareholders a priority right over the allocation of the equity proceeds available from the liquidation of the enterprise relative to common shareholders. Liquidation rights directly affect the amount of proceeds that a shareholder receives in an exit transaction and can significantly increase the return that preferred shareholders receive relative to common shareholders.

Liquidation preferences are typically expressed as a multiple of invested capital. For instance, a 1× liquidation preference indicates that investors have the right to receive their invested capital back in full before any value can be allocated to common shareholders. A 2× liquidation preference indicates that investors have the right to receive twice their invested capital amount and so on. Different series of preferred stock may have liquidation rights with different levels of seniority. As subsequent rounds of financing take place, investors in the new rounds are often able to enter into an ESE with more senior rights, and with a higher level of privilege in liquidation. Exhibit 3.1 provides the capital structure for Company Y, a sample company that has issued Series A and Series B preferred shares in addition to common stock.

Series A and Series B shares have a 1× liquidation preference. Series B shares have senior liquidation rights relative to Series A (Series B shareholders have the right to receive their invested capital back before any allocation of value is made to Series A shareholders). Exhibit 3.2 presents the allocation of proceeds under a distressed low sale and high sale scenario for Company Y. In this example, preferred shareholders must choose whether to

Type of Shares	Shares Outstanding	Issue Price	Invested Capital	Liquidation Preference per Share (x)	Liquidation Preference	Ownership %
Series A Preferred Stock	10,000,000	$1.00	$10,000,000	1.00	$10,000,000	33.33%
Series B Preferred Stock	15,000,000	$1.00	$15,000,000	1.00	$15,000,000	50.00%
Common Stock	5,000,000					16.67%
Total					$25,000,000	100.00%

EXHIBIT 3.1   Company Y – Capital Structure

	Series A/B Do Not Convert		Series A/B Convert
	Scenario 1	Scenario 2	Scenario 3
	Distressed	Low Sale	High Sale
Proceeds from Liquidity Event	$ 18,000,000	$ 28,000,000	$ 72,000,000
Allocation:			
Step 1: Liquidation Preference of Series B Preferred Stock	$ 15,000,000	$ 15,000,000	–
Step 2: Liquidation Preferece of Series A Preferred Stock	3,000,000	10,000,000	–
Step 3: Pro-rata Allocation	–	3,000,000	72,000,000
Total	$ 18,000,000	$ 28,000,000	$ 72,000,000
Total proceeds to:			
Series A Preferred Stock	$ 3,000,000	$ 10,000,000	$ 24,000,000
Series B Preferred Stock	15,000,000	15,000,000	36,000,000
Common Stock	–	3,000,000	12,000,000
Total	$ 18,000,000	$ 28,000,000	$ 72,000,000
Total proceeds %			
Series A Preferred Stock	16.67%	35.71%	33.33%
Series B Preferred Stock	83.33%	53.57%	50.00%
Common Stock	0.00%	10.71%	16.67%
Total	100.00%	100.00%	100.00%

EXHIBIT 3.2   Company Y – Liquidation Preferences under Various Scenarios

maintain their preferred shareholder status and exercise their right to a liquidation preference, or convert into common stock and participate in the allocation of enterprise value on a pro-rata basis with common shareholders.

Scenario 1 represents an exit in a distressed transaction. The enterprise is liquidated for $18 million in cash proceeds, which are sufficient to cover in full the liquidation preference of Series B shareholders and $3 million of the liquidation preference of Series A shareholders. In this scenario, only Series B shareholders recover the full value of their invested capital. Series A shareholders recover 30 cents on the dollar of their original investment, and common shareholders do not receive any proceeds.

In the low sale scenario, preferred shareholders recover their investment in full. Any proceeds in excess of the liquidation preferences are allocated to common shareholders based on their ownership percentage in the firm.

Under the high sale scenario, conversion preferences are exercised to maximize the return for investors. Series A and Series B shareholders may be better off maintaining their preferred shareholders status under Scenario 1 (distressed) and Scenario 2 (low sale), but will find it suitable to convert their preferred shares into common stock in Scenario 3 (high sale). Under the high sale scenario, the value received by each class/series of investors is proportional to their ownership interest in the company on a fully converted basis and is not affected by liquidation preferences. Indeed, liquidation preferences matter the most for investors in cases where the exit value of a company is not sufficient to cover the liquidation preferences in full. Considering that a significant share of ESEs go out of business with either a full write-off or a partial recovery of invested capital, and that low sale transactions also represent a common outcome for an ESE, the relevance of liquidation preferences and their potential impact on valuation become all the more apparent.

In a Qualified IPO scenario in which preferred shares are mandatorily converted into common stock, the liquidation preferences and most other special rights associated with preferred stock, with the exception of registration rights, are also eliminated. Accordingly, the value of liquidation preferences and other preferred stock rights often diminishes as the likelihood of a Qualified IPO increases. Generally, if a proposed IPO does not meet the requirements of a Qualified IPO, the consent of at least a majority of the holders of preferred stock is required to convert all preferred stock to common stock and permit the IPO to proceed.

It is also important to keep in mind that the specific circumstances associated to each individual exit scenario may affect the way in which the contractual rights and privileges of preferred shareholders are exercised. Particularly in a distressed scenario, shareholders that have more senior rights in enterprise value allocation may be willing to give up some of their privileges to get the junior shareholders' approval for closing a transaction and reduce the risk for costly litigation.[3]

Participation Rights Participation rights give preferred shareholders the right to share in the allocation of enterprise value beyond their liquidation preference with common shareholders while maintaining preferred shareholder status (no conversion). In a liquidity event, the holder of participating preferred stock is entitled to receive its liquidation preference first and then share pro-rata with the common shareholders in any remaining liquidation proceeds without requiring the conversion of preferred stock into common stock. The total return to preferred stock may be limited by a cap (for example, three times the original purchase price of the preferred stock) ("capped participation") or unlimited ("full participation"). If the upside is unlimited, the preferred shareholder will not have an incentive to voluntarily convert to common stock. If the upside is limited, the preferred shareholder may elect to convert the preferred stock into common stock if such conversion would result in a higher total return to the shareholder.

Preferred shares may also have no participation rights. In this case, the holder of nonparticipating preferred stock is entitled to receive only the fixed liquidation preference amount and does not share in any upside beyond its liquidation preference while preferred shareholder

---

[3]AICPA PE/VC Valuation Guide, 13.49: "When considering the impact of the rights and privileges associated with a given investment, it is important to consider how market participants would evaluate the investment, looking at the circumstances holistically, evaluating the relative positions of the holders of the various classes of equity under the scenarios being evaluated, considering the past practices of the parties, and assessing the most likely result in each scenario. One should not always assume that senior equity holders will enjoy the full benefit of their contractual rights or that a company will be liquidated in accordance with the strict priority of the rights of the holders of each class of equity as written in each of the governing agreements. [. . .] However, to the extent that ignoring or interpreting contractual rights in less favorable ways has an impact on the resulting conclusion of fair value, the fund [or valuation analyst] would document and support how the selected approach is consistent with market participant assumptions."

status is maintained. The shareholder may still elect to convert its shares to common stock if such a conversion will provide higher proceeds.

The examples in Exhibits 3.1 and 3.2 that we have previously discussed illustrate the case of an allocation to preferred shares that have no participation rights. In Exhibit 3.2, in order to continue to participate in value allocation beyond the liquidation preference, the holders of preferred stock had to convert their shares into common stock, which is convenient once the proceeds allocated to common stock have reached $1 per share.

Exhibits 3.3 to 3.5 show how the existence of participation rights affects value allocation. Exhibit 3.3 shows the capital structure of Company Y, updated with the indication of the conversion price and ratio. In this example, Series B preferred stock has seniority over Series A preferred stock and common stock while Series A stock has seniority over common stock.

Exhibit 3.4 shows the new allocation of exit proceeds, assuming now that the preferred stock of Company Y has full participation rights.

Assuming that preferred stock has full participation rights, there are three steps in our "Allocation" process: In Step 1 and Step 2, the liquidation preferences of Series B shares and Series A shares, respectively, are fulfilled. In Step 3, any remaining exit proceeds are allocated pro-rata to all shareholders based on the ownership percentage in the enterprise on a fully converted basis. For instance, in the low sale scenario, the proceeds allocated to Series A preferred are calculated as:

Total proceeds allocated to Series A Preferred

   = Liquidation Preference of Series A Preferred + Pro-rata Allocation Amount

   × Ownership Percentage of Series A Preferred on a fully converted basis

   = $10,000,000 + $3,000,000 × 33.33% = $11,000,000

And in the high sale scenario:

Total proceeds allocated to Series A Preferred = $10,000,000 + $47,000,000 × 33.33%

   = $25,666,667

Type of Shares	Shares Outstanding	Issue Price	Invested Capital	Liquidation Preference per Share (x)	Liquidation Preference	Conversion Price	Conversion Ratio	Fully Converted Ownership %
Series A Preferred Stock	10,000,000	$ 1.00	$ 10,000,000	1.00	$ 10,000,000	$ 1.00	1.00	33.33%
Series B Preferred Stock	15,000,000	$ 1.00	$ 15,000,000	1.00	$ 15,000,000	$ 1.00	1.00	50.00%
Common Stock	5,000,000	n/a						16.67%
Total					$ 25,000,000			100.00%

EXHIBIT 3.3   Company Y: Capital Structure

	Scenario 1	Scenario 2	Scenario 2
	Distressed	Low Sale	High Sale
Proceeds from Liquidity Event	$ 18,000,000	$ 28,000,000	$ 72,000,000
Allocation:			
Step 1: Liquidation Preference of Series B Preferred Stock	$ 15,000,000	$ 15,000,000	$ 15,000,000
Step 2: Liquidation Preference of Series A Preferred Stock	3,000,000	10,000,000	10,000,000
Step 3: Pro-rata Allocation	–	3,000,000	47,000,000
Total	$ 18,000,000	$ 28,000,000	$ 72,000,000
Total proceeds to:			
Series A Preferred Stock	$ 3,000,000	$ 11,000,000	$ 25,666,667
Series B Preferred Stock	15,000,000	16,500,000	38,500,000
Common Stock	–	500,000	7,833,333
Total	$ 18,000,000	$ 28,000,000	$ 72,000,000
Total proceeds %			
Series A Preferred Stock	16.67%	39.29%	35.65%
Series B Preferred Stock	83.33%	58.93%	53.47%
Common Stock	0.00%	1.79%	10.88%
Total	100.00%	100.00%	100.00%

EXHIBIT 3.4   Company Y: Preferred Stock with Full Participation Rights

Notice that also under the high sale scenario, the allocation percentages of Series A and Series B shareholders will be higher in the "full participation" case of Exhibit 3.4 (35.65% and 53.47%, respectively), in which shareholders maintain their preferred status, than in Exhibit 3.2 (33.33% and 50.00%, respectively), in which Series A and Series B preferred shares must convert into common stock in order to participate into any further allocation beyond their liquidation preference.

Exhibit 3.5 shows the allocation of exit proceeds assuming that the participation rights of Series A and Series B shareholders are capped at 2× of the initial invested capital ($20 million and $30 million for Series A and Series B, respectively).

Compared to the full participation case of Exhibit 3.4, the existence of "capped" participation rights has no effect in the distressed scenario, where proceeds are still allocated based on the liquidation preferences of the preferred stock. It also has no effect in the low sale scenario, where all shares participate pro-rata in the proceeds above the liquidation preference. It will, however, enhance the proceeds received by common shareholders in the high sale scenario in which it is convenient for preferred shareholders to convert their shares into common stock. In the high sale scenario, the results of having capped participation rights will be the same as if no participation rights were present.

Here are some conclusions that we can draw from this analysis:

- Participation rights have value for shareholders to the extent the liquidation proceeds in a liquidity event exceed the preferred stock's liquidation preference.

	Scenario 1	Scenario 2	Scenario 2
	Distressed	Low Sale	High Sale
Proceeds from Liquidity Event	$ 18,000,000	$ 28,000,000	$ 72,000,000
Allocation:			
Step 1: Liquidation Preference of Series B Preferred Stock	$ 15,000,000	$ 15,000,000	–
Step 2: Liquidation Preference of Series A Preferred Stock	3,000,000	10,000,000	–
Step 3: Pro-rata Allocation – up to cap	–	3,000,000	–
Step 4: Pro-rata Allocation – above cap	–	–	72,000,000
Total	$ 18,000,000	$ 28,000,000	$ 72,000,000
Total proceeds to:			
Series A Preferred Stock	$ 3,000,000	$ 11,000,000	$ 24,000,000
Series B Preferred Stock	15,000,000	16,500,000	36,000,000
Common Stock	–	500,000	12,000,000
Total	$ 18,000,000	$ 28,000,000	$ 72,000,000
Total proceeds %			
Series A Preferred Stock	16.67%	39.29%	33.33%
Series B Preferred Stock	83.33%	58.93%	50.00%
Common Stock	0.00%	1.79%	16.67%
Total	100.00%	100.00%	100.00%

EXHIBIT 3.5   Company Y: Allocation of Proceeds – Preferred Stock with Capped Participation Rights

- Full participation rights are the most favorable solution for preferred shareholders. When full participation rights are granted, it is generally convenient to hold on to preferred stock status and delay conversion as long as possible so as to maintain the protection offered by the liquidation preference.
- Capped participation rights provide advantages analogous to those of full participation rights to the extent the liquidation proceeds are at or below the cap. For liquidation proceeds in excess of the cap, investors will convert their shares and end up in a similar position than if the shares were nonparticipating.

Participation rights are frequently granted in the early stage of venture capital investing, when the power balance between the founders and the new investors tends to be on the side of the new investors. Full participation provisions provide the greatest advantage for preferred shareholders, but are also the least common in practice. Many ESEs that allow for participation rights will structure them with capped provisions. As a company advances in its stage of development, participation rights become less frequent and harder for new investors to negotiate.

Dividend Rights   Preferred shareholders in an ESE are often granted the right to receive stock dividends in kind as a percentage of the stock issue price. When dividends are declared, preferred shareholders generally are entitled to dividends in priority to common shareholders. After receiving dividends as a percentage of stock issue price (initial dividends), holders of preferred stock may also be entitled to participate in any dividends to be paid to the holders of common stock. In an ESE, dividends are often subject to a "when and if declared" clause, which indicates that they are only granted in a given year to the extent they have been declared by the ESE's board of directors, at the board of directors' discretion.

Dividends may be cumulative or noncumulative. Noncumulative dividends that are not declared or paid in a given year do not carry forward into or become payable in subsequent years. Combined with the "when and if declared" clause, the noncumulative clause often results in no dividends being earned at all by preferred shareholders.

Cumulative dividends give shareholders the right to add on the dividends that have been missed in one year to the dividends that are earned in a subsequent period. Cumulative dividends are rarely paid out by an ESE. In most cases they are added to the liquidation preference of the preferred stock. Cumulative dividends may significantly affect the allocation of enterprise value based on liquidation preferences. They may also affect the conversion ratio for convertible preferred stock, and result in a greater number of common shares per unit of preferred stock upon conversion.

In practice, dividend accumulation terms may be subject to restructuring upon new rounds of financing or upon conversion in a way that effectively limits their impact on value allocation. For instance, a typical "restructuring" clause may state that:

> *upon the conversion of any shares of preferred stock, all preferred stock accruing dividends related thereto shall be extinguished without payment thereof and any rights thereto shall terminate automatically.*

Exhibit 3.6 shows the impact of cumulative dividends on the capital structure of Company Y, assuming that the preferred stock has cumulative, noncompounding dividends in kind over a period of two years at an annual rate of 8% of the original issue price. In Exhibit 3.6, the liquidation preference for each series of preferred stock has been adjusted to include cumulative dividends accrued at an annual rate of 8%. The conversion ratio has also been adjusted as:

$$\text{Adjusted Conversion Ratio (ACR)} = \text{Initial Conversion Ratio} \times (1 + 2d)$$

where d = dividend rate

or

$$ACR = 1 \times (1 + 0.08 \times 2) = 1.16$$

The fully converted shares are calculated by multiplying the ACR by the original number of shares, which results in a greater ownership percentage in the company for the preferred shareholders (34.12% and 51.18% for Series A and Series B, respectively) than in the no-dividend scenario (33.33% and 50.00%, respectively).

For ESEs, "dividends" that are paid in cash typically represent a return of capital to investors rather than a distribution of profits. By definition, ESEs don't generate profits and have no profits to distribute. An ESE may still refer to a cash distribution as "dividend" in its certificate of incorporation or in a shareholder agreement.

Type of Shares	Shares Outstanding	Issue Price	Invested Capital	Liquidation Preference per Share (x)	Liquidation Preference	Cumulative Dividends	Adjusted Liquidation Preference	Adjusted Conversion Ratio	Fully Converted Shares	Fully Converted Ownership %
Series A Preferred Stock	10,000,000	$1.00	$10,000,000	1.00	$10,000,000	$1,600,000	$11,600,000	1.16	$11,600,000	34.12%
Series B Preferred Stock	15,000,000	$1.00	$15,000,000	1.00	$15,000,000	$2,400,000	$17,400,000	1.16	$17,400,000	51.18%
Common Stock	5,000,000	n/a							$5,000,000	14.71%
Total					$25,000,000				$34,000,000	100.00%

EXHIBIT 3.6 Company Y: Effect of Cumulative Dividends on Capital Structure

Antidilution Rights   Antidilution rights give preferred shareholders the right to adjust the liquidation and conversion features of their shares to prevent or reduce the dilution that would otherwise result from a subsequent round of financing at a lower valuation than in a prior financing ("down round"). For an ESE where multiple rounds of financing are likely to take place over the life of the company, antidilution rights are often very valuable and the subject of intense negotiations between the company's management and prospective preferred shareholders. From the company's perspective, the presence of antidilution rights may make negotiations with new shareholders in subsequent rounds more challenging as they have to acknowledge the equity claims of preexistent shareholders. From the perspective of preexistent shareholders, antidilution rights can provide substantial downside economic protection of their equity interest in an ESE. Let's review the effect of antidilution rights with a practical example.

Let's assume that as of January 1 of Year 1, the capital structure of Company Z, a sample ESE, consists of 8,400,000 shares of common stock held by the company's founders, and 2,000,000 shares of nonparticipating Series A Convertible Preferred stock, issued at $10 per share, with a 1 × liquidation preference and a 1 × conversion ratio. Series A shareholders have a cumulative equity interest of 19.23% of Company Z on a fully converted basis, with the remaining 80.77% for the common shareholders as illustrated in Exhibit 3.7.

On February 15, Year 1, Company Z issues a new round of 5,000,000 Series B convertible preferred shares at a price of $8 per share. Series B shares have a 1 × liquidation preference and a 1 × conversion ratio. Exhibit 3.8 presents the post-round capital structure of the company, in the absence of any antidilution rights for Series A preferred shareholders.

Series B shareholders now hold 32.47% of Company Z, and the equity ownership of Series A shareholders has been diluted from 19.23% to 12.99% on a fully converted basis.

Exhibit 3.9 presents the capital structure of Company Z assuming that Series A preferred shareholders have antidilution rights with a "full ratchet" provision.

Under the terms of a full ratchet provision, the conversion price of the previously issued preferred stock (Series A in our case) is adjusted to the price of the Series B preferred round ($8 per share). The conversion ratio of the Series A preferred stock is now 1.25× (the original $10 issue price divided by the $8 issue price of the new Series B shares). The original 2,000,000

Shares	A Shares Outstanding	B Issue Price	Invested Capital	C Liquidation Preference per Share	D Conversion Price	E Conversion Ratio	Fully Converted Shares	Fully Converted Ownership %
Series A Preferred Stock	2,000,000	$ 10.00	$ 20,000,000	$10.00	$ 10.00	1.00	2,000,000	19.23%
Common Stock	8,400,000						8,400,000	80.77%
Total							10,400,000	100.00%

EXHIBIT 3.7   Company Z: Capital Structure, January 1, Year 1

Type of Shares	Shares Outstanding	Issue Price	Invested Capital	Liquidation Preference per Share	Conversion Price	Conversion Ratio	Fully Converted Shares	Fully Converted Ownership %
Series A Preferred Stock	2,000,000	$ 10.00	$ 20,000,000	$10.00	$ 10.00	1.00	2,000,000	12.99%
Series B Preferred Stock	5,000,000	$ 8.00	$ 40,000,000	$8.00	$ 8.00	1.00	5,000,000	32.47%
Common Stock	8,400,000						8,400,000	54.55%
Total							15,400,000	100.00%

EXHIBIT 3.8   Company Z: Capital Structure, February 15, Year 1

Type of Shares	Shares Outstanding	Issue Price	Invested Capital	Liquidation Preference per Share	Conversion Price	Conversion Ratio	Fully Converted Shares	Fully Converted Ownership %
Series A Preferred Stock	2,000,000	$ 10.00	$ 20,000,000	$10.00	$ 8.00	1.25	2,500,000	15.72%
Series B Preferred Stock	5,000,000	$ 8.00	$ 40,000,000	$8.00	$ 8.00	1.00	5,000,000	31.45%
Common Stock	8,400,000						8,400,000	52.83%
Total							15,900,000	100.00%

EXHIBIT 3.9   Company Z: Capital Structure with Full Ratchet

Type of Shares	Shares Outstanding	Issue Price	Invested Capital	Liquidation Preference per Share	Conversion Price	Conversion Ratio	Fully Converted Shares	Fully Converted Ownership %
Series A Preferred Stock	2,000,000	$ 10.00	$ 20,000,000	$10.00	$ 8.57	1.17	2,333,333	14.83%
Series B Preferred Stock	5,000,000	$ 8.00	$ 40,000,000	$8.00	$ 8.00	1.00	5,000,000	31.78%
Common Stock	8,400,000						8,400,000	53.39%
Total							15,733,333	100.00%

EXHIBIT 3.10   Company Z: Capitalization Structure with Partial Ratchet – NBWA

shares of preferred stock are now convertible into 2,500,000 shares of common stock, which represent 15.72% of the company on a fully converted basis.

Exhibit 3.10 shows the capitalization structure of Company Z after the Series B round assuming that Series A shareholders have antidilution rights with partial ratchet calculated using the narrow-based weighted average (NBWA) formula.

In this case, the results for series A shareholders are less favorable than in the case of a full ratchet adjustment but still more favorable than if no antidilution provision were in place. Under the terms of a partial ratchet provision with the NBWA formula, the new conversion price of the Series A shares is calculated by taking into account both the lower issuance price of the new stock and the size of the new issuance relative to the company's outstanding preferred stock. The formula for calculating the new conversion price of the Series A preferred shares is:

New Conversion Price (NBWA) = Original issue price of Series A preferred shares

$\times (A + B)/(A + C)$

where

A = outstanding preferred capitalization prior to new round (number of shares)
B = total currency amount paid for Series B preferred shares divided by the price per share paid for Series A preferred shares
C = number of Series B preferred shares issued at the new price

In our example:

New Conversion Price (NBWA) = $10 \times [(2,000,000 + 5,000,000 \times \$8/\$10)$

$/(2,000,000 + 5,000,000)] = \$8.57$

The partial ratchet formula results in a new conversion price of $8.57 for Series A preferred shares, which in turn results in a conversion ratio of 1.17 common shares per unit of series A preferred shares, and in a 14.83% ownership interest for Series A preferred shareholders on a fully converted basis.

Exhibit 3.11 shows the capitalization structure of Company Z after the Series B round assuming that Series A shareholders have antidilution rights with partial ratchet calculated using a broad-based weighted average (BBWA) formula. This is the most common solution in ESE valuation, the least advantageous for Series A shareholders but also the solution that leaves the greatest flexibility in the negotiation of new financing rounds for the company's management.

The formula for the new conversion price now takes into account the total number of outstanding shares (common and preferred, as well as any options and warrants – none in

	Shares Outstanding	Issue Price	Invested Capital	Liquidation Preference per Share	Conversion Price	Conversion Ratio	Fully Converted Shares	Fully Converted Ownership %
Series A Preferred Stock	2,000,000	$ 10.00	$ 20,000,000	$10.00	$ 9.35	1.07	$ 2,138,889	13.76%
Series B Preferred Stock	5,000,000	$ 8.00	$ 40,000,000	$8.00	$ 8.00	1.00	$ 5,000,000	32.18%
Common Stock	8,400,000	–					$ 8,400,000	54.06%
Total							$15,538,889	100.00%

EXHIBIT 3.11 Company Z: Capital Structure with Partial Ratchet – BBWA

our case), as follows:

New Conversion Price (BBWA) = Original issue price of Series A preferred shares

$\times (A + B)/(A + C)$

where

A = outstanding total capitalization prior to new round, including common stock, preferred stock, options and warrants (number of shares)

B = total currency amount paid for Series B preferred shares divided by the price per share paid for Series A preferred shares

C = number of Series B preferred shares issued at the new price

In our example:

New Conversion Price (BBWA) = $10 \times [(10,400,000 + 5,000,000 \times \$8/\$10)$

$/(10,400,000 + 5,000,000)] = \$9.35$

In our example, the partial ratchet formula results in an adjusted conversion price for Series A preferred shares of $9.35 per share, and a conversion ratio of 1.07. This in turn results in an ownership of 13.76 % on a fully converted basis for Series A shareholders (still better than the 12.99% ownership in the lack of antidilution provisions).

A valuation analyst should consider the effect of any antidilution provision in the valuation of the equity interests in an ESE, particularly to the extent that a round of financing is already in the works and/or can be reasonably forecasted in the near term.

Redemption Rights Redemption rights give preferred shareholders the right to have their company repurchase their shares after a specified period of time (typically five years). While companies are set up to have a perpetual existence, investors may have a limited time horizon, and will often consider an exit strategy before they acquire shares of company. Redemption rights may provide an exit solution and an incentive for management to explore liquidity alternatives for the company. In an ESE, redemption rights are rarely exercised as they would involve a disbursement of company cash that may put the company at risk for survival. Even though the holders of redemption rights may not wish to force a dissolution, the ability to do so may help them influence the CEO or board of the company.

In some cases, redemption rights may be "mandatory," in that the repurchase of preferred stock by the company takes place automatically, based on contractual provisions and upon the occurrence of a triggering event or the passage of time. For instance, preferred stock may be subject to mandatory redemption at a stated date, similarly to a maturity date for a bond.

Registration Rights Registration rights grant to preferred shareholders the right to demand that the company's management exercises best effort to complete an IPO. If the company has already completed an IPO, registration rights make it possible for preferred shareholders to demand a secondary public offering of their converted shares. Registration rights may also enable holders of registrable shares to participate in the registration of any other class of shares by the company ("piggy-back rights"). Similar to redemption rights, these rights are meant to provide for an exit strategy to preferred shareholders and are rarely exercised.

Noneconomic Rights

Voting Rights Voting rights entitle each holder of outstanding shares of preferred stock to vote together with common shareholders on matters requiring a shareholder vote, and/or to vote on certain matters as a separate class. When voting together with common shareholders, the holders of preferred stock are typically entitled to cast a number of votes that is equal to the number of shares of common stock into which the shares of preferred stock are convertible as of the record date. Cumulative voting may also take place by class or series of shares. Delaware corporate law, for example, requires by default that any amendment to a corporation's certificate of incorporation receive the approval of the holders of a majority of each class of stock. The NVCA model legal documents override this provision by providing for a vote of all classes together on an as-converted basis.[4]

Board Composition Rights One of the most important noneconomic rights of preferred shareholders is the right to designate a certain number of directors to the company's board of directors. In the absence of specific provisions, the directors of the board are generally elected with the vote of a plurality of the shareholders. In order to change this "default" process, the certificate of incorporation must include an alternative voting provision, for instance, by assigning to preferred shareholders the right to elect a certain number of directors. Election and voting rights may also be placed in an investor rights agreement or voting agreement, but if they are not also included in a certificate of incorporation, their enforceability would be more limited.

In the earliest stages of a new company, the board may consist of only the founder or founders. Once the company is fully operational, boards would typically be composed of up to seven members. A typical structure for a three-person board may consist of:

- One director appointed by the founders (common shareholders) with responsibilities as CEO of the company
- One director appointed by the preferred shareholders
- One director elected by all shareholders on a fully converted basis

In a board with five directors, preferred shareholders may have the ability to elect two board directors, or, if there are multiple series of preferred shareholders, each series may have the right to appoint one director.

From a valuation perspective, board voting rights are a critical element in the assessment of whether a particular class or series of shareholders, or shareholders as a group, are in a position to exercise control over the company. A valuation analyst will typically consider the control structure of a company in the assessment, for instance, of whether preferred shareholders have the ability to modify the capital structure of a company and in determining the application and size of any control-related premiums or discounts in the valuation.

Protective Provisions and Veto Rights Protective provisions and veto rights set forth a list of actions that a company cannot take without the prior consent of preferred shareholders that

---

[4]NVCA Model Certificate of Incorporation, Sect. 3.1, Voting - General: "Except as provided by law or by the other provisions of this Amended and Restated Certificate of Incorporation, holders of Series A Preferred Stock shall vote together with the holders of Common Stock as a single class and on an as-converted to Common Stock basis."

represents a specified percentage of the outstanding preferred stock. These provisions seek to protect investors from actions by management that may dilute or diminish the value of their investment. They also serve to ensure their participation in key strategic decisions for the company, generally through the means of veto rights (the right to block a company's action). From an investor perspective, protective provisions should be set up to survive the amendments effected through a merger transaction, which may otherwise result in a new certificate of incorporation with provisions outside of the preferred shareholders' control. From an entrepreneur's perspective, it is generally best to have them in a simple structure, where all shareholders vote collectively rather than by class or series.

The consent of preferred shareholders is typically required to take actions such as:

- The liquidation, dissolution, or winding up of the company
- Mergers, acquisitions, corporate reorganizations, and transactions that effect a change of control of the company
- A filing of bankruptcy
- An IPO
- The registration of shares in a secondary offering

Corporate actions that typically require the consent of a specified percentage of preferred stock on a cumulative basis or, in many cases, on a per-class/series basis, include:

- New rounds of financing that are senior in terms of liquidation preference or have more favorable conversion rights than the already-issued shares
- Amendments to the certificate of incorporation that may alter key economic or noneconomic rights of the outstanding shares
- Employment arrangements with the grant of employee stock options or similar rights
- A declaration of dividends
- A change in the size of the board of directors
- The appointment of a new CEO
- Significant changes in the company's business, including the addition or dismission of a business line
- Transfers or exclusive licenses of the company's key technology assets and intellectual property

For a valuation analyst, it is critical to have a good understanding of these provisions to be able to adequately model the probability and timing of future liquidation events, the capital structure of the company in the calculation of the weighted average cost of capital, and its revenue growth.

Drag-Along Rights Drag-along rights allow the holders to force a sale of the company against the will of common shareholders, including the company's founders. An acquisition does not typically require the unanimous consent of all shareholders. Under Delaware law, for instance, only the consent of a majority of shareholders of the company on a fully converted basis is required. Under California law, preferred shareholders and common shareholders have to separately approve a sale based on a simple majority per class. Compared to the Delaware majority requirements, the California law grants greater protection in an ESE to the interests of founders and employees, who typically hold common stock.

Drag-along rights can significantly alter the statutory scenario and are especially relevant if the sale price of the company is at or below the liquidation preference and would not be sufficient to adequately reward common shareholders. For instance, a contractual provision may state that if the majority of the preferred shareholders agree to a sale or liquidation of the company, the holders of the remaining preferred and common stock shall consent and raise no objections to the sale. Under most state statutes, drag-along rights eliminate the possibility for minority shareholders to exercise dissenters' rights and to be able to challenge the fairness of the consideration received in an M&A transaction.

A second type of drag-along rights addresses the situation in which a founder or member of management is no longer involved in the company's operations. In this case, drag-along rights may give the remaining shareholders the right to drag along the vote of the departed founder. These rights are becoming more common as the turnover of key management personnel and workforce restructurings that involve management changes become more frequent in ESEs.

In order to be enforceable, drag-along rights must typically fulfill stringent notification requirements to protect minority shareholders and make sure they are aware of an impending transaction. In transactions that involve the sale or liquidation of the company, even when drag-along rights are present, minority investors may still find ways to delay, put restrictions on, and impose a blackout period for the transaction. They may also require a guaranteed minimum price for their shares. In any case, the majority owners must give the minority owners the same terms and conditions and price as other sellers.

Drag-along rights can significantly affect the timing and the proceeds resulting from an liquidity event for the various classes of shareholders and have a relevant impact on fair value assessment. A forced sale at a price below the liquidation preference, for instance, may well be in the interests of preferred shareholders, but may also result in no proceeds being allocated to common shareholders. The establishment of a minimum price for a sale transaction (for instance, $1.5 \times$ of the liquidation preference) may help protect the interest of the founders in the case of a distressed liquidation scenario.

Preemptive Rights   Preemptive rights provide the holders with the right to purchase a company's new shares before they are offered to other parties. For instance, the right to participate pro-rata in future rounds gives to a preferred shareholder the right to purchase a portion of any new stock offering based on the proportion that the number of shares already held bears to the company's total number of shares on a fully converted basis. If the investor chooses not to purchase its entire pro-rata share, the other investors can purchase the remaining shares pro-rata. The right to participate in future rounds gives preferred shareholders the ability to protect themselves from dilution, and restricts the ability of management to diversify the company's investor base.

The right to participate in future rounds may be accompanied by a pay-to-play provision, which mandates the conversion of preferred stock into common stock, in whole or in part, for holders that do not elect to participate in future rounds. Pay-to-play provisions may significantly reduce the expected proceeds from preferred shareholders interest in a company in a situation where an investor may have exhausted its capital reserves dedicated to add-on rounds for a company and the company still needs capital to reach a targeted sale or IPO event. To the extent the decision of current investors on whether to exercise their preemptive rights is known, it should be incorporated in the analyst's projection of the company's capitalization structure at exit in a fair value assessment.

First Refusal Rights and Tag-Along Rights   The right of first refusal gives preferred shareholders the right to purchase shares from a seller ahead of a third party, on the terms offered by the third party. If the rights are not exercised, the seller can complete the sale with the third party. First refusal rights are meant to give existing shareholders (or the company) the first opportunity to purchase shares and control the investor base of the company. If any investor declines to participate in the purchase, the others typically have a right of "oversubscription," which allows them to purchase the shares that the declining investor did not purchase.

Tag-along rights or "co-sale" rights give the holders the right to sell their shares together with other shareholders in the firm. For instance, if founders engage in a sale of their shares, the preferred shareholders with tag-along rights may also elect to enter into the sale under the same terms of the founders. These rights may help align the interest of preferred shareholders with those of the founders, reduce the liquidity of common stock held by founders and enhance the value of the preferred stock.

Management Rights   Management rights are contractual rights directly between the investor and an operating company to substantially participate in, or substantially influence the conduct of, the management of the operating company. Management rights entitle preferred shareholders to inspect a company's books and accounts, visit board meetings, discuss the company's affairs, finances, and accounts with officers, and consult with and advise management on matters relating to the company's operations. Management rights may be in place of rights to nominate board directors.

Information Rights   Preferred shareholders with information rights have the ability to access confidential information of the company, such as the company's financial statements, operating plans and budgets, and quarterly capitalization tables. These rights may be limited to investors that are not competitors of the company or to major investors that hold a minimum equity interest in the company. Information rights provide preferred shareholders timely access to critical information that may not be available to common shareholders.

OPTIONS AND OPTION-LIKE INSTRUMENTS

Options are instruments that provide the holder with the right, but not the obligation to purchase (call option) or sell (put option) an asset (referred to as an underlying, such as a share of stock) at a fixed price (the "exercise price" or "strike price") at any time during a contractually defined time period (an "American" option) or at the expiry of the time period (a "European" option).

The exercise of a call option in a strict sense is a transaction that does not involve the issuing company. No proceeds are received by the issuer, and no new shares of stock are issued. A put option, on the other hand, may be with a third-party or with the issuing company. Put option transactions with the issuing company results in a repurchase of shares by the company and directly affect the company's equity.

In an ESE, call options are typically granted to founders and employees as a form of noncash compensation, to reduce the need for compensation-related cash disbursement and to align the interests of management and key employees with that of the company's investors. They may also be granted to third party suppliers, service providers, and consultants, in exchange for key products and services. Most ESEs compensate their board directors entirely with equity in the form of stock options. These options result in a new issuance of shares upon exercise and are similar to warrants in this respect, as discussed later in this chapter.

A company may put in place an employee option plan (EOP) to promote employee stock ownership and align employee interests to those of the company. EOPs typically include a provision that indicates the maximum number of shares of common stock that may be issued pursuant to the exercise of the plan's options (the "option pool"). Options issued as compensation typically have service-based "vesting" conditions, whereby the right to exercise the options is "earned" over time, with a certain percentage of the options becoming vested after each year of employee service.

Here is a sample disclosure with a description of the option pool in an ESE's stock option plan from an ESE's annual financial statements:

> *The Company has an Employee Stock Option Plan ("Option Plan") which authorizes the issue of up to 70,000,000 class A common stock options to certain directors, officers, employees and consultants. Options issued under the plan have a maximum term of 10 years commencing from the date of original issue, unless modified by way of written agreement. Employee and non-employee options will vest equally over a four-year period commencing on the first anniversary of the grant date.*

In a typical four-year vesting scheme, 25% of the options vest at the end of Year 1 (a one-year "vesting cliff"), and 25% in each year thereafter (typically a month-by-month vest) in Years 2–4. For employees who leave the firm within one year of the start date of employment, any options granted will not vest and become worthless. Employees who stay with the firm a minimum of two years will have the right to exercise 50% of their option grants as of the end of Year 2, and an additional 25% for each of the two years thereafter. In the end, it will take an employee a total of four years to acquire the right to exercise 100% of all the options granted under the terms of its employment.

From a valuation perspective, the presence of an option pool may have a very significant effect on a ESE's capital structure and be an important factor in the dilution of investors' capital over time. Every time an option is exercised, the corresponding common shares from the option pool are reclassified from "available for issuance" to "issued and outstanding." In setting up a company's capitalization table, a valuation analyst will typically include the full option pool (stock available for issuance as well as stock already issued in relation to prior exercises) as part of the company's capitalization structure. The analyst may also consider adjusting the stock "available for issuance" in the option pool in view of expected amendments to the company's compensation agreements.

WARRANTS

Warrants are equity instruments, usually freestanding or detachable, that provide the holder with the right, but not the obligation, to purchase an asset (the underlying, such as a share of stock) at a fixed price (the "exercise price") during a contractually defined time period (an American warrant) or at the expiry of the time period (a European warrant). Warrants are similar to call options in that their value is driven by the price of the underlying security relative to the exercise price. The exercise of a warrant is a direct transaction with the issuing company, resulting in the issuance of new shares of stock in exchange for exercise proceeds. From this perspective, the employee stock options that we have described in the prior paragraph, have warrant features in that they also result in the issuance of new stock for the enterprise.

In an ESE, warrants are typically found as a boost for investors in connection with the issuance of bridge notes or preferred stock. An investor may purchase preferred stock and warrants convertible into preferred stock in a single transaction. Under U.S. GAAP, to the extent the warrants are self-standing and can be sold separately, they will also have to be identified and accounted for separately from preferred stock. Upon purchase, the investor will need to allocate the purchase price of the transaction between warrants and preferred stock, based on their relative estimated valuation. In subsequent periods, the fair value of the warrant will also have to be estimated and reported separately.

Warrants are investor instruments. They are not subject to vesting provisions and may be transferred to other parties.

Convertible Notes

Convertible notes are debt instruments that include an option to convert the repayment obligation into an alternative instrument, typically the issuer's common or preferred stock. In addition to the stated interest rate and principal amount, the terms of the convertible note establish the conversion price or ratio that dictates the number or value of shares to be received when the conversion is executed, and may also establish predetermined dates or defined events when conversion may or must take place.

Convertible notes are a common vehicle for ESE financing and provide investors with enhanced protection of invested capital relative to preferred stock. They are often used for short-term financing (one year or less), with the expectation that they will soon convert into a new round of preferred stock.

Convertible notes typically accrue interest at a rate that is below market for nonconvertible loans with similar risk characteristics. Most of the value of convertible notes for ESEs comes from their equity conversion features. Convertible notes typically give the holder the right to convert into the next round of preferred stock financing at a discount (in the 10–30% range) from the preferred stock issue price. This feature may provide a significant benefit to convertible note holders at the time of the new round.

From the perspective of the founders, one of the advantages of convertible notes is that investors do not need to agree on a valuation of the company at the financing date. A company that, for instance, believes that it is close to achieving a significant milestone, may find it more advantageous to issue a bridge convertible note to cover an immediate financing need, and wait until the milestone is reached to enter into a fully fledged preferred stock financing, presumably at a higher valuation. The terms of convertible bridge notes typically do not specify the conversion price of the notes, which is determined at the time of the preferred stock financing. A bridge note holder, on the other hand, may find itself with a smaller share of the company if the company significantly increases in value prior to the conversion round, than if it had invested in the company's equity in the first place. The discount to the new round's original issue price provides a benefit for bridge note investors that compensates them for the additional risk of a preround financing. In addition to that, investors may also demand that the purchase price of the new round be "capped" at a certain valuation for the enterprise.

As an example, let's consider an investor that enters into a bridge note of $1,000,000 in principal value, convertible into preferred stock. To protect its investment from the appreciation in value of the company's equity, the investor negotiates a conversion discount of 20% to the issue price of the next round, and a valuation cap at $5 million, calculated based on the enterprise value on a fully converted basis prior to the effect of the next round of financing. The investor is informed that the next round of financing will take place at a valuation of $8 million for the enterprise. Assuming that the company has 2,000,000 shares outstanding prior to the new round, the investor will use the lower the of (a) the conversion cap ($5.0 million) or (b) the discounted value of the enterprise prior to the new round (80% of 8 million or $6.4 million) to determine the number of shares that are received upon conversion as follows:

$$\text{Shares received upon conversion (with valuation cap)} = \text{Number of shares outstanding}$$
$$\text{prior to the new round} \times \text{Invested capital}/\text{Conversion cap}$$
$$= 2{,}000{,}000 \times 1{,}000{,}000/5{,}000{,}000 = 400{,}000$$

If the valuation cap had not been in place, the investor would have received 312,500 shares calculated as:

$$\text{Shares received upon conversion (without valuation cap)} = \text{Number of shares outstanding}$$
$$\text{prior to the new round} \times \text{Invested Capital}/\text{Discounted value of enterprise prior to the}$$
$$\text{new round} = 2{,}000{,}000 \times 1{,}000{,}000/6{,}400{,}000 = 312{,}500$$

In this example, the valuation cap results in an additional 87,500 shares for the investor.

Convertible notes carry with them certain administrative and compliance costs that may be burdensome for an enterprise with limited cash resources. Also, founders and prior VC investors may be reluctant to allow the company to enter into note agreements that have seniority rights relative to their equity interests in the company. Still, short-term bridge notes are commonly found in ESE's capital structures and can be especially useful if there is a new round of preferred stock in sight and an expectation that the company may reach a key milestone ahead of the round.

OTHER HYBRID INSTRUMENTS

Simple Agreements for Future Equity

Simple agreements for future equity (SAFE) are agreements by which an investor makes a cash investment into a company in return for the right to subscribe for new shares in the future upon the occurrence of a triggering event and at a price per share, which is not specified at the time of the initial SAFE investment. Typical terms for a SAFE may involve a valuation cap, which sets a limit to the future issuance price similarly to a valuation cap for convertible bonds, and a discount (typically between 10% and 30%) to the issuance price of the new round.

SAFEs are similar to warrants in that they qualify as equity in the company's capital structure and do not accrue interest. Compared to convertible bonds, SAFEs have typically lower transaction costs and provide greater flexibility in negotiation, as they may have customized terms for each investor and do not require the definition of a premoney valuation for the company. SAFEs were introduced in 2013 by Y Combinator, a firm that specializes in venture capital deals, as a simple and fast way to execute an initial round of financing for venture capital investors.[5] Over time, SAFEs have evolved into wholly separate financings, rather than bridges into later priced rounds, with the ability for investors and founders to calculate immediately how much ownership of the company has been sold. Some issuers have been issuing SAFEs also in crowdfunding offering, in which money is raised through soliciting relatively small individual investments or contributions from a large number of people.

It's important to note that the terms of SAFEs, and particularly the occurrence of the triggering event, have to be met in order for the investors to receive any value.[6] For example, a SAFE may be triggered if the company is acquired by or merged with another company, or if an initial public offering takes place, or if there is a new round of financing involving equity securities. There may indeed be scenarios in which the SAFE event is not triggered at all. For instance, if the trigger event is a new round of financing and the company is acquired prior to the new round taking place, the SAFE may never convert and effectively become worthless. Also, if a SAFE specifically triggers upon an offering of preferred stock, but the company subsequently raises money by instead selling more SAFEs, common stock or convertible notes, or by getting a conventional bank loan, then the SAFE will not convert despite the company having raised more capital. In cases when the trigger event does not take place, SAFE investors are unable to declare a SAFE in default and ask for repayment. From a valuation perspective, a review of the SAFE's contractual provision needs to be completed to properly incorporate these securities in a company's capitalization structure.

Keep It Simple Securities

Similarly to SAFEs, keep it simple securities (KISS) are agreements that provide the right but not the obligation to subscribe for new shares in the future at a price per share, which is not specified at the time of the initial KISS investment. Unlike SAFEs, KISS accrue interest and have a stated maturity date after which the holder may elect to convert the underlying investment amount, plus accrued interest, into a newly created series of preferred stock. They also provide enhanced downside protection rights that are similar to the rights of convertible debt, and certain noneconomic rights (information rights, and the right to participate in future company financings) that are typically offered to preferred shareholders. To this date, the use of KISS in ESEs has been limited.

CONCLUSION

The capital structure of an ESE is typically the result of a layer of multiple rounds of financing, with financial instruments that have different rights and privileges and that have different claims on enterprise value. Liquidation preferences, antidilution rights, and the voting structure of protective provisions for preferred stock are areas that should be especially monitored in terms of their potential effect on valuation and on a company's liquidation outcome.

---

[5] On SAFEs, see "Y Combinator, Quick Start Guide." The guide is available at www.ycombinator.com.
[6] U.S. Securities and Exchange Commission, Investor Bulletin: Be Cautious of SAFEs in Crowdfunding, May 9, 2017.

The early rounds are especially important in setting up the "tone" for subsequent negotiations. New investors in the company may have to balance their desire for control and ownership with management's need for financial and operational flexibility. Contractual provisions are often revised as new rounds of financing are raised. In a distressed liquidation, common shareholders may be successful in negotiating a partial allocation of liquidation proceeds even if the liquidation preference threshold of preferred stock has not yet been reached. Also, subsequent rounds of financing may lead to a renegotiation of cumulative dividend provisions to make the deal more attractive for new investors. Overall, the capital structure of an ESE is likely to change significantly over time and a dynamic modeling approach in valuation is needed to reflect its evolution over the period leading to a liquidity event.

PART Two

Enterprise Valuation

Seed Stage Valuation and the Venture Capital Method

Andreas Dal Santo

Antonella Puca

A company in the "seed" stage is a new company that is in the process of establishing its commercial operations. In this initial stage there is little or no product revenue and the company is in the process of setting up its management team. At the very inception of the company's operations, funding is typically provided by the founders and a close circle of friends and family. As the company begins to show evidence of a viable product or service, "angel" investors are likely to step in and become a primary source of funding for the company. Angel financing initially consists of relatively small investments ($50,000 to $250,000) from one or a few investors. As the company approaches its first round of venture capital financing (Series A), the size of financing rounds will typically grow to $2–$3 million, with more investors involved. The Series A round marks the graduation of the company out of its infancy and into a world with greater availability of capital and a much wider range of players, including institutional investors.

This chapter examines the approach to valuation for companies that are in the seed stage. The first section considers the market for seed stage companies, in which angel investors have a leading role. The second section presents the notion of premoney and postmoney valuation and discusses how it applies to seed-stage companies. The third section illustrates a range of methodologies that are used by angel investors in developing valuation expectations as they negotiate their seed deal. The fourth section illustrates the Venture Capital Method, which can be applied to price pre-Series A rounds, as well as later financing rounds. The fifth section presents the First Chicago Method, which adds a layer of scenario analysis to the Venture Capital Method.

From a fair value perspective, seed-stage valuation methodologies often don't have the rigor of more traditional applications of the income, market, and asset-based approach, but can still be useful to understand the perspective of an investor in a seed-stage enterprise and of founders that are "exiting" from part of their equity positions to allow for new capital to be raised. By the time of the Series A round, a "market" for the company's equity is likely to have developed, with transaction prices that may provide a stronger indication of fair value under ASC 820.

ANGEL INVESTORS AND THE MARKET FOR SEED INVESTING

The term "angel investor" has been loosely defined to identify a variety of players at the seed stage. In a strict sense, an angel investor is a high-net-worth individual who invests his or her own money, as opposed to a venture capital fund that pools together capital from third-party investors and hires a portfolio manager to manage it. Angel investors typically have a special interest in funding entrepreneurial ventures, and often also have a special industry expertise and a network of contacts that equip them particularly well to identify and help nurture promising new ventures. Paul Allen, for instance, has been an inspiring example of an angel investor: besides co-founding Microsoft Inc., Allen helped launch a number of other companies in technology, media, bioscience, and education. Allen made investments directly as an individual investor and through his family corporate arm Vulcan Inc. He also participated in venture capital investments through third-party-managed funds.

Angel investors take pride in their activity of contributing to scientific research and promoting new ideas. From this perspective, they may look at seed investing as having also a socially responsible component, targeting "returns" that may also reflect nonfinancial objectives, such as, for instance, supporting women and minority entrepreneurship, promoting health and wellness in the environment, addressing climate change, and other ESG objectives.[1]

In recent years, the definition of angel investor has broadened to include a variety of other players and sources of capital for seed-stage companies. Crowdfunding internet platforms have been used to gather very small contributions (typically $50 and up) from a large number of people, allowing small contributors to participate in a global market of seed-stage enterprises. Angel network groups, such as the Houston Angel Network, the Keiretsu Forum, and the Ben Franklin Technology Partners, pool together angel investors to allow them access to a greater variety of deals.[2] Additionally, a number of seed accelerators have developed to provide seed funding together with services that support growth. Y Combinator has been one of the pioneers in this space.[3] Founded in 2005, Y Combinator provides seed capital in the form of a $150,000 postmoney simple agreement for future equity (SAFE) investment for a 7% stake in the company when the SAFE converts, with additional funding in subsequent rounds to maintain a 7% ownership.[4] In addition, Y Combinator provides capital introduction services and training/introductions in various areas of developing a business enterprise,

---

[1]According to the Center for Venture Research (CVR), women-owned ventures accounted for 25.9% of the entrepreneurs that were seeking angel capital and 17.5% of those women entrepreneurs received angel investing in 2018. See Jeffrey Sohl, "The Angel Market in 2018: More Angels Investing in More Deals at Lower Valuations," Center for Venture Research, May 9, 2019. The CVR has been conducting research on the angel market since 1980. In the health and wellness sector, see for instance Delos, a technology real estate company based in New York (https://delos.com).

[2]Other prominent networks in the United States include: Alliance of Angels, Pasadena of Angels, Golden Seeds, New York Angels, Robin Hood Ventures, St. Louis Arch Angels, and the Maine Angels, among others.

[3]More information on Y Combinator is available on the company's website: www.ycombinator.com.

[4]SAFE is an acronym for Simple Agreements for Future Equity. These are agreements by which an investor makes a cash investment into a company in return for the right to subscribe for new shares in

as well as a broad network of connections to "alumni" firms that have gone through its entrepreneurial boot camp program. In 2015, Y Combinator created a Y Combinator Continuity Fund to continue to fund companies in their postseed stage.

Seed-stage companies have also been attracting the attention of venture capital funds that are looking for opportunities to capture a greater share of ownership and potential returns by entering at an earlier stage in the life of a company. While seed-stage investing may not be per se a primary target for many of these funds, it is more commonly becoming part of their overall investment strategy to access competitive deals early. At the same time, individual angels have continued to provide funding well after the seed stage, participating in later rounds to defend their ownership stake from dilution and sometimes enhancing their share of equity in the firm.

Corporation such as Intel, Salesforce, and Alphabet (the parent company of Google) have also been funding seed-stage companies as part of their strategic investment activity. Corporate venture capital (CVC) investment in the United States has significantly picked up starting in 2013 with a regular flow of more than 200 deals annually, and an increasing median CVC deal size that has passed the $3 million mark in 2019.[5]

Exhibit 4.1 illustrates the evolution of the angel market in the United States over the period 2007–2018.[6] While the number of investors has increased by about 30% from 2007,

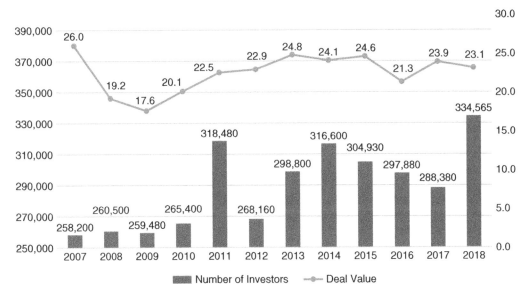

EXHIBIT 4.1   Angel Investors: Number of Investors and Deal Value ($billion)
Source: Based on data from the Center for Venture Research (CVR).

the future upon the occurrence of a triggering event and at a price per share that is not specified at the time of the initial SAFE investment. On SAFEs, see Y Combinator, Quick Start Guide. Please refer also to Chapter 3 for more information.
[5]On recent trends in corporate venture capital, see Brendan Burke, and Darren Klees, *PitchBook 2Q 2019 Analyst Note*, "The Golden Mean of Corporate Venture Capital," PitchBook Data Inc., May 16, 2019.
[6]Exhibit 4.1 is based on the studies of the Center for Venture Research directed by Jeffrey Sohl for the period 2007–2018.

the total annual investment has yet to reach the peak achieved in 2007 before the financial crisis and has remained substantially stable since 2011.

Over the period 2010–2019, the median size of the seed round has significantly increased and is now above $2 million while the size of the angel round has remained substantially stable in the $500,000 to $600,000 range (this may include contributions from more than one investor).[7]

In terms of sectors, according to the 2018 HALO report of the Angel Resource Institute, on average 40% of investments have gone to information technology enterprises, followed by healthcare (19%) and business products and services (18%).[8]

In most cases, pre-Series A investors are issued preferred stock in the company. Convertible bridge loans are a common solution, with the agreement that they will eventually convert into preferred stock upon the completion of a Series A round. SAFEs may also be negotiated as part of an angel deal. As we discussed in Chapter 3, SAFEs function like warrants in that they give rights to convert into preferred stock but they don't result in any share or convertible note issuance. Rather, they represent a contractual agreement on the share of ownership that the holder will receive upon conversion at the upcoming round. In a SAFE, valuation considerations become less relevant and the focus of the negotiation is on the share of ownership in exchange for the seed investment ticket.[9]

Premoney and Postmoney Valuation

Premoney valuation and postmoney valuation are recurring terms in the financing of early stage enterprises (ESEs). The contribution of new capital, especially in the very early stage of an entrepreneurial venture, is likely to significantly alter the equity stakes of existing shareholders and have a significant impact on investment returns.

Postmoney valuation is the valuation of a company *after* a new financing round has taken place. The postmoney valuation is based on the assumptions that all shares have equal value and that all equity interests have been converted into common stock. The postmoney valuation is calculated as the total number of shares of common stock on a fully diluted basis multiplied by the unit price of shares (common-stock equivalent) of the latest round, similarly to the calculation of market capitalization for a public company. Exhibit 4.2 illustrates the capital structure of a sample company (Company A) before and after a round of seed investing.

Before the new round, Company A had 3,500,000 shares of common stock issued and outstanding and 100,000 options granted to its employees, which could be exercised into 100,000 shares of common stock, for a total of 3,600,000 shares of common stock on a fully diluted basis. In the new round, angel investors received 400,000 shares of preferred stock, which are convertible into one share of common stock per unit. On a fully diluted basis, there are now 4,000,000 shares of common stock, with angel investors owning 10% of the

---

[7]For information on the size of angel and seed deals over time, see the quarterly releases of the PitchBook–NVCA Venture Capital Monitor.

[8]Angel Research Institute, 2018 HALO Annual Report on Angel Investment.

[9]According to the HALO 2018 report, in 2018 approximately 57% of the seed and Series A deals combined used a preferred financing instrument, while 28% were standard convertible notes, 8.6% common stock, 2.7% SAFEs, and 4.6% "Other."

Pre-Money Capital Structure:

	Shares/Units	Conversion Ratio	Shares (Fully Diluted)	Ownership % (Fully Diluted)
Common Stock – Founders	3,500,000		3,500,000	97.22%
Options	100,000	1×	100,000	2.78%
			3,600,000	100.00%

Postmoney Capital Structure:

	Shares/Units	Conversion Ratio	Shares (Fully Diluted)	Ownership % – Fully Diluted
Common Stock – Founders	3,500,000		3,500,000	87.50%
Preferred Stock – Angels	400,000	1×	400,000	10.00%
Options	100,000	1×	100,000	2.50%
			4,000,000	100.00%

EXHIBIT 4.2 Company A: Pre- and Postmoney Capital Structure

company on a fully diluted basis. Based on the $1 per unit price paid by angel investors to enter the round, the postmoney valuation of the company is:

$$\text{Postmoney valuation} = \text{Price per share} \times \text{Number of shares (fully diluted basis)}$$
$$= \$1 \times 4,000,000 = \$4,000,000$$

The **premoney valuation** is the valuation of a company *before* the new financing round. Based on the example of Exhibit 4.3:

$$\text{Premoney valuation} = \text{Postmoney valuation} - \text{Invested Capital}$$
$$= \$4,000,000 - \$400,000 = \$3,600,000$$

Exhibit 4.3 shows the median premoney valuation of pre-Series A rounds over the period 2009–2019. Median premoney valuations have increased substantially from $3.4 million in 2009 to $8.0 million in 2019, supporting the view that the seed stage may now be extending further into the company's development, and that venture capital investors tend to enter at a more advanced stage of the company's life cycle.

At all stages of the financing process for an ESE, and especially for angel investors that enter into equity at the seed stage, it is critical to be aware of the impact that dilution may have on their ownership stake in the company and, ultimately, on their potential investment returns.

For instance, it is common for seed-stage companies to offer stock options as a form of compensation to attract talented employees and preserve cash resources for use in other areas of the company's operations. As the company assembles its workforce, options may become a significant part of its overall capital structure on a fully diluted basis. Even in the absence

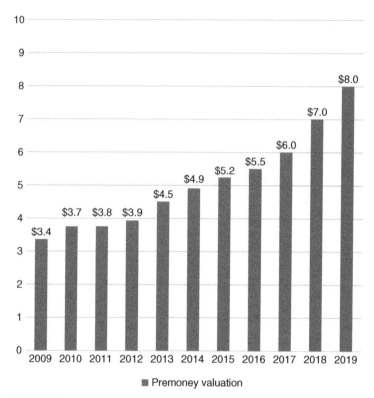

EXHIBIT 4.3   Pre-Series A Rounds: Median Premoney Valuation

of a new round, and without other adjustments, the granting of stock options has the effect of increasing the postmoney valuation of the company, as Exhibit 4.4 illustrates.

In our example, the postmoney valuation has increased by 10.0% = 400,000/4,000,000 due to the granting of 400,000 additional options, without any additional infusion of capital and actually decreasing the per share value of the company, assuming no antidilution provisions are in place.

	Shares/Units	Conversion Ratio	Shares (Fully Diluted)	Ownership % Fully Diluted
Common Stock – Founders	3,500,000		3,500,000	79.55%
Preferred Stock – Angels	400,000	1×	400,000	9.09%
Options	500,000	1×	500,000	11.36%
			4,400,000	100.00%

Postmoney valuation = $1 × 4,400,000 = $4,400,000

EXHIBIT 4.4   Effect of Stock Options Grant on Postmoney Valuation

In an article published in 2009, Luis Villalobos, founder of the Tech Coast Angels of Southern California, coined the term "valuation divergence" to represent the situation whereby the postmoney valuation of a company increases while the valuation of an individual share on a fully diluted basis increases at a lower rate or may even decrease.[10] Exhibit 4.5 illustrates the valuation divergence effect of dilution based on a seed investment of $2.10 million for a 30% stake in a company through an IPO exit in Year 7 preceded by the various rounds of financing. A successful IPO at 30× of the initial postmoney valuation ($210 million at exit/$7 million in postmoney valuation at the seed round) results in a 10× multiple of capital for the seed investor (IPO per share value of $8 divided by seed per share value of $0.80).

The 10× multiple, while still strong, is significantly lower than the 30× increase in the postmoney valuation of the company overall. The difference between the multiples (the "divergence effect") increases as the company advances in its rounds of financing, each of which enhances the dilution of the seed investors' share of the enterprise.

Exhibit 4.6 shows how even an exit at a multiple of seed postmoney valuation can in fact result in a capital loss for seed investors.

In Exhibit 4.6, the M&A exit takes place at a multiple of 5.25× for the company overall ($36.8 million in post-money valuation versus its post-money valuation at the time of the seed financing of $7 million), but angel investors have actually recovered only 88% of their original invested capital in this deal. The divergence effect focuses on the multiple of the post-money valuation at the seed stage but does not account for capital invested after the seed stage, nor for the effect on current valuation related to the timing of cash flows.

Round	Seed	Series A	Series B	Series C	Series D	IPO
$ per Share	0.80	1.00	1.50	2.00	3.00	8.00
Premoney ($million)	4.90	8.75	15.75	26.25	52.50	175.00
Money ($million)	2.10	1.75	3.94	8.75	13.13	35.00
Postmoney ($million)	7.00	10.50	19.69	35.00	65.63	210.00
Multiple of Seed Share Price		1.25	1.88	2.50	3.75	10.00
Multiple of Seed Postmoney valuation		1.50	2.81	5.00	9.38	30.00
Valuation Divergence Effect		83.33%	66.67%	50.00%	40.00%	33.33%
Shares before Round	6,125,000	8,750,000	10,500,000	13,125,000	17,500,000	21,875,000
New Shares	2,625,000	1,750,000	2,625,000	4,375,000	4,375,000	4,375,000
Shares after Round	8,750,000	10,500,000	13,125,000	17,500,000	21,875,000	26,250,000
Seed Shares	2,625,000	2,625,000	2,625,000	2,625,000	2,625,000	2,625,000
Seed Equity Ownership %	30.00%	25.00%	20.00%	15.00%	12.00%	10.00%
Seed Investment ($)	2,100,000					
Divergence = 30×/10× = 3						

EXHIBIT 4.5 Valuation Divergence Effect: Exit at a Higher Unit Price

[10]Luis Villalobos, "Valuation Divergence," Kauffman EVenturing, 2007, pp. 21–22.

Round	Seed	Series A	Series B	Series C	Series D	M&A
$ per Share	0.80	1.00	0.70	0.80	0.80	0.70
Premoney ($million)	4.90	8.75	7.35	21.00	26.25	36.75
Money ($million)	2.10	1.75	11.03	5.25	15.75	-
Postmoney ($million)	7.00	10.50	18.38	26.25	42.00	36.75
Multiple of Seed Share Price – Fully Diluted		1.25	0.88	1.00	1.00	0.88
Multiple of Seed Postmoney Valuation		1.50	2.63	3.75	6.00	5.25
Valuation Divergence Effect		83.33%	33.33%	26.67%	20.00%	16.67%
Shares after Round	8,750,000	10,500,000	26,250,000	32,812,500	52,500,000	52,500,000
Seed Shares	2,625,000	2,625,000	2,625,000	2,625,000	2,625,000	2,625,000
Seed Equity Ownership %	30.0%	25.0%	10.0%	8.0%	5.0%	5.0%
Seed Investment ($)	2,100,000					
Total additional capital ($million)	35.88					

EXHIBIT 4.6 Valuation Divergence Effect: Exit at a Lower Unit Price

SEED VALUATION: THE SCORECARD APPROACH

One of the challenges of valuing a seed-stage company is the lack of historical financial information on the company and of a solid foundation on which to base financial projections. Scorecard methodologies are an attempt to resolve this hurdle by creating a method that does not rely on the company's financial information, but rather benchmarks the company relative to other companies in its sector, geographical area, and stage of development. Scorecard methods assign a relative score to reflect the company's performance in a number of areas that are deemed strategic. The company then receives a value based on its scores and performance relative to its peers.

In this section we present four scorecard methods: the Payne method, the Risk Factor Summation method, the Berkus method, and an enhanced version of the Berkus method. These methods look at the historical valuation of companies similar to the target company as a benchmark for the target company's valuation.

The Payne and Risk Factor Summation Models are pure scorecard methods. The Berkus method in its original and enhanced versions combines elements of the scorecard approach with the Venture Capital method that we describe in the fourth section of this chapter.

Payne Scorecard

The Payne Scorecard method was described by Bill Payne in a 2001 article, and then revised in 2011.[11] Payne developed the original version of his method with reference to small seed-stage enterprises with a premoney valuation in the $1–$2.5 million range. In his method, Payne

---

[11]On the Payne Scorecard method, see William Payne, *The Definitive Guide to Raising Money from Angels* (Payne, 2006) (revised 2011).

Comparison Factor	Weight in Valuation
Strength of Entrepreneur and Team	0–30%
Size of the Opportunity	0–25%
Product/Technology	0–15%
Competitive Environment	0–10%
Marketing/Sales/Partnerships	0–10%
Need for Additional Investment	0–5%
Other Factors	0–5%

EXHIBIT 4.7   Payne Scorecard: Comparison Factors and Weight Range

lists seven qualitative factors of strategic relevance for the company's ability to survive and eventually turn into a profitable enterprise. Each of these factors is weighted based on its relative importance in the company's valuation. The weights are defined within a range, with the "Strength of the Entrepreneur and the Team" as the primary factor with a maximum assigned weight of 30%, down to "Other Factors" with a maximum weight of 5%, as illustrated in Exhibit 4.7.[12]

The factor weights need to sum up to a 100% total. The top three factors of

1. Strength of Entrepreneur and the Team
2. Size of the Opportunity, and
3. Product/Technology

account for up to 70% of the total value of the company. Regarding the primary role played by the management team in the company's valuation, Payne explains that "the management team is the most important consideration in valuing an ESE. An experienced CEO will necessarily command a higher valuation for the company. But, a CEO/founder who is clearly capable of achieving certain milestones, such as completing product development and closing the first few sales, and is willing to step aside in favor of an experienced CEO to be hired later, is also valuable."[13]

On the "Size of the Opportunity" factor, Payne notes that "investors seek to fund companies that will scale quickly to $20–$50 million in revenues or more. The importance of this factor in valuing pre-revenue companies demonstrates the criticality of scale to investors."[14]

With reference to "Product and Technology," he explains that:

It comes as a shock to all first-time entrepreneurs that their product or service represents such a small piece of the pre-money valuation. And, for high technology companies (with a valuable patent portfolio) this 15% number is low and would

---

[12]William Payne, "Valuations 101: Scorecard Valuation Methodology," blog.gust.com October 19, 2011.

[13]William Payne, *The Definitive Guide to Raising Money from Angels* (Payne, 2006) (revised 2011), p. 74.

[14]William Payne, *The Definitive Guide to Raising Money from Angels* (Payne, 2006) (revised 2011). p. 75

be perhaps 20%. In no case would the importance of the product or service exceed that of the management team or the scalability of the company. The product is important, but only as it defines the domination of a large marketplace that the company can achieve.[15]

When the weight of one or more factors is reduced/increased, the remaining factors must be adjusted for the total to equal 100%. For example, consider an investor that sets the weighting for the Size of the Opportunity factor to 15% instead of the maximum 25%. For the sum of the factors has to be equal to 100%, the 10% that was taken away from the Size of the Opportunity should increase one or more of the other factors. This can be achieved either by allocating the difference to some specific factor(s) (Modified Weighting 1) or by attributing it pro-quota to the remaining factors (Modified Weighting 2), as shown in Exhibit 4.8.

The next step in Payne's Scorecard method consists of comparing the target company to a hypothetical "average" company. Each of the factors is assigned a percentage rating relative to the benchmark company, which scores 100% in all factors. A score of greater than 100% for a comparison factor indicates that the target company outperforms the benchmark with respect to that factor. A weighting of less than 100% indicates that the target company underperforms the benchmark. The extent of the deviation will depend on the perceived magnitude of the difference as a result of the analysis of the target company versus the benchmark. A weighting equal to 100% indicates that the target company is on par with its benchmark.

As an example, let's assume that an angel investor is considering investing $400,000 in Company B. No other investor is participating in the financing round. The median premoney valuation for recent seed deals for the target company's data set is $2,300,000. Exhibit 4.9 illustrates a sample application of the Scorecard Method to Company B.

After assigning its own set of weights to the various factors based on its perspective on their valuation relevance for the target company, the investor has developed the set of Target versus Benchmark percentages in Exhibit 4.9 based on a comparison of each individual factor between the Target and the Benchmark. The values in the "Factor" column are the Target

Comparison Factor	Standard Maximum	Modified Weights 1	Modified Weights 2
Strength of Entrepreneur and Team	30.0%	35.0%	34.0%
Size of the Opportunity	25.0%	15.0%	15.0%
Product/Technology	15.0%	15.0%	17.0%
Competitive Environment	10.0%	15.0%	11.3%
Marketing/Sales/Partnerships	10.0%	10.0%	11.3%
Need for Additional Investment	5.0%	5.0%	5.7%
Other Factors	5.0%	5.0%	5.7%
Total	100.0%	100.0%	100.0%

EXHIBIT 4.8 Comparison Factor: Change in Weights

---

[15]William Payne, *The Definitive Guide to Raising Money from Angels* (Payne, 2006) (revised 2011), p. 75.

Comparison Factor	Weight	Target vs. Benchmark	Factor	
Strength of Entrepreneur and Team	30.0%	125%	0.375	
Size of the Opportunity	25.0%	150%	0.375	
Product/Technology	15.0%	100%	0.150	
Competitive Environment	10.0%	75%	0.075	
Marketing/Sales/Partnerships	10.0%	80%	0.080	
Need for Additional Investment	5.0%	100%	0.050	
Other Factors (great early customer feedback)	5.0%	100%	0.050	
Total	100%		1.155	[1]
Median premoney valuation for comparable companies			$ 2,300,000	[2]
Premoney valuation for target company			$ 2,656,500	[3] = [2] × [1]
Investment			$ 400,000	[4]
Postmoney valuation			$ 3,056,500	[5] = [3] + [4]
Required ownership			13%	[6] = [4]/[5]

EXHIBIT 4.9   Payne Scorecard – Company B

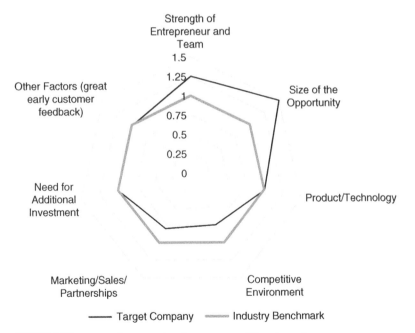

EXHIBIT 4.10   Payne Scorecard – Company and Benchmark

versus Benchmark percentages multiplied by their respective Weights. For instance, the Factor of the Strength of Entrepreneur and Team is calculated as:

$$\text{Factor of Strength of Entrepreneur and Team} = 30\% \times 125\% = 0.375$$

Based on the comparison factor analysis, Company B is superior to its benchmark as illustrated in Exhibit 4.10.

The Factor total value for Company B is:

$$\begin{aligned} \text{Factor total value} = {}& 30\% \times 125\% + 25\% \times 150\% + 15\% \times 100\% + 10\% \times 75\% \\ & + 10\% \times 80\% + 5\% \times 100\% + 5\% \times 100\% \\ = {}& 115.5\% = 1.155 \end{aligned}$$

Based on a median premoney valuation for the company's benchmark group of $2,300,000, the premoney valuation of the target company is:

$$\text{Premoney valuation of target company} = \$2,300,000 \times 1.155 = 2,656,500$$

With the new financing round of $400,000, the target company's postmoney valuation is:

$$\text{Postmoney valuation} = \$2,656,500 + \$400,000 = \$3,056,500$$

Based on a premoney valuation of $2,656,500, the investor should target at a minimum a 13% stake in Company B in its negotiation.

The Payne Scorecard is accompanied by a valuation worksheet that guides the investor in evaluating the comparison factors of the target company relative to the benchmark.[16] For instance, for the factor "Strength of the Entrepreneur and the Team," the scorecard considers issues such as the team's experience in terms of number of years in the business, leadership roles and specific operational roles, willingness to step aside for an experienced CEO, coaching flexibility, and team completeness to assess impact on the scorecard factor rating.

The results of the Payne Scorecard method are highly dependent on the characteristics of the benchmark, and the assessment of the average premoney valuation of the reference deal. The benchmark typically reflects the characteristics of a hypothetical company that is in the same phase of the business life cycle and operates in the same industry and geographical area as the target. Sourcing and analyzing data for the benchmark may be challenging. The investor must be familiar with the benchmark's data pool characteristics in order to estimate the comparison factors. Changes in market conditions need to be considered for their impact on the benchmark and the reference deal size.

Risk Factor Summation Method

The Risk Factor Summation (RFS) method was developed by the Ohio TechAngels as another type of scorecard method to apply in the premoney valuation of prerevenue companies at the

---

[16]William Payne, "Valuations 101: The Risk Factor Summation Method," November 15, 2011. Available at: blog.gust.com.

seed stage.[17] The RFS model revolves around risk assessment and its inverse relationship with company value. This approach is different from that of the Payne Scorecard method, which focuses rather on the target company's advantages or disadvantages versus its benchmark group.

The RFS method compares the target company against a peer group using a list of 12 risk factors. Each risk factor is evaluated on a scale from +2 to −2 where a score of +2 means that the target company provides extremely positive mitigation of such risk factors compared with the peer group while a score of −2 indicates that the target company offers extremely poor risk mitigation. The risk factors adjust the premoney valuation of the peer group in fixed value increments as indicated in Exhibit 4.11.

As in the Payne Scorecard method, the sum of the premoney valuation adjustments results in an increase or decrease in value relative to the median/average premoney valuation of the benchmark company/group. However, while the Payne Scorecard determines an adjustment factor expressed as a multiplier of the benchmark premoney valuation, the risk summation results in a dollar amount that is added to or subtracted from the benchmark premoney valuation.

For instance, let's assume that an angel investor is considering a seed investment of $400,000 in Company C, a company that has a great management team and is in the process of developing a product with significant revenue potential. Company C has been managing its legal/political risk effectively and has a strong sales and marketing team. However, Company C has higher business risk than its peers. Also, the company is exposed to the risk of patent infringement litigation. As compared to its benchmark, Company C has enhanced:

- Funding risk, as the company may run out of cash before it achieves the next milestone;
- International risk, as product is going to be sold mainly in emerging countries.

The risk factors based on the investor's assessment are illustrated in Exhibit 4.12.

The RFS method translates the assessment of Company C's risk into the company's premoney valuation as shown in Exhibit 4.13.

Similar to the Payne Scorecard method, this model does not need detailed financial projections as it estimates the premoney valuation from historical information available on the valuation date.

The limitations of this approach are similar to those flagged for the Payne Scorecard method. In particular,

Risk Factor Coefficient	Premoney Valuation Adjustment
2	$ 500,000
1	$ 250,000
0	$ –
−1	$ (250,000)
−2	$ (500,000)

EXHIBIT 4.11 Risk Factor Summation Method: Risk Factor Coefficients and Valuation Adjustments

[17]See William Payne, "Valuations 101: The Risk Factor Summation Method," November 15, 2011. Available at: blog.gust.com.

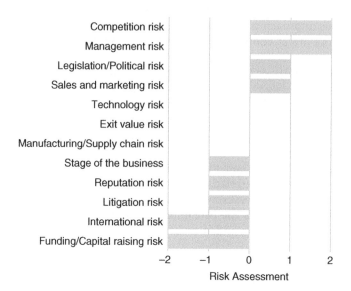

EXHIBIT 4.12   Risk Assessment: Company C

Risk Factor	Risk Assessment	Adjustment	
Management risk	Extremely positive mitigation (+2)	$ 500,000	
Stage of the business	Negative mitigation (-1)	$ (250,000)	
Legislation/Political risk	Positive mitigation (+1)	$ 250,000	
Manufacturing/Supply chain risk	Neutral (0)	$ –	
Sales and marketing risk	Positive mitigation (+1)	$ 250,000	
Funding/Capital raising risk	Extremely negative mitigation (-2)	$ (500,000)	
Competition risk	Extremely positive mitigation (+2)	$ 500,000	
Technology risk	Neutral (0)	$ –	
Litigation risk	Negative mitigation (-1)	$ (250,000)	
International risk	Extremely negative mitigation (-2)	$ (500,000)	
Reputation risk	Negative mitigation (-1)	$ (250,000)	
Exit value risk	Neutral (0)	$ –	
Total		$ (250,000)	[1]
Median premoney valuation for comparable companies		$ 2,300,000	[2]
Premoney valuation for target company		$ 2,050,000	[3] = [1] + [2]
Investment		$ 400,000	[4]
Postmoney valuation		$ 2,450,000	[5] = [3] + [4]
Required ownership		16%	[6] = [4]/[5]

EXHIBIT 4.13   Risk Factor Summation Method: Company C

- The model is rigid as it sets a fixed range of premoney adjustments; these dollar amounts should be revised up or down depending on the stage of development of the target company as well as the industry and geography it operates in.
- The same adjustments are applied to all risk factors regardless of the type of risk, target company, and benchmark characteristics.
- The list of risk factors, although broad, may need to be revised to include emerging risks, like cybersecurity risk.
- Sourcing the peer group information may be challenging or not possible at all.
- There are issues that are typical of market-based analyses, including inconsistencies between the benchmark and the target company's business.

The Berkus Method

The Berkus method was developed in the mid-1990s by David Berkus and first published in *Winning Angels* by Harvard's David Amis and Howard Stevenson with Berkus' permission in 2001.[18] The model was initially aimed at valuing technology companies in the prerevenue stage, although its application has extended to other types of companies and sectors.

In its original version, the model sets the maximum premoney value of a technology firm at $2,500,000 and breaks it down equally among five key milestones/risks as illustrated in Exhibit 4.14.[19]

Let's apply the Berkus method to Company D, a technology startup with no revenues. Company D is run by its founders and expects to begin product rollout within the next two years, once product testing is completed. An angel investor is planning to invest $250,000 in Company D and is negotiating with the founders to establish the corresponding ownership stake. Exhibit 4.15 presents a sample Berkus model for Company D.

To estimate the premoney valuation of the company, the investor must assess the degree of achievement for each of the five factors. The contribution of each factor to the premoney valuation of the company is then calculated by multiplying each maximum premoney valuation ($500,000) for the degree of achievement (%).

Milestone	Risk	Valuation
Sound idea	Innovation risk	Max $500,000
Prototype	Technology risk	Max $500,000
Quality management team	Execution risk	Max $500,000
Strategic relationships	Marketing risk	Max $500,000
Product rollout or sales	Production risk	Max $500,000

EXHIBIT 4.14 The Berkus Method: Milestones and Risk Factors

---

[18] See David Amis and Howard Stevenson, *Winning Angels: The Seven Fundamentals of Early Stage Investing* (FT Press, 2001).
[19] William Payne, "Valuations 101: The Dave Berkus Method," November 2, 2011. Available at www.blog.gust.com.

Factors	Max Premoney Valuation		Degree of Achievement	Industry Benchmark	Premoney Valuation	
Sound idea	$	500,000	100%	80%	$	500,000
Prototype	$	500,000	80%	80%	$	400,000
Quality management team	$	500,000	80%	50%	$	400,000
Strategic relationships	$	500,000	50%	25%	$	250,000
Product rollout or sales	$	500,000	0%	0%	$	-
Premoney valuation					$	1,550,000
Investment					$	250,000
Postmoney valuation					$	1,800,000
Required ownership						13.9%

EXHIBIT 4.15 Berkus Model: Company D

For example, the contribution of the prototype factor is calculated as:

$$\text{Contribution of Prototype Factor} = \$500,000 \times 80\% = \$400,000$$

The contributions of the various factors are then summed up to arrive at the premoney valuation of $1.55 million for Company D in our example. Based on a premoney valuation of $1.55 million, the investor should target at a minimum a 13.9% ownership in Company D, which would result in a postmoney valuation of $1.8 million for the company. Exhibit 4.16 shows the comparison between the percentage of achievement of Company D and the benchmark.

As the example shows, the Berkus model focuses on critical elements that the investor can evaluate and measure *at the valuation date* and on qualitative factors that are key determinants of future performance for a seed-stage enterprise. Also, the method's cap on premoney

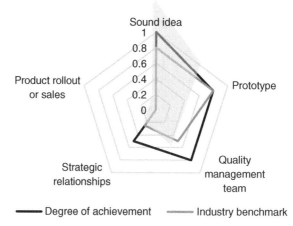

EXHIBIT 4.16 Berkus Method: Company D – Comparison to Benchmark

valuation emphasizes the importance of limiting the premoney valuation to achieve an acceptable rate of return on the investment and adequate diversification at the portfolio level.

Enhancements to the Berkus Method

In a 2016 article, Berkus indicates that the original matrix should be a suggestion rather than a rigid form.[20] Since its original version, the Berkus model has been enhanced to allow for greater flexibility in the range of milestones and risk factors that can be included in the scorecard and in the maximum value contribution that is associated to each factor. The total premoney valuation of the benchmark may also be increased to reflect the current characteristics of the industry in which the target company operates and of its peer group.

For example, the 2018 HALO report from the Angel Resource Institute shows wide variations in the average company's premoney valuation across industries in the United States as shown in Exhibit 4.17. The premoney valuation median and average across all sectors is well above the $2.5 million premoney valuation cap posited by Berkus in 2001.

Also, industries other than technology may have a different set of critical variables. For example, for a robotic surgery enterprise, prototyping and FDA approval are important factors; for service providers prototyping may not be as critical as service validation and so on.

Exhibit 4.18 shows how the Berkus method could be enhanced in the case of an investment of $500,000 in Company E, a prerevenue medical devices company.

In Exhibit 4.18, the five critical factors have been expanded to include the completion of an R&D facility and FDA approval. The maximum valuation contribution for each critical factor now varies between $500,000 and $2,000,000, reflecting their perceived value in the context of the industry and region the company operates in as well as specific company characteristics, including the stage of development. The maximum premoney value is now capped at $8,000,000, higher than the $2,500,000 of the original Berkus method.

Other Scorecard Methods

There are other scorecard methods to evaluate seed stage companies. Gautham Dingra and Christopher Olson, for instance, have proposed a franchise quality valuation score that uses

Industry	Percentage of Deals	Premoney Valuation – Average	Premoney Valuation – Median
Information Technology	38.60%	8.7	6.0
Healthcare	19.40%	8.6	5.0
Business Products and Services	18.50%	8.3	6.1
Consumer Products and Services	18.20%	7.1	5.0
Financial Services, Materials, and Other	3.40%	17.1	8.2
Energy	1.90%	32.4	12.0

EXHIBIT 4.17   Average Premoney Valuation, by Industry ($ million)

---

[20]Dave Berkus, "After 20 Years: Updating the Berkus Method of Valuation," November 4, 2016. Available at www.berkonomics.com.

Factors	Max Premoney Valuation		Degree of Achievement	Premoney Valuation	
Sound idea for pharmaceutical drug	$	2,000,000	90%	$	1,800,000
R&D facilities	$	1,000,000	40%	$	400,000
FDA approval	$	2,000,000	50%	$	1,000,000
Quality management team	$	2,000,000	80%	$	1,600,000
Strategic relationships	$	500,000	30%	$	150,000
Product rollout or sales	$	500,000	0%	$	-
Premoney valuation				$	4,950,000
Investment				$	500,000
Postmoney valuation				$	5,450,000
Required ownership					9%

EXHIBIT 4.18 Berkus Method: Company E

factors like barriers to entry, degree of competition, pricing power of customers, pricing power of suppliers, management, governance, engagement with employees, community, and government, and sustainability in company valuation.[21] The Cayenne Consulting calculator provides a premoney valuation estimate for tech start-ups and seed companies based on the responses to 25 questions.[22] The premoney valuation can range between $480,000 and $40 million, allowing the model to adapt to the different characteristics of the companies that are evaluated. Overall, the scorecard approach has proven to be highly adaptable to investor valuation needs across industries and geographies.

VENTURE CAPITAL METHOD

The Venture Capital method is used extensively in deal negotiation. As first described by Bill Sahlman of Harvard Business School in 1987, the model estimates the postmoney valuation of a company and the ownership percentage in the company that an investor may want to target in a new round to achieve its risk-adjusted return objectives.[23]

---

[21]Gautam Dhingra and Christopher Olson,"Franchise Quality Score: A Metric for Intangibles." CFA Institute: *Enterprising Investor*, August 27, 2018. Available at: https://blogs.cfainstitute.org/investor/2018/08/27/franchise-quality-score-a-metric-for-intangibles/.
[22]The questionnaire is available online on the Cayenne Consulting's website.
[23]On the Venture Capital method, see especially William Sahlman, "A Method for Valuing High-Risk, Long-Term Investments: The Venture Capital Method," Harvard Business School 9-288-006 Rev October 1, 2009; Andrew Metrick, and Ayako Yasuda, Chapter 10, "The VC Method," *Venture Capital and the Finance of Innovation*, 2nd ed. (Wiley, 2011), pp. 178–194; Robert Johnson, "Early Stage Companies and Financing Valuations: The Venture Capital Method," IESE Business School IES375, revised March 2012.

Base Case

In its basic form, the Venture Capital method estimates the postmoney valuation of a company as the value of the company at exit discounted by a discount rate that represents the annualized target return (TR) of the investment through the exit date:

$$\text{Postmoney valuation} = \frac{\text{Valuation at exit}}{(1 + \text{Discount Rate})^T}$$

where T = time to exit

For example, let's consider the situation of an angel investor that is contemplating a $500,000 investment in a company that expects to require no further capital through Year 7. The investor expects the company to have a value of $25 million at exit at the end of Year 7 and has a target return of 40% on its investment. Under the VC method, the postmoney valuation of the company is:

Postmoney valuation = $25,000,000/(1 + 0.40)^7 = $25,000,000/10.54 = $2,371,613

There is a relationship between the target return and the target total value to paid in capital (TVPI)[24] at exit based on the formula:

$$\text{Target TVPI} = (1 + \text{TR})^T$$

For example, given a seven-year time to exit and a target return of 40%, our investor may express its return objectives in terms of an implied TVPI of 10.54× at exit calculated as:

$$\text{Target TVPI} = (1 + 0.40)^7 = 10.54$$

More generally, the postmoney valuation can also be expressed as:

$$\text{Postmoney valuation} = \text{Valuation at exit/Target TVPI}$$

With a $500,000 investment over a seven-year horizon, the investor needs to obtain at a minimum a 21.1% ownership stake in the company to achieve its target return of 40%, which corresponds to a target TVPI of 10.54. The required ownership percentage is calculated as:

$$\text{Required ownership percentage} = \$500,000/\$2,371,613 = 21.1\%$$

Exhibit 4.19 shows a sensitivity analysis of the required ownership percentage to the two key variables in the model (valuation at exit and discount rate), given a contribution ticket of $500,000 and a time horizon of seven years.

---

[24] The TVPI is often designated with the generic term Multiple of Invested Capital (MOIC).

			Exit Value		
	$ 15,000,000	$ 20,000,000	$ 25,000,000	$ 30,000,000	$ 35,000,000
20%	11.9%	9.0%	7.2%	6.0%	5.1%
25%	15.9%	11.9%	9.5%	7.9%	6.8%
30%	20.9%	15.7%	12.5%	10.5%	9.0%
35%	27.2%	20.4%	16.3%	13.6%	11.7%
40%	35.1%	26.4%	21.1%	17.6%	15.1%
45%	44.9%	33.7%	27.0%	22.5%	19.3%
50%	57.0%	42.7%	34.2%	28.5%	24.4%
55%	71.6%	53.7%	43.0%	35.8%	30.7%
60%	89.5%	67.1%	53.7%	44.7%	38.3%

Time to Exit (years) 7
Investment $ 500,000

Discount Rate

EXHIBIT 4.19 VC Method Sensitivity Analysis: Effect of Exit Value and Discount Rates on Required Ownership Percentage

As Exhibit 4.19 illustrates, the required ownership percentage is highly sensitive to both the exit value and the discount rate. For instance, an increase in the discount rate from 40% to 50% would cause the required ownership percentage to move from 21.1% to 34.2%.

Venture Capital Method with Dilution

In practice, the implementation of the venture capital model presents additional layers of complexity relative to the "base" case, which depend primarily on (1) the probability that the company will fail before it reaches a successful exit and (2) the dilution effect caused by the issuance of new shares as the company moves through various rounds of financing and grants stock options to its employees.

Let's now look at a more realistic scenario, which considers the probability of failure and the dilution effect on postmoney valuation. Let's assume that Company E, a seed-stage company, is seeking $500,000 in new funding from an angel investor to support its R&D activities. The investors require an annualized return of 25% on their investment and are looking to establish a postmoney valuation of the company and an ownership percentage that will allow them to achieve the required return given their $500,000 investment ticket. In order to estimate the postmoney valuation of the company, we go through the following steps.

Step 1: Estimate a time to exit For Company E, the investor estimates a time to exit of seven years from the angel round.

Step 2: Estimate the value of the company at exit The exit value for a company under the venture capital method is estimated using one of the following approaches:

- Relative valuation based on market multiples. The investor projects the company's revenues or other suitable metric to the expected exit date. The investor then determines a multiple of revenue or other suitable multiple based on current multiples for companies that are deemed comparable to the target company. The exit value of the target company is calculated by multiplying the estimated multiple by the underlying metric.
- Discounted cash flows model. To the extent suitable projections can be made of the company's overall operations, the investor may use a discounted cash flow model for estimating the value of the company at exit. A DCF will generally not be suitable for a seed-stage enterprise.
- Average valuation of successful exits in the same industry. For a seed-stage company, in the lack of reliable revenue and cash flow projections, a common approach is to use the average valuation of successful exits in the company's environment (same industry, type of business, etc.) as an estimate for the value of the company at exit. Based on PitchBook data, the median U.S. VC-backed exit size was $377.6 million for IPOs, $100.0 million for M&A transactions, and $122.5 million for buyouts in 2019.[25] The reference valuation can be adjusted on a case-by-case basis to reflect the investor's view of the specific characteristics of the company relative to its benchmark.

In our example, the investor has used a relative valuation model to estimate the exit value of the company. The investor projects revenues of $20 million and a multiple of revenues of 6× at exit for Company E, which results in an estimated exit valuation of $120 million.

Step 3: Estimate the discount rate In the Base Case scenario, the discount rate is developed under the assumption that the company will successfully survive through its exit and achieve the projected revenue and operational metrics as the basis of its exit valuation. In the real world, however, ESEs and especially companies in the seed stage have a high probability of failure and of generating capital losses for their investors. The return that an investor requires from its investment in Company E, which is also a proxy for the company's cost of capital, depends not only on the estimated exit valuation of the company but also on the company's probability of failure.

With a probability of failure equal to zero as in our Base Case, the discount rate that needs to be applied to the exit valuation to obtain the present postmoney valuation of the company (the "Target Return") will coincide with the investor's Required Return (25% for the angel investor in Company E). Once we factor into the valuation the probability of failure, the relationship between the target return (TR) and the required return (r) starts to diverge. The relationship between TR and r can be expressed as:

$$(1 + TR)^T = (1 + r)^T / (1 - p)$$

---

[25]PitchBook Data Inc., Q4 2019 PitchBook NVCA Venture Monitor Summary.

where:

p = probability of failure
r = required return (also cost of capital)
TR = target return
T = time to exit

For example, assuming that Company E has a 60% probability of failure, the TR that the company needs to provide in order for the investor to achieve the annualized r of 25% over a seven-year time horizon is:

$$\text{Target Return} = [(1 + 0.25)^7/(1 - 0.6)]^{1/7} - 1 = [4.7684/0.40]^{1/7} - 1$$
$$= 11.9209^{1/7} - 1 = 1.4248 - 1 = 42.48\%$$

We can calculate the implied target TVPI after adjusting for the probability of failure as:

$$\text{Target TVPI} = [(1 + r)^T]/(1 - p) = (1.25^7)/(1 - 0.6) = 4.7684/0.40 = 11.92.$$

Or also, given a TR of 42.48% as:

$$\text{Target TVPI} = (1 + TR)^T = 1.4248^7 = 11.92$$

Exhibit 4.20 shows the TR and target TVPI that are associated with a range of probabilities of failure and time to exit combinations, to achieve a required return (cost of capital) for the investor of 25%.

In our example, the investor in Company E will need to target a return of 42% and a TVPI of 11.92× in order to achieve an r of 25%, given a probability of failure of 60% and a time to exit of seven years.

Step 4: Estimate the retention percentage   So far, we have assumed that the investor is able to maintain the same percentage of ownership in the company from its initial investment through exit without any addition of capital. Step 3 considers the effect of dilution on the investor's ownership of the company and on the postmoney valuation of the Company. In an ESE, each new round of financing involves the issuance of new shares, which will typically have the effect of diluting the ownership interest of the preexistent investors. Dilution also results from the issuance of stock options as a form of compensation for management and employees of the firm. The dilution effect can be especially significant for a seed-stage company, where multiple rounds of financing at increasing valuations are likely to take place prior to an exit event. The effect of dilution can be measured by a "retention" ratio, which is the ratio of the percentage of ownership held by the investor at exit (numerator) divided by the percentage of ownership held upon entry on a fully diluted basis (denominator).

For example, assuming that an investor holds 30% of the company after executing the seed round, and expects to hold 6% of the company at exit, the expected retention ratio is equal to:

$$\text{Retention ratio} = 6\%/30\% = 20\%$$

In the Venture Capital method, the retention ratio is typically an input estimated by investors based on their own experience in deal making and their perspective on ESE deals.

Required Return	25%
Invested capital	1

					Probability of Failure (p)				
		0%	10%	20%	30%	40%	50%	60%	70%
Time to Exit	1	25%	39%	56%	79%	108%	150%	213%	317%
		1.3	1.4	1.6	1.8	2.1	2.5	3.1	4.2
	2	25%	32%	40%	49%	61%	77%	98%	128%
		1.6	1.7	2.0	2.2	2.6	3.1	3.9	5.2
	3	25%	29%	35%	41%	48%	57%	70%	87%
		2.0	2.2	2.4	2.8	3.3	3.9	4.9	6.5
	4	25%	28%	32%	37%	42%	49%	57%	69% Target Return
		2.4	2.7	3.1	3.5	4.1	4.9	6.1	8.1
	5	25%	28%	31%	34%	38%	44%	50%	59%
		3.1	3.4	3.8	4.4	5.1	6.1	7.6	10.2
	6	25%	27%	30%	33%	36%	40%	46%	53%
		3.8	4.2	4.8	5.4	6.4	7.6	9.5	12.7 Target TVPI
	7	25%	27%	29%	32%	34%	38%	42%	48%
		4.8	5.3	6.0	6.8	7.9	9.5	11.9	15.9
	8	25%	27%	29%	31%	33%	36%	40%	45%
		6.0	6.6	7.5	8.5	9.9	11.9	14.9	19.9

EXHIBIT 4.20   Target TVPI and Target Returns to Achieve 25% IRR

Step 5: Estimate the postmoney value   Given the retention ratio, the exit valuation and the discount rate, we can then calculate the postmoney valuation, of Company E, as:

Postmoney Valuation of Company E = Exit valuation × Retention ratio/Target TVPI

For the seed round in Company E, our investor has estimated a retention ratio of 30%. Given an exit valuation of $120 million and target TVPI of 11.92×, we have:

Postmoney Valuation of Company E = $120,000,000 × 30%/11.92093 = $3,019,899

Assuming a seed investment of $500,000 from the angel investor, the premoney valuation of Company E is:

Premoney Valuation of Company E = $3,019,899 − $500,000 = $2,519,899

Step 6: Estimate the required ownership percentage   As a final step, the investor calculates the ownership percentage that is needed to meet the investor's goal of a required return at 25% (TR = 42.5%) and a required TVPI of 4.77x (Target TVPI = 11.92×).
The ownership percentage is calculated as:

Required ownership% = $500,000/$3,019,899 = 16.56%

[1]	Revenues at exit	$	20,000,000	input
[2]	Revenue multiple at exit		6	input
[3]	Exit value of target company	$	120,000,000	=[1] x [2]
[4]	Time to exit (years)		7	input
[5]	Probability of failure		60%	input
[6]	Retention		30%	input
[7]	Required return/Cost of capital		25.0%	input
[8]	Required TVPI		4.77	= (1 + [7])^ [4]
[9]	Target TVPI		11.92	= (1 + [7]) ^ [4]/(1 − [5])
[10]	Target return		42.5%	IRR based on [4] and [9]
[11]	Postmoney valuation—seed round	$	3,019,899	= [3] × [6]/[9]
[12]	Invested capital—seed round	$	500,000	input
[13]	Required ownership		16.56%	=[11]/[12]

*based on investor's return expectations

EXHIBIT 4.21   Venture Capital Method with Dilution: Company E

Exhibit 4.21 summarizes the steps that we have illustrated for Company E, with the related formulas.

Notes on the Venture Capital Method

The venture capital method provides a well-accepted technique for valuing ESEs, including companies in the seed stage. The VC method requires estimates of the company's revenue at exit, probability of failure for the company, and dilution, all of which can be subject to considerable uncertainty.

The model has features of the market and income approaches, both of which have significant limitations when they are applied to seed-stage enterprises. Revenue and net income projections, in particular, are subject to a high degree of projection risk. Also, the venture capital method assumes that all equity classes will effectively have equal claims on the company's value. The method treats investors and founders equally, although their interests typically have different rights and privileges, which may translate into differences in exit proceeds per share unit.

One significant limitation of the VC method is that the probability of failure/success is modeled implicitly in the TR that is used as the discount rate applied to the exit valuation. The probability of failure may be driven by systematic risk factors such as the general trend in the economy, trends in technology innovation and in the competitive landscape that cannot be diversified away, while the required rate of return (the cost of capital for the company) is much more sensitive to idiosyncratic, company-specific risk factors. Also, in the practice of deal making, the same target return is often applied consistently across investments that may have very different risk profiles. Rules of thumb are often used for the target return and target TVPI, such as a "TR of 50% and a TVPI of 10×," without considering the time horizon of the investment or the relation between the target and the required return, which is ultimately what the investor can expect to receive. This one-size-fits-all approach may result in a premoney valuation that tends to overvalue businesses that have a higher probability of failure and a longer time to exit and undervalue businesses that have a low probability of failure and a shorter time to exit relative to their peer group.

The VC model has widespread use in deal negotiation and in early stage valuation, and is especially useful at the seed stage where the implementation of traditional market, income, and asset-based approaches present special challenges. Scenario analysis and other simulation methods can be applied within a venture capital model to assess the sensitivity of the model to changing estimates and provide further insights into the distribution of outcomes.

THE FIRST CHICAGO METHOD

The First Chicago method (FCM) is named after the First Chicago National Bank that popularized it in the 1970s.[26] The FCM is an extension of the Venture Capital method and is also focused on the postmoney valuation of a company, as opposed to scorecard methodologies that focus rather on premoney valuation.

The First Chicago method estimates the postmoney value of a company using a scenario-based approach that looks at the performance of the target company under three scenarios:[27]

Success Company achieves exceptional business performance within or above management's financial projections.
Survival Company underperforms the success scenario due to delays in product approval or business pivots, resulting in higher expenses or longer time to market.
Failure Company underperforms the survival scenario and sees a continuation or a deterioration of the business resulting in capital losses or business failure.

To illustrate the model, let's apply the First Chicago method to Company F, a seed-stage enterprise that is seeking $500,000 in seed funding. Company F has no debt and is wholly owned by its founders. Exhibit 4.22 presents the postmoney valuation of Company F under the FCM in three scenarios.

Under the FCM, we have simulated three scenarios with revenues in the respective exit year that vary depending on the success of the venture. The exit value is estimated using the relative value approach, by applying different multiples to the estimated revenue at exit. We have also estimated different terms to exit, depending on the scenario, with the Failure exit taking place in Year 2, the Survival exit in Year 4 and the Success exit in Year 6.

Although we have used EV/Sales multiples in all scenarios, market participants may apply different valuation methods for different scenarios. For instance, in the success and the survival scenarios, market participants may use a combination of market multiples such as P/E and EV/EBITDA. In the failure scenario they may use an asset-based method and so forth.

---

[26] James P. Catty, *The First Chicago Method*, 2008.
[27] The number of scenarios can be larger or smaller than three depending on the assumptions pertaining to the subject company.

	Success	Survival	Failure
Revenue	$ 20,000,000	$ 3,000,000	$ 200,000
Exit year	6	4	2
Scenario probability	25%	50%	25%
Terminal value @ EV/Revenue multiple of			
1			$ 200,000
3		$ 9,000,000	
6	$ 120,000,000		
Discount rate (required return)	25%	25%	25%
Discount factor	0.2621	0.4096	0.6400
Present value (PV)	$ 31,457,280	$ 3,686,400	$ 128,000
Postmoney valuation = Probability-weighted PV	$ 9,739,520		
Investment	$ 500,000		
Required ownership	5.13%		
Premoney valuation	$ 9,239,520		

EXHIBIT 4.22   First Chicago Method: Company F

The postmoney valuation is the probability-weighted exit value of the various scenarios, discounted to present value using a single discount rate:

$$Postmoney\ valuation = 0.25 \times 120,000,000 \times 0.2621 + 0.50 \times 9,000,000 \times 0.4096$$
$$+ 0.25 \times 200,000 \times 0.6400$$
$$= \$9,739,520$$

It is important to note that the discount rate in the FCM is the r rather than the TR. This is because the probability of failure is already incorporate in the "failure" scenario and modeled separately from the TR. As discussed before, the r is typically significantly lower than the TR and can be compared to historical returns experienced by seed investors.

Based on a postmoney valuation of $9.7 million, an investment ticket of $500,000, and the other model assumptions in Exhibit 4.22, the investor has to negotiate at a minimum an ownership interest of 5.13% in order to obtain the required 25% return.

Notes on the FCM

Compared to the VC method, the FCM has the advantage of separating the modeling of the probability of failure from the discount rate applied to the company's exit value. Also, the FCM provides greater flexibility in addressing multiple scenarios with different times to exit and different base metrics and valuation methodologies from the VC method. For companies at a more advanced stage of development, the FCM can be combined with other methodologies under the income, market, and asset-based approaches and enhance their flexibility with a scenario analysis. On the downside, the FCM may bring complexity, time, and model risk into a valuation, as the analyst projects business performance and probabilities for each scenario.

The FCM can be expanded to include a broader range of scenarios, the effect of dilution, and capital structures with multiple classes of securities.

CONCLUSION

In this chapter, we have introduced a number of methods that are commonly used in the valuation of seed-stage enterprises. These methods and some of their characteristics are summarized in Exhibit 4.23.

It is important to remember that the primary goal of these methodologies at the seed stage is generally not valuation per se but rather to identify an ownership stake that is consistent with the investor required return from the investment and required multiple of invested capital (TVPI) as part of the seed round negotiations. From a fair value perspective, these methodologies can provide a framework to estimate potential transaction prices at a stage in a company's life where there may be few investors, but not yet an established market, and where estimates and projections are subject to very high uncertainty. To the extent they may lead to an actual transaction price at arm's length, these methodologies may help establish a basis for fair value measurement. For a seed-stage entity, it is important to maintain model flexibility, and consider also conclusions in terms of a range of values. A range of 15–25% for

Method	Stage	Valuation output	Class of method	Features
Payne Scorecard method	Prerevenue	Premoney	Peer comparison	Comparison with benchmark based on observable factors
Risk summation factor	Prerevenue	Premoney	Peer comparison	Comparison with benchmark with emphasis on risk factors
Berkus method 1.0	Prerevenue	Premoney	Hybrid model	Sum of valuation contributions from observable factors
Enhanced Berkus method	Prerevenue	Premoney	Hybrid model	Multiple observable factors based on industry characteristics
Venture Capital method	Pre- and Postrevenue	Postmoney	Discounted exit value	Single scenario, projection of financial performance. Discount rate incorporates risk of failure
First Chicago method	Pre- and Postrevenue	Postmoney	Discounted exit value	Multiple scenarios, projection of financial performance. Risk of failure is modeled as a separate scenario.

EXHIBIT 4.23 Valuation Methods for Seed-Stage Companies

VC required returns, for example, is unlikely to be appropriate for analyzing mature companies in an established industry, but may well be suitable to capture the broad variety of companies that fall into the VC market, from seed-stage enterprises to companies with substantial revenue and operations that are getting ready for an IPO. It is left to the analyst to identify the point within that range that is most suitable to represent the enterprise's specific features.

It is also important to emphasize the quality of management as a critical factor in the seed investor decision-making process. The importance of selecting companies with a reliable, competent, and trustworthy management team is a recurring theme in most of the readings on seed-stage valuation. For a company that is still in its infancy and where the future holds the keys to its ability to create value, confidence in management and a vision of the future for the company in the market in which it operates are key factors that drive capital allocation decisions. The investor's experience and "intelligence" form the foundations for the assessment on which such decisions are based.

CHAPTER 5

The Backsolve Method

Neil Beaton

Antonella Puca

The market approach has a privileged role under the fair value standard for its focus on market-based inputs. A common methodology under the market approach is to estimate the value of a company starting from the value of the company's individual equity interests. For a public company with shares traded on a stock exchange or in the over-the-counter market, the equity value of the company can be expressed in terms of its market capitalization, which is determined by multiplying its outstanding shares by their market prices. For private companies that do not have listed securities, the issue price of the company's own stock in a private offering often provides the most relevant market-based observable input for its equity valuation. As was discussed in Chapter 3, privately held companies typically have several classes and series of securities, with different rights and privileges. In an early stage enterprise (ESE) with a complex capital structure, a valuation of the enterprise based on a simple formula, which assigns the same value to all securities is often not suitable to generate a point estimate that complies with the fair value standard under ASC 820/IFRS 13.

This chapter presents the Backsolve method as a common method under the market approach to estimate the equity value of a company with multiple classes/series of shares starting from the price of actual transactions in the company's own stock. The Backsolve method is especially relevant in the valuation of ESEs, where transactions in the company's own stock occur relatively frequently through various rounds of financing.

The Backsolve method is a "bottom-up" approach to company valuation. Rather than developing a company's equity value and then working through an allocation method to estimate the value of the various classes/series of shares, the Backsolve method starts from the observed price of the latest transaction in the company's stock, usually a preferred round of financing, and then develops an equity value for the company that is consistent with the observed price of the last security sale. Once the model has been set up, a company's equity value can be allocated through the company's capital structure and generate value points for all other ownership interests that take into account the rights and privileges of each individual class/series of securities. From this perspective, the Backsolve method can be used both as an equity valuation method *and* as a method to allocate equity value through the company's capital structure.

The Backsolve method provides a basis also for subsequent measurements of the company's equity value, as the model built at the time of the initial transaction is "calibrated" to reflect changes in market conditions that affect the model's key inputs and assumptions over time. The AICPA PE/VC Valuation Guide places a renewed emphasis on calibration as the process of identifying the input values in the initial model that are consistent with the price of the observed transactions, and adjusting them on subsequent measurement dates to result in an equity value that is anchored to observed transactions with appropriate adjustments.[1] If a new transaction occurs, calibration requires considering the rights and preferences of each class of ownership interest in light of the new issuance, and solving for a new equity value that is consistent with the most recent transaction in the company's own debt and equity instruments.

The validity of the Backsolve method in fair value measurement relies heavily on the quality of the transaction price that is used as a basis for company valuation. A critical assumption of the Backsolve method is that the reference transaction is an arm's length transaction that provides a valid indication of the fair value of the reference security as of the transaction date (for instance, the fair value of preferred stock in the latest round). The participation of new investors to a round of financing that are not related parties of the company and its existing investors is often taken as an indication that the transaction price can be deemed to be fair value at initial recognition. On the other hand, the analyst may observe prices that come from related party transactions, financing rounds with strategic investors that are looking to obtain operational benefits above and beyond the expected financial returns from the stock or distressed transactions. Even if it has been determined that a transaction has taken place at arm's length, it may still not represent fair value if it can be shown that the exchange was not orderly because, for instance, one of the of the parties was in distress and had to prioritize the speed of the transaction over negotiating an adequate price. In such cases, transaction prices may need adjustments to get to a fair value estimate, or may also indicate that it is preferable to conduct the company's valuation using other methodologies, with the Backsolve method as an additional tool to assess whether the company's estimated value is reasonable rather than as the primary valuation method.[2]

This chapter presents a case study in the application of the Backsolve method, using a hypothetical enterprise as an example.[3] The section "The OPM Backsolve Method: A Case Study" illustrates how a valuation model can be established at the time of the first round of

---

[1]The AICPA PE/VC Valuation Guide defines calibration in the glossary as: "the process of reconciling the unobservable inputs used in a valuation technique so that the result of that valuation technique equals a specified value." As further explained in FASB ASC 820-10-35-24C, "if the transaction price is fair value at initial recognition and a valuation technique that uses unobservable inputs will be used to measure fair value in subsequent periods, the valuation technique shall be calibrated so that at initial recognition the result of the valuation technique equals the transaction price. Calibration ensures that the valuation technique reflects current market conditions, and it helps a reporting entity to determine whether an adjustment to the valuation technique is necessary (for example, there might be a characteristic of the asset or liability that is not captured by the valuation technique)."

[2]On the use of transaction prices in calibration, see also AICPA PE/VC Valuation Guide 10.31-10.43, "Inferring Value from Transactions in a Portfolio Company's Instruments." On the criteria to assess whether a transaction in the company's own stock reflects fair value, see AICPA PE/VC Valuation Guide 10.07–10.09. On fair value considerations for distressed transactions and periods of market disruption, see AICPA PE/VC Valuation Guide 4.24 and 13.20-13.24: "Significant Decrease in Volume or Activity or Distressed Transactions".

[3]Our case study is based on Case Study 10 of the AICPA PE/VC Valuation Guide, "Biotech Investments with a Complex Capital Structure – Multiple Investors' Perspective," with some modifications.

financing in the company's stock using the Backsolve method and then calibrated to estimate the company's equity value and the value of individual classes/series of shares on subsequent measurement dates. In our analysis, the Option Pricing method (OPM) is used allocate the aggregate equity value to the company's various classes/series of shares in combination with the Backsolve method. The section "Secondary Market Transaction" discusses how pricing information from secondary transactions can be integrated into a valuation that is based on the Backsolve method. The section "Estimating OPM Volatility" focuses on the estimate of equity volatility as a critical input in an OPM Backsolve model. The conclusion presents some observations on the characteristics and limitations of an OPM Backsolve method in the valuation of ESEs.

THE OPM BACKSOLVE METHOD: A CASE STUDY

The AICPA PE/VC Valuation Guide defines the Backsolve method as "a method within the market approach wherein the equity value for a privately held company is derived from a recent transaction in the company's own instruments.[. . .] The backsolve method is a form of calibration where management first estimates the other assumptions used within a valuation model, and the remaining assumption (total equity value) is then inferred from the transaction price."[4] To illustrate a practical application of the Backsolve method, we follow the progress of Boletus Biotech Inc. (Boletus), a hypothetical biotechnology company, through a series of financing rounds. Boletus has no debt (as is common for venture-backed companies), and its enterprise value (value of equity + value of debt) is the same as the company's equity value (value of preferred stock + value of common stock).

Simple Capital Structure – Calibration at Initial Measurement

On July 1 of Year 1, Boletus conducts its first round of venture-backed financing, raising $10 million in Series A preferred shares. The Series A preferred shares are issued at $1 per share, have a 1 × conversion ratio and a 1 × liquidation preference. The Series A preferred shares are nonparticipating and come with certain noneconomic rights. Exhibit 5.1 shows the company's capitalization table after the first round of financing.

The Series A round of financing qualifies as an arm's-length transaction under ASC 820. Investors in Series A preferred stock may use the issue price of $1 per share as the fair value of their preferred shares at the initial measurement date. In order to estimate the equity value of the company, we start from the "known" value of one unit of Series A preferred stock ($1 per share based on the issue price), and backsolve to the equity value of the company using an OPM model.[5]

---

[4]AICPA PE/VC Valuation Guide Glossary: "Backsolve Method."
[5]On the application of the Option-Pricing method as a valuation methodology and in allocating enterprise value, see especially Neil Beaton, *Valuing Early Stage and Venture-Backed Companies* (Wiley, 2010); and for an early formulation, see Robert Keeley, Sanjeev Punjabi, Lassaad Turki, "Valuation of Early-Stage Ventures: Option Valuation Models vs. Traditional Approaches," *Journal of Entrepreneurial and Small Business Finance* 5, no. 2 (1996): 115–138. For an early illustration of the case study in this article, see also Neil Beaton, Andreas Dal Santo, Antonella Puca, "Calibration with OPM in Early Stage Enterprises: A Fair Value Update," *Business Valuation Update* 25, no. 3 (2019): 1–8, and Andreas Dal Santo and Antonella Puca, "The Valuation of Early Stage Enterprises: A Fair Value Update," Webinar Handbook, Business Valuation Resources, December 18, 2018. The OPM Backsolve method is also discussed in AICPA Accounting and Valuation Guide, Valuation of Privately-Held

Shares	Shares Outstanding	Issue Price	Invested Capital	Liquidation Preference (x)	Conversion Ratio (x)	Fully Converted	Fully Converted %
Series A Preferred	10,000,000	$ 1.00	$ 10,000,000	1.00	1.00	10,000,000	66.67%
Common Stock	5,000,000					5,000,000	33.33%
Total						15,000,000	100.00%

EXHIBIT 5.1   Boletus Biotech Inc.: Capitalization Table, July 1, Year 1

Under the OPM, each class/series of stock is modeled as a set of call options on the company's enterprise value.[6] A call option gives to the holder the right, but not the obligation, to buy an underlying asset (the equity value of the enterprise in this case) at a certain price over a certain period of time. For a company that has debt and equity in its capital structure, the payoff to equity shareholders is effectively equal to that of the owner of a call option on the company's enterprise value, with a strike price equal to the principal amount of the company's debt and a term that coincides with the maturity date of the underlying bond.[7] Let's consider, for instance, a company that has bond debt with a principal amount of $20 million. If the company has an enterprise value of $20 million or less, any proceeds from the company's liquidation will go to satisfy the contractual rights of the bond holders. In this case, the "option" held by equity stockholders will expire worthless. If, on the other hand, the enterprise value of the company exceeds $20 million, any value above $20 million (the "strike price" or "exercise price") will go to the equity stockholders. Exhibit 5.2 illustrates the payoffs of the option at expiration for an enterprise value in the $0 to $50 million range.

Even in situations where the "call option" held by equity stockholders has zero "intrinsic value" (the company's equity would have no value if the company were to be liquidated currently), the call option associated with equity ownership may still have significant "time value" due to the possibility that the company's enterprise value in the future may exceed the redemption value of debt.

Along similar lines, the OPM can be used to allocate the equity value of a company between preferred and common stock. In this case, the strike price of the common stockholders' call option is given by the liquidation preference of the preferred stockholders, which needs to be satisfied ahead of any equity value allocation to common stock.

In its most simple (and common) form, an OPM model for equity allocation can be set up using the Black-Scholes-Merton (BSM) call option model:

$$C = S_0 e^{-qT} N(d_1) - K e^{-rT} N(d_2) \tag{5.1}$$

Company Securities Issued as Compensation (2013) and in International Valuation Standards (IVS) 200, *Businesses and Business Interests* 130.13-130.20 (2019) of the International Valuation Standards Council.

[6] Robert Merton, "On the Pricing of Corporate Debt: The Risk Structure of Interest Rates," *Journal of Finance* 29, no. 2 (May 1974): 449–470.

[7] In a theoretical framework, the bond is modeled as a zero-coupon bond, with principal due in full upon maturity. In practice, the bond's redemption value at the projected exit date can be used in the analysis.

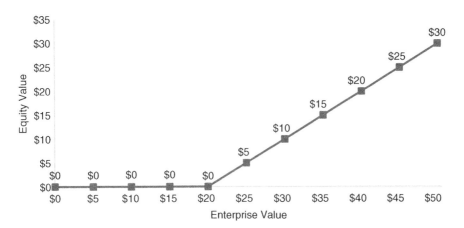

EXHIBIT 5.2 Payoff of Equity as a Call Option on the Company's Enterprise Value

where

$$d_1 = \frac{ln(S_0/K) + (r - q + \sigma^2/2)T}{\sigma\sqrt{T}} \tag{5.2}$$

$$d_2 = d_1 - \sigma\sqrt{T} \tag{5.3}$$

And where $N(x)$ denotes the standard normal cumulative distribution function, which is the probability of obtaining a value of less than x based on a standard normal distribution.[8]

The BSM formula has the following inputs:

- S_0 = Underlying asset price. The underlying asset is the equity value of the enterprise, which in our example is also the enterprise value (Boletus has no debt).
- σ = Volatility of underlying asset. In our example, equity volatility is estimated at 100%. The estimate of equity volatility is a critical input in the OPM and is discussed in greater detail in the section "Estimating OPM Volatility."
- K = Exercise price. Multiple exercise prices are determined based on the waterfall embedded in the company's capital structure, which in turn depends on the contractual rights of the various classes/series of securities. We discuss the exercise price in greater detail below.
- T = Time to exit. This input represents the expected timing of a liquidity event. In this example, we have set the time to exit at three years from the measurement date.
- r = Risk-free rate. This input is often based on the yield of government securities (U.S. Treasury securities in this case) with a matching term. We have estimated it at 2% in our example.
- q = Dividend yield. Equity securities of ESEs do not typically generate cash dividends. The value of this input in our model is zero.

---

[8]For an introduction to option pricing theory, see John C. Hull, *Options, Futures and Other Derivatives* (Pearson, 2017) (10th edition). See also Chapter 10 in this book.

	Liquidation Preference		Series A Converts	
Equity Class	**No. 1**		**No. 2**	
Series A Preferred	$	10,000,000		–
Common		–	$	5,000,000
Total	$	10,000,000	$	5,000,000
Cumulative Value				
Equity Class				
Series A Preferred	$	10,000,000	$	10,000,000
Common		–	$	5,000,000
Total	$	10,000,000	$	15,000,000
Cumulative Value per Outstanding Share				
Equity Class				
Series A Preferred	$	1.00	$	1.00
Common		–	$	1.00

EXHIBIT 5.3   Boletus Biotech Inc.: OPM Breakpoints, July 1, Year 1

One of the key inputs in the Black-Scholes-Merton OPM is the exercise price of the options, which is based on the "breakpoints" of the model, namely, the points at which there is a change in the contractual allocation of equity value among the various classes/series of shares. As indicated in Exhibit 5.3, there are two breakpoints in our example.

First, equity value is allocated to the preferred shares up to their liquidation preference of $10 million. The first breakpoint corresponds to an exercise price of $10 million, at which point the value per outstanding share is equal to $1 for preferred shares and zero for common shares. Once the liquidation preference of the preferred stock has been satisfied, value is allocated only to common stock, until the unit value of common stock is equal to the unit value of the preferred stock (Breakpoint 2). At Breakpoint 2, preferred stockholders will find it more economically feasible to convert their shares into common stock. Any equity value remaining beyond Breakpoint 2 goes pro-rata to all shareholders based on their percentage of ownership in the company on a fully converted basis.

Exhibit 5.4 and Exhibit 5.5 show the payoff diagrams of the preferred stock and common stock of Boletus, respectively, at the time of a liquidity event, based on the breakpoints identified in Exhibit 5.3.

The payoff diagrams of common and preferred stock can be replicated with a combination of options. The characteristics (such as liquidity preferences, conversion features, etc.) of each class of stock determine the class' claim on the aggregate equity value. Note that common stock receives no allocation until Boletus reaches an equity value of $10 million. For equity value above $15 million, the excess over the $15 million threshold is allocated pro-rata to the common and preferred stockholders. Exhibit 5.6 presents the OPM based on the exercise prices and other inputs that we have discussed so far, using the BSM formula to estimate the value of the call options as of each breakpoint.

The breakpoint values are inserted as an input in the "Exercise Price" line. At Breakpoint 1 (exercise price of $10 million), the incremental value assigned to the option is allocated 100% to preferred stock (breakpoint participation percentage = 100%), to reflect its

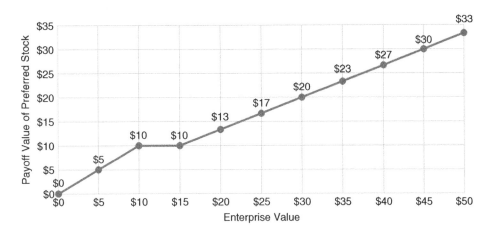

EXHIBIT 5.4 Boletus Biotech Inc.: Payoff Diagram of Preferred Stock at Exit

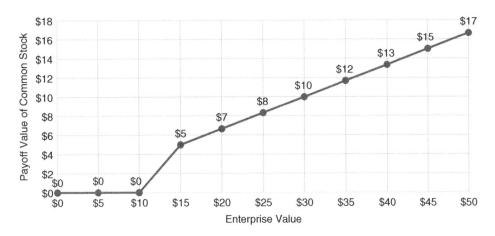

EXHIBIT 5.5 Boletus Biotech Inc.: Payoff Diagram of Common Stock at Exit

liquidation preference. At Breakpoint 2 (exercise price of $15 million), the incremental option value of $1.04 million is allocated entirely to common stock. Above the $15 million breakpoint, all incremental option value is allocated pro-rata to common and preferred stock on a fully converted basis.

Once the formulas for the model have been set up, the model is backsolved by inputting either the $10 million investment from the Series A investors or the $1 per share of the Series A preferred stock in the bottom part of Exhibit 5.6, to find the underlying asset value (the equity value of the enterprise) at the top of Exhibit 5.6.[9] In our example, the OPM results in an equity value of $13.9 million, which is consistent with a transaction price of $1 per share

---

[9]This can be done using, for instance, the "What-If" function in Excel, with the $1 per unit of pre-ferred shares or the total $10 million of the preferred shares issue price as an input and solving for the underlying asset value.

Black-Scholes-Merton Option Pricing Model				
	Total	No. 1	No. 2	End
Underlying Asset Value	$ 13,862,769	$ 13,862,769	$ 13,862,769	$ 13,862,769
Exercise Price		$ 10,000,000	$ 15,000,000	
Expected Volatility		100%	100%	
Risk-Free Rate		2%	2%	
Annualized Dividend Yield		0%	0%	
Time to Exit (years)		3	3	
$d(1)$		1.09	0.86	
$N(d1)$		0.86	0.80	
$d(2)$		(0.64)	(0.88)	
$N(d2)$		0.26	0.19	
Value of Call Option	$ 13,862,769	$ 9,499,153	$ 8,454,575	
Incremental Option Value		$ 4,363,616	$ 1,044,578	$ 8,454,575

Breakpoint Participation Percentages				
Series A Preferred Stock		100.00%	0.00%	66.67%
Common Stock		0.00%	100.00%	33.33%
Total		100.00%	100.00%	100.00%

Allocation of Incremental Option Value				
	Total Value			
Series A Preferred Stock	$ 10,000,000	$ 4,363,616	–	$ 5,636,384
Common Stock	$ 3,862,769	–	$ 1,044,578	$ 2,818,191
Total	$ 13,862,769	$ 4,363,616	$ 1,044,578	$ 8,454,575
Series A Preferred/share	$ 1.00			
Common/share	$ 0.77			

EXHIBIT 5.6   Boletus Biotech Inc.: BSM OPM, July 1, Year 1

for the Series A preferred, and with an estimated value of $0.77 per share for the common stock. Shareholders that own both classes of shares will now be expected to update the value of their common stock in a way that is consistent with the pricing of the latest round.

Simple Capital Structure – Calibration at Subsequent Measurement

Exhibit 5.7 illustrates how calibration can be applied in a subsequent measurement to estimate the value of the enterprise and the value of individual equity interests in the company. We are now at December 31 of Year 1, six months after the date of the Series A round.

In this case, we start by inputting the estimated equity value of the company as the underlying asset value. In our example, we assume that the equity value of the company is still $13.9 million and has not changed since the latest round in Series A preferred shares.[10] The model,

---

[10]In other circumstances a "rate of return" may be applied to the company's original equity value to account for the time value of money. In this case, we have assumed no value increase for purposes of demonstration.

Black-Scholes-Merton Option Pricing Model				
	Total	No.1	No.2	End
Underlying Asset Value	$ 13,862,769	$ 13,862,769	$ 13,862,769	$ 13,862,769
Exercise Price		$ 10,000,000	$ 15,000,000	
Expected Volatility		100%	100%	
Risk-Free Rate		2%	2%	
Annualized Dividend Yield		0%	0%	
Time to Exit (years)		2.5	2.5	
$d(1)$		1.03	0.77	
$N(d1)$		0.85	0.78	
$d(2)$		(0.55)	(0.81)	
$N(d2)$		0.29	0.21	
Value of Call Option	$ 13,862,769	$ 8,996,612	$ 7,826,958	
Incremental Option Value		$ 4,866,157	$ 1,169,654	$ 7,826,958

Breakpoint Participation Percentages				
Series A Preferred Stock		100.00%	0.00%	66.67%
Common Stock		0.00%	100.00%	33.33%
Total		100.00%	100.00%	100.00%

Allocation of Incremental Option Value				
	Total Value			
Series A Preferred Stock	$ 10,084,129	$ 4,866,157	–	$ 5,217,972
Common Stock	$ 3,778,640	–	$ 1,169,654	$ 2,608,986
Total	$ 13,862,769	$ 4,866,157	$ 1,169,654	$ 7,826,958
Series A Preferred/share	$ 1.01			
Common/share	$ 0.76			

EXHIBIT 5.7   Boletus Inc.: BSM OPM, December 31, Year 1

however, needs to be calibrated to reflect the conditions in place as of the subsequent measurement date of December 31, Year 1: all inputs in the BSM formula are unchanged, with the exception of the time to exit, which reflects a shorter period to exit of 2.5 years instead of 3 years. The OPM results in a unit value of $1.01 for Series A preferred stock and of $0.76 for common stock.

Simple Capital Structure – Add-on Round and Change in Inputs

The results of the OPM model are highly sensitive to the inputs in the BSM formula. Exhibit 5.8 illustrates how a change in certain key OPM inputs may affect equity value. We are now at July 1 of Year 2, one year from the initial Series A round. The company has raised an additional $10,000,000 in Series A preferred stock in May of Year 2, also a $1 per share. The round involved new investors and is deemed at fair value. The capitalization table after the new round is illustrated in Exhibit 5.8.

Exhibit 5.9 illustrates the new breakpoints, considering the liquidation preference of Series A preferred.

Shares	Shares Outstanding	Issue Price	Invested Capital	Liquidation Preference (x)	Conversion Ratio (x)	Fully Converted	Fully Converted %
Series A Preferred	20,000,000	$ 1.00	$ 20,000,000	1.00	1.00	20,000,000	80.00%
Common Stock	5,000,000					5,000,000	20.00%
Total						25,000,000	100.00%

EXHIBIT 5.8   Boletus Biotech Inc.: Capitalization Table, July 1, Year 2

	Liquidation Preference	Series A Converts
	No. 1	No. 2
Equity Class		
Series A Preferred	$ 20,000,000	–
Common	–	$ 5,000,000
Total	$ 20,000,000	$ 5,000,000
Cumulative Value		
Equity Class		
Series A Preferred	$ 20,000,000	$ 20,000,000
Common	–	$ 5,000,000
Total	$ 20,000,000	$ 25,000,000
Cumulative Value per Outstanding Share		
Equity Class		
Series A Preferred	$ 1.00	$ 1.00
Common	–	$ 1.00

EXHIBIT 5.9   Boletus Biotech Inc.: OPM Breakpoints, July 1, Year 2

Assuming no change in the inputs of the BSM formula (including time to exit at 2.5 years), and with an input price of $1 per share of Series A stock with calibration, the OPM Model would generate an equity value of $23.8 million for the company and a value of $0.77 per share for common stock as illustrated in Exhibit 5.10.

In our example, however, we estimate that the volatility has increased to 110% (from 100%), primarily due to a change in general market conditions. Also, Boletus is experiencing delays in meeting certain key milestones, which leads to an extension in the expected time to exit to four years. The risk-free rate is also adjusted to reflect the longer term to exit. Exhibit 5.11 illustrates an updated OPM model with the revised assumptions.

As a result of the change in inputs (expected volatility, risk-free rate, time to exit), the Backsolve method results in a point estimate of value of $24.3 million for the company and $0.86 per share for common stock.

Based on the OPM formula, and all other factors being equal, an increase in volatility has the effect of increasing the equity value of Boletus. The options that correspond to each breakpoint are more valuable as the volatility increases, as there is a greater probability that the equity value will reach or exceed the respective breakpoint. Similarly, an increase in the

Black-Scholes-Merton Option Pricing Model				
	Total	No. 1	No. 2	End
Underlying Asset Value	$ 23,845,964	$ 23,845,964	$ 23,845,964	$ 23,845,964
Exercise Price (Series A)		$ 20,000,000	$ 25,000,000	
Expected Volatility		100%	100%	
Risk-Free Rate		2.0%	2.0%	
Annualized Dividend Yield		0%	0%	
Time to Exit (years)		2.5	2.5	
$d(1)$		0.93	0.79	
$N(d1)$		0.82	0.79	
$d(2)$		(0.65)	(0.79)	
$N(d2)$		0.26	0.22	
Value of Call Option	$ 23,845,964	$ 14,746,286	$ 13,625,402	
Incremental Option Value		$ 9,099,678	$ 1,120,884	$ 13,625,402

Breakpoint Participation Percentages				
Series A Preferred Stock		100.00%	0.00%	80.00%
Common Stock		0.00%	100.00%	20.00%
Total		100.00%	100.00%	100.00%

Allocation of Incremental Option Value				
	Total Value			
Series A Preferred Stock	$ 20,000,000	$ 9,099,678	$ –	$ 10,900,322
Common Stock	$ 3,845,964	$ –	$ 1,120,884	$ 2,725,080
Total	$ 23,845,964	$ 9,099,678	$ 1,120,884	$ 13,625,402
Series A Preferred/share	$ 1.00			
Common/share	$ 0.77			

EXHIBIT 5.10   Boletus Biotech Inc.: Calibration to Price of New Round, July 1, Year 2

time to exit (the term of the option), results in a higher estimated equity value for Boletus: the value of the options at each breakpoint increases as the option holder has a longer time period during which the equity value of the company can reach and exceed the option's exercise price.

Complex Capital Structure – New Round of Financing

We now move forward to July 1 of Year 3. By this date, the company has already completed a Series B round of financing and is now raising additional capital in a new Series C round. Exhibit 5.12 illustrates Boletus's capitalization table after the Series B and Series C rounds.

In addition to Series A shares, the capitalization table now includes Series B preferred stock with a 1× liquidation preference and a $1.50 issue price per share. Series B ranks pari-passu with Series A, and both series are senior to common stock. Also, series B shares are convertible into common stock at a 1× conversion ratio.

Black-Scholes-Merton Option Pricing Model				
	Total	No. 1	No. 2	End
Underlying Asset Value	$ 24,293,566	$ 24,293,566	$ 24,293,566	$ 24,293,566
Exercise Price		$ 20,000,000	$ 25,000,000	
Expected Volatility		110%	110%	
Risk-Free Rate		3.0%	3.0%	
Annualized Dividend Yield		0%	0%	
Time to Exit (years)		4	4	
$d(1)$		1.24	1.14	
$N(d1)$		0.89	0.87	
$d(2)$		(0.96)	(1.06)	
$N(d2)$		0.17	0.14	
Value of Call Option	$ 24,293,566	$ 18,692,937	$ 17,999,215	
Incremental Option Value		$ 5,600,628	$ 693,723	$ 17,999,215

Breakpoint Participation Percentages				
Series A Preferred Stock		100.00%	0.00%	80.00%
Common Stock		0.00%	100.00%	20.00%
Total		100.00%	100.00%	100.00%

Allocation of Incremental Option Value				
	Total Value			
Series A Preferred Stock	$ 20,000,000	$ 5,600,628	$ –	$ 14,399,372
Common Stock	$ 4,293,566	$ –	$ 693,723	$ 3,599,843
Total	$ 24,293,566	$ 5,600,628	$ 693,723	$ 17,999,215
Series A Preferred/share	$ 1.00			
Common/share	$ 0.86			

EXHIBIT 5.11 Boletus Biotech Inc.: BSM OPM – Calibration with Updated Inputs, July 1, Year 2

The Series C preferred round raised an additional $5 million at $0.50 per share. This round also included new investors in a transaction that was considered to be conducted at fair value. Series C shares have more favorable terms than Series A and B. The Series C shares have a 2 × liquidation preference, which is senior to the claim of Series A and B shareholders. Similarly to the Series A and Series B shares, the Series C shares convert into common stock at a 1 × ratio and are nonparticipating.

Based on the new capitalization table, there are approximately 41.7 million shares on a fully converted basis, of which 48% are owned by Series A shareholders, 16% by Series B shareholders, 24% by Series C shareholders, and the remaining 12% by the common shareholders. Total invested capital is now $35 million, of which $20 million was contributed by Series A, $10 million by Series B, and $5 million by Series C shareholders. Exhibit 5.13 shows the breakpoints that reflect the contractual rights of each series of shares.

First, Series C shares receive $10 million in liquidation preference (or 2× of their invested capital of $5 million) (Breakpoint 1). The next $30 million in equity value is allocated pro-rata

Shares	Shares Outstanding	Issue Price	Invested Capital	Liquidation Preference (x)	Conversion Ratio (x)	Fully Converted	Fully Converted %
Series A Preferred	20,000,000	$ 1.00	$ 20,000,000	1.00	1.00	20,000,000	48.00%
Series B Preferred	6,666,666	$ 1.50	$ 10,000,000	1.00	1.00	6,666,666	16.00%
Series C Preferred	10,000,000	$ 0.50	$ 5,000,000	2.00	1.00	10,000,000	24.00%
Common Stock	5,000,000					5,000,000	12.00%
Total						41,666,666	100.00%

EXHIBIT 5.12   Boletus Biotech Inc.: Capitalization Table, July 1, Year 3

to satisfy the liquidation preference of the Series A and Series B shares (Breakpoint 2). After the Series A and B shares' liquidation preference is satisfied, $5 million in equity value is allocated to common shares. At an equity value of $45 million (Breakpoint 3), common shares, Series A preferred, and Series C preferred will have a value of $1 per unit. This is the point at which it will be economically viable for Series A and Series C shareholders to convert their shares into common stock, so that they can participate into any further appreciation of value. The next $17.5 million in value is allocated to Series A shares, Series C shares, and common shares pro-rata on a converted basis. At $62.5 million in equity value (Breakpoint 4), Series B shares convert into common. Any remaining enterprise value above $62.5 million is allocated pro-rata to all shareholders on a fully converted basis. Exhibit 5.14 shows the results of the OPM with the breakpoints identified earlier.

With an input issue price of $0.50 for Series C preferred shares (Series C class value of $5 million), the model backsolves to an equity value of $11.5 million, which in turn results in a value of $0.21 per unit of Series A preferred shares and $0.24 per unit of Series B preferred shares. In the model, we have reduced the risk-free-rate and the time to exit to 2% and three years, respectively. These inputs can be modified as deemed appropriate, based on the investors' expectations at the measurement date.

In applying the OPM backsolve, it is important to keep in mind that the OPM has certain limitations that affect the value relationship between the various classes and series of shares in a complex capital structure. The OPM is based on the assumption of a lognormal distribution of outcomes and may result in an overstatement of the value of the liquidation preferences of the more senior classes/series relative to the other classes/series in a complex capital structure. The potential magnitude of this distortion is greater if the OPM is calibrated to the price of the most senior class/series in a complex capital structure with different levels of seniority, and when the equity class/series used in calibration represents a small portion of the overall capitalization of the company.

One way to address this limitation is to first backsolve to an equity value under the assumption that all preferred shares have the same liquidation preferences and seniority (pari-passu). Exhibit 5.15 shows the breakpoints of Boletus on a pari-passu basis, given the unit price of Series C preferred at $0.50 per unit.

Equity Class	Series C Liquidation Preference No. 1		Series A/B Liquidation Preference No. 2		Series A/C Convert No. 3		Series B Converts No. 4	
Series A Preferred	$	–	$	20,000,000	$	–	$	10,000,000
Series B Preferred	$	–	$	10,000,000	$	–	$	–
Series C Preferred	$	10,000,000	$	–	$	–	$	5,000,000
Common	$	–	$	–	$	5,000,000	$	2,500,000
Total	$	10,000,000	$	30,000,000	$	5,000,000	$	17,500,000
Cumulative Value								
Equity Class								
Series A Preferred	$	–	$	20,000,000	$	20,000,000	$	30,000,000
Series B Preferred	$	–	$	10,000,000	$	10,000,000	$	10,000,000
Series C Preferred	$	10,000,000	$	10,000,000	$	10,000,000	$	15,000,000
Common	$	–	$	–	$	5,000,000	$	7,500,000
Total before Proceeds	$	10,000,000	$	40,000,000	$	45,000,000	$	62,500,000
Cumulative Value per Outstanding Share								
Equity Class	No. 1		No. 2		No. 3		No. 4	
Series A Preferred	$	–	$	1.00	$	1.00	$	1.50
Series B Preferred	$	–	$	1.50	$	1.50	$	1.50
Series C Preferred	$	1.00	$	1.00	$	1.00	$	1.50
Common	$	–	$	–	$	1.00	$	1.50

EXHIBIT 5.13   Boletus Biotech Inc.: OPM Breakpoints, July 1, Year 3

In Exhibit 5.15, Breakpoint 1 corresponds to the liquidation preference of Series A, Series B, and Series C on a pari-passu basis (1 × for all classes). Under the assumption of a 1 × liquidation preference, once the company reaches $37.5 million in equity value, it will be economically viable for Series C shares to convert into common stock. At a company value of $45 million and $62.5 million, Series A shares and Series B shares will convert, respectively. The equity value above $62.5 million will be allocated pro-rata to all shares.

Exhibit 5.16 shows the BSM OPM in a pari-passu scenario, which backsolves to an equity value of $23.6 million.

Notice that Breakpoint 1 now corresponds to the liquidation preference of the cumulative Series A, Series B, and Series C shares as if they had equal seniority rights (a total of $35 million in liquidation preference). In Exhibit 5.17 the equity value generated on a pari-passu basis ($23,621,876 in our model) is then allocated to the various share classes based on their actual contractual rights. Finally, the value for Series C shares as generated by the model is be discounted to calibrate to the actual Series C transaction price of $0.50 per share.

Exhibit 5.17 shows the OPM "with discount" as an alternative approach when securities with different seniority rights are present.

In Exhibit 5.17, the underlying asset value of $23,621,876 is an input into the model, which results in a value of $0.49 per share for Series A preferred, $0.54 for Series B preferred, $0.40 for common stock, and in a discount of 39.59% to match the observed transaction price of $0.50 per share for Series C preferred.

	Black-Scholes-Merton Option Pricing Model					
	Total	No. 1	No. 2	No. 3	No. 4	End
Underlying Asset Value	$ 11,467,721	$ 11,467,721	$ 11,467,721	11,467,721	11,467,721	11,467,721
Exercise Price		$ 10,000,000	$ 40,000,000	$ 45,000,000	$ 62,500,000	
Expected Volatility		100.00%	100.00%	100.00%	100.00%	
Risk-Free Rate		2.00%	2.00%	2.00%	2.00%	
Annualized Dividend Yield		0%	0%	0%	0%	
Time to Exit (years)		3.0	3.0	3.0	3.0	
$d(1)$		0.98	0.18	0.11	(0.08)	
$N(d1)$		0.84	0.57	0.54	0.47	
$d(2)$		(0.75)	(1.55)	(1.62)	(1.81)	
$N(d2)$		0.23	0.06	0.05	0.04	
Value of Call Option	$ 11,467,721	$ 7,463,771	$ 4,280,450	$ 4,015,579	$ 3,308,792	
Incremental Option Value		$ 4,003,950	$ 3,183,320	$ 264,871	$ 706,786	3,308,792

	Breakpoint Participation Percentages				
Investor					
Series A Preferred	0.00%	66.67%	0.00%	57.14%	48.00%
Series B Preferred	0.00%	33.33%	0.00%	0.00%	16.00%
Series C Preferred	100.00%	0.00%	0.00%	28.57%	24.00%
Common	0.00%	0.00%	100.00%	14.29%	12.00%
Total	100.00%	100.00%	100.00%	100.00%	100.00%

	Allocation of Incremental Option Value					
	Total Value					
Series A Preferred	$ 4,114,311	$ –	$ 2,122,213	$ –	$ 403,878	1,588,220
Series B Preferred	$ 1,590,514	$ –	$ 1,061,107	$ –	$ –	529,407
Series C Preferred	$ 5,000,000	$ 4,003,950	$ –	$ –	$ 201,939	794,110
Common	$ 762,896	$ –	$ –	264,871	100,969	397,055
Total	$ 11,467,721	$ 4,003,950	$ 3,183,320	264,871	706,786	3,308,792

	Value per Share
Series A Preferred	$ 0.21
Series B Preferred	$ 0.24
Series C Preferred	$ 0.50
Common	$ 0.15

EXHIBIT 5.14 Boletus Biotech Inc.: BSM OMP, July 1, Year 3

	Liquidation Preference	Series C Converts	Series A Converts	Series B Converts
Equity Class	No. 2	No. 2	No. 3	No. 4
Series A Preferred	$ 20,000,000	$ –	$ –	$ 10,000,000
Series B Preferred	$ 10,000,000	$ –	$ –	$ –
Series C Preferred	$ 5,000,000	$ –	$ 5,000,000	$ 5,000,000
Common	$ –	$ 2,500,000	$ 2,500,000	$ 2,500,000
Total	$ 35,000,000	$ 2,500,000	$ 7,500,000	$ 17,500,000
Cumulative Value				
Equity Class				
Series A Preferred	$ 20,000,000	$ 20,000,000	$ 20,000,000	$ 30,000,000
Series B Preferred	$ 10,000,000	$ 10,000,000	$ 10,000,000	$ 10,000,000
Series C Preferred	$ 5,000,000	$ 5,000,000	$ 10,000,000	$ 15,000,000
Common	$ –	$ 2,500,000	$ 5,000,000	$ 7,500,000
Total	$ 35,000,000	$ 37,500,000	$ 45,000,000	$ 62,500,000
Cumulative Value per Outstanding Share				
Equity Class	No. 2	No. 3	No. 4	No. 5
Series A Preferred	$ 1.00	$ 1.00	$ 1.00	$ 1.50
Series B Preferred	$ 1.50	$ 1.50	$ 1.50	$ 1.50
Series C Preferred	$ 0.50	$ 0.50	$ 1.00	$ 1.50
Common	$ –	$ 0.50	$ 1.00	$ 1.50

EXHIBIT 5.15 Boletus Biotech Inc.: OPM Breakpoints Pari-Passu, July 1, Year 3

The OPM model should reflect the provisions of the various classes/series of shares in the way they are expected to be effected through the term of the model. For instance, an analyst may expect that at the time of a subsequent round the cumulative dividend provisions will most likely be renegotiated and will no longer be in effect after the new round. In this case, the analyst would include in the model the dividend provisions as they are expected to be effected. Along similar lines, the holders of junior securities may have a significant influence on the timing and value of the company at exit, and the analyst may expect that they will be able to negotiate more favorable allocation provisions for their shares at exit in order to give their consent to a transaction under the current contractual terms. In many cases, investors that hold senior securities may also have participated in the earlier rounds and have a direct interest in making sure that junior securities receive an adequate share of exit proceeds. In this case, an OPM model that is built on the contractual provisions of the various classes/series of shares may understate the value of the junior shares when it is calibrated to the price of a senior series of shares without adjustments.

Also, a financing transaction may involve a strategic relationship in which the investor receives certain benefits over and above the value that is expected to be realized from the stock itself. For example, a pharmaceutical company may invest in Boletus to gain access to Boletus's research and draw ideas for its own research efforts. In this case, the analyst would need to assess whether it would be appropriate to adjust the input price of the latest round used as a basis of the OPM model to exclude the effect of any benefits that would not be available to a generic "market participant."

	Total	No. 1	No. 2	No. 3	No. 4	End
		Black-Scholes-Merton Option Pricing Model				
Underlying Asset Value	$ 23,621,876	$ 23,621,876	$ 23,621,876	$ 23,621,876	23,621,876	$ 23,621,876
Exercise Price		$ 35,000,000	$ 37,500,000	$ 45,000,000	$ 62,500,000	
Expected Volatility		100.00%	100.00%	100.00%	100.00%	
Risk-Free Rate		2.00%	2.00%	2.00%	2.00%	
Annualized Dividend Yield		0%	0%	0%	0%	
Time to Exit (years)		3.0	3.0	3.0	3.0	
$d(1)$		0.67	0.63	0.53	0.34	
$N(d1)$		0.75	0.74	0.70	0.63	
$d(2)$		(1.06)	(1.10)	(1.20)	(1.39)	
$N(d2)$		0.14	0.14	0.11	0.08	
Value of Call Option	$ 23,621,876	$ 12,932,744	$ 12,602,150	$ 11,721,522	$ 10,130,545	
Incremental Option Value		$ 10,689,132	$ 330,594	$ 880,628	$ 1,590,977	$ 10,130,545
		Breakpoint Participation Percentages				
Investor						
Series A Preferred		57.14%	0.00%	0.00%	57.14%	48.00%
Series B Preferred		28.57%	0.00%	0.00%	0.00%	16.00%
Series C Preferred		14.29%	0.00%	66.67%	28.57%	24.00%
Common		0.00%	100.00%	33.33%	14.29%	12.00%
Total		100.00%	100.00%	100.00%	100.00%	100.00%
		Allocation of Incremental Option Value				
	Total Value					
Series A Preferred	$ 11,879,867	$ 6,108,075	$ –	$ –	$ 909,130	$ 4,862,662
Series B Preferred	$ 4,674,925	$ 3,054,038	$ –	$ –	$ –	$ 1,620,887
Series C Preferred	$ 5,000,000	$ 1,527,019	$ –	$ 587,085	$ 454,565	$ 2,431,331
Common	$ 2,067,084	$ –	$ 330,594	$ 293,543	$ 227,282	$ 1,215,665
Total	$ 23,621,876	$ 10,689,132	$ 330,594	$ 880,628	$ 1,590,977	$ 10,130,545
	Value per Share					
Series A Preferred	$ 0.59					
Series B Preferred	$ 0.70					
Series C Preferred	$ 0.50					
Common	$ 0.41					

EXHIBIT 5.16 Boletus Biotech Inc.: BSM OPM Pari-Passu, July 1, Year 3

Black Scholes Merton Option Pricing Model					
	Total	No. 1	No. 2	No. 3	No. 4	End
Underlying Asset Value	$ 23,621,876	$ 23,621,876	$ 23,621,876	$ 23,621,876	$ 23,621,876	$ 23,621,876
Exercise Price		$ 10,000,000	$ 40,000,000	$ 45,000,000	$ 62,500,000	
Expected Volatility		100.00%	100.00%	100.00%	100.00%	
Risk-Free Rate		2.00%	2.00%	2.00%	2.00%	
Annualized Dividend Yield		0%	0%	0%	0%	
Time to Exit (years)		3.0	3.0	3.0	3.0	
$d(1)$		1.40	0.60	0.53	0.34	
$N(d1)$		0.92	0.72	0.70	0.63	
$d(2)$		(0.34)	(1.14)	(1.20)	(1.39)	
$N(d2)$		0.37	0.13	0.11	0.08	
Value of Call Option	$ 23,621,876	$ 18,230,454	$ 12,291,366	$ 11,721,522	$ 10,130,545	
Incremental Option Value		$ 5,391,422	$ 5,939,088	$ 569,844	$ 1,590,977	$ 10,130,545

Breakpoint Participation Percentages					
Investor					
Series A Preferred		0.00%	66.67%	0.00%	57.14%	48.00%
Series B Preferred		0.00%	33.33%	0.00%	0.00%	16.00%
Series C Preferred		100.00%	0.00%	0.00%	28.57%	24.00%
Common		0.00%	0.00%	100.00%	14.29%	12.00%
Total		100.00%	100.00%	100.00%	100.00%	100.00%

Allocation of Incremental Option Value					
	Total Value					
Series A Preferred	$ 9,731,183	$ –	$ 3,959,392	$ –	$ 909,129	4,862,662
Series B Preferred	$ 3,600,583	$ –	$ 1,979,696	$ –	$ –	1,620,887
Series C Preferred	$ 8,277,318	$ 5,391,422	$ –	$ –	$ 454,565	2,431,331
Common	$ 2,012,792	$ –	$ –	$ 569,844	227,283	1,215,665
Total	$ 23,621,876	$ 5,391,422	$ 5,939,088	$ 569,844	$ 1,590,977	$ 10,130,545

	Value per Share	Discount	FV per Share
Series A Preferred	$ 0.49		0.49
Series B Preferred	$ 0.54		0.54
Series C Preferred	$ 0.83	39.76%	0.50
Common	$ 0.40		0.40

EXHIBIT 5.17   Boletus Biotech Inc.: BSM OPM with Discounts, July 1, Year 3

SECONDARY MARKET TRANSACTIONS

So far, we have considered the issue price of the company's own stock (the price in the company's "primary market") as a starting point for equity valuation. Most of the ESE capital transactions take place in the form of primary market transactions between the company and its investors, with the issuance of new stock. In some cases, however, investors may also have the opportunity to purchase interests in an ESE directly from other investors, or company employees (usually founders) in the "secondary market." In a secondary market transaction, the company does not issue new securities. Rather, preexistent securities are exchanged among a buyer and a seller at terms that are privately negotiated between the parties.

There are frequently special circumstances surrounding a secondary transaction that may make it less reliable than a private market transaction as input data for a fair value measurement. For instance, a seller may be facing a need for liquidity that makes the seller willing to enter into a distressed deal, at a price lower than fair value. Secondary transactions may involve related parties, such as funds under common management, at terms that may not be at arm's length. Also, the purchase of stock in the company may be one element of a transaction that includes additional rights and privileges that should be valued separately and deducted from the transaction price.

The size of a transaction may also have an impact on the reliability of the secondary transaction price as a fair value indication. The size of secondary transactions should be evaluated as a percentage of overall shares outstanding as well as a percentage of overall shares transacted in the current period. Typically, secondary transactions that in the aggregate are for more than 10% of a company's fully diluted shares and that involve multiple buyers and sellers are seen as a significant market share in terms of their potential effect on valuation. Transactions where there is a significant gap between the date of the agreement (the trade date) and the closing (settlement), or where there is a significant time lag between the trade date and the measurement date (stale transactions) would have less impact on enterprise valuation.[11]

As an example of the impact of secondary transactions on equity value, let's go back to July 1 of Year 2 in our previous example (Exhibit 5.11). Let's now assume that, subsequent to the Series A round of preferred stock issuance at $1 per share and before the measurement date, three investors in the company had sold a total of 3,000,000 shares of Series A stock in the secondary market at an average price of $0.86 per share as indicated in Exhibit 5.18.

Let's assume that we do not have enough information to be able to determine whether these transactions were orderly transactions conducted at arm's length. Still, the transactions represent 12% of the company's shares on a fully converted basis and should be considered in the company's overall valuation.

One way to incorporate the data points provided by secondary transactions is to assign a weight to the price indications springing out of the secondary market as a factor in the

---

[11]AICPA PE/VC Valuation Guide 10.38: "For secondary market transactions, because the investor may have little information about the nature of the transactions, it may be difficult to conclude whether these transactions are orderly. Therefore, [...], these transactions may not necessarily be the sole or primary basis for measuring fair value. However, if the investor is unable to conclude that the transaction is not orderly, [...] the transaction price would need to be given some weight in measuring fair value, but that it also would be appropriate to augment the transaction price with other valuation techniques." See also AICPA PE/VC Valuation Guide 10.40: "Weighting – Secondary Market Transactions."

Secondary Transactions

Seller	Shares Sold	Unit Price	
Investor A	1,000,000	$ 0.88	$ 880,000
Investor B	1,000,000	$ 0.75	$ 750,000
Investor C	1,000,000	$ 0.95	$ 950,000
Total	3,000,000		$ 2,580,000
Average sale price			$ 0.86

EXHIBIT 5.18   Boletus Biotech Inc.: Secondary Transactions

Price Indication	Price Indication	Weight	Weighted Price Indication
Primary market	$ 1.000	0.90	$ 0.900
Secondary market	$ 0.860	0.10	$ 0.086
OPM Unit Price			$ 0.986

EXHIBIT 5.19   Boletus Biotech Inc.: OPM Unit Price

calculation of the input price of preferred stock in the OPM model. For instance, we may assign a weight of 10% of the price indication of the secondary transactions, and 90% to the price indication of the primary transactions ($1.00 per unit price of the latest round), which results in a weighted average price of $0.986 for input in the OPM (Exhibit 5.19).

The OPM model can now be run with the unit price of $0.986 per share for Series A preferred stock as an input to backsolve for an enterprise value of $23.9 million (Exhibit 5.20).

Secondary transactions may be a very relevant fair value indicator in certain circumstances, especially when a company is approaching an exit through an IPO/direct listing or an M&A transaction, even if they represent a small percentage of total capital transaction activity.

Let's take a look, for instance, at the transaction prices in shares of Slack Technologies Inc. ahead of its direct listing on June 20, 2019, on the New York Stock Exchange under the ticker symbol WORK.[12] Slack is an early player in the evolution of enterprise chat with headquarters in San Francisco (CA). Since its foundation in 2009 and ahead of its direct listing, Slack had raised $1.2 billion in the private markets. The company's postmoney valuation had increased rapidly from $280 million in Q2 of 2014 to unicorn status in Q4 of 2014 up to $7.1 billion in August 2018 (its last private round of financing). In the August/September 2018 round, Slack sold 35.9 million shares of Series H preferred stock at a price of $11.9053

---

[12]On Slack's direct listing, see Cameron Stanfill, "The Only Time Slacking Off Could Pay Off," *Pitch-Book 2Q 2019 Analyst Note*, PitchBook Data Inc., April 30, 2019. The data on Slack's trading in private transactions and on the August-September 2018 round is drawn from Slack's S 1A filing with the U.S. Securities and Exchange Commission dated May 31, 2019.

Black-Scholes-Merton Option Pricing Model				
	Total	No. 1	No. 2	End
Underlying Asset Value	$ 23,945,975	$ 23,945,975	$ 23,945,975	$ 23,945,975
Exercise Price (Series A)		$ 20,000,000	$ 25,000,000	
Expected Volatility		110%	110%	
Risk-Free Rate		3.0%	3.0%	
Annualized Dividend Yield		0%	0%	
Time to Exit (years)		4	4	
$d(1)$		1.24	1.13	
$N(d1)$		0.89	0.87	
$d(2)$		(0.96)	(1.07)	
$N(d2)$		0.17	0.14	
Value of Call Option	$ 23,945,975	$ 18,382,730	$ 17,695,945	
Incremental Option Value		$ 5,563,246	$ 686,784	$ 17,695,945
		Breakpoint Participation Percentages		
Series A Preferred Stock		100.00%	0.00%	80.00%
Common Stock		0.00%	100.00%	20.00%
Total		100.00%	100.00%	100.00%
		Allocation of Incremental Option Value		
	Total Value			
Ser A Preferred Stock	$ 19,720,000	$ 5,563,246	–	$ 14,156,754
Common Stock	$ 4,225,975	–	$ 686,784	$ 3,539,191
Total	$ 23,945,975	$ 5,563,246	$ 686,784	$ 17,695,945
Ser. A Preferred / share	$ 0.986			
Common / share	$ 0.845			

EXHIBIT 5.20   Boletus Biotech Inc.: BSM OPM with Secondary Transactions

per share. In addition, for the year ended January 31, 2019, Slack had secondary market transactions of 9,382,888 shares, representing approximately 1.9% of the total number of shares outstanding as of January 31, 2019, and 20.7% of total Slack share transactions for the year then ended. In the quarter ended January 31, 2019, Slack's secondary transactions took place at prices ranging between $17.25 and $23.41 per share.[13]

In April/May 2019, Slack's stock traded in the secondary markets within a range of $25.75–$31.50 per share. Ahead of its debut as a publicly traded company, the NYSE set Slack's reference price at $26 per share, consistently with the low price of its May secondary market trading activity. On June 20, 2019, the company started trading on the NYSE at a price of $38.5 and closed for the day at $38.62, an increase of 22.6% over the highest price in the May 2019 secondary market transactions. As of January 31, 2019, the date of the

---

[13]Information on Slack's share transactions is drawn from Slack's S-1A filing with the U.S. Securities and Exchange Commission dated May 31, 2019.

company's fiscal year-end and audited financial statements, the Q4 2018 secondary market was providing more reliable price indications for the direct listing exit price than the primary market of the August/September 2018 round.[14]

ESTIMATING OPM VOLATILITY

In our case study, we have seen how the volatility of the underlying asset (the equity value of the enterprise) is a key input in the OPM model. In the absence of an active market for the company's stock, the estimate of the equity volatility for a private company is typically based on the volatility of common stock returns of guideline public companies (GPC).

The process of estimating equity volatility within the framework of the Black-Scholes-Merton OPM involves the following steps:

Step 1: Select guideline public companies (GPC).

Step 2: Obtain/calculate the equity volatility of each GPC over the relevant term.

Step 3: Obtain/calculate the asset volatility of each GPC by removing the effect of leverage.

Step 4: Analyze GPC volatility results and estimate the asset volatility for the subject company.

Step 5 (if the subject company has debt): Adjust the asset volatility of the subject company for the effect of the subject company's leverage.

We now walk through each of these steps.[15]

Step 1: Selecting Comparable Companies

The process of selecting comparable companies for an OPM volatility estimate typically starts from a search in datasets of public company data for certain key factors of comparability with the goal of identifying a subset of GPCs that are suitable for further analysis (generally 3–10 companies). The selection of GPCs for comparison can be especially challenging for an ESE, which has risk, cash flow, and growth characteristics that may differ significantly from those of public companies in the same industry or sector. For ESEs, the key comparability factors may include, among others:[16]

- Industry and/or sector. Generally, the search is based on the North American Industry Classification System (NAICS) code or the Standard Industry Classification (SIC) code.
- Line of business and diversification

---

[14] As of November 21, 2019, Slack was trading on NYSE at $21.03 per share.

[15] On the estimate of volatility in the OPM BSM, see Neil Beaton, Stillian Ghaidarov, and William Brigida, "Volatility in the Option-Pricing Model," Valuation Strategies, 2009, also included as Appendix B in Neil Beaton, *Valuing Early Stage and Venture-Backed Companies* (Wiley, 2010); Aaron Rotkowski, "Estimating Stock Price Volatility in the Black-Scholes-Merton Model," *The Value Examiner*, November/December 2011: 13–19; AICPA PE/VC Valuation Guide Q&A 14.61: Measuring Volatility for Early Stage Companies.

[16] For a discussion of factors of comparability in selecting guideline public companies, see AICPA PE/VC Valuation Guide 5.12.

- Geographic reach
- Customers and distribution channels
- Stage of business life cycle
- Operating constraints (for instance, dependence on key customers or government regulation), seasonality of the business, barriers to entry
- Size in terms of revenues, total invested capital, postmoney valuation
- Profitability, anticipated future growth in revenue and profits
- Asset base (for instance, technology-driven intangibles versus customer-driven intangibles versus fixed assets)
- Pattern of owning versus leasing assets

The size and diversification factors have an especially relevant effect in a volatility analysis. In general, volatility tends to decrease as diversification and size increase. A large diversified company in the same sector is likely to have a significantly lower volatility of returns at the enterprise level as compared to an early-stage company that depends on the success and failure of a single product. In an ESE context, it may be appropriate to select guideline companies that may not be direct competitors but that are more similar to the subject company in size and level of diversification. In some cases, it may be appropriate to segregate a division within a GPC for comparison. Typically, once a GPC (or divisions thereof) has been selected, it continues to be used period over period unless a chance of circumstances has taken place and can be explained in the valuation documentation.

Step 2: Estimate of Individual GPC Volatility

As a next step in the volatility estimate, the analyst will typically consider the historical volatility of the GPCs over the term horizon as well as the volatility implied in the GPCs' listed option prices, if available. The historical volatility of GPCs represents the dispersion of common stock market returns over a given period of time. In an OPM context, the historical volatility of a GPC is typically measured by the annualized standard deviation of the GPC's weekly common stock price returns over the OPM term.

Exhibit 5.21 illustrates the calculation of the historical volatility for a sample company, COMP1, over a two-year period. Weekly returns are calculated based on the adjusted closing price of listed common stock using the formula LN (P_t/P_{t-1}), and the standard deviation is calculated using the STDEV formula in excel. The standard deviation is annualized using the square root of 52 (the number of weekly periods in one year), resulting in a historical annualized volatility of 21.6% for COMP1's stock returns based on a two-year return string.

For GPCs that have listed options traded in the public markets, the volatility of common stock returns can also be estimated based on the volatility that is implied in the price of their option contracts. The implied volatility of an option contract is the value of the volatility of the underlying instrument which, when input in an option pricing model (such as the BSM model) will return a theoretical value equal to the current market price of the option. Unlike the historical volatility of a GPC's common stock, which can be observed based on the historical series of stock returns, the implied volatility of an option on common stock is not directly observable. However, it can be calculated using the BSM formula for call options using Level 2 inputs, by taking the market price of an option on the GPC's common stock, entering it into the BSM formula, inputting the strike price, the time to expiration, the risk-free rate, the underlying stock price, and the dividend yield, and resolving for the volatility value.

Week	Adjusted Closing Price	Return	Week	Adjusted Closing Price	Return
YE0	21.14				
1	21.20	0.31%	53	37.90	3.78%
2	22.16	4.40%	54	38.10	0.52%
3	21.89	−1.20%	55	39.30	3.10%
4	23.04	5.13%	56	40.20	2.26%
5	23.40	1.56%	57	41.50	3.18%
6	23.52	0.48%	58	41.30	−0.48%
7	24.16	2.68%	59	41.60	0.72%
8	24.56	1.67%	60	42.75	2.73%
9	24.83	1.07%	61	41.74	−2.40%
10	24.47	−1.44%	62	44.05	5.38%
11	24.99	2.11%	63	43.59	−1.05%
12	25.27	1.08%	64	42.10	−3.47%
13	25.55	1.11%	65	41.28	−1.96%
14	25.57	0.08%	66	41.40	0.28%
15	25.49	−0.30%	67	41.46	0.15%
16	27.11	6.17%	68	44.30	6.62%
17	27.86	2.72%	69	44.70	0.91%
18	28.35	1.74%	70	45.04	0.75%
19	28.12	−0.81%	71	45.24	0.44%
20	29.01	3.11%	72	45.30	0.13%
21	30.35	4.50%	73	45.66	0.78%
22	30.82	1.56%	74	47.93	4.85%
23	30.54	−0.91%	75	48.46	1.11%
24	30.49	−0.16%	76	49.05	1.21%
25	31.63	3.66%	77	48.32	−1.50%
26	31.18	−1.44%	78	47.85	−0.98%
27	31.48	0.95%	79	49.55	3.49%
28	31.73	0.79%	80	52.43	5.67%
29	30.92	−2.58%	81	51.68	−1.45%
30	31.37	1.47%	82	51.92	0.47%
31	31.04	−1.08%	83	52.26	0.65%
32	31.41	1.19%	84	52.10	−0.30%
33	32.81	4.37%	85	52.49	0.75%
34	32.62	−0.58%	86	54.15	3.11%
35	33.56	2.83%	87	56.00	3.36%
36	34.75	3.50%	88	53.80	−4.02%
37	34.60	−0.44%	89	56.84	5.50%
38	34.38	−0.63%	90	55.68	−2.06%
39	34.86	1.38%	91	57.40	3.05%
40	36.15	3.62%	92	54.87	−4.51%
41	36.23	0.23%	93	53.20	−3.09%
42	36.96	1.99%	94	50.43	−5.36%
43	37.38	1.13%	95	48.69	−3.51%
44	38.43	2.76%	96	51.62	5.85%
45	38.91	1.27%	97	53.26	3.12%
46	39.25	0.85%	98	51.85	−2.67%
47	39.81	1.43%	99	48.96	−5.75%
48	39.67	−0.37%	100	53.09	8.10%
49	37.96	−4.39%	101	49.17	−7.67%
50	36.99	−2.60%	102	49.18	0.02%
51	36.32	−1.83%	103	44.60	−9.77%
52	36.49	0.49%	104	47.12	5.49%
			105	47.89	1.63%

STD 2Y = 21.57%

EXHIBIT 5.21 Calculation of Equity Volatility

For instance, suppose that the value of an at-the-money call option is $30.00 when the stock price is $112.50, strike price is $110.00, risk-free rate is 2.00%, and the time to expiration is two years. The implied volatility resulting from the BSM model, given the inputs above, is 43.7%.

Most listed options have a term to expiration that is significantly shorter than the term to liquidity of a typical ESE OPM, which may present some challenges as the terms of the options for volatility estimation should match the expected term to liquidity for the subject enterprise. A number of software solutions are available in the market to address this issue.

Finally, stock return volatilities for GPCs can be obtained by looking at a company's reported volatility estimate in its annual 10-K financial statement disclosures. Publicly traded companies that grant employees some form of share-based compensation are required under ASC 718 to measure the cost of all share-based payments at fair value. The financial statement footnotes of GPCs that follow ASC 718 typically include a description of how the fair value of a company's share-based compensation was determined. If the company used the BSM OPM, it would also have to disclose its estimated stock price volatility. As in the case of the implied volatility, the analyst should be wary of differences in the term covered by the volatility estimate (term per 10-K versus term to liquidity event in the ESE OPM model). A review of the 10-K volatility information can provide additional insight to better interpret the results of the historical and implied volatility analysis. Both the implied volatility and the 10-K estimates are forward looking in that they reflect expectations as to the future stock performance from the perspective of a market participant and the company's management, respectively.

Step 3: From GPC Equity Volatility to GPC Asset Volatility

The GPC volatility resulting from Step 2 represents the volatility of the GPC common stock returns ("equity" volatility). To the extent a GPC has debt in its capital structure, the GPC volatility estimate needs to be "delevered" to generate a measure of volatility at the enterprise level ("asset volatility") that can be used to compare volatilities between GPCs with different capital structures and to eventually extract a point estimate of enterprise-level volatility for the subject company. Using asset volatility removes the differences in capital structure between the comparable and subject companies and leads to a more consistent application of volatility in the OPM.

The mathematical relationship between the asset volatility and equity volatility of a company can be expressed as follows:

$$\sigma_A = \frac{1}{N(d_1)} \times \frac{E_O}{A_O} \times \sigma_E \tag{5.4}$$

where

E_O is the firm equity value at time t_0. The market capitalization of the company is typically used for this metric.

A_O is the firm asset value at time t_0. This metric represents the enterprise value of the company as the sum of its equity value and the debt value.

$N(d_1)$ is a familiar term from the BSM model and is also known as the call option's delta (a measure of the call sensitivity with respect to changes in the underlying asset value).

σ_A is the asset volatility of the firm.

σ_E is the equity volatility of the firm.

t_0 is the measurement date.

Based on Formula 1, the general relationship between equity value and asset value at time t_0 can be expressed as:

$$E_0 = A_0 \times N(d_1) - D_0 \times e^{-rT} \times N(d_2) \tag{5.5}$$

where:

  r is the risk-free rate.
  T is the option's time to expiration.
  D_0 is the value of debt.
  $d_2 = d_1 - \sigma_A \sqrt{T}$ from the Black-Scholes formula

Using Formula 5.4 within the BSM OPM model we can now calculate the asset volatilities for each of the GPCs. For instance, let's assume that COMP1 has an equity value (market capitalization) of \$1,914 million, a value of debt of \$461 million, equity volatility of 22.60%, and that the risk-free rate is 2.0%. Also assume that the debt of COMP1 consists exclusively of a zero-coupon bond with a principal that matures in two years. We can set up a BSM OPM model with the following inputs:

$$\text{Risk-free rate} = 2.0\%$$

$$\text{Strike price} = \$461 \text{ million } (D = P \text{ as principal value of debt})$$

$$T = \text{term of option} = 2 \text{ years}$$

In this model, A_0 (the underlying asset value) and σ_A (the asset volatility) are unknown. We do know, however, that σ_A relates to σ_E, which has a known value of 22.60%, as described in Formula 5.4. We also know that the OPM model generates a value for the call option that represents the payoff to the company's equity holders, namely, the equity value of our company ($E_0 = \$1,914$ million). We have therefore a system of two equations with two "unknowns" (A_0 and σ_A), which can be resolved using the Goal Seek function in Excel with a number of iterations:

$$\sigma_A = \frac{1}{N(d_1)} \times \frac{E_0}{A_0} \times \sigma_E$$

with

$$\sigma_E = 22.60\%$$

and

$$\text{Call}(A_0,\ D_0,\ T) = E_0 = \$1,914 \text{ million}$$

The model resolves for an asset value (A_0) of \$2,357 million and an asset volatility (σ_A) of 18.4%.

Volatility Analysis

Volatility of Guideline Companies	COMP1	COMP2	COMP3	COMP4	COMP5
Historical Volatility	21.6%	51.1%	74.2%	22.6%	95.6%
Implied Volatility	23.6%	62.6%	65.0%	38.3%	85.3%
Average Equity Volatility – two years	22.6%	56.9%	69.6%	30.5%	90.5%
Asset Volatility – two years	18.4%	53.1%	63.5%	30.4%	85.3%

Summary Statistics	Low	Median	High	Average	
Historical Volatility:	21.6%	51.1%	95.6%	53.0%	
Implied Volatility	23.6%	62.6%	85.3%	55.0%	
Asset Volatility	18.4%	53.1%	85.3%	50.1%	

Target ESE – Two-Year Volatility – Point Estimate = 85%

*We selected the highest value for the asset volatility of the comparable companies.
The two-year equity volatility of comparable companies is calculated as the weighted average of the implied and the historical volatility. The historical volatility is calculated using the series of weekly returns for the applicable company over the two-year period ending on the measurement date, and is annualized.

EXHIBIT 5.22 GPC Volatility Analysis

Step 4: Analytical Summary and Asset Volatility Estimate for the Subject Company

Once the steps described earlier have been completed for each of the GPCs, a table can be set up to summarize the results of the GPC's volatility analysis, for instance as shown in Exhibit 5.22.

The analyst will typically identify the high, low, median, and average of the implied and historical volatility values. It may be appropriate in some cases to exclude outliers or companies with exceedingly low volumes of trading for a period included in the return series, or which may otherwise skew the results with evidence that may reflect unorderly transactions.

In the end, the analyst will conclude on an asset volatility value to be used for the subject company. For an ESE, the analyst will tend to favor estimates in the top quartile of the GPC range and, in some cases, make adjustments to account for differences between the subject company and the selected guideline companies. These adjustments may result in an estimated volatility that is outside the observed range in certain circumstances. In our example, we have set the asset volatility of the subject company at 85%, which represents the highest value in the GPC range based on a weighted average of the GPC's historical and implied volatilities.

Step 5: From Asset Volatility to Equity Volatility

For ESEs that have little or no debt in their capital structure, Step 4 will conclude the process of volatility estimation. As we discussed in the first part of this chapter, the Backsolve method is used to estimate the equity value of a company based on its latest transaction price. Accordingly, the volatility estimate used as an input in the OPM model should be the equity volatility of the reference ESE. In the absence of debt, the value of the equity is the same as the value of the enterprise, and there is no distinction between asset volatility and equity volatility. In this situation, the estimated asset volatility that results from the GPC analysis will be a direct input in the OPM model that is used to value the subject ESE.

The identity of enterprise and equity value is no longer maintained for companies that have debt in their capital structure. The presence of debt will typically result in the need to adjust the asset volatility of the subject company to include consideration of company-specific leverage. The equity volatility can be calculated using the following formula:

$$\sigma_E = N(d_1) \times (A_0/E_0) \times \sigma_A \tag{5.6}$$

For most ESEs, corporate debt is unlikely to be a significant aspect of the company's capital structure and no adjustment for leverage at the company level will be necessary. On the other hand, the difference between asset volatility and equity volatility at the level of the guideline public companies can be significant and should be considered in the OPM model.

CONCLUSION

The OPM Backsolve method can be a suitable and defensible approach to estimate the fair value of a company's equity and of individual equity interests in the company in situations of high uncertainly concerning future enterprise value.[17] It is especially suitable for ESE valuations, to the extent it can be anchored to observed transactions in the company's securities at fair value. The results of the valuation under an OPM Backsolve method are significantly affected by the contractual rights of the different series/classes of shares. It is critical that the breakpoints in a BSM OPM model be set up to accurately reflect the rights of the various classes/series of securities in an ESE's capital structure.

Investors may end up valuing the same series of shares at different valuation points based on different inputs and assumptions. The different values may all be reasonable in terms of ASC 820/IFRS 13 even though they may be materially different. To the extent there is a later, and more senior round, it is likely that a valuation at the issue price for the earlier rounds may no longer be acceptable under ASC 820. The AICPA PE/VC Valuation Guide clearly points to the need of reconsidering the valuation of earlier rounds when the capital structure of a company changes, and that an approach that carries forward the issue price may result in a valuation that no longer reflects fair value when more senior rounds are introduced.

The equity value that results from the OPM model will typically be significantly lower than the postmoney equity value under the Venture Capital method, since the OPM framework considers the full value of the downside protection associated with the preferred stock's liquidation preferences, whereas the postmoney value calculation of the Venture Capital (VC) method assumes that all equity interests in the capital structure have the same pro-rata value. The actual value relationships between different classes/series of securities can be significantly affected by noneconomic rights such as voting rights, and by the negotiation power of the various classes/series of shareholders that are not reflected in the OPM's contractual waterfall structure.

---

[17]On the use of the OPM in various situations, see also AICPA PE/VC Valuation Guide Q&A 14.54: Use of the Option Pricing Method.

The OPM projects a single liquidity event. To the extent the analyst wants to highlight the effect of multiple liquidity events with different timings, other probabilistic models such a probability-weighted scenario analysis as discussed later in this study may provide a more flexible approach to valuation.

Generally, the allocation of equity value in an OPM waterfall does not consider the dilution impact of additional financings nor the offsetting cash raised. This is not an inherent limitation of the model, as an OPM can be modified, if desired, to include the terms of a new financing, particularly if such terms are known at the time the analyst is performing his/her work (for instance, a financing that took place in January of Year 2 for a December 31, Year 1 valuation). If a future pre-exit financing event is probable and its key terms are ascertainable, this financing can be explicitly incorporated into the OPM. Anticipated near term (within the next 12 months) compensatory stock and stock option awards can also be incorporated into the OPM.

The OMP Backsolve method is based on the well-established theory of option pricing behind the BSM model, which makes it mathematically rigorous and well-accepted in practice. The assumption of a constant equity volatility through the liquidity event and of a lognormal distribution of outcomes are simplifying assumptions, which make it easier to explain than more complex models with discrete nodes and the possibility of varying the model inputs at each node, such as the Binomial Lattice model.

The OPM Backsolve method is critically reliant on the inputs in the BSM formulas, and particularly on equity volatility, which is especially challenging to estimate. This input is likely to be developed based on the analysis of guideline public companies that may have significantly different risk, cash flow, and operational profiles from the subject company. Also, certain key adjustments may be necessary to account for leverage and for the capital structure of the guideline public companies and of the subject company.

CHAPTER 6

Discounted Cash Flow Method

John Jackman

Antonella Puca

The discounted cash flow (DCF) method is an income-based approach in which enterprise value is estimated based on the present value of the company's expected cash flows, discounted at a rate that reflects the risk of these cash flows. The credibility of the DCF method lies in a reliable cash flow forecast and well-developed discount rates. The estimate of a discount rate that considers both the prospective of the firm in acquiring its capital resources (cost of capital) and of market participants in pursuing their risk/return objectives (rate of return) is an important step in ensuring that a DCF model for an early stage enterprise (ESE) is reasonable and consistent with fair value principles.

This chapter develops a DCF model to estimate enterprise value under the fair value standards of ASC 820/IFRS 13, using a venture-backed ESE as an example. After presenting the model's components and key assumptions in some detail, the chapter shows how a DCF model can be built to reflect the special characteristics of an ESE using a scenario analysis to account for the company's risk of failure. We then discuss how a DCF model can be calibrated to estimate the fair value of the enterprise in subsequent measurement.[1] As we walk through our model, we highlight some key considerations concerning the valuation process and the documentation requirements under the Mandatory Performance Framework (MPF).[2]

In his studies of early stage valuation, Aswath Damodaran has underlined the importance of developing a realistic and internally consistent narrative on the company's path to

---

[1] For an example of how to apply calibration to the estimate of the discount rate in a DCF model, see AICPE PE/VC Valuation Guide, 10.19–10.25.

[2] As noted in Chapter 2, the Mandatory Performance Framework consists of the provisions included in the Mandatory Performance Framework for the Certified in Entity and Intangible Valuations (CEIV) Credential document and of the related guidance on the Application of the Mandatory Performance Framework (AMPF) for the CEIV Credential (collectively, the MPF), both issued in January 2017 under the umbrella of the Corporate and Intangibles Valuation Organization LLC. For an overview of the MPF, see Raymond Rath, "Advancing the Quality of Valuations," *Business Valuation Review* 36, no. 2 (Summer 2017): 48–53.

profitability and to a stage of sustainable long-term growth. The company's narrative should translate into valuation inputs and numbers in a model that can be adjusted at subsequent measurement dates as the company and market environment continue to evolve.[3]

In our example, Racoon Inc. (Racoon) is a revenue-generating company that has already completed its Series B round of financing. The company expects significant revenue growth but is still recording net losses due to a sustained level of research and development expenses and significant marketing costs for the commercialization and distribution of its products. A valuation analyst in a venture capital fund is putting together a model to value the company for financial reporting purposes under ASC 820. More than a year has passed since the company's Series B round and the valuation analyst elects to use a DCF model in valuation. The analyst estimates the model's cash flows under two scenarios:[4]

> **Scenario 1 – Survival:** The company is able to stay in business and reach its long-term mature growth stage. An IPO in Year 5 is the most likely exit for current investors and it is expected that all equity interests will eventually convert into common stock. The value of the company under the "Survival" scenario is estimated using discount rates that have been de-risked of the company's risk of failure via a probability-weighting process. The analyst assigns a 70% probability to this scenario.

> **Scenario 2 – Failure:** The company is dissolved, with equity holders receiving zero proceeds from their investment. The value of the company under the dissolution scenario is zero. The analyst assigns a 30% probability to this scenario.

The estimate of the probability of failure (or 1 minus the probability of success) is a critical estimate in the valuation of an ESE. Increasing evidence is coming to light regarding the performance of individual portfolio companies as research databases tap into the investments of venture capital funds.[5]

The availability of new research and data in this area is helping create stronger support for estimates where currently qualitative factors are most prevalent and quantitative documentation still presents many challenges.

As you review the numerical examples of this chapter, please note that most of the values in the exhibits are formula-driven and may give rise to rounding differences as the actual calculations are spelled-out in detail, which we have left unadjusted.

---

[3] Aswath Damodaran, *The Dark Side of Valuation* (Wiley, 2018). See especially Chapter 9, "Baby Steps: Young and Start-Up Companies," pp. 259–321, and Chapter 10, "Shooting Stars: Valuing Growth Companies," pp. 323–375. See also Andrew Metrick and Ayako Yasuda, "DCF Analysis of Growth Companies," *Venture Capital & the Finance of Innovation*, 2nd ed. (Wiley, 2011), pp. 195–213; Jerald Pinto, Elaine Henry, Thomas Robinson, and John D. Stowe, "Equity Asset Valuation," Chapter 6 in *Free Cash Flow Valuation* (Wiley, 2015), pp. 295–360; Joshua Rosenbaum and Joshua Pearl, "Discounted Cash Flow Analysis," Chapter 3 in *Investment Banking* (Wiley, 2013), pp. 135–190. On the DCF as it applies to private companies, see also Raymond Rath, "Private Company Valuation," Chapter 9 in *Equity Asset Valuation*, edited by Jerald Pinto and others (Wiley, 2015), pp. 527–536.

[4] See AICPA VC/PE Valuation Guide, 5.79 for a description of the "expected value technique" in the DCF approach.

[5] See for instance, Cameron Stanfill and Bryan Hanson, "VC Returns by Series Part I," *PitchBook 3Q 2019 Analyst Note*, PitchBook Data Inc., September 27, 2019.

DEVELOPING A DCF MODEL IN A SURVIVAL SCENARIO

Step 1: Choice of Model

A DCF valuation model requires three basic sets of inputs: (1) an estimated stream of cash flows to the firm's equity holders (cash flows to equity or FCFE) or to the suppliers of capital as a whole (cash flows to the firm, debt plus equity or FCFF); (2) a time horizon over which these cash flows take place; and (3) a discount rate that reflects the risk of the cash flows. For an ESE where most of the value is expected to come from future growth, all of these factors are subject to considerable estimation uncertainty.

Our model assumes that Racoon currently has no debt in its capital structure, which is common in an ESE context. In the absence of debt, all cash flows to the firm go to the firm's shareholders, and cash flows to equity and cash flows to the firm effectively coincide. As an ESE grows and turns into a "mature" company, its capital structure is likely to converge toward its industry average. In the presence of debt, the value of the firm's equity is determined by first estimating the value of the enterprise using cash flows to the firm, and then subtracting the debt component.[6]

Step 2: Estimating Future Cash Flows

The reliability of a fair value estimate under the DCF model is highly dependent on the quality of the financial data and the process used to estimate the future stream of cash flows. Managers of private companies generally command much more information about their business than external analysts. To the extent an analyst has access to management, the most common starting point in estimating future cash flows for an ESE is the prospective financial information (PFI) prepared by management or under management's direct supervision.

Management's PFI may consist of a complete set of financial statements or be limited to certain accounts. For venture capital (VC) investors, it is desirable to obtain a set of three to five years of financial projections that cover the entity's financial position, results of operations, and cash flows. These records may be challenging to obtain, though, especially for companies in the early VC stage. In some cases, management may stretch its model beyond a five-year horizon, up to the time when the company is expected to reach an exit event or a stage of stable growth.[7]

PFI can be prepared using either a "top-down" or "bottom-up" approach. In a top-down approach, management starts from an assessment of the potential market available for the company's business. Management identifies the factors that are most relevant in explaining sales/revenue trends, and projects a market share for the company and a timeline for its achievement. The assumption is that, given the existing market and potential market

---

[6]In our simplified model, we have not included an adjustment to the firm's cash flows in later years related to interest expense and corresponding tax implications on debt incurred by the firm. At our model cost of debt and D/E ratio, interest cash flow deductions are not expected to have a material impact on the total value of the firm.

[7]"Financial forecast is the prospective financial statement that present, to the best of the responsible party's knowledge and belief, an entity's expected financial position, results of operations and cash flows. A financial forecast is based on the responsible party's assumptions reflecting the conditions it expects to exist and the course of action it expects to take" (AT Section 301).

growth, the company will capture a certain percentage share of the market over the projection period. In a bottom-up approach, management starts instead from an analysis of the company's production capacity, resources, capital reinvestment needs, and cash requirements to derive projections for the company's revenue, expenses, and cash flows over the projection period. A bottom-up projection will typically include a higher level of detail, resulting in a more accurate analysis, which reflects the use of budgeting, production planning, or other internal processes.

Under the MPF, when using management-provided information, the valuation analyst should assess whether the PFI prepared by management is reasonable for use in performing a valuation.[8] The analyst should understand and document how the PFI was developed by management and which approach was used, as well as the original purpose for which the PFI was prepared. Common questions to assess the reliability of the PFI include:

- What are the drivers for the expected revenue growth (increase in price, volume, or both)?
- How does the expected revenue growth compare to industry growth?
- Is the revenue growth achievable given the current conditions of the company operations?
- Are new products or services considered in terms of forecasted revenue? If so, are the corresponding expenses reasonable?
- Are there new products under development? What is the basis for research and development expenses? Are forecasted capital expenditures consistent with the revenue growth assumptions?
- Are operating expenses consistent with historical levels? Did management differentiate between fixed and variable costs? If there are variable costs, what do costs vary against?
- Are forecasted results consistent with historical results, if not, why not?
- Is it reasonable for management to forecast a much higher or lower growth rate compared to guideline companies or other industry metrics?
- Is it reasonable for management to forecast a much higher or lower profit margin compared to guideline companies or other industry metrics?
- Are the projections reasonable in view of information from guideline companies?
- Are tax-related assumptions reasonable and is the company going to gain tax benefits from its net operating losses?

Analysts should be especially inquisitive about long-term forecasts, as they are subject to considerable estimation risk. The analyst should review each metric individually for reasonability, and in relation with each other to make sure they are internally consistent. For example, an ESE with PFI that presents aggressive growth rates and improving margins would also be expected to have a sustained rate of capital expenditures and operating expenses related to growth. If there is an indication that the company is approaching commercial viability for its product, we would expect to see an increase in operating expenses related to sales and marketing and so on.

Let's now look at how future cash flows are estimated in the valuation of Racoon. Racoon's management has prepared PFI using a bottom-up approach and has delivered to the analyst a set of balance sheet, income statement and cash flows projections for the current

---

[8] AMPF A1.4.7: The Valuation Professional's Assessment of the PFI.

calendar year and five years into the future. Management is targeting an IPO exit toward the end of Year 5.

The analyst must determine the level of detail to build into the analysis. The analyst extracts revenues, expenses, and profitability data from management's PFI schedules for Years 1–5 and then models revenues and operating expenses in Years 6–10 so that they converge to a state of stable long-term growth for the company in Year 10, generating a set of data as shown in Exhibit 6.1.

The analyst also extracts selected data from management's projected cash flows statements for Years 1–5 and models capital expenditures and incremental working capital in Years 6–10 to converge to the company's state of mature growth as shown in Exhibit 6.2.

Let's examine some of the accounts in Exhibits 6.1 and 6.2 in more detail.

Revenue

In Exhibit 6.1, the "Base" column represents revenue in the current period of $12 million. The revenue growth rates in Years 1–5 are based on management's estimates: management expects revenue growth to reach a peak in Year 3 and then decline to 30% in Year 5, when management is targeting an IPO exit. After Year 5, the analyst models revenue growth so that the growth rate gradually declines to a long-term sustainable rate of 3.0%, which is consistent with the industry average.[9]

The estimate of a company's revenue growth rate over the projection period is one of the most significant estimates in the income approach. Even minor changes in the growth rate, particularly in the early projection years for an ESE, may have a significant impact on the value of the enterprise. Under the MPF, it is important for the analyst to consider how the PFI revenue growth rates and the PFI values as a percentage of revenue compare to industry rates and percentages. A qualitative analysis may also be needed to evaluate the reasons that the entity's PFI may mirror or diverge from industry data. In a PFI that has been developed using the bottom-up approach, the analyst may want to inquire about the market share that the company is expected to capture and the timeline for the company to reach a steady growth stage, and assess whether the growth rates in the PFI are consistent with that information.

Operating Expenses

For companies that have yet to reach profitability but have a stream of revenue in sight, the operating expenses reported in the income statement are likely to include a significant component of expenditures that are incurred for developing assets that drive the company's growth. Under current accounting standards, for instance, most research and development

---

[9]In his study of the venture capital industry, Andrew Metrick and Ayako Yasuda have noted that when they go public, VC-backed firms typically have growth rates that are much higher than industry average, and that these rates decline rapidly to industry average in about five years. Andrew Metrick and Ayako Yasuda, *Venture Capital and the Finance of Innovation*, 2nd ed. (Wiley, 2011), pp. 197–198: "In the first full year after their IPO, firms grow much faster than the industry: in year 1, the median industry-adjusted growth rate is 14.7%, and the 75th percentile is 57.1%. By the fifth year after their IPO, however, this median is almost exactly 0; thus, as measured by revenue growth, we can say that the typical firm reaches "maturity" within five years after the IPO."

	Base	Management's Projections					Analyst's Model (Converge to Steady Growth in Year 10)				
		1	2	3	4	5	6	7	8	9	10
Revenue	12,000	16,800	26,880	48,384	77,414	100,639	125,396	149,472	170,099	184,387	189,919
Revenue Growth		40.00%	60.00%	80.00%	60.00%	30.00%	24.60%	19.20%	13.80%	8.40%	3.00%
Cost of Goods Sold	7,787	11,410	19,068	35,784	59,593	80,511	90,285	95,662	95,255	88,506	75,968
as % of revenue	64.89%	67.92%	70.94%	73.96%	76.98%	80.00%	72.00%	64.00%	56.00%	48.00%	40.00%
Gross Profit	4,213	5,390	7,812	12,600	17,821	20,128	35,111	53,810	74,844	95,881	113,951
as % of revenue	35.11%	32.08%	29.06%	26.04%	23.02%	20.00%	28.00%	36.00%	44.00%	52.00%	60.00%
Operating expenses ex Depreciation & Amortization	11,250	13,059	16,608	22,172	22,960	13,372	23,132	35,224	48,730	62,133	73,528
as % of revenue	93.75%	77.73%	61.79%	45.83%	29.66%	13.29%	18.45%	23.57%	28.65%	33.70%	38.72%
EBITDA	(7,037)	(7,669)	(8,796)	(9,572)	(5,139)	6,756	11,979	18,586	26,114	33,748	40,423
as % of revenue	−58.64%	−46.24%	−32.72%	−19.79%	−6.64%	6.71%	9.55%	12.43%	15.35%	18.30%	21.28%
Depreciation & Amortization	500	605	796	1,132	1,489	1,724	1,947	2,144	2,300	2,402	2,440
as % of revenue	4.17%	3.60%	2.96%	2.34%	1.92%	1.71%	1.55%	1.43%	1.35%	1.30%	1.28%
EBIT	(7,537)	(8,274)	(9,592)	(10,704)	(6,628)	5,032	10,032	16,442	23,814	31,346	37,984
as % of revenue	−62.81%	−49.25%	−35.69%	−22.12%	−8.56%	5.00%	8.00%	11.00%	14.00%	17.00%	20.00%
Taxes	—	—	—	—	—	755	1,505	2,466	3,572	4,702	5,698
as % of EBIT	0.00%	0.00%	0.00%	0.00%	0.00%	15.00%	15.00%	15.00%	15.00%	15.00%	15.00%
EBIT (1 − t)	(7,537)	(8,274)	(9,592)	(10,704)	(6,628)	4,277	8,527	13,976	20,242	26,644	32,286

EXHIBIT 6.1 Selected PFI and Analyst's Model ($ Thousand)

	Management's Projections					Analyst's Model (Converge to Steady Growth in Year 10)				
	1	2	3	4	5	6	7	8	9	10
Capital Expenditures	5,205	10,609	14,379	12,087	13,021	11,619	9,515	6,881	4,004	3,940
Incremental Working Capital	706	1,505	2,032	1,626	1,733	1,685	1,444	1,000	387	399

EXHIBIT 6.2   Selected PFI and Analyst's Model – Cash Flows Data ($ Thousand)

expenses related to intangible assets must be expensed rather than capitalized. Also, the company's costs for hiring and training specialized personnel such as software engineers and programmers that are critical for the company's growth must be expensed as incurred.

The analyst may find it useful to inquire regarding how much within the operating expenses figure consist of R&D and other expenditures related to the development of assets that drive the company's growth.[10] In order to maintain growth rates that are higher than the industry average, a company will need significant investments in growth, which the operating expense entries should reflect.

In Exhibit 6.1, operating expenses in Years 1–5 are based on management's estimates. For Years 6–10, the analyst expects that operating margin will consistently improve as revenue increases, resulting in EBIT margin of 20% in Year 10.

Depreciation and Amortization

Depreciation and amortization expenses represent noncash charges related to the company's capital assets on the balance sheet, including fixed assets, real estate, equipment (depreciation), and intangible assets (amortization). In the Racoon model, depreciation and amortization expenses for Years 1–5 are based on management's estimates. In Years 6–10, the analyst expects them to decline as a percentage of revenue to reach 1.28% in Year 10 and remain constant at that percentage thereafter.

Taxes   Taxes should consider any federal, state, or local taxes that are applicable to the company's projected taxable income. In some jurisdictions, an ESE may accumulate tax benefits in the early years, which can then be used to offset tax liabilities once the company achieves profitability. In the Racoon model, the analyst has assumed that no such tax benefits can be recognized. In Exhibit 6.1, tax expenses are first introduced in Year 5, when EBIT turns positive, and are charged at a rate of 15% of EBIT.

In many cases, the effective tax rate for a company will be lower than a straightforward cumulation of the statutory rates that are applied at its level of profitability, even in the absence of loss carryforwards. Especially for companies with international operations, tax rates tend to be significantly lower than the statutory rates.

---

[10] A company's "growth assets" may include patents, trademarks, and copyrights that relate to its core business, as well as assets that closely relate to the company's growth efforts.

Incremental Working Capital Incremental working capital consists of the cash flows invested in receivables and inventory necessary to support revenue growth. Working capital is often defined as current assets less current liabilities. For purposes of a DCF valuation, working capital is typically defined to exclude cash and any short-term debt. In Exhibit 6.2, management has made the assumption in Years 1–5 that the investment in working capital bears a constant relationship to the forecasted increase in revenue, and that an investment in working capital equal to 7% of the revenue increase year-to-year is required. For instance, in Year 2, given a projected increase in revenue ($ thousand) of $21,504 = $48,384 − $26,880, additional working capital of 7.0% × $21,504 = $1,505 is needed. The analyst continues to apply the 7% rate to the projected change in revenue in Years 6–10 and in the period after Year 10.

Capital Expenditures Capital expenditures have two components: (1) expenditures necessary to maintain existing capacity (fixed capital replacement), and (2) incremental expenditures that are necessary for growth. In the Racoon model, the capital expenditures for Years 1–5 are based on management's projections. For Years 6–10 and thereafter, the analyst models capital expenditures with the assumption that such expenditures to maintain capacity are related to the current level of revenues while expenditures for growth are related to the forecast for revenue growth. In Exhibit 6.2, capital expenditures to support current operations (fixed capital replacement) are equal to the projected D&A expense. In addition, the company is expected to reinvest for growth at a rate that will result in a revenue-to-capital multiple (incremental revenue as a multiple of invested capital) of 3.0 in stable growth, including the incremental working capital component.[11] In a given year, reinvestment at a revenue-to-capital ratio of 3.0 corresponds to reinvestment as a percentage of incremental revenue of 33.33% as follows:

$$\text{Reinvestment as a\% of Incremental Revenue}$$

$$= 1/\text{Revenue to Capital Ratio} = 1/3 = 33.33\%$$

In Years 6–10, capital expenditures as a percentage of revenue decline. In the company's mature growth stage, capital expenditures are directed primarily to maintain a company's production infrastructure rather than actively growing it. In the Racoon model, the analyst assumes that the increase in revenues and the reinvestment that creates that increase occur with a one-year lag (Year 6 capital expenditures, for instance, are based on the projected increase in revenue between Year 6 and Year 7).

Capital expenditures for Years 6–10, can then be calculated as ($ thousand):

$$\text{Capital Expenditures} = \text{Capital Replacement} + \text{Growth Capital Investment}$$

$$= \text{Depreciation \& Amortization}$$

$$+ [\text{Change in Revenue}/(\text{Revenue}/\text{Capital Ratio})$$

$$- \text{Incremental Working Capital}]$$

---

[11]For the theoretical framework and practical examples of how to use the sales/capital ratio (revenue/capital ratio in the Racoon model) to estimate the reinvestment rate of high growth companies, see especially Aswath Damodaran, *The Dark Side of Valuation* (Wiley, 2018), pp. 283, 347–348, 357–361.

In Year 10, for instance, we have:

$$\text{Capital Expenditures} = \$2,440 + [(\$189,919 \times 3\%)/3.0 - (\$399)]$$
$$= \$2,440 + \$1,899 - \$399 = \$3,940$$

Exhibit 6.3 shows the capital expenditures for Years 1–10.

Normalization Adjustments

As defined in the International Glossary of Business Valuation Terms, normalized earnings are "economic benefits adjusted for non-recurring, non-economic, or other unusual items to eliminate anomalies and/or facilitate comparisons." The estimates in Exhibits 6.1 and 6.2 may need adjustments to come to values that better represent the firm's operations for market participants. Common adjustments are made, for instance, to eliminate the effect on nonrecurring revenue or expense items, adjust the amounts of discretionary expenses that are not at arm's length (for instance, when owner compensation is above or below market rates), or reflect synergies that are to the advantage of a specific entity (for instance, a prospective buyer), but would not be available to a generic market participant. In our simplified example, we have assumed that no adjustments were necessary. Please refer to Chapter 8 for further discussion of common EBITDA and net loss adjustments.

Free Cash Flows to the Firm

We can now calculate free cash flows to the firm based on the information in Exhibits 6.1 and 6.2. Exhibit 6.4 shows the formula for the calculation of free cash flows to the firm.

In an ESE with little or no debt, interest expense is typically zero. Any debt outstanding is generally converted into equity and does not pay cash interest. Dividends, when present, are also paid in kind. For an ESE with no debt and no cash dividends, the formula for free cash flows is reduced to what is shown in Exhibit 6.5.

Free Cash Flows to the Firm (FCFF) for Racoon are presented in Exhibit 6.6.

Step 2: Discount Rate

Step 2 in the DCF model consists of estimating the discount rate that is applied to the FCFF stream to calculate its present value. From the perspective of the firm, the discount rate represents the cost that the enterprise is expected to incur to raise capital from its investors (cost of capital), whether in the form of debt (cost of debt) or equity (cost of equity) and the weighted average thereof. From the perspective of the investors, the discount rate represents the rate of return that investors demand to compensate them for giving up the use of their capital (opportunity cost and time value of money as represented by the risk-free rate) and for taking on the risk of the enterprise (investment risk as represented by a risk premium in excess of the risk-free rate). All other things being equal, companies that operate in riskier businesses should have higher costs of equity and cost of capital than companies in stable businesses. Stated another way, the higher the perceived risk of the projected cash flows, the greater the return that investors will demand to provide their capital to a company. This results in the application of a higher discount rate to the company's projected cash flows resulting in a lower present value.

		A	B	C	D = B–C	E = 7% × D	F	G = (D/A) – E + F
						in $ thousands		
Year	Source	Revenue/Capital Ratio	Revenue t + 1	Revenue t	Incremental Revenue	Incremental Working Capital	Depreciation	Total Capital Expenditures
Year 1	Management	1.90	26,880	16,800	10,080	706	605	5,205
Year 2	Management	1.90	48,384	26,880	21,504	1,505	796	10,609
Year 3	Management	1.90	77,414	48,384	29,030	2,032	1,132	14,379
Year 4	Management	1.90	100,639	77,414	23,224	1,626	1,489	12,087
Year 5	Management	1.90	125,396	100,639	24,757	1,733	1,724	13,021
Year 6	Analyst	2.12	149,472	125,396	24,076	1,685	1,947	11,619
Year 7	Analyst	2.34	170,099	149,472	20,627	1,444	2,144	9,515
Year 8	Analyst	2.56	184,387	170,099	14,288	1,000	2,300	6,881
Year 9	Analyst	2.78	189,919	184,387	5,532	387	2,402	4,004
Year 10	Analyst	3.00	195,616	189,919	5,698	399	2,440	3,940

EXHIBIT 6.3 Capital Expenditures ($ Thousand)

Operator	Component
	Net income (loss) after taxes
+	Interest expense, net of income tax (interest expense $\times$ [1 − t])
=	Net income (loss) to invested capital
+	Noncash charges against revenues (e.g. depreciation and amortization)
−	Capital expenditures (fixed assets and other operating noncurrent assets)
+ or −	Incremental working capital
+	Dividends paid on preferred shares or other senior securities (if any)
=	Free cash flows to the firm

EXHIBIT 6.4   Free Cash Flows to the Firm – With Debt

Operator	Component
	Net income (loss) after taxes
+	Noncash charges against revenues (e.g. depreciation and amortization)
−	Capital expenditures (fixed assets and other operating noncurrent assets)
+ or −	Incremental working capital
=	Free cash flows to the firm

EXHIBIT 6.5   Free Cash Flows to the Firm – Equity Only

For an ESE that has yet to achieve profitability and may still be in the process of developing viable operations, the timing and the amount of the cash flows that are projected by management are subject to considerable uncertainty and there is a high risk that the enterprise will not meet its targets. Also, the level of risk associated with the FCFF is likely to change over time as the firm moves through its various stages of growth. While using a single discount rate in a DCF model is common in practice, a more nuanced approach that adjusts the discount rate in view of the various stages in the company's development is generally more suitable for an ESE that is expected to undergo significant changes in its risk profile over the projection period.[12]

In our case study, we have identified three stages in terms of risk exposure:[13]

---

[12] The AICPA PE/VC Valuation Guide, 5.81 notes that while "most entities can be appropriately valued using a single discount rate," "some entities have evolving risk profiles and capital structures that may call for more complicated discount rate assumptions." We are of the view that the use of a dynamic model for discount rates that adapt to the evolving stage of the enterprise and to changes in capital structure is especially suitable for ESEs. On the development of a Cost of Capital that adjusts as the company moves towards its stable growth stage, see especially Aswath Damodaran, *The Dark Side of Valuation* (Wiley, 2018), pp. 290–296, 354–355.

[13] On a three-stage model in ESE valuation, see Andrew Metrick and Ayako Yasuda, *Venture Capital & the Finance of Innovation*, 2nd ed. (Wiley, 2011), as summarized on p. 212: "to perform a DCF analysis for a venture-backed company, we divide the company's life cycle into three parts: the venture period (while the company is still being funded by VCs), the rapid growth period (which immediately follows the VC exit) and the stable-growth period (when growth, margins and return on capital have settled down to industry averages)."

	1	2	3	4	5	6	7	8	9	10
EBIT $(1-t)$	(8,274)	(9,592)	(10,704)	(6,628)	4,277	8,527	13,976	20,242	26,644	32,286
+ Depreciation & Amortization	605	796	1,132	1,489	1,724	1,947	2,144	2,300	2,402	2,440
− Capital Expenditures	5,205	10,609	14,379	12,087	13,021	11,619	9,515	6,881	4,004	3,940
− Change in WC	706	1,505	2,032	1,626	1,733	1,685	1,444	1,000	387	399
= FCFF	(13,580)	(20,910)	(25,983)	(18,852)	(8,753)	(2,830)	5,161	14,661	24,655	30,387

EXHIBIT 6.6 Free Cash Flows to the Firm ($ Thousand)

- Stage 1: High growth with negative FCFF (Years 1–5). At this stage, the firm is growing revenues at rates significantly above the industry average while FCFF are negative. VC investors represent the primary source of funding for the firm, and their return expectations drive the firm's cost of capital. The discount rate is significantly above systematic risk and reflects the high-risk profile of the investment for VC market participants.
- Stage 2: Declining growth (Years 5–10). In the postexit years, and as the company moves toward a state of steady long-term growth, the discount rate is likely to decline together with the risk of the investment. The company now has access to the public capital markets. By the time the company reaches the mature growth stage, the high entity-specific risk premium no longer applies.[14] The discount rate in this stage can be modeled with a formula that makes the Year 5 discount rate gradually converge to the discount rate in the stage of steady long-term growth (Year 10+).
- Stage 3 (10+): As the company reaches a state of steady long-term growth, the discount rate will be comparable to that of guideline public companies with a similar risk profile.[15]

In our model, the discount rates have been de-risked of the risk of failure, which is modeled separately in the "Failure" scenario. The discount rates will therefore be significantly lower in the high-growth stage than if the risk of failure was still embedded in the related cash flows.

In a DCF, the discount rate is calculated as the weighted average of the enterprise's cost of equity and cost of debt (weighted average cost of capital or WACC). As noted previously, debt is typically not a significant component in an ESE's capital structure. Assuming no debt and corresponding tax deduction, the cost of capital for the ESE will coincide with its cost of equity. For enterprises with a complex capital structure including multiple classes/series of equity interests, it can be argued that the cost of equity related to preferred stock should be calculated separately from the cost of equity related to common stock, and so on for other equity interests. In practice, this is rarely done. On a case-by-case basis, a valuation analyst will need to weigh the benefits and drawbacks of adding a layer of complexity to the estimation process. For purposes of our discussion, we'll assume that all equity securities are considered as a single class, which is consistent with the expectation that they may end up being fully converted at exit, for instance in an IPO outcome.

There are two common methods for estimating the cost of equity for an enterprise: the Build-Up method and the Capital Asset Pricing method. Let's look at each methodology and how they may apply to ESE valuation.

Build-Up Method The Build-Up method assumes that the cost of equity consists of three components:[16]

---

[14] AICPA PE/VC Valuation Guide,. B.05.04: "By the time the company reaches the mature growth stage, the high entity-specific risk premium or venture capital rate of return used in calculating the discount rate would no longer apply."

[15] On modeling the stable growth phase, see Aswath Damodaran, *The Dark Side of Valuation* (Wiley, 2018), p. 350: "When you put your firm into stable growth, give it the characteristics of a stable growth firm. [. . .] With discount rates [. . .] this takes the form of using lower costs of debt and equity, and a higher debt ratio. With reinvestment, the key assumption is the return on capital that we assume for the stable growth phase."

[16] On the Build-up Method, see especially Shannon Pratt, and Roger J. Grabowski, "The Build-up Method," Chapter 9 in *Cost of Capital: Application and Examples* (Wiley, 2014), pp. 178–188.

1. Risk-free rate. The risk-free rate (RFR) is the rate of return that is available in the market on an investment that is considered free of default risk.[17] The RFR reflects the time value of money and is a nominal rate that includes expected inflation. For U.S.-based companies, this rate in the derivation of the cost of capital is typically established based on the yield to maturity of 20-year U.S. government bonds.[18] For the U.S. markets, the RFR can be obtained from the Risk-Free Rate Lookup Tool provided by Business Valuation Resources (free tool), as well as directly from federal information,[19] resources, and others. In the Racoon model, the RFR is 2.50%.

2. Systematic risk premiums. Systematic risk premiums are excess returns over the RFR that are meant to compensate market participants for risks that are systematically reflected in market prices and affect all investments in a group, not just an individual company. Under the Build-Up method, these include:

   ▪ Equity risk premium. The equity risk premium (ERP) is the average return that investors require over the RFR for accepting the higher variability in returns that are common for equity investments (i.e. the ERP reflects a minimum threshold for investors in order to be willing to invest).[20] The ERP is defined as:

   Equity Risk Premium = Expected Market Return − Risk Free Rate

   The expected market return (EMR) is typically estimated based on the historical series of returns on a broad-based, diversified portfolio of securities in the listed equity markets. In the United States, the EMR is typically measured based on the returns of the New York Stock Exchange Composite Index or the Standard & Poor's (S&P) 500 Index series. For global companies, the historical return series of the S&P Global 1200 Index or one of the MSCI Global Standard Indices are often used. In the Racoon model, the equity risk premium is estimated at 5.50%.

   ▪ Small stock risk premium (SSRP). The SSRP is the average return that investors require over the RFR for investing in a company that presents additional risk inherent to its size relative to the risk of the ERP reference portfolio, which typically consists of large company stocks. For a public company, size is generally represented by the company's market capitalization. For a private company that does not have listed securities, size may be measured by other factors that include, among others: revenue, book value

---

[17]On the risk-free rate as a component of the cost of equity, see Roger Grabowski, Carla Nunes, and James Harrington,"Risk-free Rate," Chapter 7 in *Cost of Capital: Application and Examples*, edited by Shannon Pratt and Roger J. Grabowski (Wiley, 2014), pp. 91–109.

[18]The 10-year and 30-year yields are also sometimes used, but they typically do not differ significantly from the 20-year data. The analyst should also consider the term of the risk-free rate in relation to the terms of the equity risk premium (ERP). Generally, if the 20-year yield is chosen for the RFR, then the ERP estimate should also be measured relative to 20-year yields. On the harmonization of the RFR and the ERP, see Shannon Pratt and Roger J. Grabowski, *Cost of Capital: Application and Examples* (Wiley, 2014), p. 92.

[19]The Federal Reserve (Fed) Statistical Release tracks 20-year yields. The link to its website is http://federalreserve.gov/releases/h15. The St. Louis branch of the Fed also tracks 20-year yields, see https://research.stlouisfed.org/fred2/series/GS20.

[20]On the equity risk premium, see Shannon Pratt and Roger J. Grabowski, "Equity Risk Premium," Chapter 8 in *Cost of Capital: Application and Examples* (Wiley, 2014), pp. 110–140.

of equity, net income, total assets, EBITDA, number of customers, and number of employees. In an ESE, revenues and number of employees are likely to be the key factors in size assessment and comparability. BVR's *Cost of Capital Tool* and Duff & Phelps's *Cost of Capital Navigator* use the CRSP (Center for Research in Security Prices) market return data set for estimating size premia. In the Racoon model, for example, we may assume that an SSRP of 4.0% should be used at inception, and that the small stock premium will gradually decline to zero by the time the company reaches its mature growth stage in Year 10.

- Other systematic risk premiums. These may include an industry risk premium (IRP) and a country risk premium (CRP), depending on the company's market, sources of capital, and supply chain. No other premium for systematic risk exposure is included in the Racoon model.

3. Company-specific risk premium (CSRP). The CSRP measures the individual subject company's risk characteristics relative to the typical risk characteristics of the companies that are included in the reference portfolio and that have already been reflected in systematic premium adjustments.[21] Company-specific risk adjustments may be due to the following factors, among others:
   - Variability of FCFF. If the firm's expected variability of FCFF is greater than that of the guideline companies, a CSRP premium is warranted and commonly accepted practice.
   - Leverage. Risk tends to increase as a company's D/E ratio increases.
   - Concentration of customer base.
   - Key person dependence.
   - Key supplier dependence.
   - Abnormal present or pending competition.
   - Pending regulatory changes.
   - Pending lawsuits.

Compared to the RFR, ERP, and to some extent the SSRP, the CSRP presents a much greater scope for estimation uncertainty and subjective evaluation. To the extent the Build-Up method is used in a DCF ESE valuation, it is critical for the analyst to establish a systematic process around its assessment and documentation, that includes both qualitative and quantitative considerations.

The AICPA PE/VC Valuation Guide suggests the use of calibration to the latest transaction price as a way to support the CSRP estimate. As noted in the AICPA PE/VC Valuation Guide, "Calibration is a tool which allows a CSRP to be identified at inception and provides a starting point for evaluating subsequent changes in the CSRP."[22] The MPF also notes that estimate of the CSRP is "typically the most subjective part of the derivation of the Cost of Equity capital and, therefore, documentation related to this feature should be the most extensive."[23]

For an ESE, the company-specific risk will vary depending on its stage of development and is expected to decline as the company grows and moves toward its mature stage. In fact,

---

[21] See Shannon Pratt and Roger J. Grabowski, "Company-Specific Risk," Chapter 16 in *Cost of Capital: Application and Examples* (Wiley, 2014), pp. 372–399. See especially the list of company-specific risk factors on p. 183.

[22] AICPE PE/VC Valuation Guide, 10.22.

[23] AMPF, A2.2.2.vii.

one of the advantages of using a dynamic model in the development of discount rates for an ESE is that the CSRP, and the SSRP, are likely to have limited impact on the present value of the company, since their effect is deployed mostly in the early years which are discounted at higher rates and have relatively lower impact on current fair value due to the small FCFF as a percentage of total FCFF before discounting.

Exhibit 6.7 shows the calculation of the cost of equity using the Build-Up method assuming an SSRP in the high-growth stage of 4.0%, which gradually declines to a stable long-term rate of 0.0%, and a CSRP of 8.0% in the high-growth stage, which declines to a steady-state CSRP of 1.5%.

Once the individual risk premia have been identified and measured, the cost of equity can be calculated as:

$$\text{Cost of Equity} = \text{Risk Free Rate} + \text{Systematic Risk Premia}$$
$$+ \text{Company-Specific Risk Premium}$$

For instance, in the mature growth stage starting in Year 10, we have

$$\text{Cost of Equity} = 2.5\%(\text{RFR}) + 5.5\%(\text{ERP}) + 0.0\%(\text{SSRP}) + 1.5\%(\text{CSRP}) = 9.5\%$$

The CSRP in Exhibit 6.7 has already been de-risked of the company's risk of failure, which is modeled in Scenario 2 of the valuation analysis. This results in a significantly lower value for the CSRP than if it had included the risk of failure. The annualized IRR with this method over the 10-year period is 15.89%.

The Build-Up method provides a high level of flexibility in the identification and treatment of factors that may impact the cost of equity for an enterprise, but is also subject to considerable estimation uncertainty, particularly as it pertains to the CSRP. The AICPA PE/VC Valuation Guide suggests that calibration can be used to anchor the CSRP estimate to market-based indications from the company's financing rounds.[24] The existence of a small stock factor in explaining higher target discount rates for smaller companies has also been

	RFR	ERP	SSRP	CSRP	Build-Up
Stage 1 – High Growth	2.50%	5.50%	4.00%	8.00%	20.00%
Stage 2 – Declining Growth					
Year 6	2.50%	5.50%	3.20%	4.10%	15.30%
Year 7	2.50%	5.50%	2.40%	2.54%	12.94%
Year 8	2.50%	5.50%	1.60%	1.92%	11.52%
Year 9	2.50%	5.50%	0.80%	1.67%	10.47%
Year 10	2.50%	5.50%	0.00%	1.50%	9.50%
Stage 3 – Steady State	2.50%	5.50%	0.00%	1.50%	9.50%

EXHIBIT 6.7   Cost of Equity – Build-Up Method

---

[24] AICPA PE/VC Valuation Guide, 10.22.

questioned in recent studies, although it continues to be a broadly accepted practice for financial reporting under ASC 820/IFRS 13.[25]

Capital Asset Pricing Model In its "pure" form, the capital asset pricing model (CAPM) assumes that the cost of equity consists of two components: the RFR, and the ERP, which reflects exclusively the risk related to the company's exposure to the equity markets (systematic risk).[26] Instead of having multiple risk premia as in the Build-Up method, the CAPM only recognizes the ERP, and assumes that any other risk exposure, including the company-specific risk under the Build-Up method, is "unsystematic" and can be fully eliminated by portfolio diversification. The cost of equity is described as:

$$\text{Cost of Equity} = \text{Risk-Free Rate} + \text{Beta} \times \text{Equity Risk Premium}$$

The RFR and the ERP are consistent with the inputs in the Build-Up method. Included here is Beta, which measures how the returns of a company vary in relation to the returns of a relevant market benchmark, for example, using the return of the S&P500 index (as a proxy for the U.S. equity market relative to the RFR). In this case, a Beta equal to 1.0 indicates that a 1% increase in the ERP will result in a 1% increase in the company's cost of equity. A Beta greater than 1.0 indicates that an increase by 1% in the ERP will result in an increase greater than 1% in the return of the reference company. Inversely, a Beta smaller than 1.0 means that an increase by 1% in the ERP will result in an increase smaller than 1% in the return of the reference company.

In a CAPM, Beta for an individual company is generally estimated based on an analysis of the Beta of the guideline public companies, which can be drawn from common data providers such as S&P Capital IQ, FactSet, PitchBook, Bloomberg.

For a public company that has debt in its capital structure, the Beta that is typically presented in public sources is shown after the effect of leverage (Levered Beta). The presence of debt in a company's structure amplifies the effect of any change in the ERP on the company's expected return. In order for the Betas of companies with different capital structures to be comparable, we need to remove the effect of financial leverage and calculate an adjusted asset Beta for the firm, that is, the Beta that would be expected if the company were financed only with equity capital (Asset Beta or Unlevered Beta). The Unlevered Beta is then re-levered with the specific level of financial leverage that is applicable to the company, to get to an estimate of the reference company's specific Beta value for the CAPM model.[27]

Exhibit 6.8 shows the calculation of the Beta metrics for Racoon Inc. based on a set of hypothetical guideline public companies (GPC).

---

[25]The principle that stocks with a smaller size can be expected to earn higher returns than stocks with a higher market capitalization has been subject to question by portfolio managers and in an academic context, but is still broadly accepted for financial reporting under GAAP/IFRS. The AICPE PE/VC Valuation Guide provides examples of a Cost of Capital construction that includes a small stock premium of 6.0% in 10.22-23, as part of the discussion of calibration as applied to a DCF model. Against the use of small stock premia, see Aswath Damodaran, "The Small-Cap Premium: Where is the Beef," *Musings on Markets*, April 11, 2015. See also Roger Grabowski and James Harrington, "Criticism of the Size Effect," in Chapter 15 in *Cost of Capital: Application and Examples*, edited by Shannon Pratt and Roger J. Grabowski (Wiley, 2014), pp. 331–362.

[26]Shannon Pratt and Roger J. Grabowski, "CAPM," Chapter 10 in *Cost of Capital: Application and Examples* (Wiley, 2014), pp. 189–201.

[27]Shannon Pratt and Roger J. Grabowski, "Unleveraging and Leveraging Equity Betas," Chapter 12 in *Cost of Capital: Application and Examples* (Wiley, 2014), pp. 243–268.

Company	Beta Levered	Equity Market Value ($ million)	Interest-Bearing Debt ($ million)	Tax Rate	Unlevered Beta	Enterprise Value ($ million)	Equity %	Debt %	Weighted Beta
Guideline Company 1	1.27	200	23	18.00%	1.17	223	89.89%	10.11%	0.06
Guideline Company 2	1.22	500	46	13.00%	1.13	546	91.60%	8.40%	0.14
Guideline Company 3	1.08	950	99	21.00%	1.00	1,049	90.53%	9.47%	0.23
Guideline Company 4	1.27	250	25	15.00%	1.17	275	90.81%	9.19%	0.07
Guideline Company 5	1.26	606	44	17.00%	1.19	649	93.29%	6.71%	0.17
Guideline Company 6	1.12	450	19	22.00%	1.08	469	95.92%	4.08%	0.12
Guideline Company 7	1.29	1,200	144	10.00%	1.17	1,344	89.29%	10.71%	0.34
Market-weighted industry capitalization		91.22%	8.78%		Total	4,556			1.12
Median industry capitalization		90.81%	9.19%						
Average industry capitalization		91.62%	8.38%						
Selected industry capitalization (rounded)		90.00%	10.00%						

Market cap-weighted beta	1.12
Median beta	1.17
Average beta	1.13
Selected beta – Unlevered	1.17
Tax rate	15.00%
Re-levered Beta	1.28

EXHIBIT 6.8 Beta Estimate from Guideline Public Companies

The Beta-levered column shows Beta values that can be obtained from a subscription database or other public database sets. For purposes of business valuation, Beta-levered values are typically calculated using a string of weekly returns for the guideline company and the reference portfolio over a period of two to five years. In some cases, valuation firms may develop their own calculation models to ensure that a period suitable with the specific valuation projections is considered. The equity market value is typically based on the market capitalization of the guideline company as of the valuation date. Interest-bearing debt is best measured using estimated market values, but in practice for private companies, the book value of debt is often used as a proxy. The tax rate is estimated based on the company's historical record or management's estimates. The unlevered Beta is then calculated as:

$$\text{Unlevered Beta} = \text{Levered Beta}/[1 + (1 - \text{Tax Rate}) \times (\text{Debt/Equity})]$$

As reflected in Exhibit 6.8, the median capitalization for the industry is approximately 90% equity and 10% debt. At this level of debt, the impact of financial leverage on Beta is likely to be significant. We can see from Exhibit 6.7 that the levered Beta, before the adjustment of financial leverage, is in the range of 1.08 to 1.29. At the top of the range, a 1% change in ERP will result in a 1.29% increase in the cost of equity for Guideline Company 7. Notice also that, as the debt/equity ratio increases, so generally does the levered Beta.

The unlevered Beta for each of the GPCs is also shown in Exhibit 6.8. After calculating summary statistics for our sample, including the (market cap weighted) average, the median, and straight mean, the analyst concludes on using the median value in our example model.

As a next step, the analyst needs to "re-lever" the selected asset Beta from the GPC analysis to an equity Beta for our reference company Racoon. To do so, the analyst uses the formula:

$$\text{Re-Levered Beta} = \text{Unlevered Beta} \times [1 + (1 - \text{Tax Rate}) (\text{Firm Debt/Firm Equity})]$$

To the extent the capital structure of Racoon consists exclusively of equity, the levered Beta will be equal to the unlevered Beta of 1.17. In our model, we assume that Racoon will maintain a 100% equity capitalization through Year 5, at which point its D/E ratio will start to converge toward the long-term structure of 10/90 consistent with the GPC reference group in Year 10. With a 10/90 capital structure, and a 15% tax rate, the re-levered Beta in Year 10 is:

$$\text{Re-Levered Beta} = 1.17 \times [1 + (1 - 0.15) \times (10/90)] = 1.28$$

Exhibit 6.9 shows the calculation of the cost of equity for Racoon using an RFR of 2.50%, an ERP of 5.50%, and a Beta of 1.28 as per our estimate above. With an ERP of 5.5%, each basis point increase in Beta results in 7.0 basis points of increase in the cost of equity.

The cost of equity that results from the CAPM method as described in Exhibit 6.9 is applicable to the company in the stable growth stage, once its capital structure is consistent with that of the industry. The Beta of 1.28 has been developed based on the Beta of guideline public companies that are likely to be suitable comparisons for Racoon in its mature stage. From this perspective, the cost of equity that results from the CAPM method can be looked at as the "stable growth" cost of capital to discount Year 10 cash flows and the company's terminal value in Year 10.

RFR	Beta	ERP	Cost of Equity
2.50	1.28	5.50	9.5

EXHIBIT 6.9   CAPM Method – Cost of Equity – Racoon Inc.

Modified CAPM Method   The cost of equity that results from the CAPM in its "pure" form reflects the risk of the company in its mature stage (Year 10+) and is not suitable to discount cash flows in earlier years of the ESE life, which would require a higher discount rate as in the Build-Up method.[28]

A fundamental assumption behind the CAPM is that the company's risk profile can be explained, to at least a large extent, in terms of the general trends in market prices and the company's structural correlation with the market. The CAPM assumes that a market participant will be able to eliminate other company-specific risks (for instance, the risk of not meeting a regulatory milestone, or credit risk) by holding a well-diversified portfolio of investments. Also, the CAPM assumes that markets are "efficient," and that the mechanism of demand and supply operates seamlessly in the markets to ensure that market prices fully reflect all information that may have an impact on prices as soon as the information becomes available.

For ESEs, however, company-specific factors are often more relevant drivers of valuation than factors that relate to the general market environment. All of these factors make the CAPM method in its pure form generally of limited use in the earlier stages of ESE valuation, particularly in the high growth period of Years 1–5. There are two methods for modifying the "original" CAPM that are especially suitable for ESE valuation.

Diversification-Adjusted CAPM (DA-CAPM)   This method adjusts the Beta of a company to generate a total Beta that reflects the risk under the CAPM for an equity holder who is completely undiversified.[29] As the company moves through its stages of growth, the company is expected to have access to a larger, more diversified pool of investors, and the correlation coefficient in the Beta calculation will increase accordingly. In Year 10, the market Beta (correlation coefficient of 1) will apply.

Exhibit 6.10 presents the estimate of Beta and the cost of equity under the DA-CAPM model, assuming a correlation with the market of 0.30 and a constant market Beta of 1.17 in Years 1–5 (no debt), trending in linear fashion to a Beta of 1.28 in Year 10 (D/E of 10/90).

In each year, total Beta is calculated by dividing the market Beta by its correlation factor. For instance, in Year 6, we have:

$$\text{Total Beta} = \text{Market Beta/Correlation Factor} = 1.19/0.70 = 1.70$$

---

[28] On the Modified CAPM, see especially Shannon Pratt and Roger J. Grabowski, "CAPM," Chapter 10 in *Cost of Capital: Application and Examples* (Wiley, 2014), pp. 196–199.

[29] The Total Beta method is developed and applied to the valuation of a software early stage company by Aswath Damodaran, "Baby Steps: Young and Start-Up Companies," Chapter 10 in *The Dark Side of Valuation* (Wiley, 2018), pp. 294–295.

Year	Market Beta	Correlation with Market	Total Beta	RFR	ERP	COE
Year 1	1.17	0.30	3.90	2.50%	5.50%	23.9%
Year 2	1.17	0.30	3.90	2.50%	5.50%	23.9%
Year 3	1.17	0.40	2.92	2.50%	5.50%	18.5%
Year 4	1.17	0.40	2.92	2.50%	5.50%	18.5%
Year 5	1.17	0.50	2.34	2.50%	5.50%	15.3%
Year 6	1.19	0.70	1.70	2.50%	5.50%	11.9%
Year 7	1.21	0.70	1.73	2.50%	5.50%	12.0%
Year 8	1.23	0.80	1.54	2.50%	5.50%	11.0%
Year 9	1.25	0.80	1.56	2.50%	5.50%	11.1%
Year 10	1.28	1.00	1.28	2.50%	5.50%	9.5%

EXHIBIT 6.10   Cost of Equity: Effect of No Portfolio Diversification

The annualized IRR with this method over the 10-year period of 15.44% is comparable to the annualized IRR of 15.89% that we obtain from the Build-Up method. The target rate in Year 10 of 9.52% in turn is comparable with the target rate of the "pure" CAPM method and with the Build-Up rate in Year 10.

Modified CAPM with Additional Risk Premia   The CAPM can also be modified to include consideration of an SSRP, a CSRP, and other premia as applicable:

Cost of Equity = Risk-Free Rate + (Beta × Equity Risk Premium)

+ Small Stock Risk Premium + Company-Specific Risk Premium

Exhibit 6.11 shows the discount rates that we obtain by adding the SSRP and the CSRP to the CAPM rates in our dynamic model.

For instance, in Year 6, the discount rate is calculated as:

Cost of Equity = 2.50% + (1.19 × 5.5%) + 3.2% + 2.8% = 15.03%

Cost of Equity – Modified CAPM	RFR	ERP	Beta	SSRP	CSRP	Cost of Equity Modified CAPM
Stage 1 – High Growth	2.50%	5.50%	1.17	4.00%	7.00%	19.9%
Stage 2 – Declining Growth						
Year 6	2.50%	5.50%	1.19	3.20%	2.80%	15.0%
Year 7	2.50%	5.50%	1.21	2.40%	1.12%	12.7%
Year 8	2.50%	5.50%	1.23	1.60%	0.45%	11.3%
Year 9	2.50%	5.50%	1.25	0.80%	0.18%	10.4%
Year 10	2.50%	5.50%	1.28	0.00%	0.00%	9.5%
Stage 3 – Steady State	2.50%	5.50%	1.28	0.00%	0.00%	9.5%

EXHIBIT 6.11   Modified CAPM with Additional Risk Premias

Compared to the Build-Up method, the Modified CAPM is less sensitive to the estimate of the CSRP as certain risk features that are company-specific, most notably the risk associated with leverage, are in fact incorporated in Beta. In the model of Exhibit 6.11, the CSRP declines as the company approaches its mature stage of growth, and both the SSRP and CSRP converge to zero in Year 10.

In the case of Racoon, we'll use the Modified CAPM in Exhibit 6.11 to estimate the discount rate associated with each annual cash flow in the model.

Cost of Debt

For an ESE, debt is not typically a significant component in a company's capital structure. In our model, the cost of debt becomes relevant as the company moves toward its stage of stable growth. In Year 10, we assume that the cost of debt will be consistent with the cost of debt of the GPC group. Assuming that all the GPCs have rated corporate debt from an established rating agency such as S&P, Fitch or Moody's, we can estimate a synthetic credit rating based on the GPC rating and determine a cost of debt by adding the associated default spread to the RFR. In our example, the weighted average cost of debt for Racoon is 5.5% on a pretax basis (4.68% after tax).

Weighted Average Cost of Capital

We now have all the elements for calculating the weighted average cost of capital for Racoon using the following formula:

$$\text{WACC} = [\text{Cost of Equity} \times E/(E + D)] + [\text{Cost of Debt } (1 - t) \times D/(E + D)]$$

Exhibit 6.12 shows the cost of capital for Racoon based on our dynamic four-stage model.

For instance, in Year 7 the cost of capital is calculated as:

$$\text{WACC} = [12.67\% \times 96\%] + [5.5\% \times (1 - 0.15) \times 4\%] = 12.35\%$$

Step 3: Terminal Value

The term for Racoon to reach stable, long-term growth in our model is 10 years. In order to complete the cash flow estimate, the analyst will also have to generate an estimate of a terminal value, defined as the estimated value of the firm at the end of the projection period. The estimate of terminal value is especially critical for an ESE, where terminal value often represents a very significant portion of the total value of the enterprise. For an ESE, there are two common methods for estimating terminal value.

Long-Term Growth Method   In a Long-Term Growth method (LTGM), terminal value is estimated based on the present value of estimated future cash flows. This method assumes that the company continues to operate as a going concern. After the discrete projection period, cash flows grow at a constant rate for the long term or indefinitely (in "perpetuity") and the cost of capital is also constant. Due to the mechanics of discounting, there is not a material difference in the resulting value calculation beyond 20 or 30 years of projections. A common variant of

					Cost of Capital					
	1	2	3	4	5	6	7	8	9	20
Cost of Equity	19.91%	19.91%	19.91%	19.91%	19.91%	15.03%	12.67%	11.32%	10.37%	9.52%
Proportion of Equity	100.00%	100.00%	100.00%	100.00%	100.00%	98.00%	96.00%	94.00%	92.00%	90.00%
After-tax Cost of Debt	0.00%	0.00%	0.00%	0.00%	0.00%	4.68%	4.68%	4.68%	4.68%	4.68%
Proportion of Debt	0.00%	0.00%	0.00%	0.00%	0.00%	2.00%	4.00%	6.00%	8.00%	10.00%
Cost of Capital	19.91%	19.91%	19.91%	19.91%	19.91%	14.82%	12.35%	10.92%	9.92%	9.03%
Cumulative WACC Factor	119.91%	143.78%	172.41%	206.74%	247.90%	284.65%	319.81%	354.74%	389.93%	425.14%

EXHIBIT 6.12   Cost of Capital – Racoon Inc.

the LTGM is the Gordon Growth Model (GGM), in which the terminal value is calculated as:

$$\text{Terminal Value using Gordon Growth Model} = CF_t(1 + g)/(k - g)$$

where:

CF = cash flow commensurate with k, the discount rate. In our case, the CF is measured by the Free Cash Flow to the Firm in Year 10.

k = discount rate commensurate with the free cash flow

g = long-term sustainable growth rate

t = terminal period in the explicit forecast period (Year 10 in our example)

In our example, given projected cash flows of $30,387 ($ thousand) at the end of Year 10 (Exhibit 6.6), a discount rate of 9.03%, and a growth rate of 3%, the GGM Terminal Value can be calculated as:

$$\text{Terminal Value (\$ thousand)} = (\$30,387 \times 1.03)/(0.0903 - 0.03) = \$518,919$$

It is important to note that, for some companies, the growth rate may also be negative (a firm may be projected to eventually go out of business).

Use of Earnings or Revenue Multiples Alternatively, the capitalization of a revenue or income parameter (net income, EBIT, EBITDA) may be used, determined with reference to the valuation multiples that can be observed in the market for guideline public companies. For instance, assuming the analyst selects a current GPC multiple of EBITDA of 14× as representative of the GPC group, and given Racoon's EBITDA (EBIT + Depreciation and Amortization) of $40.4 million in Year 10, the Terminal value in our example could be calculated as:

$$\text{Terminal Value (Year 10) (\$ thousand)} = 14 \times \$40,423 = \$565,922$$

A multiple method may be applied in the practice of venture capital valuation to estimate the exit value of the firm, for instance, at the end of Year 5, when the IPO event is expected to take place. The use of earnings or revenue multiples is frequent in the practice of financial reporting and in valuations related to business transactions. The IPEV Guide recognizes its frequent use in practice and notes that:

> For enterprises that have sustainable earnings, it would be more appropriate to utilize an earnings multiple; however, for enterprises that have established operations but have not yet obtained sustainable profitability, a multiple of revenue may be appropriate to determine Fair Value. A revenue multiple is commonly based on an assumption as to the "normalized" level of earnings that can be generated from that revenue. [...] This may involve the use of adjusted historic revenue, using a forecast level of revenue, or applying a sustainable profit margin to current or forecast revenues. The most appropriate revenues to use in this valuation technique would be those likely to be used by a prospective market participant purchaser of the business.[30]

Using current market multiples to estimate the terminal value or the exit value of a firm, however, has been challenged, particularly in the case of ESE valuation, as it may result in

---

[30]See IPEV Guidelines, 3.4 Multiples, "Use of Earnings Multiples" and "Use of a Revenue Multiple."

an overstatement of enterprise value. The AICPA PE/VC Valuation Guide, for instance, notes that:

> *Capitalization multiples are frequently used in calculating a terminal value for use in the income approach. However, because neither the growth rate nor the required rate of return for the stock are expected to remain constant, this method is not ideal for estimating the terminal value for early stage companies. In many cases, the cash flows provided for a portfolio company cover only the next three to five years, which is too short a time frame to bring the portfolio company into the mature growth stage. Furthermore, by the time the portfolio company reaches the mature growth stage, the high entity-specific risk premium or venture capital rate of return used in calculating the discount rate would no longer apply.*[31]

Raymond Rath further explains:

> *For a company in a high growth industry, market multiples would be expected to capture rapid growth in the near future and normal growth into the indefinite future. Using these multiples to estimate terminal value, the residual enterprise value may not be appropriate as rapid growth was incorporated twice: once in the cash flow projections over the projection period and again in the market multiple used in calculating the residual enterprise value.*[32]

The AICPA PE/VC Valuation Guide encourages the analyst to consider a variety of methods for estimating the terminal value and to select the most appropriate based on reasoned judgment.[33]

Terminal Value at Exit In addition to the terminal value at Year 10, a VC investor is also likely to focus its attention on the value of the company at exit, namely on the terminal value at the end of Year 5 in our model. From the perspective of a VC investor, the terminal value at exit (Year 5) is likely to mark the end of the holding period for the reference company and is going to drive the calculation of the investor's expected return on the investment. Under the Long-Term Growth model and the discount rates of the modified CAPM in Exhibit 6.11, the terminal value at the end of Year 5 can be estimated by discounting the cash flows in Years 6–10 back to the end of Year 5, each at its respective discount rate, and adding the discounted Year 10 terminal value as follows:

Terminal Value (Year 5) ($ thousand) = sum of:

Year 6: $-2,830/1.1482$

Year 7: $\$5,161/(1.1482 \times 1.1235)$

Year 8: $\$14,661/(1.1482 \times 1.1235 \times 1.1092)$

Year 9: $\$24,655/(1.1482 \times 1.1235 \times 1.1092 \times 1.0992)$

Year 10: $(\$30,387 + \$518,919)/(1.1482 \times 1.1235 \times 1.1092 \times 1.0992 \times 1.0903)$

$= \$347,756$

---

[31] AICPE PE/VC Valuation Guide, B.05.04.

[32] See Raymond Rath, "Private Company Valuation," Chapter 9 in *Equity Asset Valuation*, edited by Jerald Pinto, Elaine Henry, Thomas Robinson, and John D. Stowe (Wiley, 2015), p. 533.

[33] AICPA PE/VC Valuation Guide, B.05.04.

In the case of Racoon, the estimated value of the firm at the end of Year 5 is $347.8 million, which represents an implied 3.46× multiple of Year 5 revenues.

Step 4. Calculation of Present Value of FCFF

The next stage in the model consists of the calculation of the present value of the FCFF stream, by discounting the FCFF using the discount rates in Exhibit 6.12.

Exhibit 6.13 presents the calculation of the present value of FCFF over the 10-year period of the model. In our simplified model, we have assumed that annual cash flows are generated at the end of each annual period, and that the discount factor applies to the full year.[34] Note how the cost of capital decreases over time as the company benefits from: a decrease in enterprise risk as the company moves toward its stable growth phase; attracting investors that have a more diversified portfolio; decrease in operating risk; and increase in financial leverage.

STEP 5: ADJUSTMENTS

The estimated fair value of the firm should account for any adjustments which are related to assets and liabilities that are not part of the company's ordinary business activities. These may include the following.

Cash and Marketable Securities

If the cash flows are based on operating income (free cash flows to the firm) or noncash net income, cash and marketable securities that do not play a function as part of working capital have not been included in the present value and should be added to the PV as an adjustment. An ESE that has had a recent round of financing may have a significant amount of cash on hand to finance future operations. This cash needs to be added to the present value of FCFF in the enterprise valuation.

Cross Holdings in Other Companies

Minority interests in other companies need to be added. Other adjustments may need to take place for majority positions (depending on accounting method, consolidation versus equity, etc.).

Potential Liabilities (Not Treated as Debt)

There may be off-balance-sheet liabilities that may reduce the value of the firm, such as employee and customer-related lawsuits, environmental liabilities and patent infringement lawsuits.

---

[34]In the practice of valuation, it is common to assume that annual cash flows are spread evenly through the year, and the discount rate is typically adjusted to reflect cash flow earned as of mid-year (the "mid-period convention"). For simplicity, we have used the fullperiod convention in our example.

					ESTIMATED CASHFLOWS					
	1	2	3	4	5	6	7	8	9	10
FCFF	$ (13,580)	$ (20,910)	$ (25,983)	$ (18,852)	$ (8,753)	$ (2,830)	$ 5,161	$ 14,661	$ 24,655	$ 30,387
Terminal Value (end of Year)					$ 347,756					$ 518,919
Discount Factor	0.8340	0.6955	0.5800	0.4837	0.4034	0.3513	0.3127	0.2819	0.2565	0.2352
Present Value	$ (11,324)	$ (14,543)	$ (15,071)	$ (9,118)	$ (3,531)	$ (994)	$ 1,614	$ 4,133	$ 6,323	$ 129,205
PV of Cash Flows for the Firm	= $ 86,693									

EXHIBIT 6.13 Discounted Cash Flows Model–PV of Cash Flows ($ Thousand)

FIRM VALUATION	
Value of Firm – PV of Cash Flows	$ 86,693
+ Cash and Marketable Securities	$ 8,000
– Value of Debt	$ –
Value of Equity	$ 94,693

EXHIBIT 6.14 Equity Value After Adjustments ($ Thousand)

Scenario	Case	Value	Probability of Occurrence	Fair Value Contribution
Scenario 1	Survival	$ 94,693	70.00%	$ 66,285
Scenario 2	Failure	$ –	30.00%	$ –
			Fair Value Estimate	$ 66,285

EXHIBIT 6.15 Probability-Weighted Valuation ($ Thousand)

Step 6. Firm Value – Survival Scenario

Exhibit 6.14 presents the adjusted value of the firm, after considering the effect of the adjustments under Step 5 earlier. In our example, we have assumed that cash of $8 million needs to be added to the present value of future cash flows in the estimate of the company's value. No other assets or liabilities need to be included in total value under Step 5.

The estimated value of the firm under the "Survival" scenario is $94.7 million, calculated as:

$$\text{Value of Equity (after adjustments)} = \$86,693,000 + \$8,000,000 = \$94,693,000$$

Step 7. Probability-Weighted Valuation

At this point, our analyst can apply a probability-weighted method to estimate the value of the company after considering both the "survival" and the "failure" scenarios (Exhibit 6.15).

The analyst concludes that Racoon has an estimated fair value of $66.3 million as of the measurement date.

THE INVESTOR PERSPECTIVE: RECONCILING DCF RESULTS WITH THE VENTURE CAPITAL METHOD

Let's now focus on the perspective of an investor that is considering whether to buy an interest in Racoon. This investor will use the venture capital method to estimate a postmoney valuation on which to base its negotiation of an ownership interest in the firm. As we discussed in Chapter 4, the VC method starts from the "survival" case value to come to a postmoney valuation for the company that considers the probability of failure and the expected dilution effect of future financing rounds.

[1]	Initial value of target company	$ 94,693	From DCF Model: Equity Value
[2]	Exit value of target company	$ 347,756	From DCF Model: Exit Value
[3]	Time to exit (years)	5	From DCF Model: Time to Exit
[4]	Target return	29.72%	IRR based on [1], [2], and [3]
[5]	Target TVPI	3.67	$= (1 + [4])^{\wedge}[3]$
[6]	Probability of failure	30%	input
[7]	Required return	20.78%	$= \{[[5] \times (1 - [6])]^{\wedge}(1/[3])\} - 1$
[8]	Required TVPI	2.57	$= (1 + [7])^{\wedge}[3]$
[9]	Retention	60%	input
[10]	Postmoney valuation	$ 56,816	$= [2] \times [9]/[5]$

EXHIBIT 6.16 Venture Capital Method ($ Thousand)

Exhibit 6.16 presents the estimated postmoney valuation of Racoon under the venture capital method.

Items [1] and [2] show the value of the company in the survival scenario on the measurement date and at exit at the end of Year 5 based on Exhibits 6.13 and 6.14. With a time to exit of five years, an entry valuation of $94.7 million (before accounting for the probability of failure), and an exit value of $347.8 million, we can calculate a target IRR of 29.72% and a Target Multiple of Invested Capital (TVPI) of 3.67× for a VC investor. Using the VC method, and assuming a probability of failure of 30%, these performance metrics translate into a required return and required TVPI for venture capital investors of 20.78% and 2.57×, respectively. Assuming a retention rate of 60% (dilution at 40%), an exit value for the target company of $347.8 million results in a postmoney valuation of $56.8 million as of the measurement date. This amount is lower than the analyst's estimate of $66.3 million (Exhibit 6.15) due to the effect of expected dilution. An investor that acquires 10% of the company on the valuation date based on the postmoney valuation of $56.8 million and that exits at Year 5 at a valuation of $347.8 million would realize a return of 20.78%, considering both the company's probability of failure and the expected effects of dilution.

From a different perspective, a VC investor may want to know what the required ownership percentage is in the company that would allow it to obtain its minimum required return or multiple of invested capital, giving consideration to the exit valuation at Year 5 implied in the DCF model, the company's expected probability of failure, and the investor's expected dilution by the time of exit. Let's assume, for instance, that an investor is planning to contribute $1 million to Racoon in a forthcoming Series C round. The investor has a required return of 25% over a five-year time horizon, corresponding to a required TVPI of 3.05×. The investor expects the company to be valued at $347.8 million in an IPO exit in Year 5. The investor also expects a dilution of 40% (retention rate of 60%) by the time of exit, and a probability of failure with zero proceeds for the company of 30%. Given these assumptions, the investor would like to determine what is the minimum ownership share that it needs to negotiate in exchange for its $1 million investment in order to achieve its required return and required TVPI at exit. As illustrated in Exhibit 6.17, the investor in this case will need to achieve a target return of 34.2% and a target TVPI of 4.36× to reach its required return and required TVPI objectives. Given an exit valuation for the company of $347.8 million as per our DCF model, the investor needs to acquire a minimum equity stake of 2.09% of the company with its $1 million investment to reach its required return. The company's postmoney valuation should be $47.9 million or lower to justify this investment.

[1]	Exit value of target company	$ 347,756	DCF Model
[2]	Time to exit (years)	5	input
[3]	Probability of failure	30%	input
[4]	Retention	60%	input
[5]	Required return/Cost of capital	25.0%	input
[6]	Required TVPI	3.05	$= (1 + [5])^{\wedge}[2]$
[7]	Target TVPI	4.36	$= [6]/(1 - [3])$
[8]	Target return	34.2%	IRR based on [2] and [7]
[9]	Postmoney valuation	$ 47,860	$= [1] \times [4]/[7]$
[10]	Invested capital	$ 1,000	input
[11]	Required ownership	2.09%	$=[10]/[9]$

EXHIBIT 6.17   Required Return and Required Ownership ($ Thousand)

DCF MODEL AND CALIBRATION

In the case of a DCF model, similar to the OPM method under the market approach, calibration to the price of a latest financing round can help strengthen the model's profile by anchoring it to market-based inputs. While not common in current practice, a calibration model can be set up to backsolve from the implied enterprise valuation of the latest round of financing into key DCF inputs such as the CSRP or the probability of failure.[35]

Calibration can also be used to estimate the value of the company at subsequent measurement periods based on the then-current market conditions. This procedure may be especially useful if no recent rounds of financing have occurred and no recent pricing point from the company's own securities is available at the time of the subsequent measurement date.

For instance, let's assume that we are now at the end of Year 1 in the model. No other financing has occurred since the Series B round, and we are now asked to revalue Racoon. In the absence of a reliable pricing point from a recent round, we can now go back to our initial DCF model in Exhibit 6.13 and "calibrate" it by reviewing the original inputs in light of the current circumstances of our company and of the market.

Let's assume, for example, that the risk-free rate and the cost of debt need to be revised downward by 0.5% to 2.0% and 5.0%, respectively. Also, the risk of failure for the company has declined to 25%. Exhibit 6.18 illustrates the updated cost of capital for the company.

Exhibit 6.19 illustrates the updated DCF model, with cash flows discounted at the rates in Exhibit 6.18.

---

[35]The AICPA PE/VC Valuation Guide, 10.3: "Calibration to the transaction price is required when the initial transaction for an investment represents fair value" and that "in the next measurement period it typically would not be appropriate to ignore the multiple implied by the transaction [...]. Instead, at subsequent measurement dates, the valuation would consider the company's progress and changes in observable market data to estimate the fair value under current market conditions." See also AICPA PE/VC Valuation Guide 10.22: "In the discounted cash flow method, the implied transaction IRR provides strong evidence to support the company-specific risk premium, one of the most judgmental components of the WACC, or discount rate which will be used to estimate fair value at subsequent measurement dates. [...] Calibration is a tool which allows a CSRP to be identified at inception and provides a starting point for evaluating subsequent changes in the CSRP."

COST OF CAPITAL

	2	3	4	5	6	7	8	9	10
Cost of Equity	19.41%	19.41%	19.41%	19.41%	14.53%	12.17%	10.82%	9.87%	9.02%
Proportion of Equity	100.00%	100.00%	100.00%	100.00%	98.00%	96.00%	94.00%	92.00%	90.00%
After-tax Cost of Debt	0.00%	0.00%	0.00%	0.00%	4.25%	4.25%	4.25%	4.25%	4.25%
Proportion of Debt	0.00%	0.00%	0.00%	0.00%	2.00%	4.00%	6.00%	8.00%	10.00%
Cost of Capital	19.41%	19.41%	19.41%	19.41%	14.33%	11.86%	10.43%	9.42%	8.54%
Cumulative WACC Factor	119.41%	142.59%	170.26%	203.31%	232.44%	260.00%	287.11%	314.16%	340.99%

EXHIBIT 6.18 Updated Cost of Capital with Revised Inputs

	Estimated Cash Flows								
	2	3	4	5	6	7	8	9	10
FCFF	$ (20,910)	$ (25,983)	$ (18,852)	$ (8,753)	$ (2,830)	$ 5,161	$ 14,661	$ 24,655	$ 30,387
Terminal Value (end of year)									$ 565,058
Discount Factor	0.8374	0.7013	0.5873	0.4919	0.4302	0.3846	0.3483	0.3183	0.2933
Present Value	$ (17,511)	$ (18,223)	$ (11,072)	$ (4,305)	$ (1,217)	$ 1,985	$ 5,106	$ 7,848	$ 174,624
PV of Cash Flows	$ 137,234								

EXHIBIT 6.19 Calibration in Subsequent Measurement – PV of Cash Flows ($ Thousand)

Scenario	Case	Estimated Fair Value	Probability of Occurrence	Fair Value Contribution
Scenario 1	Survival	$ 143,234	75.00%	$ 107,425
Scenario 2	Failure	$ –	25.00%	$ –
			Fair Value Estimate	$ 107,425

EXHIBIT 6.20 Calibration – Scenario Analysis ($ Thousand)

The decrease in the cost of capital, which results from the decrease in the RFR and in the cost of debt, has the result of increasing the present value of FCFF to $137.2 million. Assuming a cash adjustment of $6 million, the adjusted PV of cash flows is ($ million):

$$\text{Value of Equity (Survival Scenario)} = \$137.2 + \$6.0 = \$143.2$$

The probability-weighted fair value of the company is now $107.4 million calculated as show in Exhibit 6.20.

Documentation and Disclosure Requirements

The development of a DCF model involves significant accounting estimates and relies heavily on unobservable inputs in valuation. Under ASC 820, investment companies such as VC funds are required to include in their financial statements' quantitative information about the significant unobservable inputs used in their Level 3 investments. Such requirement is usually satisfied with a table that includes, for each investment class, the aggregate fair values by valuation technique used, and, for each technique, a listing of the unobservable inputs, the range of inputs used, and a weighted average of those inputs. Examples of unobservable inputs that may have to be disclosed include:

- Revenue growth rates
- Estimates concerning capital expenditures
- Adjusted valuation multiples (revenue or EBITDA)
- Probability of failure
- Correlations
- Term to declining growth and stable growth stages
- Company-specific risk and small stock risk premia as components of the discount rate
- Cost of debt

From a financial statement reporting perspective, it is critical for management of the reporting entity, such as a VC fund, and for a valuation analyst, to be able to maintain adequate documentation in support of the key assumptions and inputs in a DCF model. The Mandatory Performance Framework (MPF) provides specific instructions on the documentation requirements concerning the discount rate derivation, the estimate of revenue growth rates, the selection of and adjustments to, valuation multiples, and the estimate of terminal value. The MPF's requirements are especially extensive concerning the documentation of the discount rates. According to the MPF, the valuation professional, at a minimum, must document in writing within the work file, among others:[36]

For the cost of equity:

- The rationale for the selection of a discount rate or model
- The source of the risk-free rate used in the calculation and the rationale for its selection
- The source or calculation of the equity risk premium and rationale for its use
- An explanation of the calculation of beta of the guideline public companies (or other industry risk adjustments) and the rationale for the method used (or rationale for the use of another source of beta) when using CAPM
- The rationale for selecting the specific beta when using CAPM, including "adjusted betas"
- The amount of size premium, the source of the premium data, and the rationale for selecting the concluded premium (even if that premium is zero) when applicable
- The amount of company-specific risk adjustment, if any, the rationale for application of the adjustment, and the objective and quantitative data sets used to develop the concluded company-specific adjustment

For the cost of debt:

- The sources of data used and the rationale for use of the sources
- The rationale to support the selection of the pretax cost of debt and any additional source documents
- The rationale for the statutory tax rate used to adjust the pretax rate to an after-tax rate, if applicable

For the capital structure:

- The capital structures of the guideline public companies, industry sector, or subject company and rationale for selection of the time frame over which they are measured
- The market participant capital structure selected in the calculation of the WACC and the rationale for its selection

CONCLUSION

In this chapter, we have seen how the DCF model can be applied to the valuation of an ESE under the fair value standard for financial reporting of ASC 820/IFRS 13 with certain key characteristics:

- The DCF model should reflect the evolution of the firm through its stages of growth over time. Key inputs such as revenue growth rates, discount rates, operating margins, reinvestment rates may change as the company moves forward in its development to eventually reach its stage of long-term stable growth.

---

[36]Application of the Mandatory Performance Framework for the Certified in Entity and Intangible Valuations Credential, A2.2: Discount Rate Derivation.

- The cash flows that are typically used in a DCF model for an ESE are the free cash flows to the firm (FCFF).
- A scenario analysis that isolates the risk of failure from the discount rate used in the DCF valuation is often advisable in an ESE valuation.
- In most cases, revenue is the key metric that is driving growth projections, expenditures, and cash flows. A DCF model for an ESE is likely to include multiple stages of growth with distinct revenue growth rates.
- Taxes are factored into the valuation based on an estimate of the company's effective or statutory tax rate. Depending on the jurisdictions, taxes may be adjusted to consider the tax benefit of net operating losses accumulated over time.
- Multiple discount rates may have to be estimated to match each "stage" in the enterprise's projection period. The company-specific risk premium is likely to be a significant component of the discount rate in the early years of the model and decline as the company approaches its mature growth stage. A diversification-adjusted CAPM, while not common in current practice for financial reporting, may provide an alternative approach that is not as reliant on a CSRP estimate for estimating the discount rate.
- The annualized discount rate through the expected VC exit event should be consistent with the target rate of return of VC investors in the "survival" scenario under the Venture Capital method. The VC method can be used to generate an estimate of the current postmoney valuation of the company that is implied in the DCF model.
- Although ESEs typically do not have debt in the current period, the analyst may want to consider including debt in the analysis. To the extent that the guideline public companies are leveraged, there may be an expectation that debt will eventually be included in the long-term capital structure of the company.
- The use of market multiples to estimate terminal value is common in practice, but may lead to double count growth and overestimate company value.
- The DCF method as a way to estimate enterprise/equity value can be combined with an allocation methodology to estimate the value of individual classes/series of shares and of other equity-like instruments.
- Calibration can be used to anchor a DCF model to the price of a transaction in the company's own shares. The DCF model can then be updated at subsequent measurement dates to reflect changes in market and company-specific conditions.

Overall, the DCF method can provide a useful tool in the valuation of an ESE, provided there is an adequate basis to develop cash flow estimates and discount rates. The DCF method is especially useful if the price points coming from the company's financing rounds are stale or reflect transactions that are not at arm's length.

CHAPTER 7

Asset Accumulation Method

Antonella Puca

Mark Zyla

The market and the income approaches to business valuation consider the enterprise as an entity in its own right, a legal "person" that can enter into contracts, assume liabilities, and hold title to assets, and that enhances the value of its individual resources with synergies to realize its business purpose. This chapter looks at the enterprise from a different perspective, as an aggregate of individual classes of assets and liabilities that maintain their own distinctive features and need to be valued on an individual basis in order to assess total enterprise value. The assed-based approach invites us to break through the corporate veil and look at individual factors that drive the value of an enterprise: How is value generated? What are the key assets of the enterprise? What are the entity's sources of capital and how are they remunerated? How are the risks of the enterprise reflected in the balance sheet and are there additional liabilities that need to be considered?

This chapter presents the application of the Asset Accumulation method (AAM) (a type of asset-based approach) to a sample early stage enterprise (ESE). Under the AAM, the equity value of the enterprise under ASC 820/IFRS 13 is equivalent to the fair value of its assets net of liabilities. The fair values of assets and liabilities are estimated using a variety of valuation methods, which often involve a combination of the cost, market, and income approaches. The AAM concludes a value for the enterprise on a controlling ownership basis and is especially suitable in enterprise valuation for an acquisition that is structured as an asset purchase transaction. It can also be used in investment valuation, generally in combination with other approaches.

As we walk through the various methodologies for asset valuation in our case study, we discuss the documentation that is required to support a valuation performed under the Mandatory Performance Framework (MPF).[1] As discussed in Chapter 2, the MPF is a framework that is designed to provide guidance on the type and amount of documentation

---

[1] The Mandatory Performance Framework consists of the provisions included in the Mandatory Performance Framework for the Certified in Entity and Intangible Valuations (CEIV) Credential document and of the related guidance on the Application of the Mandatory Performance Framework (AMPF) for the CEIV Credential (collectively, the "MPF"), both issued in January 2017 under the umbrella of the

that should be gathered in support of the analysis performed by a valuation professional in a business valuation and in the valuation of intangible assets.[2] The MPF reflects the combined effort of the American Institute of Certified Public Accountants (AICPA), the American Society of Appraisers (ASA), and the Royal Institute of Chartered Surveyors (RICS), and is mandatory for valuation analysts who hold the Certified in Entity and Intangible Valuation (CEIV) credential. More broadly, the framework can be looked at as a set of sound practices on the documentation to gather to support valuation amounts and disclosures in the financial statements, and how to meet regulatory and board due diligence requirements concerning valuation.

OVERVIEW OF THE ASSET-BASED APPROACH

The International Glossary of Business Valuation Terms defines the asset-based approach as "[a] general way of determining a value indication of a business, business ownership interest, or security using one or more methods based on the value of the assets net of liabilities."[3]

The IGBVT distinguishes the asset-based approach from the cost approach. While the asset-based approach applies to the valuation of a business enterprise, the cost approach applies to the valuation of property interests and is typically used to measure the value of individual assets (for instance, a real estate property or a patent). In an asset-based business valuation, the cost approach can be used alongside the market and income approaches to value assets which are included under the enterprise umbrella. The asset-based value of a company is also distinct from its book value, which is calculated as the net of the recorded amounts of assets and liabilities in a company's balance sheet under generally accepted accounting principles (GAAP).[4]

Corporate and Intangibles Valuation Organization. For an overview of the MPF, see Raymond Rath, "Advancing the Quality of Valuations," *Business Valuation Review* 36, no. 2 (Summer 2017): 48–53.
[2] On the valuation of intangible assets under the MPF framework, see Antonella Puca and Mark Zyla, "Valuing Intangible Assets under the Mandatory Performance Framework: A Fair Value Update," *Business Valuation Review* 38, no. 4 (Winter 2019): 1-14. For a comprehensive overview of intangible assets valuation, see Robert Reilly and Robert P. Schweihs, *Guide to Intangible Assets Valuation* (AICPA and Wiley, 2014); Mark Zyla, *Fair Value Measurement: Practical Guide and Implementation* (Wiley, 2020); Ervin Black and Mark Zyla, "Accounting for Goodwill and Other Intangible Assets," Chapter 2 in *Initial Measurement of Acquired Intangible Assets* (Wiley, 2019); Robert Reilly, "Challenges in Measuring the Fair Value of Intangible Assets," Webinar Handbook, March 4, 2014 (Business Valuation Resources, LLC, 2014). For an overview of the valuation of intangible assets for investment analysts, see also Antonella Puca and Mark Zyla, "The Intangible Valuation Renaissance: Five Methods," *Enterprising Investor* (CFA Institute, January 11, 2019). This chapter draws from earlier work of the authors on the valuation of intangible assets as referenced in this note.
[3] While not stated in a FASB standard, this definition has been adopted by a number of professional societies and organizations, including the AICPA, and is included in appendix B of Statement on Standards for Valuation Services No.1 of the AICPA.
[4] On the asset-based business valuation approach, see Robert Reilly, "What Lawyers Need to Know about the Asset-Based Business Valuation Approach," *The Practical Lawyers*, April 2017, pp. 40–64; Robert R. Reilly, "The Asset-Based Business Valuation Approach: Advanced Applications" (Part 1), *Practical Tax Strategies*, July 2018, p. 15.

One of the main challenges of the asset-based approach is that it requires the identification and a valuation assessment of assets and liabilities that may be off-balance sheet under current accounting standards, but that may still be significant drivers of value. For instance, an enterprise may have a patent that was developed internally. Under current U.S. GAAP, the costs for developing the patent would have been expensed as incurred and the patent would not be recognized in the balance sheet. Along similar lines, an enterprise may have a trademark infringement lawsuit in progress that does not meet the U.S. GAAP requirements for balance sheet reporting, but that may still have the potential to significantly affect its growth prospects. The asset-based approach takes into consideration all of the company's assets (both tangible and intangible) and liabilities (recorded and contingent) to estimate the value of the company.

The asset-based approach is typically used to provide the primary value indication in the valuation of investment companies and asset holding companies. The valuation of a venture capital fund based on its "net asset value" (the value of assets net of liabilities) is an example of an asset-based valuation. For investments in operating companies, the asset-based approach is often used in conjunction with other valuation methodologies and is mostly applied to companies that have yet to generate significant goodwill value.

The asset-based approach has often been applied in a way that emphasizes historical information and that relies heavily on the cost method to value assets at their replacement cost. From this perspective, the reliance on backward-looking, "historical" information has led to significant limitations in the use of this approach, particularly in the valuation of high-growth enterprises, where valuation is heavily reliant on projected revenue and projected free cash flows.

The AICPA PE/VC Valuation Guide, for instance, remarks that "under the going concern premise of value, the asset (or asset-based) approach, under most circumstances, is considered to be the weakest from a conceptual standpoint."[5] In the AICPA PE/VC Valuation Guide, the assed-based approach is discussed as a useful:

- Reality check on the market and income approaches, providing a "default value" if the available data for use of those other approaches are fragmentary or speculative.
- Valuation method for enterprises in the earliest stages of development, prior to raising arm's-length financing, when there may be limited (or no) basis for using the income or market approaches.
- Valuation method for enterprises that are valued primarily based on their tangible assets.[6]

It is important to keep in mind that the asset-based approach can also be applied to ESEs where intangible assets are the key driver of enterprise valuation and growth. To the extent those assets may be appropriately identified and adequate support for the selected intangible valuation method can be gathered, the asset-based approach, particularly in the AAM variant, can provide insight on a company value and growth prospects based not only on historical but also on forward-looking information.

The asset-based approach requires a significant amount of detailed information on the company's operations and of asset-specific information. The availability of information can

---

[5] AICPA PE/VC Valuation Guide 5.95.
[6] AICPA PE/VC Valuation Guide 5.95–96.

affect an analyst's ability to use this approach. Budget considerations are also relevant, as the asset-based approach often involves greater effort on the part of the analyst, and possibly the involvement of external specialists in the valuation of selected assets and liabilities (for instance, equipment, individual items of intellectual property, real estate, oil and gas reserves, certain contingent liabilities). As a result of this method, the analyst will gain useful insights into the assets that are the value drivers for the company, whether tangible or intangible, and how intangible assets such as proprietary technology, trademarks and customer relationships contribute to enterprise value.

THE ASSET ACCUMULATION METHOD: A CASE STUDY

Exhibit 7.1 presents the statement of financial condition of Nekkar Technologies Inc. (Nekkar), a hypothetical early stage technology company as of December 31 of 20X0.

In our case study, an analyst has been engaged to conduct the valuation of an equity interest in Nekkar at fair value under ASC 820 with a measurement date of December 31, 20X0. Nekkar has positive revenue but is still experiencing net operating losses and negative cash flows from operations, primarily related to capital expenditures and marketing costs. The company had a round of financing in January 20X0, which was a follow-up to a prior round at the same unit price per share and was participated in exclusively by preexistent investors. The analyst is not able to conclude on whether the issue price of the latest round represents a reliable fair value indication. The analyst elects to use the AAM as one of the methodologies to corroborate the value indications resulting from the latest round. The analyst's firm holds a significant stake in Nekkar, including a seat on the company's board of directors, and the analyst expects to have access to adequate information to be able to implement the AAM method in a cost-efficient way.

In order to complete its AAM assessment of enterprise value, the valuation analyst needs to perform the following steps:

1. Identify assets and liabilities.
2. Value the individual assets and liabilities at fair value.
3. Adjust the balance sheet to reflect the updated values of assets and liabilities.
4. Calculate the value of enterprise as the net value of its assets and liabilities.

As of the measurement date, the book value of the company is $8 million, calculated as the net of the total book value of its assets ($11 million) and the book value of its liabilities ($3 million). In this simplified example, we assume that the book value of the company's current assets and current liabilities approximates fair value and that no adjustments are necessary under the AAM for these accounts. The company holds a small amount of fixed assets and equipment, which are not deemed a material part of the business and which are left at their carrying value. The company's sources of financing consist entirely of equity capital in the form of common and preferred stock (no long-term debt).

As of December 31, 20X0, the company's intangible assets are the primary driver for its valuation. Based on interviews with management and inquiries with company's counsel, the analyst determines that there are no contingent liabilities to be added to the company's balance sheet as of the measurement date. The intangible assets, however, need to be valued at fair value and incorporated in the company's balance sheet.

	December 31, 20X0
ASSETS	
Current Assets	
Cash	$ 6,000
Other current assets	$ 2,000
Total current assets	$ 8,000
Property, plant, and equipment	$ 3,000
Total assets	$ 11,000
LIABILITIES AND SHAREHOLDERS' EQUITY	
Current liabilities	
Accounts payable	$ 3,000
Shareholders' equity	
Preferred stock	$ 20,000
Common stock	$ 2,000
Retained earnings	$ (14,000)
Total equity	$ 8,000
Total liabilities and shareholders' equity	$ 11,000

EXHIBIT 7.1 Nekkar Technologies Inc. – Balance Sheet as of December 31, 20X0 ($ thousand)

Identification of Intangible Assets

Intangible assets represent an increasingly relevant component of corporate value, and one that has been difficult to capture in corporate financial statements under GAAP.[7]

The International Glossary of Business Valuation Terms (IGBVT) defines intangible assets as "non-physical assets such as franchises, trademarks, patents, copyrights, goodwill, equities, mineral rights, securities and contracts (as distinguished from physical assets) that grant rights and privileges, and have value for the owner." For financial reporting under US GAAP, the definition is "assets (not including financial assets) that lack physical substance."[8] U.S. GAAP defines goodwill separately as "the excess of the cost of an acquired entity over the net amounts assigned to assets acquired and liabilities assumed."

The Bureau of Economic Analysis started tracking the investments in intangible capital by private enterprises as part of its GDP database in 2013 (Exhibit 7.2). BEA's measure of intangible capital includes accumulated spending on software, R&D, and intellectual property related to arts and entertainment (a "cost" perspective). Since 2012 the annual investment in intellectual property products by private enterprises in the United States has grown at a 6.0% annualized rate to $931 billion as of December 2018.

---

[7]Feng Gu and Baruch Lev, "Time to Change Your Investment Model," *Financial Analyst Journal* 73, no. 4 (2017), CFA Institute. See also Sherree DeCovny, "Assessing Value in the Digital Economy," *Enterprising Investor*, CFA Institute, April 18, 2018.
[8]FASB ASC 805-10-20 Glossary: Intangible Assets.

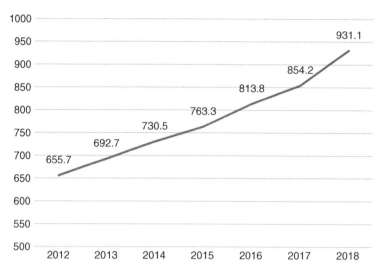

EXHIBIT 7.2   Private Investment in Intellectual Property Products (in $ Billion)
Source: U.S. Bureau of Economic Analysis, Table 1.1.5, last revised August 8, 2019.

The private investment in intellectual property products represents 33.8% of total U.S. gross private domestic investment as of year-end 2018, versus 31.2% as of year-end 2012. Over the same period, investments in structures as a percentage of total U.S. gross private domestic investment have remained substantially flat while investments in equipment have decreased (Exhibit 7.3).

Intangible assets have also grown as a share of the total value attributed to target companies in M&A transactions. According to Houlihan Lokey, intangible assets represent 35% of the purchase price allocation in the 2017 M&A transactions of public companies based on filings with the U.S. Securities and Exchange Commission, up from 31% in 2015.[9]

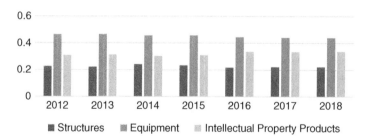

EXHIBIT 7.3   Gross Private Domestic Investment in the United States as a Percentage of Total Gross Investment
Source: U.S. Bureau of Economic Analysis, Table 1.1.5, last revised August 8, 2019.

[9]Houlihan Lokey, 2017 Purchase Price Allocation Study.

As investments in intangibles continue to grow, it is all the more critical to find suitable ways to assess the value of intangible assets as a driver of enterprise value. Both IFRS and U.S. GAAP are a "mixed" model, which generally requires a different accounting treatment for intangible assets that are acquired as part of a business combination or in other transactions, compared to intangible assets that are internally developed by the reporting entity.

Intangible assets that are internally developed typically are not recorded in an entity's balance sheet and the related costs are expensed as incurred under U.S. GAAP. Under IFRS, internally developed intangible assets are recognized only if certain criteria are met.[10]

Intangible assets may also be acquired in a business combination, which is defined as a "transaction or other event in which an acquirer obtains control of one or more businesses."[11] Intangible assets that are acquired in a business combination and that are "identifiable" must be measured at fair value at the time of the acquisition, included on the acquirer's balance sheet, and then subject to amortization and/or periodic impairment testing.[12]

Under FASB ASC 805 *Business Combinations*, in order to be "identifiable," an intangible asset needs to have at least one of the following characteristics:

1. It is separable: the asset can be separated or divided from the entity and sold, transferred, licensed, rented, or exchanged, either individually or together with a related contract, identifiable asset, or liability.
2. It arises from contractual or other legal rights, regardless of whether those rights are transferrable or separable from the entity or from other rights and obligations. In practice, it also critical that any legal rights associated with the asset be enforceable as a condition for value assignment.[13]

Exhibit 7.4 provides a list of identifiable intangible assets based on the categories cited in FASB ASC 805. This list is not meant to be exhaustive.

Intangible assets may also be acquired in a transaction that does not qualify as a business combination, either individually (for instance, the purchase of an individual patent) or as a group (for instance, in a transaction that qualifies as an asset purchase). Under U.S. GAAP, these intangibles are initially recognized based on their cost to the acquiring entity under ASC 805-50 and subsequently accounted for under ASC 350, *Intangibles – Goodwill and Other*.

The different accounting treatment of acquired versus internally developed intangible assets is likely to result in comparability issues for companies that have different growth strategies. An enterprise that has developed its portfolio of intangible assets through acquisitions is likely to have a higher share of intangibles recognized in its balance sheet (and a higher amount of goodwill) versus an enterprise that has developed its intangible assets internally, which will impact their balance sheet and profitability ratios.

A comparison of the 10-Q as of June 30, 2019, for Facebook and Alphabet (the parent company of Google Inc.), for instance, shows that reported intangible assets represent 16.5% of Facebook total assets, and 7.7% for Google, which reflects Facebook's greater involvement in acquisitions (Exhibit 7.5).

---

[10]See also Mark Zyla, *Fair Value Measurement: Practical Guidance and Implementation*, 3rd ed. (Wiley, 2020).
[11]FASB ASC 805-10-20 Glossary: Business Combination.
[12]ASC 805-10-20 Glossary: Identifiable.
[13]FASB ASC 805-10-20 Glossary: Identifiable.

Marketing-related	Trademarks
	Service marks
	Internet domain names
	Noncompete agreements
Customer-related	Customer lists
	Customer contracts and relationships
	Expected customer contract renewals
	Noncontractual customer relationships
	Contract backlog
Artistic-related	Books, magazines, newspapers, and literary works
	Plays, operas, and ballets
	Musical works such as compositions, song lyrics, and advertising jingles
	Photographs and drawings
	Video and audiovisual materials, including movies, music videos, and TV programs
Contract-based	Franchise and licensing agreements
	Construction permits
	Broadcast rights
	Favorable supplier contracts
	Employment agreements
Technology-based	Computer software
	Trade secrets
	Product patents
	Process patents

EXHIBIT 7.4 Identifiable Intangible Assets
Source: Adapted from FASB ASC 805-20-55-11 to 51.

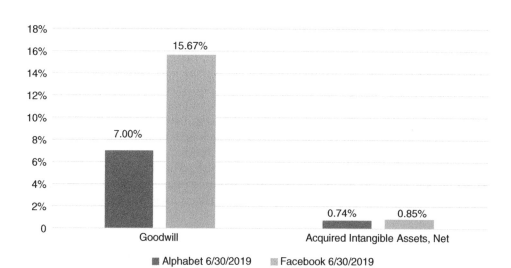

EXHIBIT 7.5 Facebook and Alphabet – Intangibles as a % of Total Assets
Source: Data based on SEC 10Q June 30, 2019.

The identification of the intangibles that need to be added to the balance sheet is a key step in the application of the AAM. The MPF emphasizes that, while the responsibility for the identification lies with management, the valuation professional should be actively involved in this process and document the process as well as the conclusions reached in the engagement files. The documentation should be sufficient for an external party to be able to understand the rationale for inclusion or exclusion from the valuation analyses of certain assets and how the assets were classified based on the table above. Among others, the analyst should be able to explain how the assets meet the separability, legal, and contractual criteria of ASC 805.[14]

Valuation of Intangible Assets

Let's now go back to Nekkar and see how we can incorporate its intangible assets in the company's valuation under the AAM. Based on discussions with management and a review of the company's operations, the analyst has identified the following intangible assets for the company:

a. Customer relationships
b. Trade name
c. Proprietary software
d. Undeveloped patent
e. In-progress research and development
f. Noncompetition agreements
g. Assembled workforce

Under ASC 820, the analyst must estimate the fair value of intangible assets assuming their "highest and best use" (HABU) by market participants, considering the use of the assets as "physically possible," "legally permissible," and "financially feasible" at the measurement date.[15]

Nekkar has developed a technology platform that is used internally to support the company's operations. If market participants consider the HABU of the asset to be in a different function, for instance, in a different type of process where it will produce greater fair value, then the fair value measurement would have to reflect the market participant alternative value. Nekkar has also developed a patent for a web-based application and a related software that are used by the company in combination. To the extent a market participant would consider the two intangible assets separately in a market transaction, the HABU of the assets would be as separate assets under ASC 820 and each asset would be valued on a stand-alone basis.

For assets that are developed internally, the projected financial information (PFI) at the basis of asset valuation may have to be adjusted to exclude entity-specific synergies. For instance, let's assume that Nekkar is in the process of developing an algorithm for data extraction and analysis that the company is planning to sell externally. If used by Company B, a strategic buyer, the algorithm may provide cash flow benefits by enhancing the functionality of Company B's existing data platform. To the extent the projected cash flows from the enhancement are entity-specific, the portion of the synergies available just to the acquiring

---

[14]AMPF A3.2.4: Identified Assets and Liabilities.
[15]ASC 820-10-35-10B.

entity and no other market participant should be excluded from the projected cash flows used to assess the fair value of the intangible under ASC 820.[16]

In our case study, we go over some of the more common methods for valuing intangibles within the framework of the cost, market, and income approach under ASC 820 and of the related documentation requirements under the MPF.[17] One of the key considerations in the selection of a method to value an intangible asset is the way in which the asset adds value to the enterprise. Assets such as copyrights, trademarks, and patents, for instance, may be directly associated to a revenue stream and/or may have a market value based on an estimate of the price that a market participant would be willing to pay to acquire their cash flows or use the asset in its operations. Typically, the intangible asset which is the key driver of revenue for the firm will use an income approach such as the Capitalized Excess Earnings method (CEEM) or the Multiperiod Excess Earnings method (MEEM). Assets such as assembled workforce and computer software that has been internally developed specifically for internal use have value primarily in view of their contribution to the overall operations of the firm and may best be valued using a cost approach (reproduction cost, replacement cost, or trended historical cost). Under the MPF, the valuation analyst should document the criteria for selection of a particular valuation method for each identified intangible asset.[18]

Customer Relationships: Multiperiod Excess Earnings Method   For Nekkar, customer relationships are the primary driver of value. The company expects its revenue growth to come primarily from an increase in the number of users of its technology platform while the revenue per user is expected to remain substantially stable over time. To reflect the relevance of customer relationships in Nekkar's valuation, the analysts elect to measure the fair value of customer relationships using the Multiperiod Excess Earnings Method (MPEEM).

The MPEEM method is a variation of the discounted cash flow analysis. Instead of focusing on the entity as a whole, the MPEEM isolates the cash flows that can be associated with a single intangible asset and measures fair value by discounting them to present value. The MPEEM is typically applied to a single asset, which is identified as the primary driver of value for a firm and where the related cash flows can be isolated from the overall cash flows of the firm. This is often the case for ESEs and for technology firms that maintain a competitive advantage by successfully deploying a strategic intangible asset. Proprietary technology and customer relationships are examples of assets that may be primary generators of cash flows and may be suitable for fair value measurement using the MPEEM. Intangible assets classified or designated as operating rights, including, for instance, FCC and other government granted licenses (for example, wireless or broadcast spectrums, casino licenses, certificates of need), commercial franchises (such as fast-food restaurants), and governmentally granted monopolies or franchises (such as in the cable industry) may also be valued using the MPEEM or a variation of the MPEEM often referred to as the "Greenfield Method."

---

[16]Natahn DiNatale and Mark Zyla, "Case Studies in Purchase Price Allocations," *Business Valuation Resources*, 2016.

[17]See also James R. Hitchner, "Valuation of Intangible Assets," Chapter 21 in *Financial Valuation: Applications and Models* (Wiley, 2011); and Gary Trugman, "Valuing Intangible Assets: An Overview," Chapter 20 in *Understanding Business Valuation* (AICPA, 2017).

[18]AMPF A1.3.4: Considerations for Selection and Reconciliation of Approaches and Methods – Documentation Requirements.

The MPEEM typically involves the following steps:

1. Project financial information attributable to the specific asset or group of related assets (cash flows/revenue, expenses).
2. Subtract the portion of cash flows attributable to all other assets through a contributory asset charge (CAC). The CAC is a form of economic rent for the use of all other assets in generating total cash flows and is composed of the required rate of return on all other assets and an amount necessary to replace the fair value of certain contributory intangible assets.[19]
3. Calculate the cash flows attributable to the intangible asset after the CAC adjustment subject to valuation and discount them to present value.

Exhibit 7.6 illustrates the valuation of customer relationships using the MPEEM model for Nekkar.

The analyst starts by projecting a revenue stream based on the revenue generated by existing customer relations over their projected life. In this example, we have assumed no growth in revenues from existing customers. As time goes by, we estimate that the revenue from its current customers will be eroded at an annual rate of 20% of existing revenues. Under simplified assumptions, operating expenses are assumed to be a constant 85% of revenues net of erosion. Depreciation is an allocated charge and is estimated at 10% of EBITDA. Taxes are estimated at a rate of 23% of EBIT. The CAC line reflects an allocation of charges that relates to general expenses of the company. It would typically also include a component that is associated with the firm's goodwill value. In this simple model, the contributory asset charges are reported as a single line. In practice, a separate CAC is calculated for each relevant asset, including CACs on PP&E (property, plant, and equipment), working capital, assembled workforce, and other assets as suitable.

The adjusted net earnings after taxes, depreciation, and CAC allocations are then discounted to present value using the mid-period convention (we are assuming that the stream of income is earned at a steady rate during the year), and an estimated discount rate of 20%. It is important to note that the discount rate in this model is the rate that represents the risk of the specific intangible being valued, which is likely to be different from the weighted average rate of return on assets representing a blend of the various types of tangible and intangible assets in the company.

In Period 2, for instance, the present value of adjusted net earnings is calculated as:

$$\text{PV of Adjusted Net Earnings (Year 2)} = \text{Adjusted Net Earnings}/(1 + \text{Discount Rate})^{1.5}$$

$$= \$1,088,650/(1.2^{1.5})$$

$$= \$1,088,650/1.3145 = \$828,157$$

The sum of the present value of customer earnings after taxes, depreciation, and the CAC allocation for each year in the model ($3,399,532 in our example) is then increased by

---

[19]On the estimate of CACs in the MPEEM, see especially Appraisal Foundation VFR Valuation Advisory #1: Identification of Contributory Assets and Calculation Economic Rent (with Toolkit), 2010.

	Year 1	Year 2	Year 3	Year 4	Year 5	Year 6	Year 7	Year 8
Revenues	$ 30,000,000	$ 30,000,000	$ 30,000,000	$ 30,000,000	$ 30,000,000	$ 30,000,000	$ 30,000,000	$ 30,000,000
Customer Erosion 20.0%	80%	64%	51%	41%	33%	26%	21%	17%
Existing Customer Revenue	$ 24,000,000	$ 19,200,000	$ 15,360,000	$ 12,288,000	$ 9,830,400	$ 7,864,320	$ 6,291,456	$ 5,033,165
Operating Expense	$ 20,400,000	$ 16,320,000	$ 13,056,000	$ 10,444,800	$ 8,355,840	$ 6,684,672	$ 5,347,738	$ 4,278,190
EBITDA	$ 3,600,000	$ 2,880,000	$ 2,304,000	$ 1,843,200	$ 1,474,560	$ 1,179,648	$ 943,718	$ 754,975
Depreciation	$ 360,000	$ 288,000	$ 230,400	$ 184,320	$ 147,456	$ 117,965	$ 94,372	$ 75,497
EBIT	$ 3,240,000	$ 2,592,000	$ 2,073,600	$ 1,658,880	$ 1,327,104	$ 1,061,683	$ 849,347	$ 679,477
Taxes 23.0%	$ 745,200	$ 596,150	$ 476,928	$ 381,542	$ 305,234	$ 244,187	$ 195,350	$ 156,280
CAC	$ 1,134,000	$ 907,200	$ 725,760	$ 580,608	$ 464,486	$ 371,589	$ 297,271	$ 237,817
Adjusted Net Earnings	$ 1,360,800	$ 1,088,650	$ 870,912	$ 696,730	$ 557,384	$ 445,907	$ 356,725	$ 285,380
Discount Periods	0.5	1.5	2.5	3.5	4.5	5.5	6.5	7.5
Discount Factor 20.0%	0.9129	0.7607	0.6339	0.5283	0.4402	0.3669	0.3057	0.2548
Present Value	$ 1,242,235	$ 828,157	$ 552,104	$ 368,070	$ 245,380	$ 163,587	$ 109,058	$ 72,705
Total PV $ 3,399,532								
TAB $ 467,297	TABM	1.1375						
Fair Value $ 3,866,829								
Fair Value (rounded) $ 3,867,000								

EXHIBIT 7.6 Valuation of Customer Relationships – MPEEM

the estimated value of the tax amortization benefit (TAB) that would result from the amortization of the asset. In our example, the TAB is calculated as the present value of the tax savings resulting from an eight-year amortization of the asset. In calculating the amortization adjustments, analysts need to make an estimate of the corporate tax rates that would be applicable for "market participants" and estimate their impact on intangible amortization over the period considered in the valuation. The formula for the TAB is:

$$\text{TAB} = \text{INT} \times [(n/(n - (PV\,(r, n, -1) \times (1 + r)^{0.5} \times t))) - 1]$$

where:

$$\text{TAB} = \text{tax amortization benefit}$$
$$\text{INT} = \text{intangible asset value}$$
$$n = \text{number of years}$$
$$t = \text{tax rate}$$
$$r = \text{discount rate}$$

The factor $PV\,(r, n, -1) \times (1 + r)^{0.5}$ represents the present value of an annuity of \$1 over $n = 8$ years at the discount rate r, using the mid-period convention.

In our example:

$$PV\,(r, n, -1) \times (1 + r)^{0.5} = PV(20\%, 8, -1) \times (1 + 20\%)^{0.5} = 4.2034$$

and

$$\text{TAB} = 3,399,532 \times [(8/(8 - (4.2034 \times 23\%)) - 1)]$$
$$= \$3,399,532 \times [(8/7.0332) - 1]$$
$$= \$3,399,532 \times 0.1375 = \$467,297$$

The TAB can also be expressed as a multiplier (TABM). In our case:

$$\text{TABM} = 1 + (\text{Tax Amortization Benefit/Present Value of Adjusted Net Earnings})$$
$$= 1 + 0.1375 = 1.1375$$

We can now calculate the fair value of customer relationships as:

$$\text{Fair Value of Customer Relationships} = \text{PV of Adjusted Net Earnings}$$
$$+ \text{Tax Amortization Benefit}$$
$$= \$3,399,532 + 467,297 = \$3,866,829$$
$$= \$3,867,000 \text{ (rounded)}$$

To the extent a market participant would factor the TAB into the valuation, it is appropriate to include the TAB when estimating the fair value of an intangible asset regardless of whether the asset was developed internally, acquired in a taxable or nontaxable transaction, and regardless of whether the company itself would have enough taxable income to take advantage of the TAB. Under the MPF, the valuation professional should document at a minimum whether the TAB is appropriate based on the market participant tax jurisdiction requirements, how the amortization method (straight-line or accelerated) and the amortization term were determined, and the rationale for the tax rate and the discount rate used in the calculation.[20]

The attrition rate (customer erosion rate) is an especially sensitive metric for the valuation of customer-related intangible assets. Typically, this rate is estimated based on revenue or per-unit projections that take into account historical attrition for the entity, as well as industry and competitor customer attrition rates. Under the MPF, the valuation professional should document the process and rationale for determining historical and future attrition rates, how the attrition data concerning the industry and competitors was gathered and analyzed, the extent of reliance on the data provided by management, and the extent of independent analysis performed.[21]

In an MPEEM, the estimated life of the projection period can have a significant effect on the concluded value of the asset. As noted in the MPF, for customer-related intangible assets, the projected cash flows approach but never arrive at zero, which would imply an infinite projection period. In our example, the valuation professional would be required to document the methods, assumptions, and inputs used to determine when the life of the projected period should be truncated (Year 8 in this case). The MPF also requires that the valuation professional document any discussions with company management and the company's auditors about materiality considerations that may have affected the estimate life of the projection period.[22]

The assessment of the CAC can be especially challenging in an MPEEM model. The required returns on contributory assets must be consistent with an assessment of the risk of individual asset classes and should reconcile overall to the enterprise Weighted Average Return on Assets (WARA) and the Weighted Average Cost of Capital (WACC) as we discuss later in this chapter. Under the MPF, in performing a MPEEM valuation, the valuation analyst should document at a minimum the process for identifying and valuing the contributory assets and the support for the required rates of return on and of contributory assets.

The MPF has substantial documentation requirements concerning the individual CACs, which depend on the type of asset (working capital, land, other fixed assets, intangible assets valued with the relief-from-royalty method discussed below, assembled workforce and other intangibles) generating the charge. For the CAC related to the assembled workforce, (an asset that is not reported separately but rather included in goodwill as we discuss later), the MPF requires a documentation, at a minimum, of the assumptions used to estimate the fair value of the assembled workforce, how the required rate of return on the asset has been assessed, and how the value of the workforce and of the related CAC were ultimately calculated.[23]

---

[20] AMPF A3.85: Tax Amortization Benefits – Documentation Requirements.

[21] AMPF, A3.5.3: Customer-related Intangible Assets: Documentation Requirements.

[22] AMPF, A3.4.5: Life for Projection Period – Documentation Requirements.

[23] AMPF, A3.7.3: Contributory Asset Charges – Documentation Requirements. A useful checklist for the MPF documentation requirements for CACs can be found in "Work File Checklist for Contributory Asset Charges," *Business Valuation Update*, September 2018: 21–22.

Trade Name: Relief from Royalty Method   A trade name identifies the name of the company or business. Trade names that function as a source identifier of a company's goods or services may be entitled to protection under the trademark law. In the United States, a trade name cannot be registered at the federal level under the Lanham Act, but can be registered under state law. The Lanham Act and common law can still provide some protection from unfair competition for trade names. While still in the preprofit stage, an ESE may already have a well-recognized trade name in the market, which enhances the strength of its customer relationships.

Trade names typically have a market value and can be subject to agreements that allow for third-party use in exchange for a royalty fee. Accordingly, our analyst has elected to measure the fair value of Nekkar's trade name using the Relief from Royalty method (RRM). The RRM determines value by reference to the hypothetical royalty payments that would be saved through owning the asset, as compared with licensing the asset from a third party. The theory behind the RRM is that an entity that owns an intangible asset has a valuable right since the entity does not have to pay a third party a license fee for the right to use that intangible asset. The RRM is often applied to assets such as domain names, trademarks, trade names, licensed computer software, in-progress research, and development, which can be associated to a specific revenue stream and where data on royalty/license fees can be obtained from other market transactions.

The valuation of an intangible using the RRM method typically involves the following steps:

1. Project financial information for the overall enterprise, including revenue, grow rates, tax rates, and estimates. The underlying information is generally obtained from the entity's management.
2. Estimate a royalty rate that is suitable for the intangible asset based on an analysis of royalty rates from publicly available information for similar intangible assets and of the industry in which the entity operates.
3. Estimate the useful life of the asset.
4. Apply the royalty rate to the estimated revenue stream.
5. Estimate a discount rate for the after-tax royalty savings and discount to present value.

The RRM contains assumptions from both market (royalty rate) and income approach (estimate of revenue, growth rates, tax rates, discount rate). Exhibit 7.7 presents a model for the valuation of Nekkar's trade name using the RRM method.

The analyst starts by setting up a stream of projected revenue over the estimated term of the trade name (15 years in our example), based on management's projections. Under the MPF, the analyst is responsible for evaluating whether prospective financial information (PFI) provided by management is reasonable and properly supported. In cases where the PFI is deemed not representative of expected value, the analyst may elect to adjust the projections, have management revise them or also use an entirely different approach from the RRM.[24] The analyst should understand and document how the revenue projections were developed by management: whether a bottom-up or a top-down approach was used and whether they were prepared using market participant assumptions. If historical information is available, the analyst should complete a comparison of prior forecasts against actual results. It is also important to compare the revenue projections to industry expectations, for

---

[24]AMPF A1.4.7: The Valuation Professional's Assessment of the PFI.

B. Valuation Model

VALUATION OF TRADE NAME - ROYALTY RELIEF METHOD

	Year 1	Year 2	Year 3	Year 4	Year 5	Year 6	Year 7	Year 8	Year 9	Year 10	Year 11	Year 12	Year 13	Year 14	Year 15
Revenues	$30,000,000	$40,500,000	$54,675,000	$71,077,500	$88,846,875	$106,616,250	$122,608,688	$134,869,556	$141,613,034	$145,861,425	$150,237,268	$154,744,386	$159,386,717	$164,168,319	$143,283,325
Growth Rate	35.00%	35.00%	35.00%	30.00%	25.00%	20.00%	15.00%	10.00%	5.00%	3.00%	3.00%	3.00%	3.00%	3.00%	3.00%
Pre-tax royalty savings	$300,000	$405,000	$546,750	$710,775	$888,469	$1,066,163	$1,226,087	$1,348,696	$1,416,130	$1,458,614	$1,502,373	$1,547,444	$1,593,867	$1,641,683	$1,432,833
Less: taxes	$(69,000)	$(93,150)	$(125,753)	$(163,478)	$(204,348)	$(245,217)	$(282,000)	$(310,200)	$(325,710)	$(335,481)	$(345,546)	$(355,912)	$(366,589)	$(377,587)	$(329,552)
Royalty savings	$231,000	$311,850	$420,998	$547,297	$684,121	$820,945	$944,087	$1,038,496	$1,090,420	$1,123,133	$1,156,827	$1,191,532	$1,227,278	$1,264,096	$1,103,282
Partial period	1.00	1.00	1.00	1.00	1.00	1.00	1.00	1.00	1.00	1.00	1.00	1.00	1.00	1.00	1.00
Period	0.50	1.50	2.50	3.50	4.50	5.50	6.50	7.50	8.50	9.50	10.50	11.50	12.50	13.50	14.50
Present value factor	0.9129	0.7607	0.6339	0.5283	0.4402	0.3669	0.3057	0.2548	0.2123	0.1769	0.1474	0.1229	0.1024	0.0853	0.0711
PV of royalty savings	$210,873	$237,232	$266,886	$289,127	$301,174	$301,174	$288,625	$264,573	$231,501	$198,705	$170,555	$146,393	$125,654	$107,853	$78,444

Sum of PV of savings	$3,218,771	Royalty rate 1.00%
TAB	$274,324	Long-term growth rate 3.00%
Preliminary value	$3,493,095	Tax rate 23.00%
Concluded value (rounded)	$3,493,000	Discount rate 20.00%
		Remaining useful life – years 15

EXHIBIT 7.7 Valuation of Trade Name – RRM

instance, by comparing revenue growth rates to industry growth rates.[25] In our example, revenues are expected to grow at 35% in Years 2 and 3, and then gradually decline to a long-term sustainable rate of 3.0%, which is deemed consistent with industry averages.

From the overall firm revenue, a pretax stream of royalty savings is estimated by applying a royalty rate (1% in our case) to each annual estimated revenue figure. The posttax stream is then calculated by deducting the estimated tax at a 23% from the pretax royalty savings. For instance, in Year 2, we have:

$$\text{Royalty Savings (Year 2)} = (\text{Estimated Firm Revenue} \times \text{Royalty Rate})(1 - \text{Tax Rate})$$

$$= (\$40{,}500{,}000 \times 1.0\%)(1 - 23\%) = \$311{,}850$$

The royalty savings value is then discounted to present value using the mid-period convention (we are assuming that the stream of income is earned gradually during the year), at an estimated discount rate of 20%. As in the valuation of customer relationships, the discount rate reflects the risk of the specific intangible being valued, which is likely to differ from the WARA.

In Period 2, the present value of the royalty savings is calculated as:

$$\text{PV of Royalty Savings (Year 2)} = \text{Royalty Savings}/[(1 + \text{Discount Rate})^{1.5}]$$

$$= \$311{,}850/1.20^{1.5} = \$311{,}850/1.3145 = \$237{,}232$$

The sum of the present value of royalty savings over the period (\$3,218,771) is then increased by the TAB to incorporate the value of the tax benefit resulting from the amortization of the asset. The TAB is calculated as the present value of the tax savings resulting from a 15-year amortization of the asset.

In our example:

$$PV(r, n, -1) \times (1 + r)^{0.5} = PV(20\%, 15, -1) \times (1 + 20\%)^{0.5} = 5.1217$$

and

$$\text{TAB} = \$3{,}218{,}771 \times [(15/(15 - 5.1217 \times 23\%)) - 1]$$

$$= \$3{,}218{,}771 \times [(15/13.8220) - 1]$$

$$= \$3{,}218{,}771 \times 0.0852 = \$274{,}324$$

The TAB can also be expressed as a multiplier (TABM). In our case:

$$\text{TABM} = 1 + (\text{Tax Amortization Benefit}/\text{Sum of Present Value of Annual Savings})$$

$$= 1 + 274{,}324/3{,}218{,}771 = 1 + 0.0852 = 1.0852.$$

---

[25] AMPF A1.4.4: Understanding Management's Approach to Developing the PFI.

We can now calculate the fair value of the trade name as:

$$\text{FV of Trade Name} = \text{Sum of preliminary value of savings} + \text{TAB} = \$3,218,771 + \$274,324$$
$$= \$3,493,095 = \$3,493,000 \text{ (rounded)}$$

The royalty rate is an especially sensitive input in the RRM model. Information on royalty rates can be found, among others, in databases such as ktMINE (www.ktmine.com), Royalty Source (www.royaltysource.com), RoyaltyStat (www.royaltystat.com), Thomson Reuters Recap IQ (recap.com/recap-iq), and Royalty Connection (www.royaltyconnection .com). Filings with the U.S. Securities and Exchange Commission for publicly traded companies that have similar types of assets can also be useful.

Royalty rates are typically established by negotiation: the same license may result in different royalty rates depending on the relative strength and negotiating ability of the market participants. In establishing an appropriate rate, it's important for the valuation professional to consider the unique facts and circumstances associated with the fields of use of the intangible asset being valued. A similar asset in a different industry is likely to be subject to a different regulatory, performance, and competitive environment, which may significantly affect the value of the asset. Also, the scope of the rights granted may vary by license type, from an outright sale to the nonexclusive license for restricted uses. A consideration of scope may result in adjustments to the database information.

Under ASC 820, observed royalty rates in actual arm's-length negotiated licenses are preferable relative to rates determined based on a rule of thumb or other more subjective methods. Under the MPF, the valuation professional should make sure to document in the work file, at a minimum, the search criteria used to sort through the selected royalty rate databases, the process used in analyzing the third-party licensing agreements and the rationale for selecting or excluding certain agreements, from the list and the support for the selection of the royalty rate used.[26]

Proprietary Software: Replacement Cost Method Less Obsolescence

Nekkar has developed a proprietary software that is used internally to facilitate its administrative and risk management functions. The fair value of Nekkar's proprietary software is estimated using the replacement cost method.[27] This method starts from an assessment of the replacement cost new for the intangible asset, defined as "the cost to construct, at current prices as of the date of the analysis, an intangible asset with equivalent utility to the subject intangible, using modern materials, production standards, design, layout and quality workmanship."[28] The replacement cost is then adjusted for an obsolescence factor as it affects the subject intangible asset. A simple replacement cost model for acquired software, which adjusts for obsolescence, is shown in Exhibit 7.8.

---

[26]AMPF A3.6.3: Royalty Rates – Documentation Requirements.
[27]On the cost method in intangible asset valuation, see especially American Institute of Certified Public Accountants, Business Valuation Committee, Best Practices in Intangible Asset Valuation – Cost Approach Methods and Procedures, AICPA: 2020.
[28]Robert Reilly and Robert P. Schweihs, *Guide to Intangible Asset Valuation* (AICPA, 2014), p. 221.

Module in Place	Lines of Code		Standard LOC per Hour	Hours to Re-create
Module A		43,000	3	14,333
Module B		36,000	4	9,000
Total				23,333
	Blended hourly rate			$ 100.80
	Reproduction cost			$ 2,352,000
	Less: obsolescence factor		25.00%	$ (588,000)
	Before-tax replacement cost			$ 1,764,000
	Less: taxes		23.00%	$ (405,720)
	After-tax replacement cost before amortization			$ 1,358,280
	Amortization benefit multiplier			
	Discount rate		20.00%	
	Tax rate		23.00%	
	Tax amortization period		4	
	Present value of annuity over period		2.8358	
	Amortization benefit			$ 264,631
	Fair value of software			$ 1,622,911
	Fair value of software (rounded)			$ 1,623,000

EXHIBIT 7.8 Proprietary Software – Replacement Cost New

Nekkar's proprietary software consists of two modules which are estimated to involve respectively 43,000 and 36,000 lines of code (LOC) to reproduce. Based on the company's historical experience, the analysts estimate that a coder can execute three lines of code per hour for Module A and four lines of code per hour for Module B, which results in a total number of hours of 23,333 for the two modules combined. The total number of hours is then multiplied by the estimated blended rate per hour to obtain the reproduction cost of the software of $2,352,000.

The blended hourly rate is a key input in the model and is calculated as shown in Exhibit 7.9.

The blended hourly rate includes an entrepreneurial profit component in estimating the asset's replacement cost, which reflects the expectation that the developer will receive not only a return *of* all the costs associated with the development, but also a return *on* those

Components	Rate	Amount
Blended hourly salary		$ 60.00
Benefits	30%	$ 18.00
Overhead	15%	$ 9.00
Opportunity cost of development	18%	$ 10.80
Entrepreneurial profit	5%	$ 3.00
Blended hourly rate		$ 100.80

EXHIBIT 7.9 Valuation of Proprietary Software – Blended Hourly Rate

costs as an incentive to develop the asset in the first place. In addition, the blended hourly rate incorporates an opportunity cost, to compensate the owner of the asset for the risk and resources employed in the asset development and detracted from other uses. The inclusion of an opportunity cost of development and of the entrepreneurial profit are justified in a fair value context to the extent that market participants would indeed be willing to pay more than the base replacement cost for the asset. The historical cost adjusted for the opportunity cost of development and the entrepreneurial profit will more closely resemble a market price and serve as a better base than the "unburdened" cost of replacement to estimate fair value.

As a next step, the analyst considers the effect of obsolescence on the asset value. Acquired software may be operationally functional but may also have lost value as a result of new products or services that are more efficient or operationally superior. The obsolescence of software products is generally related to:

1. Functional obsolescence: Changes in hardware, or other software changes to the system, obsolete the functionality of the software.
2. Technological obsolescence: The sales and/or support for the company software terminates as the original supplier no longer sells the software as new, is unable to expand or renew licensing agreements, or no longer supports its maintenance.
3. Logistical obsolescence: Digital media obsolescence, formatting, or degradation limits or terminates access to software.

Other common causes of obsolescence for tangible assets, such as physical deterioration and location obsolescence (typical of real estate), do not typically have a material effect on intangible assets.

The estimate of the obsolescence percentage (25% in this case) is based on the expected remaining useful life of the software (four years) and is a critical factor in the model. This estimate is typically developed based on inquiries with technical management personnel that should be documented under the MPF.[29]

In the next step, we calculate the after-tax replacement cost before amortization by subtracting the estimate tax at a 23% rate from the before-tax estimated replacement cost:

After-tax replacement cost before amortization = $1,764,000 × (1 − 0.23) = $1,358,280

The final step in the valuation considers the tax impact of the asset's amortization. Considering a discount rate of 20% and an amortization period for the asset of four years, the inclusion of the asset in the balance sheet would generate an estimated tax benefit of $264,631 over the life of the asset, due to the reduction in taxes for the inclusion of the additional asset-related amortization expense in the company's income statement. The analyst will need to evaluate whether it is indeed appropriate to include a tax adjustment depending on whether a market participant would be likely to incorporate it in an estimate of value.

We can then calculate the fair value of proprietary software as:

$$\text{Proprietary Software, at fair value} = \$1,358,280 + \$264,631 = \$1,622,911$$

$$= \$1,623,000 \text{ (rounded)}$$

---

[29] AMPF A3.4.5: Life for Projection Period: Documentation Requirements.

Undeveloped Patent – Real Option Pricing

In addition to technology that is currently in commercial use, Nekkar holds a patent on computer software that is still undeveloped. The issuance of a patent reflects the determination that an invention must be new and nonobvious. The issuance of a patent, however, is only a step on the road to the commercial viability of an invention. In many cases, further technical developments are needed to make the invention applicable for commercial use. Also, a study of commercial viability may be needed to determine whether there are opportunities for developing a market and for profit generation. The decision of "going to market" is typically followed by substantial marketing expenses to establish a company's presence in the target market. In some cases, a company may prefer to hold on to a patent and wait until more clarity on market opportunities is obtained. In other cases, the patent has to remain "undeveloped" until the necessary scientific testing and regulatory approvals for commercial use are received (for instance, an FDA approval for a new drug). A company may determine that the patent has currently a negative net present value, and decide to shelve it for the time being.

Intangible assets that have the potential to create cash flows in the future but do not right now, such as undeveloped patents, have option characteristics that make them suitable to be valued using a real option pricing model. For a real option to have significant economic value, there has to be a restriction on competition in the event of the contingency. This is typically the case for patents, which give the owner the right, but not the obligation, to exclude others from making, using, selling, offering for sale, or importing the patented invention. An undeveloped patent may have a zero "intrinsic" value if the net present value of the underlying project is deemed to be zero or negative at the measurement date (the cost of development exceeds the expected value of the product sales). Still, the patent may have considerable "time" value, related to the possibility that the net present value of the project will turn out to be positive at some point over the life of the patent.

An option pricing model may be most suitable to capture the time value component of a patent that is not currently generating cash flows for the firm, but may have the potential to do so in the future.[30] In our example, Nekkar has a patent for a new application that has currently been set aside in view of the significant uncertainty concerning its commercial potential and the additional technical development and marketing costs that will be necessary to make it commercially viable. In our case, the analyst elects to value the patent using the BSM option pricing model with the following inputs:

- Current Price of Underlying = PV of cash flows from introducing the application now (Current Price). The analyst estimates this input at $20 million.
- Exercise Price = PV of cost of developing and marketing the application platform for commercial use. The analyst estimates this input at $25 million based on information obtained from management's and from the company's technical staff and from a review of the company's cost accounting records.
- Term to Expiration = Patent Life = 8 years. The term to expiration should reflect the time period over which the patent is likely to produce value for a market participant.

---

[30]See also, Mark Zyla, "Advanced Valuation methods for Measuring the Fair Value of Intangible Assets," Chapter 9 in *Fair Value Measurement* (Wiley, 2020); A. Pakes, "Patents as Options: Some Estimates of the Value of Holding European Patent Stocks," *Econometrica* 54 (1986): 755–784.

This may be significantly less than the term of the legal protection afforded to the patent under patent rights.

- Risk-free Rate = 2.0%. The risk-free rate is an observable input that typically comes from the rate on virtually risk-free government securities that match the term of the patent.
- Volatility of Underlying = 60%. This is based on the analyst's estimate.
- Dividend Yield = Expected Cost of Delay = $1/t = 6.67\%$. This is just the inverse of the time input value and represents the loss of value that the patent is subject to as it approaches the end of its term life.

Using the BSM model for a European call option and the aforementioned inputs, our analyst obtains a fair value for Nekkar's undeveloped patent of $2,832,000 (rounded).

As in the case of stock options, one of the challenges in the valuation of real options in the BSM model is the assessment of the volatility for the underlying. Real options also require an estimate of the exercise price (the cost of developing the patent in our example), and the current price of the underlying (the present value of the cash flows from developing the patent now). While there is judgment involved in the application of option pricing models to intangible assets, there is also a significant amount of guidance and industry practice that has developed over time and that the analyst can refer to for implementation.

Real option pricing models can provide an elegant modeling solution for patent valuation. Especially in the case of patents, it is also important for a valuation analyst to keep in mind the legal content and enforceability of the patent's rights. The existence in the market of potentially blocking patents, for instance, may significantly affect a patent's value and result in litigation that makes the patent invalid or unenforceable. The status of any pending or legal actions surrounding the patent under review should be carefully monitored. In order for the patent to maintain its value, the licensor must be prepared to enforce and be capable of enforcing the patent protection against infringers, which may involve a significant cost. The valuation analysts may want to obtain a written management representation as to the validity and enforceability of a key patent in connection with an independent valuation appraisal.

Noncompetition Agreements: With and Without Method

Nekkar has noncompete agreements in place with its executive and technical employees. Noncompete agreements are contracts between an employer and an employee or contract workers that restrict the employee from sharing proprietary information or from starting up a competing business. Noncompete agreements are typically valued using the With and Without method (WWM). The WWM estimates the value of an intangible asset by comparing two discounted cash flow models – one that represents the status quo for the business enterprise with the asset in place, and the other that assumes that the intangible asset is not in place. The difference in value between the two scenarios can be attributed to the intangible asset. In the case of Nekkar, the analyst determines that the noncompete agreements that exist as of the valuation date should be valued on a combined basis.

The fair value of the company's noncompete agreements is $1,024,000 and is presented in Exhibit 7.10.

		With Noncompete			Without Noncompete		
		Year 1	Year 2	Year 3	Year 1	Year 2	Year 3
Revenues, Net		$ 30,000,000	$ 40,500,000	$ 54,675,000	$ 30,000,000	$ 40,500,000	$ 54,675,000
Revenue Growth		35%	35%	30%	35%	35%	30%
% Decline in Revenues Due to Competition					10.00%	8.00%	6.00%
$ Decline in Revenues Due to Competition		$ -	$ -	$ -	$ (3,000,000)	$ (3,240,000)	$ (3,280,500)
Total Projected Revenues, Net		$ 30,000,000	$ 40,500,000	$ 54,675,000	$ 27,000,000	$ 37,260,000	$ 51,394,500
Expenses	85.00%	$ 25,500,000	$ 34,425,000	$ 46,473,750	$ 22,950,000	$ 31,671,000	$ 43,685,325
EBITDA		$ 4,500,000	$ 6,075,000	$ 8,201,250	$ 4,050,000	$ 5,589,000	$ 7,709,175
Depreciation		$ 450,000	$ 607,500	$ 820,125	$ 405,000	$ 558,900	$ 770,918
EBIT		$ 4,050,000	$ 5,467,500	$ 7,381,125	$ 3,645,000	$ 5,030,100	$ 6,938,258
Taxes	23.00%	$ 931,500	$ 1,257,525	$ 1,697,659	$ 838,350	$ 1,156,923	$ 1,595,799
Debt-Free Net Income		$ 3,118,500	$ 4,209,975	$ 5,683,466	$ 2,806,650	$ 3,873,177	$ 5,342,458
Plus: Depreciation		$ 450,000	$ 607,500	$ 820,125	$ 405,000	$ 558,900	$ 770,918
Less: Capital Expenditures		$ 75,000	$ 101,250	$ 131,625	$ 67,500	$ 93,150	$ 123,727
Less: Incremental Working Capital		$ 25,000	$ 30,000	$ 35,000	$ 22,500	$ 27,600	$ 32,900
Cash Flows to Invested Capital		$ 3,468,500	$ 4,686,225	$ 6,336,966	$ 3,121,650	$ 4,311,327	$ 5,956,748
Mid-Period		0.5	1.5	2.5	0.5	1.5	2.5
Present Value Factor	20.00%	0.9129	0.7607	0.6339	0.9129	0.7607	0.6339
Present Value of Cash Flows to Invested Capital		$ 3,166,293	$ 3,564,932	$ 4,017,245	$ 2,849,664	$ 3,279,737	$ 3,776,210
Sum of PV of DFCF		$ 10,748,470			$ 9,905,611		
Preliminary Value of Noncompete Agreement		$ 842,859					
TAB		$ 181,160					
Fair Value		$ 1,024,019					
Fair Value (rounded)		$ 1,024,000					

EXHIBIT 7.10 Valuation of Noncompete Agreement – WWM Method

The valuation of a noncompete agreement requires a detailed review of the agreement terms. Typically, the analyst will gain insight from the company's management on the impact of the agreement on existing customers, revenue growth, and profitability. Management's insight is critical in identifying the revenue stream that is affected by the agreement and the related estimated revenue growth rate.

For noncompete agreements, the life of the projection period (three years in this case) is typically contract-based. The estimation of the percentage decline in revenues due to competition on the other hand represents a key challenge in the model. The MPF does not specifically discuss noncompete agreements and the WAW method. However, we are of the view that the decline in revenue for a noncompete agreement is conceptually similar to attrition in customer-related intangible assets and should be documented accordingly. From this perspective, the process for selecting the decline rate and its changes over time (from 10% in Year 1 to 6% in Year 3 for Nekkar), and the related discussions with management, should be documented by the valuation professional as part of the engagement workpapers.[31]

Once total projected revenues are estimated under the with and without noncompete scenario, the same percentage deductions for expenses, including depreciation, are applied to come to a debt-free net income figure. After adjusting for depreciation, capital expenditures, and incremental working capital, the cash flows to invested capital for each of the years in the noncompete agreement term are estimated. These cash flows are discounted to present value, using a discount rate that reflects the risk specifically associated to the noncompete agreement (20% in our case). As mentioned previously, we have used the mid-period convention (income is considered earned at midpoint during the year, or at an equal rate throughout the year). The present value of each cash flow to invested capital is summed up under the two scenarios of (1) with the noncompete ($10,748,470) and (2) without the noncompete ($9,905,611). The preliminary value of the noncompete agreement is estimated as the difference between these two amounts or:

$$\text{Preliminary value of noncompete agreement} = \text{PV of cash flows with the noncompete}$$
$$- \text{PV of cash flows without the noncompete}$$
$$= \$10,748,470 - \$9,905,611$$
$$= \$842,859$$

After considering the effect for the TAB, the estimated fair value of the noncompete agreement is $1,024,019 or $1,024,000 (rounded) in our example.

IN-PROCESS RESEARCH AND DEVELOPMENT

Nekkar has In-Process Research and Development (IPRD), which is valued using the replacement cost approach as presented in Exhibit 7.11. The fair value of IPRD is calculated as the

---

[31]See AMPF A3.5.3: Customer-related Intangible Assets – Documentation Requirements.

In-Process Research and Development

	Rate	Value
Cost of process R&D (actual expenses incurred)		$ 3,000,000
Opportunity cost	20.00%	$ 600,000
Entrepreneur's profit	5.00%	$ 150,000
Total replacement cost		$ 3,750,000
Fair value of in-process research and development		$ 3,750,000

EXHIBIT 7.11 Valuation of In-Process Research and Development – Replacement Cost

sum of the actual R&D expenses incurred to date with a component for the opportunity cost and for the entrepreneurial profit, similarly to what we have discussed earlier in the valuation of proprietary software. We have not considered taxes in this simplified example.

The actual expense incurred in Exhibit 7.11 may include certain sunk costs related to failed efforts that are not directly attributed to the prototypes currently being pursued, but that may have contributed indirectly to value generation as part of the research effort. Assumptions regarding the valuation of research would ordinarily be disclosed in a valuation report.

Assembled Workforce

The assembled workforce may represent a significant component of value in an ESE. The assembled workforce is typically valued using a replacement cost – new methodology. Under U.S. GAAP, the assembled workforce is considered a component of goodwill and is a contributory asset for purposes of the MPEEM method.

Nekkar has seven employees as of the valuation date. Our analyst estimates the fair value of the assembled and trained workforce at $1,555,000 using the model in Exhibit 7.12.

The fair value of Nekkar's assembled workforce consists of two components: the cost of recruiting a new workforce with similar characteristics and the cost of training it so that it can perform at the same level of efficiency as the current team.

The analyst estimates a cost of recruiting per employee that includes base salary, any fringe benefits, the percentage of base salary paid to an external recruiter (if applicable), the cost associated with the company's human resource staff interviewing and processing the new hire, and any cost of advertising. Training costs are then estimated based on the amount of time that a replacement employee of comparable skills will need to be in training. The estimate of training costs considers also the efficiency rate during the training period (92% versus a 100% expected from a fully trained employee).

Summary of Valuation Methodologies for Intangible Assets Exhibit 7.13 provides a summary of the cost, market, and income approach models as they typically apply to the main classes of intangible assets.

Employee Classification	Average Annual Salary	Fringe Benefits	Average Annual Salary with Benefits (1)	Total Hiring Cost per Employee (2)	Number of Employees	Total Hiring Cost
Executive	$ 200,000	$ 60,000	$ 260,000	$ 46,800	2	$ 613,600
Technical	$ 140,000	$ 42,000	$ 182,000	$ 32,760	3	$ 644,280
Sales	$ 130,000	$ 39,000	$ 169,000	$ 30,420	1	$ 199,420
Administrative and Other	$ 35,000	$ 10,500	$ 45,500	$ 8,190	1	$ 53,690
Total						$ 1,510,990

Employee Classification	Average Annual Salary with Benefits	Percent Effective	Number of Months Until Full Productivity	Inefficiency Training Costs (3)	Direct Training Costs (4)	Total Training Costs per Employee	Number of Employees	Total Training Cost
Executive	$ 260,000	92.00%	3	$ 5,200	$ 5,200	$ 10,400	2	$ 20,800
Technical	$ 182,000	92.00%	3	$ 3,640	$ 1,820	$ 5,460	3	16,380
Sales	$ 169,000	92.00%	3	$ 3,380	$ 1,690	$ 5,070	1	5,070
Administrative and Other	$ 45,500	92.00%	3	$ 910	$ 455	$ 1,365	1	1,365
								$ 43,615

Total	$ 1,554,605
FV of Assembled Workforce (rounded)	$ 1,555,000

EXHIBIT 7.12 Valuation of Assembled Workforce – Replacement Cost

ASSET	Primary	Secondary	Tertiary
Patents	Income	Market	Cost
Technology	Income	Market	Cost
Copyrights	Income	Market	Cost
Assembled workforce	Cost	Income	Market
Internally developed woftware	Cost	Market	Income
Brand name	Income	Market	Cost
Customer relationships	Income	Cost	Market

EXHIBIT 7.13   Intangible Assets – Summary of Valuation Methodologies

PUTTING IT ALL TOGETHER

Once all assets and liabilities have been appropriately identified and valued at fair value, the next step in the asset-accumulation model consists of adjusting the company's balance sheet to include the identified assets, liabilities, and related valuations.

Exhibit 7.14 presents the original balance sheet, the adjustments, and the adjusted balance sheet for Nekkar as of the valuation date.

Based on Exhibit 7.14, the equity value of Nekkar using the AAM is $26.1 million, a more than threefold increase relative to its unadjusted book value. The adjusted equity value of Nekkar includes the fair value of the assembled workforce as a component of goodwill. The AMM provides a "floor" for the valuation of the equity of an enterprise as a going concern, which can be integrated with other valuation techniques as a basis for a valuation conclusion. It should also be noted that the accumulated deficit of Nekkar turns into a surplus as a result of the revaluation. Approximately $18.1 million of expenses included in the accumulated deficit are effectively reclassified and capitalized as intangible assets in the balance sheet.

In situations where intangible assets are difficult to identify and/or the necessary information to reliably assess value cannot be obtained, the valuation analyst can obtain a preliminary indication of value for the company's equity by assuming that the company's retained losses to date ($14 million for Nekkar) represent built-up intangible value that can be posted to the balance sheet. Using this shortcut, the adjusted equity value of Nekkar would be $22 million (the total invested capital). While this preliminary indication does not have the rigor of a full analysis under AAM, it can still be useful as a reasonableness check of the results of the AAM and as a reference point for comparison to the results of other valuation approaches.

As a final step, we want to make sure that the discount rates that we have used to value the individual asset classes under the AAM, as summarized in an overall weighted-average return on assets or WARA, are consistent with the weighted average cost of capital (WACC) for the firm, and with the internal rate of return (IRR) that an investor would expect from an investment in Nekkar as a portfolio company. The WARA, WACC, and IRR represent three different perspective, of looking at the discount rate. The WARA considers the discount rate from the asset perspective, as the rate that needs to be applied to a stream of cash flows to get to the present value of the company's assets. The WACC focuses on liabilities and shareholders' equity side of the balance sheet, and reflects the cost of attracting and retaining

	Unadjusted	Adjustments	Adjusted
ASSETS			
Current assets			
Cash	$ 6,000		$ 6,000
Other current assets	2,000		2,000
Total current assets	8,000		8,000
Property and equipment, net	3,000		3,000
Intangible assets			
Customer relationships		3,867	3,867
Trade name		3,493	3,493
Proprietary software		1,623	1,623
Undeveloped patent		2,832	2,832
In-progress research and development		3,750	3,750
Noncompete agreement		1,024	1,024
Total intangible assets			16,589
Goodwill (assembled workforce)		1,555	1,555
Total assets	$ 11,000		$ 29,144
LIABILITIES AND SHAREHOLDERS' EQUITY			
Current liabilities			
Accounts payable	$ 3,000		$ 3,000
Shareholders' equity			
Preferred stock	20,000		20,000
Common stock	2,000		2,000
Accumulated surplus (deficit)	(14,000)	18,144	4,144
Total equity	8,000		26,144
Total liabilities and shareholders' equity	$ 11,000		$ 29,144

EXHIBIT 7.14 Asset Accumulation Method – Nekkar Technologies Inc. – December 31, 20X0 – Adjusted Balance Sheet (in $ thousand)

capital in the form of debt and equity to the firm. The IRR reflects the perspective of investors in search of return from their investment in the debt and equity of a portfolio company. Ultimately, WARA, WACC, and IRR have to reconcile into a single rate that harmonizes the interests of market participants.

Exhibit 7.15 presents a WARA/WACC/IRR reconciliation based on Nekkar's adjusted balance sheet.

In this simplified example, the analyst estimates that the return on assets (ROA) for net working capital and other tangible assets is 2.5% and 8.0%, respectively, and that the identified intangible assets, with the exception of the assembled workforce, have a ROA of 20%. The assembled workforce, as a component of goodwill, has a higher estimated ROA at 23%.

Assets:	Fair Value	Return on Asset	Return
Net working capital	$ 5,000,000	2.50%	$ 125,000
Other tangible assets	3,000,000	8.00%	240,000
Customer relationships	3,867,000	20.00%	773,400
Trade name	3,493,000	20.00%	698,600
Proprietary software	1,623,000	20.00%	324,600
Undeveloped patent	2,832,000	20.00%	566,400
Noncompete agreement	1,024,000	20.00%	204,800
In-progress research and development	3,750,000	20.00%	750,000
Assembled workforce	1,555,000	23.00%	357,650
Total	$ 26,144,000		$ 4,040,450
		WARA	15.45%
		WACC	18.50%
		IRR	19.00%

EXHIBIT 7.15   WARA-WACC-IRR Reconciliation: Nekkar Technologies Inc. – December 31, 20X0

Based on the fair value and ROA associated with each asset, we can now calculate the contribution of each asset to the WARA. For customer relationships, for instance, we have:

$$\text{Contribution to WARA of customer relationships} = \text{Fair Value of Customer Relationships}$$
$$\times \text{Asset-Specific ROA}$$
$$= \$3,867,000 \times 20\% = \$773,400$$

The WARA is the weighted sum of the individual return contributions divided by the total fair value of assets as follows:

$$\text{WARA} = \text{Total return contributions/Total assets at fair value}$$
$$= \$4,040,450/\$26,144,000 = 15.45\%$$

In our case study, we assume that Nekkar has a WACC of 18.5% and an IRR of 19% as a result of a separate assessment. The difference between the WARA and the WACC gives us a sense of the goodwill component (in excess of the value of the assembled workforce in our case) that is embedded in our asset-based valuation. Exhibit 7.16 shows a calculation of the embedded goodwill, given the WARA and the analyst's estimated WACC.

The difference between the WACC and the WARA represents the contribution of goodwill (in excess of the assembled workforce component) to the value of the enterprise under the AAM. Based on identified assets at fair value of $26,144,000, and on an estimated goodwill ROA of 23% (as used in the assembled workforce valuation) the difference in total return between the WACC and the WARA of $796,190 can be capitalized into an estimated goodwill

WACC	18.50%	[1]
WARA	15.45%	[2]
Diff	3.05%	[3] = [1] − [2]
Total identified assets	$ 26,144,000	[4]
Total return at WACC	$ 4,836,640	[5] = [1] × [4]
Total return at WARA	$ 4,040,450	[6] = [2] × [4]
Goodwill return	$ 796,190	[7] = [5] − [6]
Goodwill estimated cost of capital	23.00%	[8]
Goodwill – Additional	$ 3,461,696	[9] = [7]/[8]
Goodwill – Assembled workforce	$ 1,555,000	[10]
Total goodwill	$ 5,016,696	[11] = [9] + [10]
Adjusted total assets	$ 29,605,696	[12] = [4] + [9]
Goodwill %	16.95%	[13] = [11]/[12]

EXHIBIT 7.16 Implied Goodwill from WARA/WACC Reconciliation: Nekkar Technologies Inc. – December 31, 20X0

value of $3,461,696. The total goodwill adjustment of $5,016,696 (including the assembled workforce component) represents approximately 16.95% of the adjusted total asset value of Nekkar ($29,605,696, including goodwill). The analyst deems that a goodwill estimate of 16.95% is reasonable for Nekkar. It's important to note that the analyst does not have to adjust the fair value results of the asset-based method to include the implied goodwill ($3,461,696 in our case, which represents goodwill in excess of the value of the assembled workforce). Rather, the implied goodwill can provide a suitable check of reasonableness for the results of the asset-based method relative to the indications that come from a WACC estimate.

In our example, there is also a significant difference between the WARA and the IRR. As in the WARA–WACC comparison, the difference does not necessarily have to result in a revision in the fair value of the company from the value indicated by the asset-based method. The WARA–IRR difference confirms the fact that the WARA provides a "floor" for the company equity value and that it should be integrated, when possible, with other valuation methodologies more closely aligned with market-based inputs. A difference of about 3.5% between the WARA and the IRR may be an indication that the market is currently seeing more value in the company than what has been reflected in the asset-based valuation. It could be an indication that perhaps not all value-carrying assets have been captured in the adjusted balance sheet, or that market participant expectations are somewhat "overheated" for Nekkar or for the overall venture capital market, and that they may eventually have to converge toward lower expected returns. Even when no adjustment to the AAM fair value conclusion is made, the reason for any significant differences among the WARA, the WACC, and the IRR should be evaluated critically for its implications in terms of valuation. Under the MPF, the analyst must document in writing the reconciliation of the WARA to the WACC. If these cannot be reconciled, the MPF mandates that work files include documentation of the steps and analysis undertaken by the valuation professional that illustrates the attempted reconciliation, and an explanation about why the disparity exists.[32]

CONCLUSION

The AAM can provide insight into the drivers of value for an ESE with an approach that incorporates forward-looking as well as historical information. Under the AAM, intangible assets are identified and analyzed to determine their contribution to the value of the enterprise, typically using a combination of the income, market, and cost approaches. For valuation analysts, the MPF provides guidance on the key variables and the depth of documentation that should be gathered to adequately support a valuation conclusion under the fair value standard of ASC 820/IFRS 13. Aside from being a requirement for professionals that hold the CEIV certification, the MPF represents a set of sound practices for any valuation analyst that engages in valuations at fair value, and should assist in increasing the efficiency of the valuation process in transaction due diligence, board valuation reviews, and in the financial reporting and audit process.

---

[32] AMPF A3.9: Discount Rate/IRR/WARA.

CHAPTER 8

Non-GAAP Metrics in ESE Valuation

In recent years, the range of company performance measures used in valuation has been expanded to include a variety of metrics outside the framework of generally accepted accounting principles (GAAP). The combination of non-GAAP metrics (NGMs) with financial metrics based on GAAP has become a powerful tool to evaluate a company's growth prospects, its strategic direction, and its performance relative to its peers. NGMs are often a significant factor into management's compensation and provide insight into the incentives that drive management's strategic decisions.[1] In this chapter, we provide an overview of some of the most common NGMs that are used in early stage enterprise (ESE) valuation, a definition that covers a broad category of measures of a company's performance that are not included in corporate financial statements.

The first section of this chapter presents an overview of Non-GAAP Financial Measures (NGFM), a subgroup of NGMs, which adjust a GAAP line item (generally revenue, earnings, or cash flows from operations) by adding or subtracting other GAAP accounts. We have already seen examples of NGFMs in earlier chapters. For instance, Free Cash Flows to the Firm is an NGFM that adjusts GAAP net income (loss) to generate a cash flow measure commonly used in DCF modeling. Common measures of profitability based on financial statements earnings such as EBITDA (Earnings Before Interest, Taxes, Depreciation and Amortization), EBIT (Earnings Before Interest and Taxes) and EBIT $(1 - t)$ are also NGFMs. NGFMs like Adjusted EBITDA or Adjusted Net Loss are often used as a tool in the evaluation of management performance, and may require further adjustments to be meaningful indicators of "normalized" or "recurring" measures for ESE valuation purposes.

NGMs also include other metrics such as average revenue per customer/user, same store sales, occupancy rate, and number of paid customers, which are not derived from financial statements amounts or, in the case of ratios, have at least one of the components that is not drawn from the company's financial statements.[2] The second section of this chapter discusses

---

[1]According to a recent survey of Audit Analytics, 68% of S&P 500 companies use non-GAAP measures for executive compensation. See Audit Analytics, "Pros and Cons of Using Non-GAAP Metrics for Executive Compensation Including ESG Consideration," June 11, 2019.

[2]The AICPA PE/VC Valuation Guide provides a case study of how other metrics, such as the revenue run rate and cash burn, can be used to assess the status of a company, and its progress toward achieving

some of the "Other Metrics" that are most relevant in ESE valuation. Trends in number of users, gross billings, annual recurring revenues, and revenue run rates can provide useful insight into the company's ability to meet its performance targets.

In this chapter we illustrate some examples of NGMs from ESE registration filings ahead of an IPO offering in the United States (Form S-1 or S-1A). The companies that we discuss typically combine significant growth and a broad consumer base with net losses and a new business model that is rapidly evolving, and all fall into our ESE classification at the time of their pre-IPO filings. In registration filings, NGMs are often included in the management discussion and analysis and in other disclosures outside of the audited financial statements. NGMs are not covered by the auditor's opinion on the financial statements. Professional standards require that the auditor read the information in a registration statement that is not included in the company's audited financial statements and be alert to material inconsistencies. The auditor may also be asked to provide "comfort" to the underwriters regarding the reconciliation between a non-GAAP metric and a GAAP account included in the registration statement in a separate "comfort letter." The Public Company Accounting Oversight Board (PCAOB) is currently exploring whether to enhance auditor's responsibility for NGMs beyond the current standards.[3]

NON-GAAP FINANCIAL MEASURES

As defined by SEC Regulation G and IOSCO guidance, a non-GAAP financial measure is:

> *a numerical measure of a registrant's historical or future financial performance, financial position, or cash flows that (i) excludes amounts, or is subject to adjustments that have the effect of excluding amounts, that are included in the most directly comparable measure calculated and presented in accordance with GAAP in the statement of income, balance sheet or statement of cash flows (or equivalent statements of the issuer); or (ii) includes amounts, or is subject to adjustments that have the effect of including amounts, that are excluded from the most directly comparable measure so*

---

its milestones. See AICPA Case Study 12: High Value Early Stage E-Commerce Start-Up in a High Risk, High Opportunity Market," C.12.1-C.12.53.

[3]Under current PCAOB standards, auditors do not have responsibilities to perform procedures related to information presented in corporate earnings releases, investor presentations, and other communications, such as calls with analysts and information on the company's website. Company performance measures that are included in an annual report outside the financial statements, for example, in management's discussion and analysis of financial condition and results of operations, are considered "other information" and are subject to the requirements of PCAOB AS 2710, *Other Information in Documents Containing Audited Financial Statements*. The PCAOB has currently a research and standard-setting project in place on the *Auditor's Role Regarding Other Information and Company Performance Measures, Including Non-GAAP Measures*. The objective of the project is to "evaluate the auditor's role in relation to other information and company performance measures, including non-GAAP financial measures, and explore whether there is a need for guidance, changes to PCAOB standards, or other regulatory action" (PCAOB website at www.pcaob.org as of December 1, 2019).

calculated and presented. A Non-GAAP financial measure does not include financial measures required to be disclosed by GAAP, Commission rules, or a system of regulation of a government or governmental authority or self-regulatory organization that is applicable to the registrant.[4]

According to a study published by Audit Analytics, 97% of S&P500 companies present NGMs in the document that contains their annual financial statement filing.[5] In a 2016 survey, the CFA Institute has noted that more than 60% of the respondents always or often use non-GAAP financial measures (NGFM) in their investment decision-making process, and many investors have expressed that they find NGFM reporting to be a useful input for predicting future cash flows and valuing reporting companies.[6]

In an ESE, net loss or negative EBITDA are typically adjusted in valuation by the exclusion/inclusion of items that are considered nonrecurring, infrequent, and unusual in nature to get to a stronger measure of core performance. Generally, if the nature of the charge is such that it is reasonably likely to recur within two years, or there was a similar charge or gain within the prior two years, there is a good case for considering the charge as a recurring item and leaving it unchanged for valuation purposes. In the lack of a standard definition for Adjusted Net Loss or Adjusted EBITDA, it is important to be aware of differences in definition between companies that may need further adjustments for comparability.

Adjusted Net Loss

Exhibit 8.1 presents a comparison of the Adjusted Net Loss calculation of Crowdstrike Holding Inc. (Crowdstrike) and Cloudflare Inc. (Cloudflare), two companies that are active in the cybersecurity software industry and that have conducted their IPO in 2019 on the NASDAQ exchange in the United States. The data in the exhibit is drawn from the registration statement that the companies filed ahead of their IPO.

Both companies start with the financial statement Loss from Operations to arrive at a Non-GAAP Loss from Operations. The adjustments include:

- Stock-based compensation. This adjustment backs out from the GAAP Loss from Operations the value of the stock granted to the company's employees. From a valuation perspective, there is a strong case for considering stock-based compensation as a recurring item, and not treating it as an adjustment in the calculation of "base" net loss figures. Adjusting stock-based compensation expenses while calculating either adjusted net loss or other NGFMs is especially common in the information technology sector.
- Amortization of acquired intangibles. Under current accounting standards, intangible assets that are acquired as part of a business combination must be amortized over their remaining life. To the extent acquisitions are a recurring and structural aspect of a company's growth strategy, a valuation adjustment for the amortization of acquired intangibles would typically not be appropriate for valuation purposes. On the other hand, if the

---

[4]Code of Federal Regulation, Title 17, Chapter 2, Part 244, Regulation G, Section 244.101.
[5]"Audit Analytics, Long-Term Trends in Non-GAAP Disclosures: A Three-Year Overview," October 10, 2018.
[6]CFA Institute, "Investor Uses, Expectations, and Concerns on Non-GAAP Financial Measures," CFA Institute: 2016.

(US$ in thousand) Year ended January 31	Crowdstrike			(US$ in thousand) Year ended December 31	Cloudflare		
	2017	2018	2019		2016	2017	2018
Revenue	$ 52,745	$ 118,752	$ 249,824	Revenue	$ 84,791	$ 134,915	$ 192,674
Loss from operations	$ (90,556)	$ (131,440)	$ (136,864)	Loss from operations	$ (17,029)	$ (9,730)	$ (84,899)
Adjustments:				Adjustments:			
Stock-based compensation expense	$ 1,994	$ 12,343	$ 20,505	Stock-based compensation expense	$ 5,700	$ 2,755	$ 27,347
Amortization of acquired intangible assets	$ 97	$ 628	$ 583	Amortization of acquired intangible assets	$ 38	$ 462	$ 517
Acquisition-related expenses	$ -	$ 167	$ -				
Non-GAAP loss from operations	$ (88,465)	$ (118,302)	$ (115,776)	Non-GAAP loss from operations	$ (11,291)	$ (6,513)	$ (57,035)
Non-GAAP operating margin	–168%	–100%	–46%	Non-GAAP operating margin	–13%	–5%	–30%
Revenue growth rate		125.14%	110.37%	Revenue growth rate		59.11%	42.81%

EXHIBIT 8.1   Adjusted Loss from Operations – Crowdstrike and Cloudflare

Source: Based on data from Crowdstrike Holdings Inc., Form S-1A filed June 6, 2019 and Cloudflare Inc., Form S-1A filed September 11, 2019.

company has engaged in a one-off acquisition, an adjustment for acquired intangibles may be appropriate in valuation.

- Acquisition-related expenses. As in the case of the amortization of intangible assets, the valuation treatment of this item, which may include substantial legal, accounting, and consulting fees related to business acquisitions, should depend on whether it is expected to be recurring versus nonrecurring. In this case, the inclusion of an adjustment for valuation purposes seems appropriate, given that it only applies to one of the three years in the series for Crowdstrike.

Adjusted net loss as reported by management can also be useful in an ESE valuation as an indication of the progress that the company is making toward meeting its milestones and performance objectives.

Adjusted EBITDA

Adjusted EBITDA starts from the value of net income (loss in an ESE) as reported in the financial statements and adjusts it to come to a measure that reflects the company's operating performance before the effect of financial leverage (interest), taxes, and noncash expenses related to asset amortization and depreciation. Exhibit 8.2 compares the Adjusted EBITDA of Uber and Lyft from their pre-IPO registration statements.

Items [1]–[3] in the list of adjustments are typical of all EBITDA calculations, and reverse the effect of interest, taxes, and depreciation/amortization on net loss. Items [4] and [5] are analogous to the stock-based compensation expense and acquisition-related adjustments that we have discussed with reference to Adjusted Net Loss. The other items are specific to the reference company and may reflect a different definition of Adjusted EBITDA across companies.

In the case of Uber, the Adjusted EBITDA measure includes a significant "Other Income" adjustment of $4.99 billion in 2018, which effectively turns the reported net income of $1 billion into a $1.8 billion Adjusted EBITDA Loss. By digging a little deeper in the registration statement, we find out that the other income includes:

- A nonrecurring gain on divestitures from operations in Southeast Asia and Russia of $3.2 billion.
- An unrealized gain on investments of $1.5 billion, net of a $0.5 billion change in fair value of embedded derivatives. Gains and losses on investments and derivatives at fair value are a common adjustment to EBITDA figures, and need to be evaluated on a case-by-case basis to determine their appropriateness in view of their recurring versus nonrecurring nature from a valuation perspective.
- Foreign currency exchange losses of $45 million. Foreign currency remeasurements are generally adjusted in valuation if they relate to exposures from investment activities that are not part of a firm's "core" business. An adjustment may not be appropriate in valuation if the foreign exchange exposure is generated through regular operating activities of the company.

		Uber			Lyft		
Line	Year ended December 31	2016	2017	2018	Year ended December 31	2016	2017	2018
	Net income (loss)	$ (370)	$ (4,033)	$ 997	Net income (loss)	$ (682.8)	$ (688.3)	$ (911.3)
	Adjustments:				Adjustments:			
[1]	Interest expense	$ 334	$ 479	$ 648	Interest income, net	$ (7.0)	$ (20.2)	$ (66.5)
[2]	Benefit from (provision for) income taxes	$ 28	$ (542)	$ 283	Provision for income taxes	$ 0.4	$ 0.6	$ 0.7
[3]	Depreciation and amortization	$ 320	$ 510	$ 426	Depreciation and amortization	$ 0.5	$ 2.6	$ 18.8
[4]	Stock-based compensation expense	$ 128	$ 137	$ 172	Stock-based compensation	$ 9.4	$ 9.5	$ 8.6
[5]	Acquisition and financing-related expenses	$ -	$ 4	$ 15	Costs related to acquisitions	$ -	$ -	$ 3.5
[6]	Income (loss) from discontinued operations, net of income taxes	$ (2,876)	$ -	$ -				
[7]	Net income (loss) attributable to redeemable noncontrolling interest, net of tax	$ -	$ -	$ (10)				
[8]	Income (loss) from equity method investments, net of tax	$ -	$ -	$ 42				
[9]	Other income (expense), net	$ (139)	$ 16	$ (4,993)	Other income, net	$ (3.2)	$ (0.3)	$ (0.7)
[10]	Legal, tax, and regulatory reserves and settlements	$ 49	$ 440	$ 340				
[11]	Asset impairment/loss on sale of assets	$ 9	$ 340	$ 237				
[12]	Restructuring charges	$ -	$ 7	$ (4)				
					Changes to insurance reserve	$ 17.2	$ -	$ 3.4
	Adjusted EBITDA	$ (2,517)	$ (2,642)	$ (1,847)	Adjusted EBITDA	$ (665.5)	$ (696.1)	$ (943.5)

EXHIBIT 8.2 Adjusted EBITDA – Uber and Lyft ($ Million)

Source: Based on data from Uber Technologies Inc. Form S-1A filed April 26, 2019; Lyft Inc., Form S-1A filed March 27, 2019.

Other adjustments for Uber include:

- Asset impairments. The impairment of intangible assets is required under U.S. GAAP when an asset's carrying value exceeds its recovery amounts. Impairments of assets under the property, plant, and equipment accounts are also required when circumstances indicate that an asset's carrying book value cannot be recovered.
- Asset sales. One-off asset sales are also common EBITDA adjustments. In Uber's schedule, asset sales are combined with asset impairments in a single entry.
- Legal, tax, and regulatory reserves and settlements. For Uber, the increase in these reserves and settlements reflect the greater exposure of the company to regulatory scrutiny, litigation, and governmental investigation in recent years. To the extent these costs become part of the ordinary way for Uber of doing business, they may not need an adjustment to come to a normalized EBITDA figure for valuation purposes.

In the end, the Adjusted EBITDA that is reported in the S-1 does provide useful information to the analyst to identify areas that may warrant a normalization adjustment in valuation. It is important to keep in mind that the criteria that guide management's definition of Adjusted EBITDA may not necessarily coincide with the valuation analyst's approach in identifying what is recurrent and part of the company's ordinary operations. The analyst in fact may want to include certain items that are ordinary, but not part of what management sees as the company's "core" business (for instance, in the case of Uber, some of the legal reserves and settlements, and foreign currency exposure that relate to the company's operating activities). For both Uber and Lyft, the adjustments included in the Adjusted EBITDA measure in 2018 have the result of depicting a less favorable picture of the firm than the unadjusted GAAP measures.

Billings

Billings represent the total amount of current and future revenue that has been invoiced to customers in the current period. Billings can be calculated on a gross basis, before any deduction for items such as sales commissions, taxes, and product returns, or on a net basis. Gross billings differ from GAAP revenues in that (a) revenue may be recognized over the life of the contract as services are performed and products delivered under GAAP rules, while billings are calculated as of the contract date and (b) only a portion of gross billings actually ends up being recognized as revenue due to deductions, which may include sales commissions, product returns, etc. Net billings can be calculated by adding unearned revenue to GAAP revenue. For instance, Slack Technologies Inc. describes "Calculated Billings" in its S-1 as follows:

> *Calculated Billings consist of our revenue plus the change in deferred revenue in a given period. The Calculated Billing metric is intended to reflect sales to new paid customers plus renewals and additional sales to existing paid customers. Our management uses Calculated Billings to measure and monitor our sales growth because we generally bill our paid customers at the time of sale, but may recognize a portion of the related revenue ratably over time. Only amounts invoiced to a paid customer in a given period are included in Calculated Billings. We generally bill our paid customers at the time of sale, but may recognize a portion of the related revenue ratably over time.*[7]

---

[7]Slack Technologies Inc. Amendment N.3 to Form S-1 Registration Statement under The Securities Act of 1933, Registration 333-231041, filed on May 31, 2019.

	Year Ended January 31,		
	2017	2018	2019
Revenue:	$ 105,153	$ 220,544	$ 400,552
Add: Total deferred revenue, end of period	$ 56,984	$ 125,453	$ 241,873
Less: Total deferred revenue, beginning of period	$ (18,747)	$ (56,984)	$ (125,453)
Calculated billings	$ 143,390	$ 289,013	$ 516,972

EXHIBIT 8.3   Slack Technologies, Inc. – Calculated Billings ($ Thousand)
Source: Based on data from Slack Technologies, Inc. Form S-1A, filed May 31, 2019.

Slack provides a reconciliation of revenue to calculated billing as shown in Exhibit 8.3.

Cash Burn

For an ESE, the availability of cash and the ability of the company to access new funding as needed is critical to its survival. To that extent, metrics that provide a representation of the company's liquidity position and cash strength are significant indicators of the company's ability to sustain its operations and eventually be able to reach profitability. Cash burn is a common cash-based metric that represents the amount of cash used by the company over a specified period, typically a month. A monthly cash burn rate of $0.5 million, for example, indicates that the company needs $0.5 million in cash, net of any cash inflow from revenue, for its monthly operations. Given the amount of cash at hand (for instance, $5 million), a company with a cash burn of $0.5 million will run out of cash in 20 months (5.0/0.5 = 20), assuming it continues to deploy cash at the current levels. For companies that are running on negative cash flows from operations, the cash burn is a key indicator of company's sustainability and of the likelihood and timing of a new round of financing. When looking at the cash burn is also important to consider the company's forecasts of cash flows from operations. The cash burn can rapidly deteriorate if the company engages in high capital expenditures to sustain growth without increasing revenues accordingly. Conversely, a reduction in cash burn while the company is experiencing revenue growth may be an indication that the company is achieving economies of scale and is on a solid path to profitability.

OTHER METRICS

NGMs also include metrics that are derived from:

- Data that is outside the GAAP financial statements (for instance, the number of active users of a technology platform); or
- The division of a GAAP number by this data (for instance, revenue per user); or
- A GAAP number as a percentage of it (for instance, revenue as a percentage of bookings).

These Other Metrics (OM) are industry and often company-specific metrics. A clear understanding of how they are defined and constructed is critical for comparability over time and among companies and for their use in valuation. For an ESE, in the lack of profitability, OMs tend to focus on metrics related to revenue and company's size in terms of number of customers/users and market share. The OM umbrella also includes metrics that represent the company's performance in terms of environmental, social, and governance (ESG) factors. The consistent measurement of some of these factors and the way in which they can influence valuation is a matter of debate. We conclude with a note on additional OMs that are industry- or company-specific and may be useful to evaluate a company's progress toward the achievement of its milestones.

Bookings

Bookings represent the total amount of revenue stated in a signed customer contract. Bookings reflect the contractual obligation of the company's customers to pay the company for its products and services, independently of when those services will be invoiced or performed. Bookings differ from billings in that the revenue stated in a customer agreement may not be invoiced all at once. For instance, a company may have a new three-year agreement with a customer for $300,000 in total revenue ($300,000 in bookings) signed in Year 1 that is invoiced in three annual tranches of $100,000 each. In this case, the company will record in relation to the contract:

Year 1: $300,000 of Bookings and $100,000 of Billings

Year 2: $0 in Bookings and $100,000 in Billings

Year 3: $0 in Bookings and $100,000 in Billings

Bookings are an indication of the scale of a company's product or service offering, which ultimately impacts revenue. Bookings can be calculated on a gross basis, before any deduction for items such as taxes, sales commissions, and customer discounts, or on a net basis. Gross bookings are typically not an NGFM in that they cannot be reconciled to a GAAP measure just by adding or subtracting another GAAP account. There may be more than unearned revenue in the adjustment. As such, we rely on management's definition and reporting to understand the nature of this NGM and its potential impact on a company's valuation.

Exhibit 8.4 shows bookings as reported by Lyft and Uber in their S-1 pre-IPO registration statements.

Based on Exhibit 8.4 it appears that bookings as a percentage of revenue fall within a relative narrow comparability range between the two companies. In the case of Lyft, the growth rate of bookings has significantly declined in 2018 relative to prior year, while for Uber it has declined at a slower pace. The picture somewhat changes, however, once we realize that the two companies define bookings in materially different ways.

	Lyft		
	Year Ended December 31,		
	2016	2017	2018
Bookings ($ Million)	$ 1,905	$ 4,587	$ 8,054
Revenue as a Percentage of Bookings	18.0%	23.1%	26.8%
Growth Rate of Bookings		140.8%	75.6%

	Uber		
	Year Ended December 31,		
	2016	2017	2018
Bookings ($ Million)	$ 19,236	$ 34,409	$ 49,799
Revenue as a Percentage of Bookings	0.0%	0.0%	0.0%
Growth Rate of Bookings		178.9%	144.7%

EXHIBIT 8.4   Bookings – Lyft and Uber

Source: Based on data from Uber Technologies Inc. Form S-1A filed April 26, 2019 (Bookings and Growth Revenue of Bookings) and Author based on S-1A data (Revenue as Percentage of Bookings); Lyft Inc., Form S-1A filed March 27, 2019.

For Lyft, bookings as the aggregate charges of rides on the company's platform, *net* of the following deductions:

- Any pass-through amount paid to drivers and regulatory agencies, including sales tax and other fees such as airport and city fees, as well as tips, tolls, cancellation, and additional fees;
- The aggregate amount of market-wide price adjustment promotions offered to ridesharing riders, and
- Any discounts for renters of bikes and scooters.

For Uber, on the other hand, bookings are reported *gross* of any applicable tools, fees, taxes, and amounts paid by shippers for Uber Freight shipments, without adjustment for consumer discounts and refunds, and various driver benefits and incentives. Uber's gross bookings do not include tips earned by drivers.

Number of Customers   The number of customers (also called users or subscribers, depending on the industry) is an important metric for most ESEs, as they work to scale their operations and expand in their target market. Scalability is a critical feature for a company that is planning to leverage off technology to achieve profitability and it's common to find significant amounts of money being deployed even at an early stage in sales and marketing expenses directed at increasing the number of customers as a key condition for the company's survival. The number of customers can be dissected and analyzed in multiple ways to identify trends, formulate financial projections, and manage strategic decisions. Let's take, for instance, the example of Slack Technologies Inc., a software company that went public in June 2019 on the New York Stock Exchange. Slack developed a real-time collaboration app and platform

	Slack Technologies Inc.		
As of January 31	2017	2018	2019
Paid Customers	37,000	59,000	88,000
Paid Customers > $100,000	135	298	575
Net Dollar Retention Rate	171%	152%	143%
Year ended January 31	2017	2018	2019
Revenue ($ thousand)	$ 105,153	$ 220,554	$ 400,552
Revenue Growth		109.75%	81.61%
Paid Customers Growth Rate		59.46%	49.15%
Paid Customers > $100,000 Growth Rate		120.74%	92.95%

EXHIBIT 8.5 Slack Technologies Inc. – Revenue and Selected Key Business Metrics ($ in Thousands)
Source: Based on data from Slack Technologies Inc. Form S-1A filed May 31, 2019.

and had 2019 revenues of $400.6 million, a net loss of $138.9 million, and an IPO reference valuation of $15.7 billion based on an IPO reference price of $26 per share.[8] In its pre-IPO S-1 registration statement, Slack gives us an insight into its "Key Business Metrics," including what is shown in Exhibit 8.5.

Based on Slack's S-1A, paid customers had increased at annual rates of 59.5% and 49.2% in 2018 and 2019, respectively, but paid customers defined as those organizations with annual subscriptions of more than $100,000 increased at a much faster pace of 120.7% and 93.0% over the same period, respectively. The growth in the number of large customers can help explain the company's increase in revenue by 109.7% and 81.6% in 2018 and 2019, respectively.

The net dollar retention rate complements the paid customer metrics by reflecting the ability of the company to retain and grow the business from existing customers. As defined by Slack, the net dollar retention rate measures the total current period revenue divided by the total prior period revenue for the customers that were with the firm as of the end of the prior period and includes the change of scope in the existing customers subscriptions. As competition in Slack's marketplace continues to grow, Slack's ability to sustain its retention rates at increasing levels of profitability is likely to be a critical factor in turning it into a stable, viable business.

Exhibit 8.6 reports similar metrics for Pinterest Inc., a company with an image-sharing online platform that went public in April 2019 on the New York Stock Exchange. Pinterest was founded in 2008 and has a more stable net dollar retention rate. As in the case of Slack both the net dollar retention rate and the increase in paid customers (especially above the $100,000 revenue mark) point to a rapid growth phase, which in Pinterest's case was enhanced by the approaching of its IPO event.

---

[8]Slack closed at $38.62 on June 20, 2019, its first day of trading, and was trading below its reference price as of September 30, 2019.

	Pinterest Inc.		
As of December 31	2017	2018	2019
Paid Customers	9,793	9,444	10,806
Paid Customers > $100,000	144	132	203
Net Dollar Retention Rate	134%	136%	139%
Year ended December 31	2017	2018	2019
Revenue ($ thousand)	$ 298,870	$ 472,852	$ 755,932
Revenue Growth		58.21%	59.87%
Paid Customers Growth Rate		−3.56%	14.42%
Paid Customers > $100,000 Growth Rate		−8.33%	53.79%

EXHIBIT 8.6   Pinterest Inc. – Revenue and Selected Key Business Metrics
Source: Based on data from Pinterest Inc. Form S-1A filed April 8, 2019.

Active Users   In social medial, online retail, and other internet-oriented industries it is common to distinguish "active users", who have logged in, visited a site, and perhaps completed an online transaction, from users who may have registered on an internet platform but have not executed any transactions or have not engaged with the online community.[9] There is not a broadly accepted, standardized definition of active user. A company may focus on:

- Daily active users (DAU) – typical for businesses where users are expected to interact on a daily basis (email, calendar, games).
- Weekly active users (WAU) – typical for businesses with weekly frequency (forums and social communities, mobile apps, productivity, and analytics tools).
- Monthly active users (MAU) – typical to many business-to-business applications where users are expected to interact a few times a month or less (email providers, accounting, and bookkeeping).

Pinterest includes both MAU and WAU in its key metrics. As stated in its pre-IPO registration statement, Pinterest defines monthly active users (MAUs) as "logged-in Pinterest users who visits our website or opens our mobile application at least once during the 30-day period ending on the date of measurement," and weekly active users (WAU) as "logged-in Pinterest users who visits our website or opens our mobile application at least once during the seven-day period ending on the date of measurement." Pinterest explains that MAUs are the primary metric by which the company measures the scale of its active user base and that it actively monitors the relationship of WAUs to MAUs.

As noted in the registration statement, Pinterest indicates that user growth trends, which are reflected in the number of MAUs, are a key factor that affects the company's revenue and

---

[9]For a discussion and practical example of how non-GAAP valuation metrics can be used in the valuation of social media companies, see Mark Zyla, "Social Media: Who Owns It and What Is it Worth?," Webinar Handbook, Business Valuation Resources LLC, February 23, 2017.

financial results, and that as their user base and the quality of their users grow, the company believes that the potential to increase its revenue grows as well.

Active users include both existing, recurring users (existing users) as well as new users that approach the company's internet platform for the first time. The retention rate of a company's active users (existing and new) is a key metric in assessing the value of a company's customer relationships and their potential revenue generation for the firm over time. User growth trends, which are reflected in the number of users, are a key factor that may affect revenue and financial results.

Revenue-Based Metrics

Revenue-based NGMs are critical in driving ESE performance. In combination with the number of customers and considering customer retention rates, these metrics are useful tools in valuation.

Annual Recurring Revenue   Among revenue-based metrics, annual recurring revenues has a prominent place as an indication of the "core" operating performance for a company. Annual recurring revenue may take as a starting point a company's annual revenue (a GAAP figure) and subtracting the amount that is not deemed recurring (a non-GAAP figure). Alternatively, it may be calculated as the monthly recurring revenue (MRR) (monthly revenue less nonrecurring component), typically from the most recent month at period end, multiplied by 12, or also as the daily recurring revenue (DRR) multiplied by 365. The annual recurring revenue may provide a more suitable basis for a revenue multiplier, for instance, in the estimate of a potential acquisition price, than the unadjusted GAAP revenue.

Revenue Run Rate   For a high-growth company, revenue data that is even a few months old may not provide an adequate basis to project future revenues. In high-growth circumstances, companies often report a revenue run rate, which estimates revenues based on the revenues over a closer and shorter time horizon from the measurement date. For instance, an annual revenue run rate (ARR) may be calculated by taking the revenue of the last full quarter and multiplying it by 4, or using revenues for the latest month multiplied by 12. A time lag can also be incorporated in the analysis, for instance, by using the average of monthly revenues over the past six months multiplied by 12, or quarterly revenues with a three-month lag.

Revenue per User (RPU)   The revenue per user (RPU) ratio is a common metric for companies that generate revenue through subscription services, such as social media companies or data service providers. RPU is defined as the amount of revenue divided by the number of users. There is not a standardized definition of RPU. The RPU ratio can be defined over an annual period, a monthly, weekly, or even daily time frame. Pinterest, for instance, uses average revenue per user (ARPU) as a key metric, which is defined as total revenue in a given geography divided by the average number of monthly active users (MAU) in that geography. Pinterest presents ARPU on a U.S. and international basis because it monetizes users in different geographies at different average rates.

	Year 1	Base Year
Operating Information		
Number of existing users/subscribers	4,200	3,000
Gross billings	$ 34,500,000	$ 30,000,000
Cash		$ 5,000,000
Net revenue	$ 31,050,000	$ 27,000,000
% of operating expenses spent acquiring new users	40.00%	
% of operating expenses spent on corporate expenses	25.00%	
% of operating expenses spent servicing existing users	35.00%	
Corporate tax rate	15.00%	
Growth rate in general corporate expenses for next 10 years	15.00%	

EXHIBIT 8.7   Company A – Inputs

In the paragraphs that follow, we illustrate how to build a simple business valuation model using RPU as a key driver of the valuation.[10] Let's assume that Company A has 3,000 users in the base year, and expects to have 4,200 users by the end of Year 1. Total gross billings are expected to increase from $30.0 million in the base year to $34.5 million in Year 1. The company currently has cash at hand of $5 million and is still incurring operating losses. Of the company's operating expenses, 40% are expected to relate to new user acquisition, 35% to the retention and development of business from existing users, and 25% are general corporate expenses not related to a specific user base. The company has a corporate tax rate of 15% and expects general corporate expenses to grow over the next 10 years at an annual rate of 15%. Exhibit 8.7 summarizes these company-level inputs.

Our valuation analysis consists of four steps:

Step 1. Estimate of Value of Current Users. Company A expects to have 4,200 users at the end of Year 1, with an expected life of 10 years. Each year, there is an 85% probability that a user will continue its relationship with the company and a 15% probability that its relationship with the company will terminate (an annual renewal probability for current users of 85%). Also, the volume of business generated by each user that continues its relationship with the company is expected to grow at a rate of 15% per year. The discount rate of the current users cash flows is estimated at 15%. Exhibit 8.8 presents a summary of inputs in the valuation of current users for Company A.

---

[10]In building this model, we have referred to the models developed by Aswath Damodaran for the valuation of Uber Technologies Inc, modified to reflect the specific features of our hypothetical ESE and for other characteristics. See especially Asworth Damodaran, "User/Subscriber Economics: An Alternative View of Uber's Value," June 28, 2017, available at https://aswathdamodaran.blogspot .com/2017/06/usersubscriber-economics-alternative.html; and Aswath Damodaran, "Uber's Coming Out Party: Personal Mobility Pioneer or Car Service on Steroids?," April 15, 2019, available at: https://aswathdamodaran.blogspot.com/2019/04/ubers-coming-out-party-personal.html. We have also referred to the analysis of social media companies in Mark Zyla "Social Media: Who Owns It and What Is it Worth?" Webinar Handbook, Business Valuation Resources LLC, February 23, 2017.

Current Users	
Revenue share of gross billings	90.00%
Lifetime of a user/subscriber	10
Annual renewal probability	85.00%
Growth rate in annual revenues/user	15.00%
Growth rate in operating expenses/user	13.65%
Discount rate	15.00%
Cost of service as % of revenue	45.50%

EXHIBIT 8.8   Valuation of Current Users – Inputs

Exhibit 8.9 presents the valuation of current users for Company A based on these assumptions, and assuming a risk-adjusted discount rate of 15%.

The model in Exhibit 8.9 has 10 annual periods in addition to the base year, which correspond to the 10 years of the expected life of existing users. Line [1] represents the survival rate of the base year users as of the end of each annual period. For each annual period, the survival rate is calculated by multiplying the rate in the prior period by the probability of survival at 85%. For example, in Year 2, membership survival is:

$$\text{Membership Survival (Year 2)} = 0.85 \times 85\% = 0.7225$$

In Line [2], gross billings per user are estimated using the prior year figure multiplied by the growth rate of annual revenue per user of 15%. For example, for Year 2 we have:

$$\text{Gross Billings per User (Year 2)} = \$11{,}500 \times 1.15 = \$13{,}225$$

In Line [3], net revenues per user are calculated by multiplying the estimated gross billings per user for the period by the revenue share of gross billing of 90.0%. For instance:

$$\text{Net Revenues per User (Year 2)} = \$13{,}225 \times 0.90 = \$11{,}903$$

In Line [4], operating expenses per user are estimated by multiplying the prior-year operating expenses per user in [4] by the growth rate of operating expenses of 13.65% (input):

$$\text{Operating Expenses per User (Year 2)} = 4{,}654 \times 1.1365 = \$5{,}289$$

Operating profit per user in [5] is calculated as the difference between net revenues per user and operating expenses per user. We can then determine the survival-adjusted operating profit in [6] as the operating profit per user [5] multiplied by the membership survival rate [1]. For example, in Year 2 we have:

$$\text{Survival Adjusted Operating Profit (Year 2)} = \$6{,}614 \times 0.7225 = \$4{,}778$$

Value of Existing Customers

	Base Year	1	2	3	4	5	6	7	8	9	10
[1] Membership survival	1.0000	0.8500	0.7225	0.6141	0.5220	0.4437	0.3771	0.3206	0.2725	0.2316	0.1969
[2] Gross billings/user	$ 10,000	$ 11,500	$ 13,225	$ 15,209	$ 17,490	$ 20,114	$ 23,131	$ 26,600	$ 30,590	$ 35,179	$ 40,456
[3] Net revenues/user	$ 9,000	$ 10,350	$ 11,903	$ 13,688	$ 15,741	$ 18,102	$ 20,818	$ 23,940	$ 27,531	$ 31,661	$ 36,410
[4] Operating expenses/user	$ 4,095	$ 4,654	$ 5,289	$ 6,011	$ 6,832	$ 7,764	$ 8,824	$ 10,029	$ 11,397	$ 12,953	$ 14,721
[5] Operating profit/user	$ 4,905	$ 5,696	$ 6,614	$ 7,677	$ 8,909	$ 10,338	$ 11,994	$ 13,911	$ 16,134	$ 18,708	$ 21,689
[6] Survival-adjusted operating profit		$ 4,842	$ 4,778	$ 4,714	$ 4,651	$ 4,587	$ 4,523	$ 4,460	$ 4,396	$ 4,333	$ 4,270
[7] After-tax operating profit/user	$ 4,169	$ 4,115	$ 4,061	$ 4,007	$ 3,953	$ 3,899	$ 3,845	$ 3,791	$ 3,737	$ 3,683	$ 3,629
[8] Discount factor		0.9325	0.8109	0.7051	0.6131	0.5332	0.4636	0.4031	0.3506	0.3048	0.2651
[9] Present value		$ 3,838	$ 3,293	$ 2,826	$ 2,424	$ 2,079	$ 1,783	$ 1,528	$ 1,310	$ 1,122	$ 962
[10] Value per existing user =	$ 21,165										
[11] Number of existing users =	3,000										
[12] Value of Existing Users	$ 63,493,762										

EXHIBIT 8.9 Company A – Valuation of Existing Users

New Users	
Cost of acquiring new user (estimate)	$ 15,600
Growth rate in number of total users (Years 1–5)	40.0%
Growth rate in number of total users (Years 6–10)	10.0%
Growth rate in number of total users (Years 11+)	2.5%
Discount rate	18.0%
Growth rate in cost of acquiring new user = Inflation rate	1.5%

EXHIBIT 8.10   Valuation of New Users – Inputs

After deducting taxes at 15% rate, the present value of each annual profit figure in [9] and the total value per existing user of $21,165 in [10] are calculated using a risk-adjusted discount rate of 15% (input) and the mid-period convention in the discount factor. Finally, we compute the value of existing users by multiplying the unit value of $21,165 by the number of existing users in the base year:

$$\text{Value of Existing Users} = \text{Unit value} \times \text{Number of users in Base Year}$$

$$= \$21,165 \times 3,000$$

$$= \$63.5 \text{ million}$$

Step 2. Estimate of Value of New Users. Company A is expected to expand its user base over time. Exhibit 8.10 presents the key inputs for the valuation of Company A's new users.

The number of total users is expected to grow at a rate of 40% and 10% in Years 1–5 and Years 6–10, respectively, and continue to grow at the risk-free rate of 2.5% after that in perpetuity. The number of new users is expected to reflect the change in total users, after adjusting for any churning effect. Each new user comes with a cost of acquisition of $15,600 for the company, which is also expected to grow at an estimated annual inflation rate of 1.5%. For each year, the value added by new users is then discounted at the risk-adjusted discount rate of 18%, using the mid-period convention. Notice that the discount rate for new users is higher than the discount rate that is used to discount revenue from current users due to the higher risk profile of net revenue from new users. Exhibit 8.11 illustrates the valuation of new users for Company A.

In the base year, the value of a new user to the company is simply the difference between the value of an existing user and the cost of acquisition as follows:

$$\text{Value per new user Base Year} = \$21,165 - \$15,600 = \$5,565$$

In Exhibit 8.11, the value per new user [Line 3] is expected to growth annually at the inflation rate of 1.5% (input). For instance, the value per new user in Year 1 is:

$$\text{Value per new user Year 1} = \$5,565 \times 1.015 = \$5,648$$

					Value of New Users						
	Base Year	1	2	3	4	5	6	7	8	9	10
[1] Total users	3,000	4,200	5,880	8,232	11,525	16,135	17,748	19,523	21,475	23,623	25,985
[2] New users		1,650	2,310	3,234	4,528	6,339	4,034	4,437	4,881	5,369	5,906
[3] Value per new user	$ 5,565	$ 5,648	$ 5,733	$ 5,819	$ 5,906	$ 5,995	$ 6,085	$ 6,176	$ 6,268	$ 6,362	$ 6,458
[4] Value added by new users		$ 9,319,293	$ 13,242,715	$ 18,817,898	$ 26,740,233	$ 37,997,871	$ 24,543,170	$ 27,402,449	$ 30,594,835	$ 34,159,133	$ 38,138,672
[5] Terminal value (new users)											$ 27,472,147
[6] Discount factor		0.9206	0.7801	0.6611	0.5603	0.4748	0.4024	0.3410	0.2890	0.2449	0.2075
[7] Present value		$ 8,579,104	$ 10,330,277	$ 12,440,310	$ 14,982,288	$ 18,042,230	$ 9,875,967	$ 9,344,506	$ 8,841,645	$ 8,365,844	$ 13,617,469
[8] Value Added by New Users	$ 114,421,640										

EXHIBIT 8.11 Valuation of New Users

The number of new users is calculated as the number of Total Users in Year T less the number of Total users in Year T-1 adjusted by the churning rate. For instance, in Year 1 we have:

Number of new users Year 1 = Total Users (Year 1) − Total Users (Base Year) after churn

$$= 4,200 - 3,000 \times 0.85 = 1,650$$

We can then calculate the value added by new users as the number of new users [Line 2] multiplied by the value per new user [Line 3].

The terminal value for new users is then determined as:

$$\text{Terminal Value} = \left[\left(\text{Value per User}_{10} \times \text{Number of Users}_{10} \times g \right) \times (1 + i) \right] / (k - g)$$

where

$$k = \text{discount rate} = \text{cost of capital for new users} = 18.0\% \,(\text{input})$$

$$g = \text{growth rate} = 2.5\% \,(\text{input})$$

$$i = \text{inflation rate} = 1.5\%$$

or

$$\text{Terminal value } new \text{ users} = [\$6,458 \times 25,985 \times 2.5\% \times (1 + 1.5\%)]/(18.0\% - 2.5\%)$$

$$= \$27.5 \text{ million}$$

Notice that after Year 10, all users are deemed to be new users for purposes of the calculation of terminal value. The total value of new users can then be calculated as the sum of the terminal value and the value of the Year 1–Year 10 stream discounted using the mid-period convention in line [7] of Exhibit 8.11, for a total of $114.4 million.

Step 3. Estimate of the Value Drag of Corporate Expenses. The third step in the valuation considers the effect on the firm's valuation of corporate expenses that are not directly correlated with the revenue per user figures. These may include, for instance, fixed administrative costs, expenses related to property and equipment, and other fixed costs for the firm. General corporate expenses are expected to increase at an annual rate of 15% in our model (input) and are discounted using the discount rate of current users at 15%. As illustrated in Exhibit 8.12, the Value Drag of Corporate Expenses is estimated at $112.0 million in our model.

Step 4. Firm Valuation. Step 4 puts the results of Steps 1–3 together to come to a valuation of the firm's equity at $70.9 million, resulting from the combination of its three components: value from current users, value from new users, and value drag from other corporate expenses, as shown in Exhibit 8.13.

Exhibit 8.14 summarizes all the steps that we have illustrated so far, and provides a narrative for the company's development for Years 1–10.

It is important to note that the value of the firm in this model corresponds to the result of a DCF model in a "success" scenario: it does not consider the probability of failure for the company.

	Base Year	1	2	3	4	5	6	7	8	9	10
Value Drag of Corporate Expenses											
Corporate Expenses	$ 6,750,000	$ 7,762,500	$ 8,926,875	$ 10,265,906	$ 11,805,792	$ 13,576,661	$ 15,613,160	$ 17,955,134	$ 20,648,404	$ 23,745,665	$ 27,307,515
After-tax Corporate Expenses		$ 6,598,125	$ 7,587,844	$ 8,726,020	$ 10,034,923	$ 11,540,162	$ 13,271,186	$ 15,261,864	$ 17,551,144	$ 20,183,815	$ 23,211,388
Terminal Value (Corporate Expenses)											$ 190,333,378
Discount Factor		0.9325	0.8109	0.7051	0.6131	0.5332	0.4636	0.4031	0.3506	0.3048	0.2651
PV of Corporate Expenses		$ 6,152,783	$ 6,152,783	$ 6,152,783	$ 6,152,783	$ 6,152,783	$ 6,152,783	$ 6,152,783	$ 6,152,783	$ 6,152,783	$ 56,605,606
Value Drag of Corporate Expenses	$ 111,980,656										

EXHIBIT 8.12 Company A – Value Drag of Corporate Expenses

Value of Existing Users	$ 63,496,762
Value of New Users	$ 114,421,640
– PV of Corporate Expenses	$ (111,980,656)
+ Cash	$ 5,000,000
+ Cross Holdings	$ -
– Debt	$ -
Value of Equity	$ 70,934,746

EXHIBIT 8.13   Company A – Firm Valuation

ESG Metrics

The incorporation of ESG factors in the investment process has become a large and fast-growing market segment of the finance industry, which is estimated to represent more than a quarter of the total assets under management globally.[11] As of September 30, 2019, the Principles for Responsible Investing, the United Nations–supported organization dedicated to support ESG principles by companies and investors, had more than 2,300 signatories, covering more than $80 trillion in assets under management.[12] Large European institutional investors such as Norway's Government Pension Fund Global and the Dutch retirement fund ABP have traditionally been leaders in implementation, with growth spreading more recently also in the private wealth and retail investor market. According to a recent survey by the Alternative Investment Management Association and the Cayman Alternative Investment Summit, alternative investment funds are also an area of growth for ESG integration, with an estimated allocation of at least $59 billion to responsible investments and a 50% increase in demand from either current or prospective investors relative to the prior year.[13]

Venture capital funds have also been responsive to the increasing interest of institutional investors for ESG integration in their investment portfolios. An increasing number of tools that target private equity and venture capital firms, their portfolio companies, and investors in providing ESG data collection and reporting solutions has been coming to market, in response to the lack of a single industry standard.[14] The Institutional Limited Partner Association (ILPA) in the United States has published a template for fund-level reporting of portfolio company metrics, including ESG. The ILPA Portfolio Metrics Reporting Template includes a taxonomy with itemized material ESG factors and key performance indicators.[15]

According to a recent survey of the Alternative Investment Management Association, when asked what is the biggest challenge to adopting responsible investment strategies,

---

[11]An earlier version of this section is included in Antonella Puca, "Metriche di Performance per gli Investimenti ESG," Chapter 4 of *Investimenti ESG*, CFA Society Italy and AP Advisor Private, September 2018, pp. 50–61.

[12]PRI Data available at: https://www.unpri.org/pri/about-the-pri.

[13]AIMA and Cayman Alternative Investment Summit, "From Niche to Mainstream: Responsible Investment and Hedge Funds," AIMA and CAIS: 2018.

[14]See, for instance, the launch in 2018 of IHS Markit Global ESG Data Reporting Platform.

[15]The ILPA reporting template is available at: https://ilpa.org/reporting-template/.

Existing Users	
Inputs	
Net revenue/user	$ 9,000
Operating expenses/user	$ 4,095
Operating profit/user	**$ 4,905**
CAGR in revenue/user	15.00%
Annual renewal rate	85.00%
User life	10.00
Discount rate	15.00%

Output	
Value/User	$21,165
Number of existing users	3,000
Value of existing users	**$ 63,493,762**

Existing users have a life of 10 years. Operating margins on exiting users are strong and stable as most of the operating expenses are variable.

+

New Users	
Inputs	
Cost of acquiring user	$ 15,600
Value of new user	$ 5,565
Growth rate in total users (1–5)	**40.00%**
Growth rate in total users (6–10)	10.00%
Discount rate	18.00%

Output	
Number of users in year 10	25,985
Number of new users (10 years)	42,688
Value of new users	**$ 114,421,640**

The ability of the company to add new users is critical to its success. The cost of acquiring new users is high.

−

Corporate Expenses	
Inputs	
Corporate expenses	$ (6,750,000)
CAGR – Next 10 years	15.00%
Discount rate	**15.00%**

Output	
PV of corporate expenses	**$(111,980,656)**

Corporate expenses are continuing to grow, driven by sales and marketing expenses and research expenses.

=

Value of operating assets	$ 65,934,746
+ Cash	$ 5,000,000
+ Cross holdings	$ –
– Debit	$ –
Value of equity	**$70,934,746**

EXHIBIT 8.14 Company A – Valuation Summary

45.1% of respondents mention "inadequate methodologies for the calculation of sustainability risks" and 44.0% the "lack of relevant disclosures from companies."[16] Along similar lines, a recent Swiss Sustainable Investment Market Study identifies financial performance concerns as a relevant barrier to ESG investments for asset managers, and the top barrier for further adoption by investors (voted 3.9 on a scale of 5).[17] These findings contrast with the latest academic findings that show that sustainable investments are on average at least as profitable as traditional investments in terms of financial performance.[18] How then should we incorporate ESG factors in the valuation of a portfolio company and how is it that we get such different perspectives?

The lack of a set of standards for measuring the effect of ESG factors on value of a portfolio company investment and evaluating ESG performance is a well-known issue in the industry, and one that regulators, ESG standard setting organizations, investors, asset managers, and a variety of service providers such as rating agencies and data providers are working to address.

The assessment of ESG value contribution typically starts from the identification of material ESG factors that characterize each company included in a fund's portfolio. Exhibit 8.15 presents a list of some common ESG factors that may be used to generate an ESG evaluation

Environmental (E)	Social (S)	Governance (E)
Biodiversity/land use	Community relations	Accountability
Carbon emissions	Controversial business	Anti-takeover measures
Climate change risks	Customer relations/product	Board structure/size
Energy usage	Diversity issues	Bribery and corruption
Raw material sourcing	Employee relations	CEO duality
Regulatory/legal risks	Health and safety	Executive compensation schemes
Supply chain management	Human capital management	Ownership structure
Waste and recycling	Human rights	Shareholder rights
Water management	Responsible marketing and R&D	Transparency
Weather events	Union relationships	Voting procedures

EXHIBIT 8.15 Material ESG Factors
Source: Based on data from University of Oxford and Arabesque Partners: From the Stockholder to the Stakeholder: How Sustainability Can Drive Financial Outperformance, 2015.

[16] AIMA and Cayman Island Alternative Investment Summit, "From Niche to Mainstream: Responsible Investment and Hedge Funds," 2018.
[17] Swiss Sustainable Finance, CFA Institute Research Foundation, and CFA Society Switzerland, *Handbook on Sustainable Investments: Background Information and Practical Examples for Institutional Asset Owners*, 2017.
[18] Alexander Zanker, "The Performance of Sustainable Investments: An Overview of Academic Studies," Chapter 4 in *Handbook on Sustainable Investments: Background Information and Practical Examples for Institutional Asset Owners* (CFA Institute Research Foundation, 2017).

model (or "rating") based on the three pillars of ESG. Each of these factors may or may not be relevant depending on company-specific characteristics.

Each of the factors in Exhibit 8.15 is further articulated in key data points ("key performance indicators," or KPIs) that can be quantitative or qualitative, and become the basis for the ESG ranking system. The identification and quantification of KPIs is typically where issues in comparability and performance measurement arise. There is currently a great deal of variability in how ESG KPIs are defined and measured among companies and different lines of business. Let's take, for instance, the "diversity" factor under Social. One may find two companies that identify an ESG KPI as the percentage of their workforce that is female. However: Who are they considering within their population? Is it only full-time employees or also part time? Are they considering all the workforce at any level, or only nonmanagement employees? Similarly, are they excluding any area within the firm (for instance, employees in "noncore operations")?[19] These are just examples of how an ESG KPI may take very different meanings depending on how it is interpreted by each individual company. These differences may not be apparent without additional questioning of management and may affect ESG ratings in ways that are noncomparable for investors.

Other examples of social KPIs may include, for instance, the number of staff trained on health and safety standards within the last year and the number of work-related injuries ("health and safety"), the total amount of corporate or group donations to local nonprofit organizations and the number of lawsuits in which the company is involved (community), and the full-time staff voluntary turnover rates (human capital). Based on KPIs as reported by the companies and often additional information obtained independently, index developers and rating agencies will generate an ESG rating for each company using a model that has proprietary features. For instance, MSCI assigns a rating on an AAA-CCC scale to more than 6,400 companies based on its own set of proprietary standards, which are then used also to compare companies with their peers. As noted, it's important for investors to be aware that the input data in this process may present comparability challenges to begin with, and that differences in definition and measurement methods need to be taken into account in evaluating the comparability of ESG rating systems.

In the United States, the Department of Labor has clarified that ESG factors may indeed be considered in the investment decision-making process, but that fiduciary agents must not sacrifice returns or incur enhanced risks to promote collateral objectives of ESG policy.[20] The UK Law Commission has taken a more favorable position toward ESG investments, stating that there are no impediments for fiduciary agents that consider ESG factors that are, or could be, material factors from a financial perspective.[21] In any case, the expectations concerning risk-adjusted returns are critical in the decision of integrating ESG factors into an investor's portfolio.

---

[19]Excerpt from an interview with Damian Regan, Trust and Transparency Solutions Leader, PwC Middle East in Antonella Puca, "Metriche di Performance per gli Investimenti ESG," Chapter 4 of *Investimenti ESG*, CFA Society Italy and AP Advisor Private, September 2018, pp. 50–61.

[20]U.S. Department of Labor, "Interpretive Bulletin Relating to the Fiduciary Standard under ERISA in Considering Economically Targeted Investments," 29 CFR Part 2509, 2015 and Field Assistance Bulletin No. 2018 01, April 23, 2018.

[21]Fiduciary Duties of Investment Intermediaries, UK Law Commission 2014.

There is currently a broad range of studies that addresses the performance of ESG factors and their impact on investment valuation. In a study published by the *Journal of Sustainable Finance and Investment* in 2015, Gunnar Friede, Timo Busch, and Alexander Bassen have gathered more than 2,000 empirical analyses of ESG performance to show that the empirical case in favor of ESG investments has very solid foundations, and that about 90% of the empirical studies shows a non-negative correlation between ESG portfolio metrics and metrics of financial performance, with the majority of the studies reporting positive results.[22]

At a minimum, the evidence provided by these empirical studies indicates that the selection of ESG factors is unlikely to have a material negative impact on absolute, as well as risk-adjusted performance. As we look through a variety of other indices, the results on performance, including risk-adjusted performance, are still somewhat controversial. It can be argued that a long-term horizon is necessary to evaluate the financial effectiveness of ESG integration. For instance, neglecting sustainability issues can indeed turn out to have a substantial impact on a company's business operations over the longer term, or suddenly jeopardize the survival of a firm all-together (tail-risk). From a risk perspective, it has been emphasized that companies with high ESG ratings are more likely to be primary drivers for strategic product and business model integration and have a better work environment to attract and retain talent. Also, the reduction in the risk of legal settlements and fines may be a significant factor to improve performance over the longer term. More information and greater standardization of data are desirable to adequately determine the impact of ESG metrics on investment valuation and performance, both in financial and in ESG-specific qualitative terms.

Other Metrics

The metrics that we have just reviewed are some of the most common examples of NGMs that may apply to companies in a variety of industries. Other metrics have been developed that are industry- or company-specific. For instance, in the pharmaceutical sector it is common to include in investor reports schedules that classify products by their stage in the FDA approval process or that give a detailed description with quantitative data concerning the results of their FDA-related testing. The number of patents filed or the number of publications that cite a company's product may provide evidence of a company's recognition as a leader in its sector and of its effort to develop a pipeline of new products. Exhibit 8.16, for instance, shows a table extracted from the S-1A registration statements of 10X Genomics, a life science company, which lists the peer-reviewed scientific publication using the company's products as a performance metric. These additional NGMs may provide relevant information to assess the company's performance in terms of its ability to reach its own strategic milestones in a valuation analysis.

---

[22]Gunnar Friede, Timo Busch, and Alexander Bassen, "ESG and Financial Performance: Aggregate Evidence from More than 2000 Empirical Studies," *Journal of Sustainable Finance and Investment* 5, no. 4 (2015): 210–233.

Research area	Number of articles	Percentage
Developmental Biology	112	17%
Immunology	88	14%
Cancer Research	72	11%
Computational Method	62	10%
Neuroscience	51	8%
Genome Assembly	41	6%
Cell Biology	37	6%
Other	33	5%
Assay Method	31	5%
Cell Atlas	31	5%
Genetic Health	29	5%
Microbiology	13	2%
Population Genetics	13	2%
Agrigenomics	11	2%
Conservation Biology	10	2%
Reproductive Biology	7	1%

EXHIBIT 8.16 10X Genomics – Peer-Revewed Scientific Publications Disclosure
Source: Based on data from 10X Genomics Inc. Form S-1A filed September 10, 2019.

CONCLUSIONS

NGMs have become a relevant component of the information that a valuation analyst may want to consider in developing an estimate of value for an ESE. NGMs can provide useful insights into a company's strategic direction, management's goals, the company's competitive position and risk of failure, and its progress toward the achievement of its operational and financial milestones. NGMs can be integrated into an analysis based on the income-, market-, or asset-based approaches to clarify the context and enhance the explanatory power of the analyst's valuation conclusion and to highlight how it fits into the company's overall trajectory toward profitability. Given the general lack of standardized definitions for NGMs, an understanding of how an NGM is defined for a specific reference company is often a first step when interpreting NGM data or comparing them across companies. ESG metrics represent a promising area in terms of their effectiveness as a value indicator for the company, and of the sustainability of a company's operations. It is also important to keep in mind that NGMs are often used by management to track the company's performance and their own performance for compensation purposes. As such, some of these metrics may need adjustments to come to normalized values that are more appropriate in a valuation context.

PART Three

Valuation of Financial Instruments

Allocation of Enterprise Value

In the preceding chapters, we have examined how valuation models under the income-, market-, and asset-based approaches can be used to estimate of the value of an early stage enterprise (ESE) under the fair value standard. This chapter focuses on how to allocate the enterprise value through the company's capital structure to estimate the value of a partial ownership interest in the company in the form of common or preferred stock. For a company that has a simple capital structure consisting exclusively of common stock with equal ownership rights, the unit value of common stock can be determined by dividing the enterprise value by the number of common shares issued and outstanding as of the measurement date. As the company grows into a more complex entity, with multiple layers of equity interests and debt, a methodology for the allocation of enterprise value to the various stakeholders in the company needs to be developed by taking into account the rights and privileges of the various types of ownership interests.

In this chapter, we distinguish three methods for allocating enterprise value and valuing equity interests in a company:[1]

1. The Option Pricing Method (OPM). This method allocates the current equity value of the firm to the various classes of equity using option pricing models. We have discussed the OPM in Chapter 5 of this book as a method that can be used both to estimate equity value and to allocate equity value to individual classes/series of equity interests in the company.
2. Scenario-Based Method (SBM). Under the Scenario-Based Method, a discrete set of future scenarios is projected for the enterprise, and a future value for the enterprise and its equity interests is estimated under each scenario. For an ESE, common future outcomes might include an IPO, a merger or sale, a dissolution, or continued operation as a private

---

[1]On the methodologies for enterprise value allocation, see IPEV Guidelines, 3.10, IVS 200 *Businesses and Business Interests* 130.5-130.25 and AICPA PE/VC Valuation Guide, 8.18–8.79; Q&A 14.52: Use of the PWERM; Q&A 14.53: Use of the Current Value Method; Q&A 14.54: Use of the Option Pricing Method; Q&A 14.59: Use of the OPM as the Fund's Standard Approach for All Portfolio Companies. On the implementation of the enterprise valuation allocation methods, see especially AICPA PE/VC Valuation Guide, Case Study 10, Biotech Investment with a Complex Capital Structure – Multiple Investors' Perspectives.

company until a later exit date. The three basic types of Scenario-Based methods are discussed in the first section of this chapter, Scenario-Based Methods.

3. The Current Value Method (CVM). This method allocates the equity value of the enterprise to the various equity interests as if the enterprise were to be sold on the measurement date. The Current Value method is presented in the second section of this chapter, Current Value Method.

In our examples, we assume that enterprise value is equal to equity value (no debt and no other adjustments). We conclude with some notes comparing the three methods and a few suggestions for their implementation.

SCENARIO-BASED METHODS

Scenario-Based methods rely on scenario analysis to expand the range of outcomes that are considered in the valuation of an enterprise and its equity interests and resolve some of the uncertainty that is embedded in a single scenario estimate.[2] Combined with calibration, Scenario-Based methods can be anchored to transaction prices and provide a sound basis in a fair value assessment. To the extent Scenario-Based methods are based on a discrete set rather than a continuous distribution of outcomes, they are generally not suitable for valuing stock options, warrants, and other option-like instruments.[3]

The AICPA PE/VC Valuation Guide and the IPEV Guidelines distinguish three methods for scenario analysis in the valuation of a company's equity interests: simplified scenario analysis (SSA), full scenario analysis (FSA), and relative value scenario analysis (RVA).

For a firm in its early stages of development, an SSA based on a bimodal scenario (IPO or dissolution with no proceeds) and which considers all shares on a fully converted basis (all shares have the same value after conversion) may be appropriate. In this chapter, the section, Simplified Scenario Analysis, presents an SSA with a bimodal scenario.

As the company develops, an FSA may be more suitable to capture the nuances in the company's capital structure and its exit opportunities. In an FSA, the equity value of the enterprise is estimated under each scenario and allocated to each class/series of equity interests based on their rights and privileges under that particular scenario. The allocated value is then discounted to present value using rates that reflect the risk profile of the individual class/series of equity interests based on the expected company's capital structure at exit. The value of each class/series of equity interests is then determined as the probability-weighted (PW) average of the point estimates that result under each scenario.[4] In the section, Full Scenario Analysis, we develop an FSA using both a top-down (from enterprise value to the value of individual equity instruments) and a bottom-up approach (from the issue price of the latest round to enterprise value).

---

[2]On scenario-based methods in ESE valuation, see especially Neil Beaton, "Application of the Probability-Weighted Expected Returns Method," Chapter 5 in *Allocating Enterprise Value*; Chapter 5 in *Valuing Early Stage and Venture-Backed Companies* (Wiley, 2010), pp. 89–105.
[3]AICPA PE/VC Valuation Guide 8.35.
[4]The full scenario analysis is also known as the probability-weighted expected return method (PWERM).

Under a relative value analysis, the value of the various classes/series of shares is estimated based on the value of a reference class, generally at a discount relative to the value of the more senior class of shares. The section Relative Value Analysis illustrates an RVA.

Scenario analysis can also be combined with the OPM method in a "hybrid" approach.[5] The hybrid approach is discussed later in this chapter.

Under the various approaches, we show how to set up a calibration model and how calibration can be used in fair value measurement at subsequent measurement dates in scenario-based modeling.

Simplified Scenario Analysis

Bimodal Scenario For a very early stage company, it is typical for venture capital market participants to assume an exit scenario with only two outcomes ("bimodal" scenario):

1. IPO scenario: the company goes public, and all equity instruments convert into common stock based on their conversion ratios. This approach assumes that all shares have equal value upon the IPO, on a fully converted basis.
2. Dissolution with no proceeds: the company liquidates with a de minimis or no residual value. All equity interests become worthless.

Exhibit 9.1 illustrates a simplified analysis with a bimodal scenario for sample Company A.

Inputs			Estimated Future Proceeds	Probability	
Target revenue multiple	6	Dissolution	–	70.0%	–
Targeted revenues at exit	$ 60,000,000	IPO future proceeds	$ 360,000,000	30.0%	$ 108,000,000
Time to exit (years)	5	Probability-weighted future proceeds			$ 108,000,000
Discount rate	20.00%	Dilution adjustment			$ 43,200,000
Expected dilution	40.00%	Proceeds after dilution adjustment			$ 64,800,000
		Discount factor			0.40188
		Present value of the enterprise			$ 26,041,667

EXHIBIT 9.1 Company A – Bimodal Scenario

---

[5] IPEV Guidelines, 3.10 and AICPA PE/VC Valuation Guide, 8.18–8.79 discuss the hybrid method as a separate methodology. We present the Hybrid method as a type of scenario-based methodology in our discussion.

Let's review the key assumptions in Exhibit 9.1 in some detail:

Scenario Probabilities: In this example, we estimate that Company A has a 70% probability of a dissolution outcome with a full loss of investment for equity holders and a 30% probability of an IPO.

IPO Future Proceeds: Future proceeds from the IPO are calculated as the product of the target revenue at exit (estimated at $60 million) and the target revenue multiple of 6. The target revenue multiple can be developed based on an analysis of recent IPO activity in the industry. The revenue multiple is sensitive to the market overall conditions at the expected time of exit. A change in market conditions (for instance, a decline in the level of IPO activity and in the IPO industry valuation multiples) may negatively affect the proceeds from the investment that are eventually realized. Target revenues at Exit are based on the analyst's revenue growth expectations.

Time to Exit: The time to exit for the IPO scenario is expected to be five years.

Discount Rate: The discount rate is assumed to be 20.0%.

Expected Dilution: The model includes consideration of the expected dilution that is deemed likely to occur as the company goes through its various rounds of financing ahead of an exit event. Given that we are dealing with an ESE, the expected dilution is a significant component of valuation, and a dilution adjustment at 40% of the future proceeds from liquidation is deemed appropriate.

As indicated in Exhibit 9.1, the model results in an estimated enterprise value of $26.0 million using the simplified scenario approach.

Simulation Analysis with a Bimodal Scenario The results of the model are highly dependent on the key inputs in the model, which are subject to significant uncertainty. By running a simulation analysis, we can examine how the estimated enterprise value changes as a result of changes in key inputs and come to a better understanding of the estimation risk involved in our model.

Exhibit 9.2 presents a simulation analysis that shows the enterprise values resulting from various combinations of expected dilution and time to exit. Given all other inputs, an acceleration of one year in the time to exit (four years instead of five), results in an increase of approximately 20.0% in the enterprise value to $31,250,000 relative to the base case ($26,041,667). An increase of 10 basis points in the expected dilution rate will cause a decrease in enterprise value of 16.7%.

Calibration at Inception with a Bimodal Scenario Let's now assume that sample Company A has just completed a round of Series A preferred stock financing at $1.0 per share. The preferred stock has a 1 × liquidation preference and a conversion ratio of 1×. Immediately after the round on June 30 of Year 1, Company A has the capital structure shown in Exhibit 9.3.

Based on the price of the latest round, and assuming that all shares have equal value on a fully converted basis, we can calculate the postmoney enterprise valuation of the company as follows:

$$\text{Postmoney valuation} = \text{Number of shares} \times \text{Series A Issue Price per Share}$$

$$= 25,000,000 \times \$1 = \$25,000,000$$

We can now set up a calibration model that we can use at future measurement dates for Company A by inputting the postmoney valuation of $25 million in the model of Exhibit 9.1 and backsolving to one of its key inputs (the probability of an IPO exit in our example) (see Exhibit 9.4).

In Exhibit 9.4, the probability of an IPO exit is calculated at 28.8% using the "What IF" function in Excel, so that the model results in a value of $25 million for the enterprise.

		Dilution %		
		30%	40%	50%
	4	$ 36,458,333	$ 31,250,000	$ 26,041,667
Time to Exit	5	$ 30,381,944	$ 26,041,667	$ 21,701,389
	6	$ 25,318,287	$ 21,701,389	$ 18,084,491

EXHIBIT 9.2   Enterprise Value with Bimodal Scenario – Sensitivity Analysis

Type of Interest	Number of Shares	Issue Price	Liquidation Preference per Share	Conversion Ratio	Fully Converted Shares	Fully Converted %
Series A Preferred	20,000,000	$ 1.00	$ 1.00	1	20,000,000	80.00%
Common Stock	5,000,000				5,000,000	20.00%
Total					25,000,000	100.000%

EXHIBIT 9.3   Company A – Capitalization Table – June 30, Year 1

Inputs			Estimated Future Proceeds	Probability	
Target revenue multiple	6.0	Dissolution	–	71.2%	–
Target revenue at exit	$ 60,000,000	IPO future proceeds	$ 360,000,000	28.8%	$ 103,680,000
Time to exit (years)	5	Probability-weighted future proceeds		100.0%	$ 103,680,000
Discount rate	20.00%	Dilution adjustment			$ 41,472,000
Expected dilution	40.00%	Proceeds after dilution adjustment			$ 62,208,000
		Discount factor			0.40188
		Present value of enterprise			$ 25,000,000

EXHIBIT 9.4   Company A – June 30, Year 1 – Bimodal Scenario – Calibration to the Series A Postmoney Valuation

Calibration at Subsequent Measurement with a Bimodal Scenario

Once the calibration model has been set up, it can be used at subsequent measurement dates to estimate the value of individual equity interests on a fully converted basis. For instance, let's assume that we are now in Year 2 for Company A. An analysis of market- and company-specific risk factors indicates that as of June 30 of Year 2:

- The company is on target to meet its revenue estimates and key milestones. The target revenue at exit is deemed appropriate to reflect current conditions. We estimate that the probability of an IPO exit has increased from 28.8% to 35%.
- The IPO market has deteriorated and IPO market multiples have generally declined. As a result, the target revenue multiple has been decreased from 6.0 to 5.0.
- The time to exit has decreased to four years due to the passage of time.
- The expected dilution is unchanged at 40%.
- The risk-free rate has increased by 0.5%, and the discount rate has been adjusted accordingly to 20.5%.

Using the updated inputs above, we obtain an enterprise value of $29.9 million and a value per share on a fully diluted basis of $1.20 as of June 30, Year 2 as per Exhibit 9.5.

Strengths and Weaknesses of the Simplified Scenario Analysis An SSA can be a suitable approach for equity valuation at the early VC stage, particularly if calibration to the price of a Series A round of financing can be used, and the model established based on the initial round is then updated to reflect changes in market and enterprise conditions at subsequent measurement dates. The effectiveness of an SSA relies to a large extent on the assumption that all shares of the company will eventually convert, and that they have all equal value on a fully converted basis. The analyst may want to compare the unit share price that results from the model on a fully converted basis with the price that investors would be willing to pay if a new round

Inputs			Estimated Future Proceeds	Probability	
Target revenue multiple	5	Dissolution	–	65.0%	–
Target revenue at exit	$ 60,000,000	IPO future proceeds	$ 300,000,000	35.0%	$ 105,000,000
Time to exit (years)	4	Probability-weighted future proceeds		100.0%	$ 105,000,000
Discount rate	20.50%	Dilution adjustment			$ 42,000,000
Expected dilution	40.00%	Proceeds after dilution adjustment			$ 63,000,000
		Discount factor			0.47430
		Present value of the enterprise			$ 29,880,810
		Present value of the enterprise (rounded)			$ 29,900,000
		Value per share (rounded)			$ 1.20

EXHIBIT 9.5 Company A – June 30, Year 2 – Bimodal Scenario – Calibration at Subsequent Measurement

of financing were to take place as of the measurement date as a check for reasonableness of the model's results.

Full Scenario Analysis

As a company approaches the timing of an exit event and develops its capital structure through multiple rounds of financing, a simplified bimodal scenario analysis will most likely no longer be adequate to capture the complexity of the company's prospective outcomes. An FSA is likely to be more suitable under a more complex set of circumstances, particularly if the company is close to an exit and the timing and expected proceeds under various exit scenarios may be reasonably forecasted.

Top-Down Approach An FSA for the valuation of equity interests in a company using a top-down approach involves the following steps:

1. Identify scenarios and assign probabilities of occurrence.
2. Estimate future equity value under each scenario.
3. Allocate the equity value under each scenario to each class/series of shares.
4. Discount the value of each class/series of shares under each scenario to present value using a risk-adjusted discount rate.
5. Calculate the value of each class/series of shares as the probability-weighted average of their present value under each scenario.

We now review each step in some details with reference to a sample Company B. The company has a complex capital structure consisting of 3,600,000 Series A preferred shares with a liquidation preference of $3 per share, 4,500,000 Series B shares with a liquidation preference of $4 per share, and 8,400,000 shares of common stock. Series B shares are senior to Series A shares and common stock, and Series A shares are senior to common stock. All preferred shares are nonparticipating and convertible into common stock at a 1 × conversion ratio (Exhibit 9.6).

The company has engaged a valuation analyst to provide a fair value for the equity interests in the company using an FSA.

Investor	Number of Shares Outstanding	Issue Price	Liquidation Preference per Share	Total Liquidation Preference	Fully Converted Shares	Fully Converted %
Series A Preferred	3,600,000	$ 3.00	$ 3.00	$ 10,800,000	3,600,000	21.82%
Series B Preferred	4,500,000	$ 4.00	$ 4.00	$ 18,000,000	4,500,000	27.27%
Common Stock	8,400,000				8,400,000	50.91%
Total				$ 28,800,000	16,500,000	100.000%

EXHIBIT 9.6 Company B – Capitalization Table

Step 1: Identify Scenarios and Probabilities of Occurrence The valuation analyst identifies three potential outcomes for Company B: a dissolution scenario with a 10% probability of occurrence, a low sale in one year with an 80% probability of occurrence, and a high sale in two years with a 10% probability of occurrence. An IPO transaction can also be modeled as a separate scenario. The probabilities of occurrence are typically assessed based on input from management and from a review of current and historical exit activity in the industry.

Step 2: Estimate Future Equity Value under Each Scenario In our example, the analyst estimates the future proceeds associated to the low sale and the high sale scenarios at $30 million and $100 million, respectively. The dissolution scenario will not generate any proceeds.

Step 3: Allocation of Future Equity Value As a next step, the analyst allocates the expected future proceeds under each scenario to each class/series of shares, based on the respective contractual provisions, as described in Exhibit 9.7.

Note that each scenario in Exhibit 9.7 generates its own allocation waterfall. Under the low sale scenario, $28.8 million in proceeds are allocated to fulfill the liquidation preferences of preferred stock, and common stock receives the $1.2 million residual. The high sale scenario, on the other hand, allows all classes of shares to participate in value allocation. The preferred shares are converted into common stock and the equity proceeds are allocated pro-rata to all shares on a fully converted basis.

Step 4: Discount to Present Value under Each Scenario We can now calculate the present value of each share class under each scenario by discounting the allocated proceeds at a rate that reflects the risk associated to each class/series as well as the different time horizon of the individual scenarios (one year for the low sale scenario and two years for the high sale scenario). As inputs in the model, the analyst estimates the discount rates in Exhibit 9.8.

The Series B preferred class has a lower discount rate than Series A preferred class and common shares as it is the most senior class, with the added protection of a senior liquidation preference. The discount rate is highest for common stock, which is exposed to the greater potential variability of proceeds as the most junior class.

Scenario	Series A	Series B	Common	Total	Probability
Dissolution	–	–	–	–	10.00%
Low sale	10,800,000	18,000,000	1,200,000	30,000,000	80.00%
High sale	21,818,182	27,272,727	50,909,091	100,000,000	10.00%

EXHIBIT 9.7 Company B – Allocation of Expected Future Proceeds

Discount Rate – A Preferred	20.00%
Discount Rate – B Preferred	16.00%
Discount Rate – Common	27.50%

EXHIBIT 9.8 Company B – Discount Rates

Exhibit 9.9 presents the calculation of the present value per class/series of shares under the low sale and the high sale scenarios for Company B.[6]

The formula for the discount factor is:

$$\text{Discount Factor} = 1/(1+k)^t$$

where: k = class-specific discount rate
          t = scenario-specific time to exit

For instance, for Series A under the low sale scenario, the discount factor is calculated as:

$$\text{Discount Factor} = 1/(1+0.20) = 0.83333$$

The lower discount factor associated to the high sale scenario reflects its longer time horizon to exit (two years) versus the low sale scenario (one year).

Step 5: Probability-Weighted Average of Each Class/Series of Shares   We can now provide an estimate of the value of each class/series of shares as of the measurement date by calculating the PW present value for each class/series as presented in Exhibit 9.10.

For instance, the present value of Series A shares is calculated as:

Present Value of Series A shares = Present Value per Class Low Sale

   × Probability of Low Sale Occurrence + Present Value per Class High Sale

   × Probability of High Sale Occurrence = $9,000,000 × 80\% + \$15,151,515 × 10\%$

   = $8.7 million (class) or $2.42 per share

If we go back to the enterprise level, assuming no debt and adjustments to the equity value, we have a valuation of approximately $27.0 million from the sum of the values of each individual class/series of shares:

Enterprise Value (No Debt) = $8,715,152 + \$14,440,601 + \$3,884,603 = \$27,040,356$

	Series A	Series B	Common	Total
Future Value per Class – Low Sale	$ 10,800,000	$ 18,000,000	$ 1,200,000	$ 30,000,000
Future Value per Class – High Sale	$ 21,818,182	$ 27,272,727	$ 50,909,091	$ 100,000,000
Discount Factor – Low Sale	0.8833	0.8621	0.7843	
Discount Factor – High Sale	0.6944	0.7432	0.6151	
Present Value per Class – Low Sale	$ 9,000,000	$ 15,517,241	$ 941,176	
Present Value per Class – High Sale	$ 15,151,515	$ 20,268,079	$ 31,316,626	

EXHIBIT 9.9   Company B – Present Value per Class/Series of Shares

---

[6]It may be argued that under the high sale scenario all classes should be discounted at the common stock discount rate, as under the high sale scenario all preferred stock is converted into common stock.

	Series A	Series B	Common
Present Value per Class – Low Sale	$ 9,000,000	$ 15,517,241	$ 941,176
Probability of Occurrence – Low Sale	80%	80%	80%
Present Value per Class – High Sale	$ 15,151,515	$ 20,268,079	$ 31,316,626
Probability of Occurrence – High Sale	10%	10%	10%
Present Value per Class – Probability-Weighted	$ 8,715,152	$ 14,440,601	$ 3,884,603
Number of Shares	3,600,000	4,500,000	8,400,000
Present Value per Share	$ 2.42	$ 3.21	$ 0.46

EXHIBIT 9.10   Company B – Probability-Weighted Value of Equity Interests

Bottom-Up Approach with Calibration at Inception   Let's now assume that Company B has just completed a Series C round of financing and that the analyst intends to set up a calibration model using an FSA linked to the issue price of the Series C round of $4.0 per share with the inputs shown in Exhibit 9.11.

The capitalization table of Company B after the Series C round is shown in Exhibit 9.12.

The analyst calibrates the model that we have seen in Steps 1–5 to the issue price of the Series C round. The issue price of Series C shares is used as an input in the scenario-based model, which resolves for the probability of a high sale using the Goal Seek function in Excel as shown in Exhibit 9.13.

Time to Exit (years) – Low Sale	1.00
Time to Exit (years) – High Sale	2.00
Discount Rate – A Preferred	20.00%
Discount Rate – B Preferred	16.00%
Discount Rate – C Preferred	15.00%
Discount Rate – Common	27.50%
Expected Dilution	0.00%
Probability of dissolution scenario	10.00%
Expected Future Proceeds – Low Sale	$ 40,000,000
Expected Future Proceeds – High Sale	$ 150,000,000

EXHIBIT 9.11   Company B – Full Scenario Analysis Post-Series C Round – Inputs

Investor	Number of Shares Outstanding	Issue Price	Liquidation Preference per Share	Total Liquidation Preference	Fully Converted Shares	Fully Converted %
Series A Preferred	3,600,000	$ 3.00	$ 3.00	$ 10,800,000	3,600,000	16.74%
Series B Preferred	4,500,000	$ 4.00	$ 4.00	$ 18,000,000	4,500,000	20.93%
Series C Preferred	5,000,000	$ 4.00	$ 4.00	$ 20,000,000	5,000,000	23.26%
Common Stock	8,400,000				8,400,000	39.07%
Total				$ 48,800,000	21,500,000	100.00%

EXHIBIT 9.12   Company B – Capitalization Table after Series C Round

Scenario	Proceeds	Probability	Series A	Series B	Series C	Common
Dissolution	–	10.00%	–	–	–	–
Low Sale	$ 40,000,000	41.62%	2,000,000	18,000,000	20,000,000	–
High Sale	$ 150,000,000	48.38%	25,116,279	31,395,349	34,883,721	58,604,651
Total						

	Total		Series A	Series B	Series C	Common
Future Value per Class – Low Sale	$ 40,000,000		$ 2,000,000	$ 18,000,000	$ 20,000,000	$ –
Future Value per Class – High Sale	$ 150,000,000		$ 25,116,279	$ 31,395,349	$ 34,883,721	$ 58,604,651
Discount Factor – Low Sale			0.8333	0.8621	0.8696	0.7843
Discount Factor – High Sale			0.6944	0.7432	0.7561	0.6151
Present Value per Class – Low Sale			$ 1,666,667	$ 15,517,241	$ 17,391,304	$ –
Present Value per Class – High Sale			$ 17,441,860	$ 23,331,859	$ 26,377,105	$ 36,050,535
Present Value per Class – Probability-Weighted	$ 64,320,015		$ 9,132,267	$ 17,746,342	$ 19,999,634	$ 17,441,771
Present Value per Share			$ 2.54	$ 3.94	$ 4.00	$ 2.08

EXHIBIT 9.13   Company B – Full Scenario Analysis with Calibration to Issue Price of Series C Shares

The model results in an enterprise/equity value of $64.3 million for the company, and a unit value of $2.54, $3.94, and $2.08 for Series A preferred, Series B preferred, and common shares, respectively.

Calibration at Subsequent Measurement with a Full Scenario Analysis   The model that we have set up based on the Series C issue price can be used to estimate fair value in subsequent measurement dates by calibrating the inputs to reflect company-specific developments as well as significant changes in market and industry conditions. For instance, let's assume that six months after the Series C round, the company has not yet been able to find a buyer and has not met a significant operating milestone. The model is then updated to reflect: (1) an increased probability for a low sale scenario (60% instead of 42%) and (2) an increase in the time horizon to exit, which is now set at two years for both a low sale and a high sale. All other input factors remain unchanged. Exhibit 9.14 illustrates the updated inputs.

Exhibit 9.15 presents the results of the calibrated model at subsequent measurement.

To the extent there is now a single point estimate for the time horizon (all scenarios have a time horizon of two years), only one discount factor needs to be calculated for each class, resulting in a different present value per class for the low sale scenario. The model generates an equity value of $48.9 million for the enterprise. The value allocation to each class of shares reflects the impact of the liquidation preferences of each class of preferred stock.

Inputs:	
Time to Exit (years) – All Scenarios	2.00
Discount Rate – A Preferred	20.00%
Discount Rate – B Preferred	16.00%
Discount Rate – C Preferred	15.00%
Discount Rate – Common	27.50%
Expected Dilution	0.00%
Expected Future Proceeds – Low Sale	$ 40,000,000
Expected Future Proceeds – High Sale	$ 150,000,000
Probability – Liquidation Scenario	60.00%
Probability – Low Sale Scenario	30.00%

EXHIBIT 9.14   Company B – Full Scenario Analysis Post-Series C Round – Calibration at Subsequent Measurement – Inputs

Scenario	Proceeds	Probability	Series A	Series B	Series C	Common
Dissolution	–	10.00%	–	–	–	–
Low Sale	$ 40,000,000	60.00%	$ 2,000,000	$ 18,000,000	$ 20,000,000	$ –
High Sale	$ 150,000,000	30.00%	$ 25,116,279	$ 31,395,349	$ 34,883,721	$ 58,604,651
	Total		Series A	Series B	Series C	Common
Future Value per Class – Low Sale	$ 40,000,000		$ 2,000,000	$ 18,000,000	$ 20,000,000	$ –
Future Value per Class – High Sale	$ 150,000,000		$ 25,116,279	$ 31,395,349	$ 34,883,721	$ 58,604,651
Discount Factor – All Scenarios			0.6944	0.7432	0.7561	0.6151
Present Value per Class – Low Sale			$ 1,388,889	$ 13,376,932	$ 15,122,873	$ –
Present Value per Class – High Sale			$ 17,441,860	$ 23,331,859	$ 26,377,105	$ 36,050,535
Present Value per Class – Probability-Weighted	$ 48,893,624		$ 6,065,891	$ 15,025,717	$ 16,986,855	$ 10,815,161
Present Value per Share			$ 1.68	$ 3.34	$ 3.40	$ 1.29

EXHIBIT 9.15   Company B – Full Scenario Analysis Post-Series C Round – Calibration at Subsequent Measurement

Relative Value Analysis

Instead of using a full waterfall allocation as presented in Exhibit 9.15, we can simplify the process of estimating the value of each class/series of shares by identifying a reference class and valuing the other classes/series of shares at a discount relative to that class. For instance, let's consider a sample Company C with the capitalization table in Exhibit 9.16.

Investor	Number of Shares Outstanding	Issue Price	Liquidation Preference per Share	Total Liquidation Preference	Fully Converted	Fully Converted %
Series A Preferred	20,000,000	$ 1.00	$ 1.00	$ 20,000,000	20,000,000	23.53%
Series B Preferred	30,000,000	$ 1.50	$ 1.50	$ 45,000,000	30,000,000	35.29%
Series C Preferred	30,000,000	$ 2.00	$ 2.00	$ 60,000,000	30,000,000	35.29%
Common Stock	5,000,000				5,000,000	5.88%
Total				$ 125,000,000	85,000,000	100.00%

EXHIBIT 9.16 Company C – Capitalization Table

The reference class is typically the most senior in a company's capital structure: Class C in our case. At the date of the Series C round, the analyst determines that in the dissolution scenario (20% probability) all shares will be worthless. In the high sale scenario (40% probability), all shares will receive the same proceeds on a fully converted basis, and have a value of $3 per share. In the low sale scenario (40% probability), the analyst estimates that Series C will recover in full its liquidation preference and be valued at $2 while Series A preferred, Series B preferred, and common stock will be valued at a 40%, 20%, and 50% discount, respectively relative to Class C, in consideration of their respective seniority. Exhibit 9.17 shows the valuation of each class/series of shares that results from a relative value analysis.

	Probabilities of Occurrence	Series C Value	Series A Value	Series B Value	Common Value
Dissolution	20%	$ 0.00	$ 0.00	$ 0.00	$ 0.00
Low Sale	40%	$ 2.00	$ 1.20	$ 1.60	$ 1.00
High Sale	40%	$ 3.00	$ 3.00	$ 3.00	$ 3.00
Class/Series Value per Share		$ 2.00	$ 1.68	$ 1.84	$ 1.60

EXHIBIT 9.17 Company C – Relative Value Analysis

Hybrid Method

Under the hybrid method, scenario analysis is combined with the application of an option-pricing model to allocate the estimated equity value of a company to the various classes/series of shares. For instance, let's consider a sample company D for which two potential outcomes are identified:

- An IPO exit in one year with an 40% probability of occurrence. All shares are expected to convert and value is allocated to each class/series of shares on a fully converted basis. The allocated value of future proceeds is then discounted to present value using separate discount rates for each class/series of shares, to reflect their specific risk profile.

Investor	Number of Shares Outstanding	Issue Price	Liquidation Preference per Share	Total Liquidation Preference	Fully Converted Shares	Fully Converted %
Series A Preferred	12,000,000	$ 1.00	$ 1.00	$ 12,000,000	12,000,000	13.79%
Series B Preferred	50,000,000	$ 1.00	$ 1.00	$ 50,000,000	50,000,000	57.47%
Common Stock	25,000,000				25,000,000	28.74%
Total				$ 62,000,000	87,000,000	100.000%

EXHIBIT 9.18   Company D – Capitalization Table

Inputs	
IPO Target Proceeds	$ 400,000,000
IPO Probability	40%
IPO Time to Exit	4
Alternative Exit Proceeds	$ 120,000,000
Alternative Exit Probability	60%
Time to Exit (years)	3
Discount Rate – Series A preferred	20.00%
Discount Rate – Series B preferred	18.00%
Discount Rate – Common	25.00%

EXHIBIT 9.19   Company D – Hybrid Method – Inputs

- A sale in three years (Alternative Exit) with a 60% probability of occurrence. In the Alternative Exit scenario, the analyst estimates the present value of the enterprise at $120 million. Equity value is allocated to each class/series of shares using an OPM model.

Exhibit 9.18 presents the capitalization table of Company D as of the measurement date. Series B preferred shares have a liquidation preference with seniority relative to Series A preferred. Preferred stock is senior relative to common stock and is nonparticipating.

In setting up our scenario analysis under the Hybrid Method, we use the inputs in Exhibit 9.19.

Based on the capitalization table in Exhibit 9.18, an OPM under the Alternative Exit scenario can be set up as shown in Exhibit 9.20.

The OPM model in Exhibit 9.20 has three breakpoints. The first breakpoint corresponds to the liquidation preference of the Series B shares of $50 million. The second breakpoint corresponds to the liquidation preference of the combined preferred stock at $62 million. The third breakpoint occurs at an equity value of $87 million: at this point all shares will have a value of $1. Series A and Series B shares will convert and any value above the $87 million threshold in the model will be allocated pro-rata to all shares. Based on Exhibit 9.20, the OPM model results in a present value of $1.27, $1.49, and $1.22 per unit for Series A preferred, Series B preferred, and common shares, respectively.

Under the IPO scenario, all shares will have equal value at exit on a fully converted basis, calculated as:

Value of each share at exit (IPO scenario) = $400,000,000/87,000,000 = $4.5977

	Black-Scholes-Merton Option Pricing Model				
	Total	No. 1	No. 2	No. 3	End
Underlying Asset Value	$ 120,000,000	$ 120,000,000	$ 120,000,000	$ 120,000,000	120,000,000
Exercise Price		$ 50,000,000	$ 62,000,000	$ 87,000,000	
Expected Volatility		100%	100%	100%	
Risk-Free Rate		2.00%	2.00%	2.00%	
Annualized Dividend Yield		0%	0%	0%	
Time to Exit (years)		3.0	3.0	3.0	
d(1)		1.41	1.28	1.09	
N(d1)		0.92	0.90	0.86	
d(2)		(0.33)	(0.45)	(0.65)	
N(d2)		0.37	0.33	0.26	
Value of Call Option	$ 120,000,000	$ 92,890,646	$ 88,954,825	$ 82,120,386	
Incremental Option Value		$ 27,109,354	$ 3,935,821	$ 6,834,439	$ 82,120,386
Breakpoint Participation Percentages					
Series A Preferred		0.00%	100.00%	0.00%	13.79%
Series B Preferred		100.00%	0.00%	0.00%	57.47%
Common		0.00%	0.00%	100.00%	28.74%
Total		100.00%	100.00%	100.00%	100.00%
Allocation of Incremental Option Value					
Total Value					
Series A Preferred	$ 15,262,771	– $	3,935,821	$ –	$ 11,326,950
Series B Preferred	$ 74,304,978	$ 27,109,354	$ –	$ –	$ 47,195,624
Common	$ 30,432,251	– $	– $	6,834,439	$ 23,597,812
Total	$ 120,000,000	$ 27,109,354	$ 3,935,821	6,834,439	$ 82,120,386
Value per Share					
Series A Preferred	$ 1.27				
Series B Preferred	$ 1.49				
Common	$ 1.22				

EXHIBIT 9.20 Company D – Alternative Exit Scenario – Allocation of Equity Value under the OPM Method

Exhibit 9.21 presents the probability-weighted value of each class/series of shares, after considering the probability of occurrence of each scenario (IPO versus Alternative Exit). The model results in an estimated fair value of $1.65, $1.84, and $1.48 for Series A preferred, Series B preferred, and common stock shares, respectively.

The hybrid method can be especially appropriate if the capital structure of the company includes instruments such as options and warrants. Also, the model allows for greater

Calculation of per-share value

	Alternative Exit		IPO Exit				
	Present Value per Share	Probability of Occurrence	Future Value per Share	Discount Factor	Present Value per Share	Probability of IPO	PW Value
Series A Preferred/share	$ 1.27190	60.00%	$ 4.59770	0.48225	$ 2.21726	40.00%	$ 1.65
Series B Preferred/share	$ 1.48610	60.00%	$ 4.59770	0.51579	$ 2.37144	40.00%	$ 1.84
Common/share	$ 1.21729	60.00%	$ 4.59770	0.40960	$ 1.88322	40.00%	$ 1.48

EXHIBIT 9.21   Company D – Hybrid Method – Probability-Weighted Valuation

flexibility in allocating equity value to the various classes/series of securities under different scenarios than under a "pure" full scenario or an SSA. A disadvantage of the hybrid model is that it typically requires a large number of assumptions and may be overly complex.

Selecting a Method for Scenario Analysis

Exhibit 9.22 summarizes the characteristics of the various types of scenario analysis that we have discussed in this chapter, with reference to the stage of enterprise development in which they are most likely to be applied.

The complexity of the method used should be appropriate to the company's stage of development. An FSA provides greater insights into a company's future outcomes than other methods of scenario analysis but is also more complex and costly to implement. This approach is most appropriate when market participants are likely to place value on the liquidation preference and other contractual features that distinguish the various classes of equity interests in a complex capital structure. It may also be appropriate when a company is close to an exit and the exit outcomes can be projected with reasonable accuracy, particularly if the company does not plan to raise additional capital ahead of an exit event. A simplified bimodal scenario analysis may be more suitable for an early venture capital (VC) enterprise with a simple capital structure and may be able to provide reasonable results at a lower cost. An RVA may also be appropriate when a company has a complex capital structure but is still somewhat far away from an exit event while continuing to raise capital in new rounds. The hybrid approach may be most useful in situations where the analyst may want to differentiate the modeling approach under the various scenarios and use the OPM model for calibration to a recent transaction price as one of the scenarios. The primary limitation of scenario-based methods, and especially FSA, is that they can be complex to implement and require detailed assumptions about future potential outcomes.[7]

---

[7]On the limitation of scenario-based methodologies in enterprise valuation, see especially AICPA PE/VC Valuation Guide 8.34: "Estimates of the probabilities of occurrence of different events, the dates at which the events will occur, and the values of the company under and at the date of each event may be difficult to support objectively. The methods may involve complex construction of probability models

Type of Scenario Analysis	Use	Number of Outcomes	Considers Liquidation Preferences of Preferred Stock	Treatment of Future Rounds	Considers Multiple Discount Rates on a per-Class/Series Basis	Suitable to Value Option-like Payoffs	Stage of Development
Simplified Scenario	Equity valuation and/or allocation	Binary	N	Dilution discount	No	No	Start-up (Series A round)
Full Scenario	Equity valuation and/or allocation	Two or More	Y	Modeled in the capital structure	Yes, if desired	No	Any stage; most suitable if an enterprise is close to an exit event, future proceeds can be estimated with reasonable accuracy under various scenarios, and no additional financing rounds are expected ahead of exit
Relative Value Scenario	Allocation only	Two or More	Yes, in terms of a discount relative to reference series	Dilution discount	Yes, if desired	No	More advanced stages and complex capital structures
Hybrid Method	Equity valuation and/or allocation	Two or More	Y	Modeled in the capital structure	Yes, if desired	Yes	More advanced stages and complex capital structures

EXHIBIT 9.22 Approaches to Scenario Analysis – Comparative Table

CURRENT VALUE METHOD

Description and Uses

The Current Value method (CVM) assumes that the company is dissolved or sold on the measurement date, and that the proceeds from dissolution or sale are then allocated to the various classes/series of shares based on the class/series liquidation preferences or conversion values, whichever would be greater. The CVM approach assumes that the company has no growth potential, and that the pay-off of any option-like instruments (options, warrants, the option component in a convertible preferred or bond) reflects exclusively the option's intrinsic value, with no value assigned to the option's time component.

Under fair value standards, the CVM is appropriate in only two cases:[8]

1. When a liquidity event is imminent (sale or dissolution) and expectations about the future of the company as a going concern are virtually irrelevant. For instance, a company is about to be sold in a cash transaction with no contingent payments and there is virtually no uncertainly concerning the sale price and the timing of the transaction. In this circumstance, the contractual sale price discounted to present value can be used as the equity value in the allocation. Alternatively, a company may be anticipating an imminent dissolution due to poor performance, government intervention, or by management decision. In this case, the expected liquidation value of the company can be used as the equity value in the allocation.
2. When the equity interest to be measured has seniority over the other classes of equity in the company and the investors who hold the senior class of equity have the power and may have the interest to force a sale of the company at the measurement date, which would allow them to realize the allocated value from the CVM. In this situation, the allocated value under the CVM model represents a "low case" scenario for these investors, who could exercise their power to effect a forced liquidation in case other potential exit outcomes would result in a lower payout for their interests.

In practice, either of these two situations is a rare occurrence for an ESE. Most sales of enterprises in their early stages of development provide for sale proceeds that are at least in part related to the company's growth potential, typically in the form of future payments that are contingent upon the company reaching contractually defined milestones and profitability metrics. In the case of a dissolution due to unavailability of funding, poor performance, or similar factors, equity shareholders typically recover minimal or no proceeds after all liquidation expenses are accounted for. Also, the exercise of forced liquidation or forced sale rights is unlikely to occur in an ESE where most of the value is tied to the expectation of future growth. Rather, senior shareholders have an interested in collaborating with the company to support its capital raising efforts and enhance its growth.

Let's now go over a practical application of the current value method for a sample Company E.

A Case Study

Company E is a software development firm with capitalization as shown in Exhibit 9.23.

---

and might depend heavily on subjective management assumptions. To the extent possible, calibration should be used to mitigate these issues."

[8] AICPA PE/VC Valuation Guide 8.58; Q&A 14.53: Use of the Current Value Method.

Investor	Number of Shares	Issue Price	Liquidation Preference per Share	Total Liquidation Preference	Fully Converted Shares	Fully Converted %
Series A Preferred	20,000,000	$ 1.00	$ 1.00	$ 20,000,000	20,000,000	50.00%
Series B Preferred	10,000,000	$ 1.50	$ 1.50	$ 15,000,000	10,000,000	25.00%
Common Stock	10,000,000				10,000,000	25.00%
Total				$ 35,000,000	40,000,000	100.00%

EXHIBIT 9.23 Company E – Capitalization Table

	Series A	Series B	Common	Total
Step 1 – Series B Liquidation Preference	$ –	$15,000,000	$ –	$ 15,000,000
Step 2 – Series A Liquidation Preference	$ 15,000,000	$ –	$ –	$ 15,000,000
			–	
	$ 15,000,000	$ 15,000,000	$ –	$ 30,000,000
Value per Share	$ 0.75	$ 1.50	$ –	

EXHIBIT 9.24 Company E – Current Value Method

The company's capital structure consists of 10 million shares of common stock, 20 million shares of Series A preferred stock, and 10 million shares with liquidation rights of $1.0 per share and of Series B preferred stock with liquidation rights of $1.5 per share. Series B has seniority rights relative to Series A. Preferred stock has seniority rights relative to common stock. All preferred shares are nonparticipating. Assuming that the company is sold in exchange of $30 million in cash proceeds to be received three months from the measurement date, a CVM would allocate value to the company's equity interests based on their liquidation preferences as shown in Exhibit 9.24.

Under the current method, Series B shares will receive the full value of their liquidation preference while Series A preferred will only be able to recover proceeds of $0.75 per share. Common stock has zero value. These results reflect a valuation that attributes no value to the company's upside potential. Even in early-stage companies, and also in situations where proceeds from a sale or from an asset liquidation are not enough to cover all of the preferred rights, it is still likely that common stock will be allocated some value, even if minimal.

Compared to the OPM, the CVM provides for a higher unit value of preferred stock relative to common stock, which is allocated no value under the CVM. In the OPM model common stock would still receive some value based on the possibility (however remote) that the company may indeed reach a valuation above the liquidation preferences of common and preferred even over a short time horizon of three months under a normal distribution of outcomes.

CONCLUSION

Exhibit 9.25 summarizes some of the characteristics of the three allocation methods that we have discussed in this chapter.

Type of Allocation Method	Use	Forward Looking	Number of Outcomes	Considers Liquidation Preferences of Preferred Stock	Treatment of Future Rounds	Considers Multiple Discount Rates on a per-Class/ Series Basis	Suitable to Value Option-like Payoffs	Key Challenge	Stage of Enterprise
OPM	Equity valuation and/or allocation	Yes	Single	Y	Generally, does not include dilution impact of future financing, except for rounds already in the workings as of the measurement date	No	Yes	Volatility of underlying equity; time to exit	Any stage, with adjustments if small rounds have high seniority and outsized liquidation preferences
Scenario Methods	Equity valuation and/or allocation	Yes	Two or More	Depends on scenario	Modeled in the capital structure	Yes, if desired	No, except for hybrid variant	Scenario probabilities; estimate of future proceeds and time to exit under each scenario; estimate of discount rates	Any stage
Current Value	Equity valuation and/or allocation	No	Single	Y	No	No	No	Estimate of current value of enterprise	Distressed scenario, sometimes very early stage

EXHIBIT 9.25 Methods for the Allocation of Enterprise Value – Comparative Table

The OPM and the scenario-based methods, particularly the FSA for companies at a later VC stage and in its hybrid version, are broadly used in the valuation of ESEs while the current method is used only in specified circumstances as indicated in the AICPA PE/VC Valuation Guide. The OPM method in particular has gained broad acceptance in the valuation of preferred and common stock interests and as a way of estimating volatility to value warrants and options that have preferred or common stock as their underlying. Scenario methods are especially relevant when a company's valuation is binary in nature, for instance for a company in the biotech sector whose valuation is likely to be significantly affected by the results of the regulatory approval process. Scenario methods are also suitable when there is an expectation of significant dilution due to future rounds and the analyst has a reasonable basis for making estimates on the expected dilution percentage. Finally, both the OPM and the Scenario-Based methods are forward looking in that they base the current value of the enterprise on its estimated valuation at a future point (or points) in time. The Current Value method, on the other hand, focuses on the enterprise in the state in which it can be observed as of the measurement date. For an ESE, a valuation under the CVM that does not consider the company's growth potential is rarely appropriate.

CHAPTER 10

Valuation of Options and Warrants

Options and warrants are a common feature in the capital structure of early stage enterprises (ESEs). We typically start seeing options being issued as the company approaches the first round of venture capital financing. In many cases, they are used as a tool by companies with limited cash resources to attract an expert workforce by allowing participation in the equity's upside potential. In a capital raising transaction, warrants can provide a potential return booster for investors, as an add on to stock or debt securities. Over time, and as the firm continues to grow, options and warrants may have a significant effect on the allocation of value among employees, management, and investors in the firm.

In this chapter, we address the valuation of options and warrants in an ESE. The first section, General Principles of Option Valuation, recalls some basic principles in option valuation.[1] The second section, Valuation of Options in a Complex Capital Structure, illustrates the valuation of options using an enterprise value allocation model. This section expands the discussion of the Option Pricing Model (OPM) introduced in Chapter 5 by considering options as part of the company's capital structure. The third and fourth sections, Valuations of Options as Stand-Alone Instruments using the Black-Scholes-Merton (BSM) model and the binomial lattice model (BLM), respectively. The fifth section, Valuation of Warrants, highlights some special features in the valuation of warrants. While the principles of option valuation can generally be applied to warrants as well, warrants have specific characteristics that require adjustment in the application of models developed for option pricing. In our discussion, we consider options within a capital structure that consists exclusively of equity (no debt).

---

[1]For an introduction to Option Pricing, see the classic textbook of John C. Hull, *Options, Futures and Other Derivatives*, 10th ed. (Pearson, 2017). For a primer on the Black-Scholes-Merton Option Model, see also the course A Valuers Guide to the Black Scholes Option Model of the International Institute of Business Valuers (2019). The course can be accessed at www.iibv.org. On the valuation of options and options-like instruments of portfolio company investments, see AICPA PE/VC Valuation Guide B.09.01-B.09.17: Valuation Issues – Stand-Alone Option-like Instruments.

GENERAL PRINCIPLES OF OPTION VALUATION

Options and warrants are "derivative" instruments, as they "derive" their value from the value of an underlying asset. In an ESE, the "underlying asset" is the company's common stock or a specific series of preferred stock. Call options and warrants give the holder the right, but not the obligation, of purchasing a certain quantity of the underlying asset at a fixed price (the "strike price" or "exercise price") on a specific date (European-style call option/warrant) or at any time on or before that date (American-style call option/warrant). On the expiration date, a call option/warrant has two possible outcomes:

1. The strike price (K) is higher than the price of the underlying stock (S): the call option/warrant expires worthless.
2. The price of the underlying stock (S) is higher than the strike price (K): the call option/warrant is exercised and its payoff is equal to S-K.

For instance, let's assume that a call option on common stock has a strike price of $1 and that the common stock at expiration has a value of $1.20 per share. In this case, the holder of the option will be better off exercising the option, with a net payoff of $1.20 − $1.00 = $0.20. If, on the other hand, the value of common stock at expiration had been $0.50 per unit, it would have been more convenient for the option holder to let the option expire worthless.

Prior to the expiration date, the value of an option/warrant consists of two components: the "intrinsic" value and the "time" value. The intrinsic value represents the value of the option as if it were exercised currently. For instance, assuming that a call option on common stock has a strike price of $0.50 and that the current value of one share of common stock is $1.20, the intrinsic value of the option is $0.70 = $1.20 − $0.50. This particular option is "in the money," since it would have an immediate positive payoff if it were exercised today. Generally, however, a market participant will be willing to pay more for a call option than the mere intrinsic value, to reflect the possibility that at some point between now and the expiration date the value of the underlying stock could increase and make the option even more valuable. The "time value" of the option will increase as the time interval between the valuation date and the expiration date increases. Even for "American-style" options, which can be exercised at any time on or before the expiration date, an early exercise is almost never convenient, as the option holder would give up the time value component of the instrument by exercising it before the expiration date. If there is an expectation that the value of the option will decrease, the most efficient way to act on it is to sell the option.

Call options and warrants are typically valued with reference to one of two fundamental frameworks for option pricing: the BSM model and the BLM. Since an early exercise is almost never economically convenient for the option holder in an ESE, a European-style option model (exercise at expiration) is generally applied also in the valuation of American-style options (exercise at any time on or prior to expiration).

VALUATION OF OPTIONS IN A COMPLEX CAPITAL STRUCTURE

In an ESE, options are often part of a complex capital structure that may include multiple layers of preferred stock with different features and liquidation preferences alongside common stock. One methodology for option valuation in an ESE is to consider options as part of the company's overall capital structure. We can then use one of the methodologies for enterprise value allocation that we have reviewed in Chapter 9 to establish how much value is going to

Shares	Shares/Options Outstanding	Issue Price	Invested Capital	Liquidation Preference (x)	Conversion Ratio (x)	Fully Converted	Fully Converted %
Series A Preferred Stock	10,000,000	$ 1.00	$ 10,000,000	1.00	1.00	10,000,000	55.56%
Options on Common Stock – strike $0.4	3,000,000				1.00	3,000,000	16.67%
Common Stock	5,000,000					5,000,000	27.78%
Total						18,000,000	100.00%

EXHIBIT 10.1   Company A: Capital Structure

be allocated to the reference options within the company's expected distribution waterfall. This methodology is most suitable for plain vanilla options with a term that coincides with the expected term to exit of the allocation model.

For instance, let's assume that the valuation analyst has estimated the value of a sample Company A at $20.2 million as of the measurement date and that Company A has the capital structure illustrated in Exhibit 10.1.

On the valuation date, Company A has 10 million shares of nonparticipating Series A preferred stock outstanding with a liquidation preference of $10 million that can be converted into 10 million shares of common stock. It also has 5 million shares of common stock outstanding, and 3 million options on common stock, which give to their holders the right, but not the obligation, to purchase one share of common stock each at $0.4 per share (strike price). The options expire at the end of Year 2 from the measurement date.

The analyst elects to use a BSM OPM to allocate enterprise value to the various equity interest in the company. Exhibit 10.2 illustrates the breakpoints of the OPM. Breakpoint 2

	Liquidation Preference	Options Exercise	Series A Converts
Equity Class	No. 1	No. 2	No. 2
Series A Preferred Stock	$ 10,000,000	$ -	$ -
Options on Common Stock	$ -	$ -	$ 1,800,000
Common Stock	$ -	$ 2,000,000	$ 3,000,000
Total	$ 10,000,000	$ 2,000,000	$ 4,800,000
Cumulative Value			
Equity Class			
Series A Preferred Stock	$ 10,000,000	$ 10,000,000	$ 10,000,000
Options on Common Stock	$ -	$ -	$ 1,800,000
Common Stock	$ -	$ 2,000,000	$ 5,000,000
Total	$ 10,000,000	$ 12,000,000	$ 16,800,000
Cumulative Value per Outstanding Share			
Equity Class			
Series A Preferred Stock	$ 1.00	$ 1.00	$ 1.00
Options on Common Stock	$ -	$ -	$ 0.60
Common Stock	$ -	$ 0.40	$ 1.00

EXHIBIT 10.2   Company A: OPM Value Allocation – Breakpoints

	Black-Scholes-Merton Option Pricing Method				
	Total	No. 1	No. 2	No .3	End
Underlying Asset Value	$ 20,200,000	$ 20,200,000	$ 20,200,000	$ 20,200,000	$ 20,200,000
Exercise Price		$ 10,000,000	$ 12,000,000	$ 16,800,000	
Expected Volatility		80%	80%	80%	
Risk-Free Rate		2.0%	2.0%	2.0%	
Annualized Dividend Yield		0%	0%	0%	
Time to Exit (years)		3.0	3.0	3.0	
$d(1)$		1.24	1.11	0.86	
$N(d1)$		0.89	0.87	0.81	
$d(2)$		(0.31)	(0.44)	(0.68)	
$N(d2)$		0.38	0.33	0.25	
Value of Call Option	$ 20,200,000	$ 14,463,857	$ 13,771,469	$ 12,386,322	
Incremental Option Value		$ 5,736,143	$ 692,388	$ 1,385,147	$ 12,386,322

	Breakpoint Participation Percentages			
Series A Preferred Stock	100.00%	0.00%	0.00%	55.56%
Options on Common Stock	0.00%	0.00%	37.50%	16.67%
Common Stock	0.00%	100.00%	62.50%	27.78%
Total	100.00%	100.00%	100.00%	100.00%

		Allocation of Incremental Option Value			
	Total Value				
Series A Preferred Stock	$ 12,617,433	$ 5,736,143	$ -	$ -	$ 6,881,290
Options on Common Stock	$ 2,583,817	$ -	$ -	$ 519,430	$ 2,064,387
Common Stock	$ 4,998,750	$ -	$ 692,388	$ 865,717	$ 3,440,645
Total	$ 20,200,000	$ 5,736,143	$ 692,388	$ 1,385,147	$ 12,386,322
Series A Preferred/share	$ 1.26				
Options on Common/unit	$ 0.86				
Common/share	$ 1.00				

EXHIBIT 10.3   Company A: OPM Value Allocation

corresponds to the point in which the options are going to be exercised (common stock price of $0.40 = strike price). At Breakpoint 3, when Series A converts, the option unit value will be $0.60 (common stock price of $1.00 less the strike price of $0.40).

The analyst uses the BSM OPM to allocate enterprise value, with the following inputs:

Underlying asset value: $20.2 million (enterprise value)

Strike prices: as per breakpoints

Time to exit: 3 years

Risk-free rate: 2.0%

Expected volatility of underlying: 80%

Exhibit 10.3 illustrates the BSM OPM and the resulting unit values for the company's equity interests. As can be expected, the greatest share of value is allocated to preferred stock, because of its liquidation preference and its right to convert into common stock if the enterprise value exceeds their liquidation preference. In this model, preferred stock receives a value allocation of $12.6 million, or $1.26 per share while common stock is valued at $1.00 per share. Based on an estimated enterprise value of $20.2 million, the value of the options is $0.86 per unit. Based on a strike price of $0.40 and a common share value of $1.00, the options are "in the money" and have an intrinsic value of $0.60 ($1.00 − $0.40) and a time value of $0.26 ($0.86 − $0.60).

VALUATION OF OPTIONS AS STAND-ALONE INSTRUMENTS: THE BSM MODEL

One limitation of using the OPM as illustrated in Exhibit 10.3 is that the term of the options (two years) does not correspond to the expected term to exit for Company A (three years), which is an input in the model (see row "Time to Exit" in Exhibit 10.3). In this specific instance, an option unit value of $0.86 assumes that the options have longer time to expiration than their contractual term of two years.

For options with more complex features such as options with inputs that do not reflect the inputs of the BSM OPM in terms of volatility, time to expiration, and risk-free rate, the BSM OPM as illustrated in the prior paragraph is likely not to be appropriate. In the example of Exhibit 10.4, a model that considers the reference option as a stand-alone instrument, and that models its specific term to expiration of two years, is likely to provide more reliable results than the BSM OPM that we have illustrated in Exhibit 10.3.

The valuation of plain vanilla options as stand-alone instruments is typically performed using the BSM model for a European call option with the following inputs:

- S_0 = Underlying asset value: estimated value of a share of common or preferred stock, depending on the type of option.
- K = Exercise price or strike price: contractual input, which represents the fixed price at which the underlying unit of stock can be purchased under the terms of the option agreement.
- T = Term: contractual time to expiration of the option.
- σ = Volatility of underlying asset: volatility of common or preferred stock returns, depending on the underlying asset.
- r = Risk-free rate: set to match the time to expiration of the option.
- D = Dividend yield: equity securities of ESEs do not typically generate cash dividends. The value of this input is typically is zero.

Exhibit 10.4 illustrates the valuation of an option on common stock as a stand-alone instrument using the BSM model. The option has an exercise price of $0.40 and a contractual term to expiration of two years. We estimate that the volatility of common stock is 80%. We

Option Valuation - BSM model	
Inputs	
Common stock price	$ 1.00
Exercise price	$ 0.40
Volatility of common stock	80.00%
Risk-free rate (2 years)	1.80%
Term to expiration	2.00
Value of option (BSM)	$0.69

EXHIBIT 10.4   Valuation of Call Option Using the BSM Model

then obtain the two-year risk-free rate of 1.8% from market observation, and we estimate value of common stock as of the valuation date at $1.00 dollar per share.

The call option value the results from the BSM model represents the present value of the expected option payoff at expiration, using the risk-free rate as the discount rate. In the absence of dividends, the call option value can be expressed in the BSM model as

$$C = S_0 N(d_1) - Ke^{-rT}N(d_2)$$

where

$$d_1 = \frac{\ln(S_0/K) + (r + \sigma^2/2)T}{\sigma\sqrt{T}}$$
$$d_2 = d_1 - \sigma\sqrt{T}$$

And where $N(x)$ denotes the standard normal cumulative distribution function, which is the probability of obtaining a value of less than x based on a standard normal distribution.

Given the inputs in Exhibit 10.4, we have

$$d_1 = \frac{\ln(1/0.4) + (0.018 + 0.8^2/2)2}{0.8\sqrt{2}}$$
$$= 1.5923/1.1314 = 1.4074$$
$$d_2 = 1.4074 - 1.1314 = 0.2760$$
$$N(d_1) = 0.9203$$
$$N(d_2) = 0.6087$$

This results in:

$$C = 1 \times 0.9203 - 0.40e^{-0.018\times2} \times 0.6087 = \$0.69$$

Exhibit 10.5 shows the effect on the value of the option of increasing each of the inputs by 20%, with all other inputs left unchanged.

Option Valuation - BSM model

Inputs						
Common stock price	$ 1.00	$ 1.20	$ 1.00	$ 1.00	$ 1.00	$ 1.00
Exercise price	$ 0.40	$ 0.40	$ 0.48	$ 0.40	$ 0.40	$ 0.40
Volatility of common stock	80.00%	80.00%	80.00%	0.96	80.00%	80.00%
Risk-free rate	1.80%	1.80%	1.80%	1.80%	2.16%	1.80%
Term to expiration	2.00	2.00	2.00	2.00	2.00	2.40
Value of option (BSM)	$ 0.69	$ 0.87	$ 0.64	$ 0.72	$ 0.69	$ 0.70
% change		27.19%	−6.49%	5.02%	0.25%	2.60%

EXHIBIT 10.5 Option Valuation: BSM Model – Effect of Input Change

Input	Impact of Input Increase
Underlying asset value	Increase
Exercise price	Decrease
Time to expiration	Increase
Volatility of underlying	Increase
Risk-free rate	Increase

EXHIBIT 10.6   Option Valuation: BSM Model – Impact of Input Increases

We can see from Exhibit 10.5 that as the price of the underlying asset (the common stock price in our example) increases, so will the option value, while an increase in the option's strike price (exercise price) will result in a lower value for the option. This is because a higher strike price will make it less likely for the option to be "in the money" and exceed the common stock price at expiration. As the volatility of the option increases, the likelihood that over time the price of the underlying asset will exceed the option price will increase as well. It's interesting to note that an increase in the risk-free rate will also cause the call option to increase in value, albeit to a significantly smaller extent than the other factors. This is because as interest rates grow, the financial benefit of holding a leveraged call option position instead of having to finance the full value of the underlying asset increases as well. Finally, the longer the time to expiration, the more valuable a call option is: this is due to the fact that as time increases it becomes more likely that the common stock price will exceed the strike price over the term of the option, a positive effect on value that more than offsets the decrease in present value due to a higher discount factor.

Exhibit 10.6 summarizes the effect of an increase in the key inputs on the value of a call option.

Volatility Estimate in a Complex Capital Structure

In a company with a complex capital structure, the equity volatility of the company is effectively an average of the volatilities of each class/series of equity interests. Each class/series of shares will have a volatility that reflects its contractual features and liquidation preferences relative to the other classes. In general, we expect the volatility of preferred stock with seniority in the capital structure to be lower than that of common stock, which is more exposed to fluctuations in value related to the overall performance of the business enterprise. Along similar lines, senior series of preferred stock will have a lower volatility than the more junior series. In a complex capital structure, using the equity volatility of the firm as an input in a BSM model for option valuation will typically understate the value of a call option on common stock and overstate the value of a call option on senior preferred stock.

One way to increase the accuracy of our option model is to use the relationship between equity and asset volatility to estimate the volatility of an individual class/series of shares.[2]

---

[2]Neil J. Beaton, Stillian Ghaidarov, and William Brigida, "Option Pricing Model," *Valuation Strategies*, November–December 2009. See also AICPA Valuation Guide B.08.07.

Following Merton's formulation, and as we discussed in Chapter 5 with reference to the OPM Backsolve method, the relationship between equity and asset volatility can be expressed as:

$$\sigma_E = N(d_1) \times (A_0/E_0) \times \sigma_A$$

where

σ_E is the equity volatility of the firm
σ_A is the overall enterprise volatility
E_0 is the value of the firm's equity
A_0 is the enterprise value of the firm (debt + equity)

$N(d_{1C})$ is the delta value of equity (the sensitivity of the equity value of the firm to changes in enterprise value).

In the case of common stock, this relationship becomes:

$$\sigma_c = N(d_{1C}) \times (E_0/C_0) \times \sigma_E$$

where

σ_c is the volatility of common stock
σ_E is the overall equity volatility of the firm
E_0 is the value of the firm's equity
C_0 is the value of the firm's common stock
$N(d_{1C})$ is the delta value of the call option (the sensitivity of the call option on common stock to changes in the value of the firm's overall equity).

For preferred stock we have:

$$\sigma_p = N(d_{1p}) \times (E_0/P_0) \times \sigma_E$$

where

σ_p is the volatility of preferred stock
σ_E is the overall equity volatility of the firm
E_0 is the value of the firm's equity
P_0 is the value of the firm's preferred stock
$N(d_{1p})$ is the delta value of the call option (the sensitivity of the call option on preferred stock to changes in the value of the firm's overall equity)

In the absence of an active market for a company's preferred and common stock, we can obtain the value of the variables σ_c and σ_p from a BSM OPM. Exhibit 10.6 revisits the BSM OPM that we have introduced in Exhibit 10.3 with the addition of the Incremental Delta [$N(d1)$] in correspondence of each breakpoint. In the Allocation of Incremental Delta section of Exhibit 10.6, the Incremental $N(d_1)$ is allocated to each class/series of shares based on the allocation percentages associated with each breakpoint.

In Exhibit 10.6 the Delta factors of common and preferred stock represent the sensitivity of the value of common and preferred stock, respectively, to changes in equity value (=enterprise value in our example). These delta factors are a linear combination of the Deltas of the

	Black-Scholes-Merton Option Pricing Method				
	Total	No. 1	No. 2	No. 3	End
Underlying Asset Value	$ 20,200,000	$ 20,200,000	$ 20,200,000	$ 20,200,000	$ 20,200,000
Exercise Price		$ 10,000,000	$ 10,000,000	$ 16,800,000	
Expected Volatility		80%	80%	80%	
Risk-Free Rate		2.0%	2.0%	2.0%	
Annualized Dividend Yield		0%	0%	0%	
Time to Exit (years)		3.0	3.0	3.0	
$d(1)$		1.24	1.11	0.86	
$N(d1)$		0.89	0.87	0.81	
$d(2)$		(0.31)	(0.44)	(0.68)	
$N(d2)$		0.38	0.33	0.25	
Value of Call Option	$ 20,200,000	$ 14,463,857	$ 13,771,469	$ 12,386,322	
Incremental Option Value		$ 5,736,143	$ 692,388	$ 1,385,147	$ 12,386,322
Incremental $N(d1)$		0.1068	0.0262	0.0593	0.8076

	Breakpoint Participation Percentages			
Series A Preferred Stock	100.00%	0.00%	0.00%	55.56%
Options on Common Stock	0.00%	0.00%	37.50%	16.67%
Common Stock	0.00%	100.00%	62.50%	27.78%
Total	100.00%	100.00%	100.00%	100.00%

	Allocation of Incremental Option Value				
	Total Value				
Series A Preferred Stock	$ 12,617,433	$ 5,736,143	$ -	$ -	$ 6,881,290
Options on Common Stock	$ 2,583,817	$ -	$ -	$ 519,430	$ 2,064,387
Common Stock	$ 4,998,750	$ -	$ 692,388	$ 865,717	$ 3,440,645
Total	$ 20,200,000	$ 5,736,143	$ 692,388	$ 1,385,417	$ 12,386,322

	Allocation of Incremental Delta				
	Total Delta				
Series A Preferred Stock	0.5555	0.1068	-	-	0.4487
Options on Common Stock	0.1568	-	-	0.0222	0.1346
Common Stock	0.2876	-	0.0262	0.0371	0.2243
Total	1.0000	0.1068	0.0262	0.0593	0.8076

	Value	Delta
Series A Preferred/share	$ 1.26	0.5555
Options on Common/unit	$ 0.86	0.1568
Common/share	$ 1.00	0.2876

EXHIBIT 10.7 OPM with Volatility per Class of Shares

individual calls in the model using the breakpoint allocation percentages for the delta allocation of each call as follows:

Common Stock Delta

$$= 0.0\% \times 0.1068 + 100\% \times 0.0262 + 62.50\% \times 0.0593 + 27.78\% \times 0.8076 = 28.76\%$$

Preferred Stock Delta

$$= 100\% \times 0.1068 + 0.0\% \times 0.0262 + 0.0\% \times 0.0593 + 55.56\% \times 0.8076 = 55.55\%$$

Exhibit 10.7 illustrates the calculation of implied volatility for common and preferred stock based on the Delta values calculated above and using the asset/equity volatility formula.

	[1] Delta	[2] Equity Value	[3] Class/Series Value	[4] = [2]/[3]	[5] Equity Volatility	[6] Implied Volatility = [1] × [4] × [5]
Series A Preferred Stock	0.5555	$ 20,200,000	$ 12,617,433	1.6010	80%	0.7115
Common Stock	0.2876	$ 20,200,000	$ 4,998,750	4.0410	80%	0.9299

EXHIBIT 10.8   Implied Volatility

Inputs:	Stand-Alone	From Firm OPM (Exhibit 10.3)	Difference
Common stock value	$ 1.00		
Exercise price	$ 0.40		
Volatility of common stock	92.99%		
Risk-free rate	1.8%		
Term to expiration	2.00		
Value of option (BSM)	$ 0.71	$ 0.86	−17.21%

EXHIBIT 10.9   Option Valuation with Adjusted Volatility

We can now use the estimated volatility of 92.99% and the unit value for common stock that comes out of the BSM OPM to calculate the value of the option using the BSM model as shown in Exhibit 10.9.

Using the BSM model to value our call option as a stand-alone instrument, we obtain a value of $0.71, which is 17.62% less than the value that results from the Firm OPM. The difference is due to the interaction of three factors: a higher volatility input (92.99% for common stock instead of 80.0% for the enterprise), which has the effect of increasing the option value, a lower term to expiration (the option's actual contractual term of two years versus the three-year time to exit of the firm's BSM OPM), which has the effect of decreasing the value of the option, and a lower risk-free rate (1.8% instead of 2.0%) to match the shorter option term. The decrease in option value associated with a shorter term to expiration more than offsets the effect on option value of an increase in volatility and in the risk-free rate, with the result that the value of the option is lower overall if we use a stand-alone BSM model than if we value the option using the OPM at the firm level.

VALUATION OF OPTIONS AS STAND-ALONE INSTRUMENTS: THE BINOMIAL LATTICE MODEL

An alternative approach to the valuation of stock options as stand-alone instruments using the BSM model is to use a BLM instead. The BLM is based on the assumption that the term of an option can be divided into a series of small but distinguishable time intervals of length δt. In a BLM, each step can be modeled separately and have its own specific time interval, risk, and volatility features. The BLM is especially suitable for valuing path-dependent options, and options that have more complex features, such as barriers, multiple strike prices at different points in time, or an early exercise feature. In a BLM, at each time interval, the price of the underlying stock can have only one of two motions: it can either move "up" by the multiplier u or it move "down" by the multiplier d. The magnitude of the up and down moves is based on the length of the time interval and on the stock's estimated volatility and is calculated as:

$$u = e^{\sigma \sqrt{\delta t}}$$
$$d = e^{-\sigma \sqrt{\delta t}}$$

As the volatility of the underlying stock and the time intervals increase in size (for instance, moving from one day to one month), the up and down movements will also widen.

The probability of an up movement is denoted by p and the probability of a down movement is $1 - p$, where p is defined as:

$$p = (a - d)/(u - d)$$

where

$$a = e^{r\sqrt{\delta t}}$$
$$\text{and } r = \text{risk-free rate}$$

For example, starting with a current stock price of S_0 at time t_0, the stock price at time t_1 can be either:

$$S_u = S_0 \times u$$

or

$$S_d = S_0 \times d$$

We can extend the analysis one more step, and build a three-step tree such as that shown in Exhibit 10.9. The tree can then be extended as desired to cover all time intervals in the analysis.

Once the full tree for the stock prices has been created (the "Asset Tree"), we can derive the value of the option by starting at the end of the tree and working backward to t_0. For

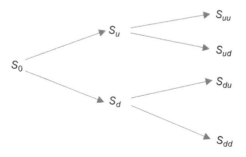

EXHIBIT 10.10   Binomial Lattice Tree – Three Steps

Inputs		
[1] Common stock – current value	$ 1.00	
[2] Exercise price	$ 0.40	
[3] Volatility of common stock	80.00%	
[4] Term (in years)	1	
[5] Annual dividend rate	0.00%	
[6] Risk-free rate	1.80%	
[7] Steps in year	12	
Calculations:		
[8] Total steps in term	12	= [4] × [7]
[9] Step volatility	23.09%	= [3] × SQRT [1 / [7]]
[10] u = Up move	1.2598	= EXP [9]
[11] d = Down move	0.7938	= 1/[10]
[12] RFR = Interval discount rate	0.0015	= [6]/[8]
[13] RFR = Interval discount risk factor	1.0015	= EXP [12]
[14] pu = Probability of up move	0.4457	= ([13] – [11])/([10] – [11])
[15] pd = Probability of down move	0.5543	= 1 – [14]

EXHIBIT 10.11   Binomial Lattice Model – Inputs

each ending stock price, there is also an ending value for the option, which is either its value as-if exercised (the value of the underlying stock is higher than the exercise price) or zero (the option expires worthless). Eventually, by working back through all the nodes, we obtain the value of the option at time zero.

Let's turn now to an example of a binomial pricing model for a sample option on common stock.[3] Let's assume that we have a call option with a strike price of $0.40 that can be exercised into one share of common stock. The value of common stock as of the measurement date is $1.00 per share. The ESE is incurring losses and has no expectation to pay dividends over the term of the option. The volatility of common stock is estimated at 80%. We now walk through each of the steps in a binomial lattice model.

Step 1. Inputs and Model Set Up

Exhibit 10.10 presents the characteristics of our option on common stock and the key inputs in our binomial lattice model based on the option's features.

Step 2. Build the Asset Tree

We now have all the inputs to build the Asset Tree, which represents the projected value of one share of common stock in the company as of each month-end, starting from the current value of $1.00 per share and up to the expiration of the option one year from the valuation date as presented in Exhibit 10.11.

---

[3]For an example of a binomial lattice model in option valuation, see also AICPA PE/VC Valuation Guide B.09.04–B.09.11.

Asset Tree

Period	0	1	2	3	4	5	6	7	8	9	10	11	12
Value of Common Stock	$ 1.00	$ 1.26	$ 1.59	$ 2.00	$ 2.52	$ 3.17	$ 4.00	$ 5.04	$ 6.34	$ 7.99	$ 10.07	$ 12.68	$ 15.98
		$ 0.79	$ 1.00	$ 1.26	$ 1.59	$ 2.00	$ 2.52	$ 3.17	$ 4.00	$ 5.04	$ 6.34	$ 7.99	$ 10.07
			$ 0.63	$ 0.79	$ 1.00	$ 1.26	$ 1.59	$ 2.00	$ 2.52	$ 3.17	$ 4.00	$ 5.04	$ 6.34
				$ 0.50	$ 0.63	$ 0.79	$ 1.00	$ 1.26	$ 1.59	$ 2.00	$ 2.52	$ 3.17	$ 4.00
					$ 0.40	$ 0.50	$ 0.63	$ 0.79	$ 1.00	$ 1.26	$ 1.59	$ 2.00	$ 2.52
						$ 0.32	$ 0.40	$ 0.50	$ 0.63	$ 0.79	$ 1.00	$ 1.26	$ 1.59
							$ 0.25	$ 0.32	$ 0.40	$ 0.50	$ 0.63	$ 0.79	$ 1.00
								$ 0.20	$ 0.25	$ 0.32	$ 0.40	$ 0.50	$ 0.63
									$ 0.16	$ 0.20	$ 0.25	$ 0.32	$ 0.40
										$ 0.12	$ 0.16	$ 0.20	$ 0.25
											$ 0.10	$ 0.13	$ 0.16
												$ 0.08	$ 0.10
													$ 0.06

EXHIBIT 10.12 Binomial Pricing Model – Asset Tree

At the end of Period 1, the stock can have one of two values:

$$S_u = \$1.00 \times u = \$1.00 \times 1.2598 = \$1.26$$

or

$$S_d = \$1.00 \times d = \$1.00 \times 0.7938 = \$0.79$$

At the end of Period 2, we have three possible values for S as follows:

$$S_{uu} = S_u \times u = \$1.26 \times 1.2598 = \$1.59$$

$$S_{dd} = S_d \times d = \$0.79 \times 0.7938 = \$0.63$$

$$S_{du} = S_{ud} = \$1.26 \times 0.7938 = \$0.79 \times 1.2598 = \$1.00$$

Note that the tree recombines in the sense that an up movement followed by a down movement leads to the same stock price as a down movement followed by an up movement $(S_{du} = S_{ud})$.

We can then complete the tree using the same procedure at each step.

Step 3. Determine the Values of the Option at Expiration

Based on the Asset Tree that we have built in Step 2, we can now determine the value of our call option under each possible stock value outcome at expiration. For each outcome, our option can either be exercised into common stock or expire worthless. To the extent the stock price at expiration is in excess of the option's strike price, it will be convenient for the call option holder to exercise the option. On the other hand, the holder of the option will let the option expire if the strike price exceeds the stock price.

A	B	C = MAX (A − B, 0)
Stock Price	Exercise Price	Option Payoff
$ 15.98	$ 0.40	$ 15.58
$ 10.07	$ 0.40	$ 9.67
$ 6.34	$ 0.40	$ 5.94
$ 4.00	$ 0.40	$ 3.60
$ 2.52	$ 0.40	$ 2.12
$ 1.59	$ 0.40	$ 1.19
$ 1.00	$ 0.40	$ 0.60
$ 0.63	$ 0.40	$ 0.23
$ 0.40	$ 0.40	$ -
$ 0.25	$ 0.40	$ -
$ 0.16	$ 0.40	$ -
$ 0.10	$ 0.40	$ -
$ 0.06	$ 0.40	$ -

EXHIBIT 10.13   Option Value at Expiration

For example, for each stock price at Period 12, we can calculate a single point estimate of the value of the option. For $Su^{12} = \$15.98$, we have

$$Cu^{12} = MAX\,[(Su^{12} - Exercise\ Price),0] = MAX(\$15.98 - \$0.40,0) = \$15.58$$

Using the same procedure, we can calculate all other option values in Period 12 as shown in Exhibit 10.12.

Step 4. Building the Call Option Tree

We can now build the Call Option Tree, starting from the values calculated in Period 12 and working back through the model in a process called backwardation to estimate the value at t_0. At each juncture or "node," the value of the option is calculated as the weighted average of the values of the immediately following period, discounted at the risk-free rate. Exhibit 10.13 illustrates the tree for our sample option.

Let's take a look at some of the values in greater detail. For instance, let's consider the value of 12.28 (Cu^{11}) in Period 11. Starting from node Cu^{11}, our option can take one of two possible values in Period 12:

$$Cu^{12} = \$15.58$$

or

$$Cu^{11}d = \$9.67$$

Asset Tree

Period	0	1	2	3	4	5	6	7	8	9	10	11	12
Value of	$0.63	$0.88	$1.20	$1.61	$2.12	$2.78	$3.60	$4.64	$5.95	$7.59	$9.67	$12.28	$15.58
Common		$0.44	$0.62	$0.87	$1.19	$1.60	$2.12	$2.78	$3.60	$4.64	$5.95	$7.59	$9.67
Stock			$0.29	$0.43	$0.62	$0.87	$1.19	$1.60	$2.12	$2.77	$3.60	$4.64	$5.94
				$0.18	$0.28	$0.42	$0.61	$0.86	$1.19	$1.60	$2.12	$2.77	$3.60
					$0.10	$0.16	$0.26	$0.41	$0.60	$0.86	$1.19	$1.60	$2.12
						$0.05	$0.09	$0.15	$0.25	$0.40	$0.60	$0.86	$1.19
							$0.02	$0.04	$0.07	$0.13	$0.23	$0.39	$0.60
								$0.00	$0.01	$2.00	$0.05	$0.10	$0.23
									$-	$-	$-	$-	$-
										$-	$-	$-	$-
											$-	$-	$-
												$-	$-
													$-

EXHIBIT 10.14   Call Option Tree

We can calculate the value of the option at Step 11 as the probability weighted average of these two possible outcomes in Step 12, discounted to present value as of the end of Period 11 as follows:

$$Cu^{11} = 0.4457 \times 15.58/1.0015 + 0.5543 \times 9.67/1.0015 = \$6.93 + \$5.35 = \$12.28$$

where:

$$p_u = 0.4457 \text{ and } p_d = (1 - p_u) = 0.5543$$

We can complete the tree by moving backward period by period, until we reach the value of the option at the measurement date of $0.63. For the same option, the BSM model would return a value of $0.64. The shorter the time interval between periods in the BLM, the closer the results to those of the BSM model.

One of the advantages of the BLM as compared to the BSM is that it allows for much greater flexibility in reflecting more complex option features and expectations about the path of the underlying equity value, including barrier-related constraints.

For an ESE, an adjustment for barriers may be suitable as a way to incorporate in the analysis a liquidation scenario or an early exit through a corporate restructuring transaction or an IPO. These barriers may indeed significantly affect the present value of the option and its ultimate payoff, beyond the contractual features of the option.

VALUATION OF WARRANTS

Similar to call options, warrants are instruments that provide the owner with the right, but not the obligation, to acquire shares of a company at a fixed price (the "exercise price") on the expiration date (European-style warrant) or at any time during the term of the warrant (American-style warrant). Since it is a right and not an obligation, the holder can choose not to exercise the right and allow the warrant to expire. An important difference between warrants and options is that warrants are actually equity securities of the company: upon the warrant exercise, the company will issue new shares, while options can only be exercised against previously issued equity securities (the total number of securities issued and outstanding will not be affected by the option exercise). In the case of warrants, the company receives proceeds from warrant exercise, which will increase its enterprise value.[4]

In an ESE, warrants are often issued in conjunction with other securities to enhance the attractiveness of a preferred stock or convertible debt offering. Having the additional benefit of warrant coverage can be very attractive for investors. The value of warrant coverage can vary greatly depending on the other terms negotiated. In some cases, warrants are already in the money at issuance, and may have a nominal strike price of a cent to the dollar. In others, they may be issued with an at-the-money or out-of-the-money strike price. In addition, in some cases preferred stock may be issued, but the related warrants may be exercisable into common stock. In the next chapter we discuss how to approach the disaggregation of the value of warrants from the value of its related securities in the case of a joint issuance.

A warrant can be valued as part of a BSM OPM similarly to options as we discussed in the first section, General Principles of Option Valuation. The BSM OPM already accounts for the dilution effect of the warrant by considering its effect on the number of fully converted shares at exit and by deducting the warrant's exercise price from its payoff in setting up the various breakpoints. As in the case of options, the warrant value that results from a BSM OPM is more reliable when the terms of the warrant are aligned with the terms of the model and when the equity volatility of the enterprise is a reasonably accurate proxy for the volatility of the underlying asset in the warrant valuation. Generally, a stand-alone approach using the BSM model or a BLM is likely to be more appropriate for warrant valuation than valuing the warrant as part of an OPM waterfall allocation.

The valuation of a warrant may require some modifications to the BSM European call option formula as follows:[5]

1. The stock price S_0 is replaced by $S_0 + W\frac{n}{N}$.
2. The volatility in the BSM model is the combined volatility of underlying stock and warrants (equity volatility).
3. The formula is multiplied by a dilution factor: $N/(N+n)$.

---

[4]In an ESE, employee stock options that involve the issuance of new shares are assimilated to warrants from a valuation perspective. As stated in the AICPA PE/VC Valuation Guide 13.80: "Many instruments that are typically referred to as call options – for example employee stock options or ESOs – are in fact warrants as defined herein, due to the fact that the holder's exercise is a direct transaction with the issuer that results in the issuance of new shares."

[5]To the extent market participants expect that the issuance of new stock upon warrant exercise will affect the value of the underlying stock, a dilution adjustment should be incorporated in the warrant valuation. See AICPA PE/VC Valuation Guide 13.80: for a publicly traded company, "If the market price of the underlying common stock does not anticipate the impact of warrants, for example if the transaction has not yet been announced to the public markets, then the valuation model should incorporate adjustments for the dilution of the warrant. If the issuing company is privately held, and the underlying stock has been valued without considering the dilutive impact, the selected warrant valuation model should include an adjustment for such dilution."

BSM Inputs	
Common stock value	$ 1.00
Exercise price	$ 0.40
Volatility of common stock	80.00%
Term (in years)	2
Annual dividend rate	0.00%
Risk-free rate	1.80%
Number of common shares upon exercise (all warrants)	300,000
Number of common shares outstanding	10,000,000

EXHIBIT 10.15   Warrant Valuation – Inputs

where

W = warrant value

N = number of outstanding shares before warrant exercise

n = number of shares to be issued upon warrant exercise

The resulting formula is:

$$W = \frac{N}{N+n}\left[\left(S_0 + W\frac{n}{N}\right)N(d_1) - Ke^{-rT}N(d_2)\right]$$

with

$$d_1 = \frac{ln\left(\left(S_0 + W\frac{n}{N}\right)/K\right) + (r + \sigma^2/2)T}{\sigma\sqrt{T}}$$

and

$$d_2 = d_1 - \sigma\sqrt{T}$$

In the modified BSM formula for warrant valuation, the term W is included on both the left and the right side of the equation. This creates a circular reference, which can be solved numerically. For instance, given the inputs in Exhibit 10.15 for a warrant that can be exercised in one share of common stock, the modified BSM formula resolves for an adjusted underlying price S_{0ADJ} = $0.9960 and a warrant unit value of $0.6768.

Warrants may also be valued using the BLM. The probability and timing of a change of control may have a significant effect on a warrant payoff. A change of control will typically cause the life of the warrant to be truncated and may cause the warrant to be repaid based on an alternative contractual formula. Also, the warrant contract may include a provision whereby the strike price may be adjusted down if the underlying stock is issued at a lower price in a subsequent round. The BLM can be adjusted to incorporate these features, if there is a reasonable expectation that they may be considered by market participants in the valuation. In a BLM, the dilution effect is typically factored into the payoff of the warrant at each node. Alternatively, a scenario-based approach that identifies, for instance, a separate "change of control" scenario with an associated probability of occurrence and estimated proceeds can also be developed.

CONCLUSION

In an ESE, options and warrants may have a significant impact on enterprise value allocation and are often a key component of the firm's capital raising and talent retention strategy. A valuation analysis of these instruments will typically start from a careful consideration of their contractual features in the context of the overall capital structure of the enterprise. In the dynamic environment in which an ESE typically operates, it's important to consider how these contractual features are expected to be implemented in practice in the life of the company. The potential impact of an exit event, a change of control transaction, and a term renegotiation may have to be considered within the valuation framework, even for instruments that have plain-vanilla contractual features and for which a BSM may be at first sight most appropriate. In a BSM model, warrants and stock options issued to employees and other stakeholders that result in the issuance of new shares upon exercise will typically require a dilution adjustment to the standard BSM call option formula.

CHAPTER 11

Valuation of Debt Securities

In an early stage enterprise (ESE), debt financing can be challenging to obtain. ESEs may not have adequate collateral and guarantees to offer for the issuance of a commercial line of credit or unsecured bond financing. An ESE may, however, be able to attract capital from certain specialized players in the private debt markets, such as venture banks, specialty finance companies, and venture capital funds. In most cases, ESE debt financing will take the form of convertible notes. Similarly to preferred stock, convertible notes may convert into equity and participate in the company's equity upside potential. Convertible notes have seniority rights in the company's proceeds from liquidation or insolvency relative to all equity classes and may accrue interest over their time horizon. As companies develop an institutional investor base, a history of customer adoption, and revenue growth, they may also find ways to access mezzanine debt financing without conversion features. Even for companies that have not yet issued debt, a valuation analysis may include debt in the company's projected capital structure at exit and will typically include debt in the company's capital structure at later stages of development in a discounted cash flow (DCF) model.

A debt instrument may be valued from the perspective of a debt holder, for example, as an instrument in a venture capital fund portfolio, or from the perspective of an equity holder, as a liability that needs to be subtracted from enterprise value to get to the value of the total equity of the firm (Exhibit 11.1).

This chapter considers the valuation of debt instruments in an ESE both from the perspective of a debt holder and in the context of equity valuation, with a focus on the valuation of convertible notes as the most common type of debt instruments in ESE financing.[1] After reviewing some key principles of debt valuation, we illustrate the valuation of convertible notes from the perspective of a debt holder. In the absence of dividends and borrowing costs, convertible notes may be valued using a discounted cash flows method, as a combination

---

[1]On the valuation of private debt, see AICPA PE/VC Valuation Guide Chapter 6: "Measures of the Value of Debt Instruments"; Andreas Dal Santo and Antonella Puca, *The Valuation of Private Debt Investments: A Fair Value Update*, Webinar Handbook, Business Valuation Resources, LLC, February 12, 2019. For a general introduction to bond valuation, see also Frank Fabozzi and Steven V. Mann, "Introduction to Fixed Income Analytics," Chapter 5 in *Yield Measures*, 2nd ed. (Wiley, 2010) and Frank Fabozzi, *Bond Markets, Analysis & Strategies* (9th ed.) (Pearson, 2015).

VALUE OF DEBT	
The Debt Holder Perspective	**The Equity Holder Perspective**
The price at which the debt instrument would transact between market participants in an orderly transaction at the measurement date	The value of the liability that market participants would subtract from the total enterprise value to establish the fair value of the equity interests in an orderly transaction at the measurement date

EXHIBIT 11.1   Valuation of Debt – The Debt Holder and the Equity Holder Perspective

of a straight debt security and a call option. Convertible notes may also be valued using an option-pricing model such as the Black-Scholes-Merton (BSM) model, or a binomial lattice model. We consider the valuation of bridge notes under the "as if converted" method and with warrants attached. We then discuss broker-dealer quotes in ESE valuation. The final section is dedicated to the valuation of debt for the purpose of valuing equity.

GENERAL PRINCIPLES OF DEBT VALUATION

Measures of the Value of Debt

In our analysis, we refer to a variety of measures of the "value" of debt, which may or may not represent fair value from the perspective of a debt holder.[2] Exhibit 11.2 presents some common measures of value for debt instruments.

The par value and the face value of debt are based on the contractual provisions of the debt indenture. The par value (or principal value) of debt is the amount of debt principal as stated in the bond indenture. The par value is the basis on which the calculation of coupon interest (if any) is performed, and represents the amount that the bond holder will eventually receive at the maturity date of the bond.

The face value of debt is the sum of par value and accrued interest as of the measurement date. For instance, assuming that a bond has a maturity of two years, a par value at maturity

Par Value	Notional value of debt
Face Value	Par Value + Accrued Interest
Book Value	Par Value – Original Issue Discount + Debt Issuance Cost
Payoff Amount	Value of debt if repaid at the measurement date
Traded Prices	Actual transaction prices reported from traders/brokers/pricing services

EXHIBIT 11.2   Measures of Value for Debt Instruments

---

[2] AICPA PE/VC Valuation Guide Chapter 6: Measures of the Value of Debt Instruments. For an introduction to bond valuation, see also Frank Fabozzi and Steven V. Mann, "Introduction to Fixed Income Analytics," Chapter 5 in *Yield Measures*, 2nd ed. (Wiley, 2010); and Frank Fabozzi, *Bond Markets, Analysis & Strategies*, 9th ed. (Pearson, 2015).

of $2 million and a paid-in-kind (PIK) interest accrual of 8% a year, the face value of the bond at the end of Year 1 is:

Face Value = Par Value + PIK Accrued Interest = $2,000,000 × 1.08 = $2,160,000

Book value is the value of debt that is inscribed in the company's official books and records under the applicable accounting standards. From the perspective of the issuing corporation, book value is generally equal to par value less the original issue discount plus debt issuance costs. Book value is sometimes used to value debt as a step in equity valuation.

Payoff value (or redemption value) is the amount that an investor would receive (and the company pay) if debt was repaid at the measurement date. Debt that is repaid prior to maturity typically receives less than the principal amount. This discount component distinguishes the bond payoff value from the par value discussed earlier. The payoff value may be relevant in certain scenarios where an exit is expected to take place prior to maturity.

Traded price is the price that results from actual transactions in the market or that reflects the price at which broker-dealers are willing to transact in a particular instrument at the measurement date. A traded price often provides the most suitable indication of fair value under ASC 820. Getting information from brokers or from actual market transaction does not necessarily mean, however, that the price point received is indicative of fair value. A price analysis is still needed to establish if the traded price is reflective of an actual transactions or intent to transact in an orderly market and if it indeed qualifies as a fair value indication under ASC 820/IFRS 13.

Measures of Bond Yield

The return on a bond investment is expressed as a bond yield, namely as a percentage of bond value.[3] Different types of "bond yield" can be determined based on the type of bond value that is used in the return formula. Common bond yield metrics include:

Coupon yield. The coupon yield is the annual interest rate established when the bond is issued. The coupon yield represents the coupon interest expressed as a percentage of the original investment in a bond. For instance, if a bond is purchased at $1,000 and receives $50 in interest income every year, the coupon yield on the bond is 5.0%. The amount of coupon interest in turn is calculated based on the bond indenture as a percentage of the bond's par value. The coupon yield is determined at purchase (or issuance from the issuing company's perspective) and does not change over the life of the instrument.

Current yield. The current yield is the bond's coupon interest amount divided by the bond's current price. For instance, assuming that a bond has a par value of $1,000, a current price of 98 cents to the dollar, and a coupon interest of 5.0% payable annually, the current yield of the bond is:

Current yield = $50/$980 = 5.10%

---

[3] On Yield Measures, see Frank Fabozzi and Steven V. Mann, Chapter 5 in *Yield Measures, Introduction to Fixed Income Analytics*, 2nd ed. (Wiley, 2010), pp. 109–140.

The current yield at a point in time depends on the current value of the reference bond. To the extent the bond price increases and given the amount of coupon interest, the current yield will decline. For bonds that are issued at par and held to maturity, the current yield will converge toward the coupon yield over time.

> *Yield to maturity (YTM).* The YTM is the return on the bond that the investor expects to receive if the bond is held through maturity, assuming that the bond will fulfill the terms of the bond indenture and that any interest paid will be reinvested at the same YTM rate as the current bond.

Exhibit 11.3 presents the contractual cash flows and the calculation of the YTM for a bond issued on January 1, 2020, with a par value of $20 million, a coupon rate of 5.5% per annum paid semiannually, a term to maturity of three years, and a price at issuance of 98.35. The bond has a YTM of 6.2% (annualized), which is calculated as the internal rate of return, which makes the net present value of the bond's stream of cash flows equal to zero.

In Exhibit 11.3, each cash flow over the time horizon of the bond has been discounted to present value using the YTM as the discount rate. In practice, the risk of each cash flow depends on the combination of the risk associated with the passage of time (represented by the risk-free rate) and the risk of the counterparty failing to meet its obligations (counterparty credit risk). With greater accuracy, a bond can be seen as a string of individual cash flows, each of which can be valued using its own discount rate, including a risk-free rate and a counterparty credit risk rate that is specific to the time horizon of that particular cash flow. Exhibit 11.4 shows that a YTM of 6.2% for our bond is compatible with an upward trending yield curve where the discount rate used for each annual cash flows gradually increases as the discount term increases, from a six-month rate of 5.75% (annualized) to a three-year rate of 6.60% (annualized) for the cash flows on the maturity date.

> *Yield to call (YTC).* YTC applies to bonds that can be called by the issuer and is the return that will make the present value of the cash flows to the call date equal to the price/fair value of the bond on the measurement date. This calculation takes into account the impact on a bond's yield of a call prior to maturity and should be performed using the first date on which the issuer could call the bond. Callable bonds may have multiple call-in dates at various price points. In this case, the YTC will have to specify which of the call-in dates it refers to (yield to first call, yield to next call, etc.).

Date	Interest	Principal	Net Cash Flows
1/1/2020		$ (19,670,000)	$ (19,670,000)
7/1/2020	$ 550,000		$ 550,000
1/1/2021	$ 550,000		$ 550,000
7/1/2021	$ 550,000		$ 550,000
1/1/2022	$ 550,000		$ 550,000
7/1/2022	$ 550,000		$ 550,000
1/1/2023	$ 550,000	$ 20,000,000	$ 20,550,000
		YTM	6.20%

EXHIBIT 11.3   Yield to Maturity

Date	Interest	Principal	Net Cash Flows	Discount Rate	Discount Factor	PV Cash Flow
1/1/2020	$ 550,000	$ -	$ 550,000		1.0000	$ (19,670,000)
7/1/2020	$ 550,000	$ -	$ 550,000	5.75%	0.9724	$ 534,843
1/1/2021	$ 550,000	$ -	$ 550,000	6.05%	0.9443	$ 519,363
7/1/2021	$ 550,000	$ -	$ 550,000	6.20%	0.9163	$ 503,975
1/1/2022	$ 550,000	$ -	$ 550,000	6.30%	0.8887	$ 488,812
7/1/2022	$ 550,000	$ -	$ 550,000	6.40%	0.8616	$ 473,883
1/1/2023	$ 550,000	$ 20,000,000	$ 20,550,000	6.60%	0.8345	$ 17,149,124
		YTM	6.20%			

EXHIBIT 11.4   Yield to Maturity – Yield Curve Trending Upward

To illustrate the computation, let's assume that our bond is callable by the issuer at the end of Year 2 at par. The YTC in this case is 6.49% calculated as the internal rate of return, which generates a net present value of zero for the bond cash flows through the call date of January 1, 2022 (Exhibit 11.5).

Yield to Put. When a bond is putable, the yield to put can be calculated as the interest rate that will make the present value of the cash flows to the first put date equal to the current value plus accrued interest. For our sample bond, assuming a put date of July 1, 2021, the yield to put is 6.79% as illustrated in Exhibit 11.6.

Date	Interest	Principal	Net Cash Flows
1/1/2020	$ -	$ (19,670,000)	$ (19,670,000)
7/1/2020	$ 550,000		$ 550,000
1/1/2021	$ 550,000		$ 550,000
7/1/2021	$ 550,000		$ 550,000
1/1/2022	$ 550,000	$ 20,000,000	$ 20,550,000
		YTC	6.49%

EXHIBIT 11.5   Yield to Call

Date	Interest	Principal	Net Cash Flows
1/1/2020	-	$ (19,670,000)	$ (19,670,000)
7/1/2020	$ 550,000		$ 550,000
1/1/2021	$ 550,000		$ 550,000
7/1/2021	$ 550,000	$ 20,000,000	$ 20,550,000
		YTP	6.79%

EXHIBIT 11.6   Yield to Put

VALUATION OF CONVERTIBLE NOTES: DECOMPOSITION AND YIELD METHOD

Let's now turn our attention to the valuation of convertible notes from the perspective of a debt holder in an ESE. To develop an analytical framework for valuing a convertible note, a common approach is to decompose the note into its component parts.[4] Let's consider, for example, Convertible Note A with a par value of $10 million, a maturity term of four years from issuance and an interest rate of 4% (Paid-In-Kind, accrued annually). Note A is convertible into 80,000 shares of common stock (conversion ratio = 80,000) at a conversion price per share of $125 = $10,000,000/80,000. Convertible Note A can be analyzed as a combination of two instruments:

1. An option-free note with a par value of $10,000,000, a maturity term of four years from issuance, and a PIK interest rate of 4% per year.[5]
2. A call option on 80,000 shares of common stock at a strike price of $125 dollar per share, with a term of four years at issuance.

In our example, we assume that Convertible Note A was issued on January 1 of Year 1 and that the measurement date is December 31 of Year 1. The convertible note has three more years to maturity, and the embedded call option has a remaining term of three years.

Convertible Note A – Valuation of Option Component

The option component of Convertible Note A can be valued using the BSM formula for a call option.[6] Exhibit 11.7 illustrates the calculation of the value of the option component of the note using the following inputs:

- Common stock value as of the measurement date: $60 (analyst estimate)
- Common stock volatility: 70% (analyst estimate)
- Exercise price: $125 (equal to conversion price – contractual)
- Term of the option: three years (contractual)

---

[4]On the valuation of convertible notes, see AICPA PE/VC Valuation Guide B.10.01-B.10.16. On the bifurcation of the option and straight debt components, see AICPA PE/VC Valuation Guide B.10.05: "The value of a convertible instrument with a specified conversion price is essentially equal to the value of the debt-like host instrument based on market participants' current required yield for debt-like instruments with similar credit quality and terms (excluding the conversion option), plus the value of the option to convert, except that there is an interaction between the credit risk and the stock price." For a case study that illustrates the decomposition method in bond valuation, see AICPA PE/VC Valuation Guide C.14.73-89: Investment 3 – Investment in Second Lien Convertible Debt – Prim Solutions.
[5]PIK interest on convertible bonds typically compounds semiannually or annually. In our simplified example, we assume that PIK is $400,000 per year.
[6]AICPA PE/VC Valuation Guide B.10.05: "The value of the option embedded in a convertible instrument is similar to other options and is affected by the same factors: value of underlying alternative asset (stock price); strike price (redemption value if the holder chooses not to convert); term (typically the time remaining until the redemption date); risk-free rate (risk-free rate of interest appropriate for the term); volatility of the underlying asset (expected annual standard deviation of stock or comparable company stocks)."

[1] Common Stock Value	$ 60	BSM Input
[2] Common Stock Volatility	70.00%	BSM Input
[3] Exercise Price = Conversion Price	$ 125	BSM Input
[4] Term (in years)	3	BSM Input
[5] RFR	1.65%	BSM Input
[6] Call Option Value	$ 16.62	Output BSM Formula
[7] Number of Options	80,000	Conversion ratio
[8] Position Value – Option Component	$ 1,329,600	= [6] × [7]

EXHIBIT 11.7   Convertible Note A – Option Component

- Risk-free rate: 1.65% (RFR over a three-year horizon – market-based input)
- Dividend yield: zero

In Exhibit 11.7, Items [1]–[5] represent the inputs in the BSM formula. Item [6] is the unit value of the option resulting from the BSM model ($16.62 in our example). The call option unit value is then multiplied by the conversion ratio of 80,000 to obtain the value of the overall option component at $1,329,600.

Convertible Note A – Valuation of Straight Debt Component

In order to estimate the value of the straight debt component of Convertible Note A, we use the yield method. Under the yield method, the cash flows from the note are estimated and then discounted at the YTM. The yield method involves the following three valuation steps.

Step 1: Defining Time Horizon   The time horizon in the yield method reflects the period from the measurement date to the maturity date of the bond or to the date in which the bond is expected to convert into common stock. In our example, we assume that the bond has a time horizon of three years and will remain outstanding through its contractual maturity date.

Step 2: Estimating Cash Flows   Cash flows for a debt instrument are estimated based on the expected cash flows of the instrument, which may or may not coincide with the contractual cash flows as defined in the note indenture. In an ESE, convertible notes typically do not pay cash interest. Rather, interest is accrued and paid in kind (PIK interest) as an addition to principal or with shares of the underlying stock, with periodicity that is contractually defined. Notes with a PIK interest provision will typically generate cash flows only at the time of the original investment, to reflect the cash-out related to the purchase price, and at the time in which the position is closed, at which point the note may be converted into common or preferred shares (cash flow = value of the converted stock position less any conversion price) or may pay back its principal amount and PIK interest, in whole or in part.

In our example, we assume that Convertible Note A has a purchase price equal to the value of the note under the yield method on the measurement date. Convertible Note A is expected to return the full amount of principal and accrued PIK interest in cash at the maturity date.

Step 3: Estimating Discount Rate   The discount rate under the yield method has two components:

1. Risk-free rate: For corporate notes, the risk-free rate is typically based on the swap rate curve, which represents the fixed interest rate that a participant in the interest rate swap market would be willing to provide in exchange for the floating rate on the principal amount over the terms of the swap, assuming that no money is exchanged at contract initiation. Floating rates in the swap market are based on a short-term interest rate, which is deemed virtually risk-free.
2. Counterparty-credit-risk (CCR) rate: The CCR rate depends on the credit profile of the reference company and the seniority and collateral features of the individual debt instrument. A synthetic credit risk analysis is typically performed to assess the CCR embedded in an individual debt issuance. A synthetic credit risk analysis is a quantitative analysis that assigns a credit rating to a debt instrument based on a comparison of the reference company's risk profile with that of comparable companies with rated debt. A synthetic credit analysis will typically assign a corporate family rating (CFR) to the reference company, and then a rating to the individual debt issuance, which is assessed relative to the CFR. Senior unsecured bonds of a corporation are typically rated at the CFR. Secured bonds typically are rated one notch better than the CFR (e.g. BB+ instead of BB), while subordinated bonds may be two to three notches below the CFR. Once a credit rating for a particular bond issue has been assigned, the CCR rate is assessed within the range that is associated to the assigned rating.

As of December 2019, 10 credit-rating agencies are recognized by the U.S. Securities and Exchange Commission as "nationally recognized statistical rating organizations." Exhibit 11.8 shows the ratings assigned to debt issues by S&P Global Rating, Moody's Investor Services Inc., and Fitch Ratings Inc.

For ESE debt, a synthetic credit analysis presents special challenges. Some of the key metrics considered by the major credit ratings, such as EBIT/net debt (a key solvency metric), EBIT/revenues (a key operating margin metric), and EBIT/average capital (a return on capital metric), for instance, are not meaningful in a situation where EBIT is expected to be negative over the note term. Funds that hold ESE debt instruments as a significant part of their portfolio may find it more suitable to use internally developed models that are customized for the characteristics of ESEs. For an ESE, the credit analysis may emphasize cash and revenue-related metrics, as well as trends in operating margins that can provide indications on the company's risk of failure, including:

- Cash burn. As discussed in Chapter 8, this metric provides a key reference point for estimating the probability of default in an ESE. It is often calculated as a monthly rate, as the total cash outlay over the period (month, quarter, year) divided by the number of months in the period. Alternatively, the numerator may include net cash outflows (the amount of cash disbursed, including cash paid for capital expenditures net of cash generated by the company's operations). Cash burn provides an important indicator of the ability of the company to sustain its operations without additional infusion of external funding.
- Revenue growth rate. The revenue growth rate measures the change in revenue over time, on a historical and/or perspective basis. The trend in revenue growth as well as revenue

	S&P	MOODY'S	FITCH	
INVESTMENT GRADE	AAA	Aaa	AAA	Prime
	AA+	Aa1	AA+	Very high
	AA	Aa2	AA	credit
	AA–	Aa3	AA–	quality
	A+	A1	A+	High credit
	A	A2	A	quality
	A–	A3	A–	
	BBB+	Baa1	BBB+	Good credit
	BBB	Baa2	BBB	quality
	BBB–	Baa3	BBB–	
NON-INVESTMENT GRADE	BB+	Ba1	BB+	
	BB	Ba2	BB	Speculative
	BB–	Ba3	BB-	
	B+	B1	B+	Highly
	B	B2	B	speculative
	B–	B3	B–	
	CCC+	Caa1	CCC+	Substantial risks
	CCC	Caa2	CCC	Extremely speculative
	CCC–	Caa3	CCC–	
	CC	Ca	CC	Default or
	C	C	C	near-default
	D		D	

EXHIBIT 11.8   Rating Scales from Best to Worst Rating

growth projection may provide significant insight into the ability of the company to stay in business and eventually achieve profitability.

- Trend in gross margin. The gross margin measures the difference between revenue and cost of goods sold as a percentage of revenue. The trend in gross margin can provide indications on the company's progress toward profitability and on its ability over time to achieve self-sustaining operations. In an ESE, there is an expectation that the gross margin will improve over time, as a company achieves economies of scale and makes its production process more efficient.
- Trend in operating margin. The operating margin is a profitability ratio measuring revenues after operating and nonoperating expenses as a percentage of total revenues.

The operating margin is also referred to as return on sales as it reflects how much of the sales revenue is left after covering for operating expenses. An operating margin that increases over time is an indication that the firm is making progress toward achieving self-sustaining operations and improving its debt-servicing profile.

- Trends in non-GAAP metrics. Trends in industry-specific metrics such as customer acquisition costs, attrition rates, active users, annual recurring revenue, number of customers, revenue run rates, and other non-GAAP metrics as discussed in Chapter 8 can also provide useful signals of the company's progress toward profitability and a sustainable business model.
- Other factors. To the extent the survival of the company depends on the ability to access external funding for financing growth, a consideration of trends in the venture capital markets and of qualitative factors such as management's expertise and history of successful financing are also very relevant in assessing the credit profile of an ESE.

The CCR rate that corresponds to the assessed synthetic rating is typically expressed as a spread over the swap rate (risk-free rate). Assuming in our example an estimated swap spread of 8.0%, and a swap rate of 1.6%, the total discount rate for the note is:

Discount rate = Risk-free rate (Swap rate)

+ Counterparty Credit Risk Rate (Swap spread) = 1.60% + 8.00% = 9.60%

Step 4: Calculating the Value of the Straight Debt Component The value of the straight debt component in Convertible Note A can now be estimated as illustrated in Exhibit 11.9. Given a YTM of 9.60%, and the interest and principal payoff structure as described in the Exhibit 11.9, we can backsolve for the principal cash outflow at the end of Year 1 from issuance of $8,410,000. We can then add the accrued interest as of the valuation date at the end of Year 1 (accrual in Year 1 of $400,000 = 4% × $10,000,000), and estimate the fair value of the straight debt component at the end of Year 1 at $8,810,000 = $8,410,000 (principal) + $400,000 (accrued interest).

Convertible Note A – Valuation of Combined Instrument

We can now estimate the fair value of Convertible Note A as a combined instrument by summing the value of the call option component at $1,329,600 with the value of the straight bond component of $8,810,000, including $400,000 in accrued interest, resulting in a total fair value for the note of $10,139,600 as of December 31 of Year 1.

Date of Cash Flow	Interest	Principal	Net Cash Flow
December 31, Year 1	$ (400,000)	$ (8,410,000)	$ (8,810,000)
December 31, Year 4	$ 1,600,000	$ 10,000,000	$ 11,600,000
		IRR	9.60%

EXHIBIT 11.9   Convertible Note A – Valuation of Straight Debt Component

VALUATION OF CONVERTIBLE NOTES: CALIBRATION WITH THE YIELD METHOD

So far, we have presented the yield method as a valuation method that can be implemented also in the absence of actual transaction prices in the reference note or other equity interests in the company. To the extent market transactions in the reference note or equity instruments in the company have taken place, those transactions need to be taken into account in valuation under the fair value standard of ASC 820/IFRS 13.[7] As discussed in Chapter 5, for an ESE, the most reliable evidence of "market" prices is likely to come from the transactions between the company and its investors. A recent transaction price in a convertible note, for instance, can be used to "backsolve" into the key variables for note valuation such as the implied YTM and the inputs in the BSM model for the option component of the note. Once a calibration model has been set up based on the initial transaction price of the note (purchase price or issue price), the input variables can be updated at subsequent measurement dates to reflect changes in market conditions and in the credit risk profile of the company.

As an illustration of calibration using the latest transaction price, let's assume that a venture capital fund had purchased Convertible Note A at a price of $10,139,600 on December 31 of Year 1, and that the analysis in Exhibit 11.7 and Exhibit 11.9 reflects the initial calibration model of the note value at the time of purchase. We are now at December 31 of Year 2, and we want to reassess the value of the note by adjusting the inputs of the calibration model to current conditions. As a first step, we reassess the value of the option component of the note using the BSM model. Let's assume that the common stock value is now $70 per share, the volatility of the underlying stock has decreased from 70% to 65%, primarily due to a decrease in volatility for the overall market. The risk-free rate has increased from 1.65% to 2.00%, also driven by market conditions. The term of the option is now two years instead of three due to the passage of time. Using the BSM formula for a European call option, we can calculate the value of the option component of Convertible Note A as illustrated in Exhibit 11.10.

The call option component has now a value of $1,097,600, which represents a decrease of 17.45% relative to the December 31, Year 1 price. In this case, the increase in value related to an increase in the underlying asset value was more than offset by the combined effect of the decrease in volatility and decrease in time to exit, all factors that point to a lower value of the call option component.

Inputs:	
[1] Underlying asset value	$ 70.00
[2] Volatility of underlying asset	65.00%
[3] Exercise Price = Conversion Price	$ 125
[4] Term (in years)	2
[5] Risk-free rate	2.00%
[6] Conversion ratio	80,000
Results:	
[7] Call option value	$ 13.72
[8] Position Value - Option Component	$ 1,097,600 = [6] x [7]

EXHIBIT 11.10 Convertible Note A – Calibration – Valuation of Option Component

---

[7]See especially AICPA PE/VC Valuation Guide 5.52-5.55: Transactions in the Portfolio Company's Interests.

Date	Interest	Principal	Net CF
December 31, Year 2	$ (800,000)	$ (8,819,000)	$ (9,619,000)
December 31, Year 4	$ 1,600,000	$ 10,000,000	$ 11,600,000
		IRR	**9.80%**

EXHIBIT 11.11   Convertible Note A – Calibration – Valuation of Straight Debt Component

We can now look at the debt component of Convertible Note A. Compared to the calibration model established on December 31, Year 1, the date of purchase, we determine that the risk-free rate has increased to 2.0% while the swap spread on the bond has decreased from 8.0% to 7.8%, due primarily to an improvement in the company's credit risk profile, resulting in an estimated YTM for the debt component of 9.8%.

The bond yield as of the valuation date can be measured relative to the bond yield at the initial transaction date by observing:

- The change in credit quality for the reference company.
- The change in credit spreads for comparable debt instruments, considering the characteristics of the reference company's debt relative to the comparable traded debt, including seniority, strength of covenants, reference company performance, quality of collateral, maturity, early redemption features, or optionality, and any other differences that a market participant would consider in determining its fair value.
- For fixed rate debt, the change in the reference rate matching the remaining maturity of the debt (that is, the change in the reference swap rate or treasury rate).

The value of the debt component can now be calculated by inputting in a yield model the amount of accrued interest at the measurement date of $800,000, the redemption value at par+ accrued interest of $11.6 million, the estimated YTM at 9.80%, and solving for the cash outflow related to the principal value of the debt component. The resulting value for the straight debt component is $9,619,000, including $8,819,000 of principal and $800,000 in accrued interest, as illustrated in Exhibit 11.11

The total value of Convertible Note A at the subsequent measurement date of December 31, Year 2, is now $10,716,600 calculated as:

$$\text{Value of Convertible Note A} = \text{Value of Option Component}$$
$$+ \text{Value of Straight Debt Component}$$
$$= \$1,097,600 + \$9,619,000 = \$10,716,600$$

VALUATION OF CONVERTIBLE NOTES: THE OPTION PRICING METHOD

An alternative approach to the valuation of convertible notes considers the reference bond as a combined instrument within a company's overall capital structure and uses the option pricing method to allocate a portion of the enterprise value to the note based on its claim as part of the company's waterfall.[8] This approach is less common in practice than the yield method, but is sometimes used in situations where estimating a bond yield may be especially challenging, where the debt profile is very similar to that of preferred stock, or in the context of valuing debt for the purpose of valuing equity. Exhibits 11.12–11.15 illustrate this methodology with a practical example.

Let's assume that Sample Company has a capital structure on January 1 of Year 1 as represented in Exhibit 11.12.

Sample Company has Convertible Note B outstanding with a par value of $5 million. The note was issued at par and is convertible into 5 million shares of Series A preferred stock of the company (conversion ratio = 1). Convertible Note B accrues paid in-kind interest

Investor	Shares/ Principal Outstanding	Issue Price/ Par	Invested Capital	Accrued Interest/ Dividends	Liquidation Preference	Conversion Ratio (x)	Fully Converted Shares	Fully Converted %
Series A Preferred Stock	10,000,000	$1.00	$10,000,000	6%	$10,000,000	1.00	10,000,000	28.57%
Convertible Note B	5,000,000	$1.00	$5,000,000	8%	$5,000,000	1.00	5,000,000	14.29%
Common Stock	20,000,000						20,000,000	57.14%
Total							35,000,000	100.00%

EXHIBIT 11.12 Sample Company – Capital Structure

Investor	Shares/ Principal Outstanding	Issue Price/Par	Invested Capital	Accrued Interest/ Dividends	Liquidation Preference	Conversion Ratio (x)	Fully Converted Shares	Fully Converted %
Series A Preferred Stock	10,000,000	$1.00	$10,000,000	6%	$11,910,160	1.00	11,910,160	31.17%
Convertible Note B	5,000,000	$1.00	$5,000,000	8%	$6,298,560	1.00	6,298,560	16.48%
Common Stock	20,000,000						20,000,000	52.34%
Total							38,208,720	100.00%

EXHIBIT 11.13 Sample Company – Capital Structure Including Accrued Dividends and Interest

---

[8]The use of the portfolio company's enterprise value, including debt, as the underlying asset in an OPM framework is discussed in AICPA PE/VC Valuation Guide, 6.25–26, Q&A 14.48: Using the Zero Coupon Bond Equivalent for Including Debt in the Option Pricing Method, and 8.48.c.: "under this approach, the zero coupon bond equivalent of the debt is modeled as the first breakpoint, modeling the total equity as a call option on the enterprise value." The zero coupon bond equivalent of the debt is the future payoff amount for the debt such that the modeled valued of the debt (the value allocated to the first breakpoint) equals its fair value.

Equity Class	Note Preference No. 1	Series A Liquidation Preference No. 2	Bond and Series A Convert No. 3
Series A Preferred Stock	$ –	$ 11,910,160	$ –
Convertible Note B	$ 6,298,560	$ –	$ –
Common Stock	$ –	$ –	$ 20,000,000
Total	$ 6,298,560	$ 11,910,160	$ 20,000,000

EXHIBIT 11.14   Sample Company – OPM Breakpoints

(PIK interest) at a rate of 8% per year and has a senior liquidation preference relative to preferred stock. PIK interest is included in the liquidation preference as it accrues. Preferred stock has senior liquidation rights relative to common stock, is nonparticipating, and accrues dividends at a rate of 6% per year. Dividends on preferred stock are cumulative and are added to the liquidation preference and conversion basis of the stock on an accrual basis.

The enterprise value of Sample Company has been estimated at $40 million using a discounted cash flow model. The company has no debt aside from Convertible Note B. Management expects an exit event to take place approximately three years from the measurement date. Exhibit 11.13 illustrates the company's capital structure adjusted for the interest/dividends that are expected to have accrued as of the exit date (three years from the valuation date) based on the existing contracts. To the extent accrued interest/dividends are expected to have an impact on the enterprise value allocation at exit, their effect needs to be incorporated in the capital structure of the company that is used for valuation.

We can now apply an option pricing model similar to the one described in Chapter 5, with the difference that it now also includes convertible debt as part of the allocation waterfall. Based on the capital structure in Exhibit 11.13, we have the following breakpoints (Exhibit 11.14).

The first breakpoint corresponds to the note par value of $6,298,560, including $1,298,560 of PIK interest accrual over the three-year period to exit:

$$\text{Note par value at exit}$$

$$= \text{Par Value of the Bond} \times (1 + \text{Interest Rate})^{\text{Number of Years to Exit}}$$

$$= \$5,000,000 \times 1.08^3 = \$6,298,560$$

After the note has received its par value, including accrued interest, the next $11.910,160 million in proceeds are allocated to preferred stock to fulfill its own liquidation preference (including $1,910,160 in accrued PIK dividends). Following that, $20 million are allocated to common stock, until all shares have reached a threshold of $1 per unit in allocated value. At this point, Series A preferred stock and the Convertible Note B will convert. Any value above the $38,208,720 threshold will be allocated pro-rata to all classes on a fully converted basis. Notice that in this example the fully converted ownership percentages in Exhibit 11.13 are calculated after taking into account the accrued dividend and interest on preferred stock and convertible notes, respectively. Over time, the effect of dividend and interest accruals may be significant in terms of enterprise value allocation between the different classes/series of shares.

Black-Scholes-Merton Option Pricing Method				
	Total	No. 1	No. 2	End
Underlying Asset Value	$ 40,000,000	$ 40,000,000 $ 40,000,000	$ 40,000,000	$ 40,000,000
Exercise Price		$ 6,298,560	$ 18,208,720	$ 38,208,720
Expected Volatility		70%	70%	70%
Risk-Free Rate		1.6%	1.6%	1.6%
Annualized Dividend Yield		0%	0%	0%
Time to Exit (years)		3	3	3
$d(1)$		2.17	1.29	0.68
$N(d1)$		0.99	0.90	0.75
$d(2)$		0.96	0.08	(0.53)
$N(d2)$		0.83	0.53	0.30
Value of Call Option	$ 40,000,000	$ 34,411,910	$ 26,844,913	$ 19,246,130
Incremental Option Value		$ 5,588,090	$ 7,566,997	$ 7,598,783 $ 19,246,130

Breakpoint Participation Percentages				
Series A Preferred		0.00%	100.00%	0.00%	31.17%
Convertible Note		100.00%	0.00%	0.00%	16.48%
Common		0.00%	0.00%	100.00%	52.34%
Total		100.00%	100.00%	100.00%	100.00%

Allocation of Incremental Option Value Total Value				
Series A Preferred	$ 13,566,269	$ -	$ 7,566,997	$ -	$ 5,999,272
Convertible Note	$ 8,760,740	$ 5,588,090	$ -	$ -	$ 3,172,650
Common	$ 17,672,991	$ -	$ -	$ 7,598,783	$ 10,074,208
Total	$ 40,000,000	$ 5,588,090	$ 7,566,997	$ 7,598,783	$ 19,246,130
Series A Preferred/share	$ 1.36			
Convertible Note B/unit of principal	$ 1.75			
Common/share	$ 0.88			

EXHIBIT 11.15 Sample Company – Enterprise Value Allocation – BSM Option Pricing Method

We can now use the BSM option pricing method to allocate enterprise value to the various classes/series of shares and calculate the value of Convertible Note B accordingly, as illustrated in Exhibit 11.15.

With an enterprise value of $40 million, an asset volatility of 70%, and a risk-free rate of 1.6%, and using the breakpoints identified in Exhibit 11.14 as exercise prices, we obtain a value for Convertible Note B of $1.75 per unit of principal as of the valuation date. It is important to note that the volatility used in this model is the asset volatility of the enterprise, which is not affected by financial leverage. Also, the analyst should consider the possibility that investors may renegotiate the allocation of enterprise value at exit in a way that may result in a greater share of the value to be allocated to the common equity class.

VALUATION OF CONVERTIBLE NOTES: CALIBRATION WITH THE OPM BACKSOLVE

The transaction price of a convertible note is not typically used as the initial input in an Option Pricing method (OPM) backsolve model, primarily due to the distortions in the estimated enterprise value that are likely to result from the fact that convertible notes are senior securities in a complex capital structure, and that they are often a small share of ownership on a fully converted basis. There are, however, circumstances in which the issue price of a convertible note may affect an OPM model indirectly, because of its impact on the price of the stock that is used as an input in the OPM model.

For instance, let's assume that on January 1 of Year 2 Sample Company has issued Convertible Note C with a par value of $10 million and a term to maturity of 1 year. Convertible Note C is a short-term bridge loan that is expected to convert into a new forthcoming round of Series B preferred shares. Convertible Note C accrues PIK interest at 8% per annum and is convertible into Series B preferred stock upon issuance at a conversion discount of 20%.

On April 1 of Year 2, the Series B preferred stock issuance takes place as scheduled. Convertible Note C is converted into 12,750,000 Series B shares, including accrued interest and after the 20% conversion discount:

$$\text{Number of Series B shares upon conversion: } [10,000,000 + 10,000,000 \times 8\% \times 3/12]/(1 - 20\%) = 12,750,000$$

In addition, the same investors purchase additional 15,000,000 shares of Series B preferred stock at a price of $1 per share.

For purposes of the OPM model, the "transaction price" of the new round of Series B preferred as of April 1 can now be calculated using a weighted average price that considers both the issue price of 15,000,000 shares at $1 per share and the price of $0.78 per share that results from the conversion of the Convertible B Bonds as shown in Exhibit 11.16.

The weighted average price of Series B preferred stock at issuance is now $0.90 per unit, a 10% discount relative to the contractual issue price of $1.0 per share. To the extent there

	Invested Capital	Discount	Accrued Interest	Shares Issued	Unit Price	Weighted Average Price
Convertible Note C	$ 10,000,000	20%	$ 200,000	12,750,000	$ 0.78	$ 0.36
Series B Preferred – New Shares	$ 15,000,000	n/a	n/a	15,000,000	$ 1.00	$ 0.54
Total	$ 25,000,000			27,750,000		$ 0.90

EXHIBIT 11.16 Weighted Average Issue Price of Series B Preferred Stock

is identity in the investor group between Convertible Note C and Series B Preferred stock financing, the weighted average price may provide in some cases a more suitable indication of unit price for the overall transaction than if the contractual issue price of $1 per share had been used. The valuation analyst can then use the unit price of $0.90 per share as an input in its OPM backsolve model, to generate a value for the company's equity and for the other equity interests in the firm that can be used at subsequent measurement dates for calibration. Alternatively, the analyst may determine that the contractual $1.0 per share price should be used, and the 20% discount granted to Convertible Bond B holders should not be factored into the base OPM backsolve price as the discounted price does not represent fair value. This may be the case, for instance, if the new round includes new investors as market participants that enter at the $1 per share contractual price, and/or if the converted shares represent a small percentage of the overall round volume.

VALUATION OF CONVERTIBLE NOTES: BINOMIAL LATTICE MODEL

One of the limitations of the methods that rely on the BSM model as discussed so far is that they do not consider the correlation between the credit risk of the convertible note and the underlying stock price, which tends to understate the value of the conversion option. In the BSM model, the strike price of the conversion option is set to be equal to the face value of the bond as a proxy for the fair value of the bond. The face value of the bond, however, is a fixed contractual amount while the fair value of the bond is a variable amount that is correlated with the company's stock price. As the stock price of a company increases (together with the value of the conversion option), its credit risk profile also improves and the fair value of the bond increases as well. Conversely, a deterioration in a company's credit profile is likely to be accompanied by a decrease in the company's equity value (and related conversion option).[9]

Also, the BSM model is based on a single point estimate for key inputs such as the term to exit, volatility, and discount rate (risk-free rate), which makes it less suitable to value convertible notes with more complex features such as prepayment and early conversion options, dilution adjustments, mandatory conversion rights, embedded put rights, or restricted dates that require greater modeling flexibility.

For convertible notes with more complex features and where the correlation between credit risk and underlying equity value may be significant, a common approach to address the limitations of the BSM model is to use a binomial lattice model.[10] Compared to the BSM model, a binomial lattice model allows for greater flexibility of terms and can better incorporate the interaction between credit risk and stock price.

Let's look now at an example of a binomial lattice model for a convertible note. Convertible Note C has a principal value of $1,000 and a term to maturity of two years. The bond is convertible at maturity into 100 shares of preferred stock, which have an estimated

---

[9]AICPA PE/VC Valuation Guide B.10.10.14: "Even if the instrument is issued at par, treating the face amount as the aggregate strike price incorporates a portion of the market value of the embedded option into the strike price. This simplification results in overstating the strike price, thus understating the value of the conversion option."

[10]AICPA PE/VC Valuation Guide B.10.06-B.10.13 provides an example of convertible bond valuation using a binomial lattice model.

value per share of $10 at the measurement date t_0. In this simplified example, let's assume that Convertible Note C is a zero-coupon bond with no other contractual features that are relevant for valuation. We now walk through each of the steps of the binomial lattice model.

Step 1: Inputs and Model Setup

Exhibit 11.17 presents the characteristics of our Convertible Note C and the key inputs in our binomial lattice model.

Since the note is convertible into preferred stock, the volatility of preferred stock must be used, which may be significantly lower than the overall equity volatility of the company. In this simplified model, the term to maturity has been divided into eight steps with a time interval of three months each. In practice, a binomial lattice model relies on a large number of small binomial movements for its accuracy.

Inputs [5], [7], [8], and [9] are the familiar inputs that we also find in the BSM model. In a binomial lattice model, we need to adjust the annualized volatility of the underlying equity (50%) and estimate the volatility that applies to the specific time interval used in the valuation ("step volatility" over three months in our example). To do so, we multiply the annualized volatility by the square root of time (the number of steps in one year), as follows:

$$\text{Step volatility} = \text{Annualized volatility} \times \text{SQRT} (1/4) = 25.00\%$$

Convertible Note Features:		
[1] Principal value of note	$	1,000
[2] Coupon rate		0.00%
[3] Term to maturity – years		2
[4] Conversion price = strike price	$	10
Other Inputs:		
[5] Preferred stock – current value	$	10
[6] Credit spread		11.50%
[7] Volatility		50.00%
[8] Annual dividend rate		0.00%
[9] Risk-free rate		3.50%
[10] Steps in year		4
Calculations:		
[11] Conversion ratio – number of shares	100	= [1]/[4]
[12] Total steps in term	8	= [3] × [10]
[13] Step volatility	25.00%	= [7] × SQRT [1/[10]]
[14] u = Up move	1.2840	= EXP [13]
[15] d = Down move	0.7788	= 1/[14]
[16] RFR = Equity payoff interval discount rate	1.75%	= [9] × SQRT [1/[10]]
[17] RFR = Equity payoff interval discount risk factor	1.0177	= EXP [16]
[18] Debt payoff discount rate	15.00%	= [6] + [9]
[19] Debt payoff interval discount rate	7.50%	= [18] × SQRT [1/[10]]
[20] Debt payoff interval discount rate factor	1.0779	= EXP [19]
[21] pu = Probability of up move	0.4728	= ([17] − [15])/([14] − [15])
[22] pd = Probability of down move	0.5272	= 1 − [21]

EXHIBIT 11.17 Convertible Note C – Binomial Lattice Model – Inputs and Model Setup

The up move and the down moves are calculated as:

$$u = e^{0.25} = 1.2840 \text{ (rounded)}$$

and

$$d = e^{-0.25} = 0.7788 \text{ (rounded)}$$

One fundamental assumption in our model is that a different discount rate should be used for equity payoffs (if the bond converts into equity) versus debt payoffs (if the bond receives proceeds based on its principal value). The equity payoffs are discounted using the risk-free rate (adjusted to match the time interval) while the debt payoffs incorporate also counterparty credit risk by adding the credit spread to the risk-free rate.

The probability of up and down moves is calculated as follows:

$$P_u = e^{r\sqrt{\delta t}} - d/u - d = e^{0.015\sqrt{1/4}} - 0.7788/1.2840 - 0.7788 = 0.4728$$
$$P_d = 1 - 0.4728 = 0.5272$$

Step 2: Build the Asset Tree

We now have all the inputs to build the Asset Tree, which represents the projected value of one share of preferred stock in the Sample Company as of each quarter-end, starting from the current value of $10.00 per share and up to the maturity date of the bond as illustrated in Exhibit 11.18.

At the end of Period 1, the stock can have one of two values:

$$S_u = \$10 \times u = \$10 \times 1.2840 = 12.84$$

or

$$S_d = \$10 \times d = \$10 \times 0.0779 = \$7.79$$

Asset Tree Period	0	1	2	3	4	5	6	7	8
Value of Underlying Equity	$10.00	$12.84	$16.49	$21.17	$27.18	$34.90	$44.85	$57.55	$73.89
		$7.79	$10.00	$12.84	$16.49	$21.17	$27.18	$34.90	$44.82
			$6.07	$7.79	$10.00	$12.84	$16.49	$21.17	$27.18
				$4.72	$6.07	$7.79	$10.00	$12.84	$16.49
					$3.68	$4.72	$6.07	$7.79	$10.00
						$2.87	$3.68	$4.72	$6.07
							$2.23	$2.87	$3.68
								$1.74	$2.23
									$1.35

EXHIBIT 11.18 Preferred Stock – Asset Tree

At the end of Period 2, we have three possible values for S as follows:

$$S_{u2} = S_u \times u = \$12.84 \times 1.2840 = \$16.49$$

$$S_{ud^2} = S_d \times d = \$7.79 \times 0.0779 = \$6.07$$

$$S_{du} = S_{ud} = \$12.84 \times 0.7788 = \$7.79 \times 1.2840 = \$10.00$$

Note that the tree recombines in the sense that an up movement followed by a down movement leads to the same stock price as a down movement followed by an up movement ($S_{du} = S_{ud}$).

We can then complete the tree using the same procedure at each step.

Step 3: Determine the Values of the Convertible Note at Maturity

Based on the Asset Tree that we have built in Step 2, we can now determine the value of the convertible note under each possible stock value outcome. For each outcome, our note can either convert into equity or receive principal as stated in the note indenture. To the extent the conversion value of the note is in excess of its principal value, it will be convenient for the note holder to convert. Vice versa, the note holder will be better off receiving its principal value if it exceeds its conversion value.

For each stock price at Period 8, we can calculate a single point estimate of the value of the note. For instance, for $S = \$73.89$, we have

$$\text{Note value} = \text{MAX (Note conversion value, Note principal value)}$$

with:

$$\text{Note conversion value} = \text{Unit share price} \times \text{number of shares upon conversion}$$
$$= \$73.89 \times 100 = \$7,389$$

and

$$\text{Note principal value} = \$1,000$$

The note value can be calculated as:

$$\text{Note value} = \text{MAX} (\$7,389, \ \$1,000) = \$7,389$$

Using the same procedure, we can calculate all other note values in Step 8 as shown in Exhibit 11.19.

Step 4: Building the Convertible Note Tree

The next step consists of building the Convertible Note Tree, starting from the values calculated in Period 8 and working back through the model in backwardation to estimate the value at t_0. At each node, the value of the note is calculated as the weighted average of the equity and debt payoffs from the immediately following period, which are discounted at the

Step 8 - Note Value

A Stock Price	B = A × 100 Conversion Value	C Principal Value	D = MAX (B, C) Note Value
$ 73.89	$ 7,389	$ 1,000	$ 7,389
$ 44.82	$ 4,482	$ 1,000	$ 4,482
$ 27.18	$ 2,718	$ 1,000	$ 2,718
$ 16.49	$ 1,649	$ 1,000	$ 1,649
$ 10.00	$ 1,000	$ 1,000	$ 1,000
$ 6.07	$ 607	$ 1,000	$ 1,000
$ 3.68	$ 368	$ 1,000	$ 1,000
$ 2.23	$ 223	$ 1,000	$ 1,000
$ 1.35	$ 135	$ 1,000	$ 1,000

EXHIBIT 11.19 Convertible Note D – Value at Maturity

respective rates (risk-free rate for equity payoffs and risk-free rate + credit spread for bond payoffs). Exhibit 11.20 illustrates the full Convertible Note Tree for Convertible Note C.

Let's take a look at some of the values in greater detail. For instance, let's consider the value of 5,755 (B_0u^7) in Period 7. Staring from node B_0u^7, our bond can take one of two possible values in Period 8:

$$B_0u^8 = 7,389 \text{ or } B_0u^7d = 4,482$$

We can calculate the value of the bond at Step 7 as the probability weighted average of these two possible outcomes in Step 8, discounted to present value as of the end of Q7 as follows:

$$B_0u^7 = p\, B_0u^8/RFR + (1-p)\, B_0u^7d/RFR$$

$$= 0.4728 \times \$7,389/1.0177 + 0.5272 \times \$4,482/1.0177$$

$$= \$3,433 + \$2,322 = \$5,755$$

where:

$$
\begin{aligned}
B_0u^8 &= \$7,389 \\
B_0u^7 &= \$4,482 \\
p &= 0.4728 \\
(1-p) &= 0.5272
\end{aligned}
$$

Notice that both payoffs for B_0u^7 at the terminal Step 8 represent equity payoffs from the conversion of the Note into equity. Accordingly, both the $7,389 payoff and the $4,482 payoff are discounted using the equity discount risk factor for the relevant period of 1.0177 (three-month risk-free rate).

Let's now look at the value of the Note at $B_0d^7 = \$928$. This value is calculated as the probability-weighted average of the two terminal values $B_0d^8 = \$1,000$ and $B_0d^7u = \$1,000$ as follows:

$$B_0d^7 = 0.4728 \times 1,000/1.0779 + 0.5272 \times 1,000/1.0779 = \$439 + \$489 = \$928$$

Period	0	1	2	3	4	5	6	7	8	
Value of Convertible Note	$ 967	$ 1,234	$ 1,598	$ 2,081	$ 2,703	$ 3,490	$ 4,482	$ 5,755	$ 7,389	Convert to Equity (E)
		$ 420	$ 625	$ 895	$ 1,229	$ 1,621	$ 2,082	$ 2,673	$ 3,433	
		$ 166	$ 278	$ 450	$ 698	$ 1,025	$ 1,408	$ 1,808	$ 2,322	
		$ 145	$ 111	$ 67	$ 25	$ -	$ -	$ -	$ -	
		$ 236	$ 220	$ 185	$ 125	$ 57	$ -	$ -	$ -	
			$ 804	$ 987	$ 1,247	$ 1,609	$ 2,095	$ 2,718	$ 3,490	$ 4,482 — Convert to Equity (E)
			$ 250	$ 404	$ 626	$ 919	$ 1,263	$ 1,621	$ 2,082	
			$ 72	$ 134	$ 243	$ 428	$ 715	$ 1,097	$ 1,408	
			$ 197	$ 166	$ 115	$ 51	$ -	$ -	$ -	
			$ 285	$ 284	$ 264	$ 211	$ 117	$ -	$ -	
				$ 721	$ 838	$ 1,008	$ 1,257	$ 1,620	$ 2,117	$ 2,718 — Convert to Equity (E)
				$ 120	$ 218	$ 384	$ 641	$ 983	$ 1,263	
				$ 18	$ 40	$ 86	$ 184	$ 397	$ 854	
				$ 255	$ 236	$ 189	$ 105	$ -	$ -	
				$ 328	$ 344	$ 349	$ 327	$ 239	$ -	
					$ 707	$ 781	$ 879	$ 1,024	$ 1,255	$ 1,649 — Convert to Equity (E)
					$ 36	$ 77	$ 165	$ 356	$ 766	
					$ -	$ -	$ -	$ -	$ -	
					$ 309	$ 313	$ 239	$ 215	$ -	
					$ 362	$ 391	$ 421	$ 454	$ 489	
						$ 741	$ 799	$ 861	$ 928	$ 1,000 — Receive Principal (D)
						$ -	$ -	$ -	$ -	
						$ -	$ -	$ -	$ -	
						$ 350	$ 378	$ 407	$ 439	
						$ 391	$ 421	$ 454	$ 489	
							$ 799	$ 861	$ 928	$ 1,000 — Receive Principal (D)
							$ -	$ -	$ -	
							$ -	$ -	$ -	
							$ 378	$ 407	$ 439	
Source:	E up						$ 421	$ 454	$ 489	
	E down							$ 861	$ 928	$ 1,000 — Receive Principal (D)
	D up							$ -	$ -	
	D down							$ -	$ -	
								$ 407	$ 439	
								$ 454	$ 489	
									$ 928	$ 1,000 — Receive Principal (D)
									$ -	
									$ 439	
									$ 489	
										$ 1,000 — Receive Principal (D)

EXHIBIT 11.20   Convertible Note C – BLM Tree

Both payoffs are debt payoffs and the discount rate is accordingly the discount rate of debt, which includes consideration of counterparty credit risk.

As we proceed backward in the model, it's important to keep track of the type of payoffs that go into the overall value of the Note at each node in order to apply the appropriate discount rate. For instance, let's look at $B_0u^3d^3 = \$1,024$ in Period 6. This value is calculated as the probability weighted average of $B_0u^4d^3 = \$1,255$ and $B_0u^3d^4 = \$928$ as follows:

$$B_0u^3d^3 = 0.4728 \times 766/1.0177 + 0.4728 \times 489/1.0779 + 0.5272 \times 928/1.0779 = \$1,024$$

In this case, the payoffs associated with $B_0u^3d^4 = 928$ consist entirely of debt payoffs which are discounted using the debt discount factor of 1.0779. On the other hand, the payoffs associated with $B_0 u^4 d^3 = 1,255$ are in part equity payoffs (\$766) and in part debt payoff (\$489). Accordingly, the discount factor is set to match the respective payoff type.

Along similar lines, the Convertible Note Tree can be completed, resulting in a value of Convertible Note D of \$967 as of the measurement date.

Use of Binomial Lattice Model in ESE Valuation

The binomial lattice model can be used effectively to model convertible notes with more complex features such as prepayment options and mandatory conversion. In these cases, the Convertible Note tree will be adjusted to reflect the desired characteristics and the expected payoff of the Note under each possible outcome for the underlying stock price. For instance, a provision to mandatorily redeem the bond as the underlying stock price first reaches \$40 per share would put a cap to the model in Steps 6, 7, and 8 at an equity price of \$40 in our example based on Exhibit 11.18.

While developed to value primarily stand-alone option instruments, the binomial lattice model has become a widely accepted and commonly used tool in the valuation of convertible notes. In most cases, ESE convertible notes tend to have noncomplex features, with short-term conversion terms that generally coincide with the maturity of the bond. In such cases, the binomial lattice model is unlikely to result in a value that is significantly different from a BSM approach. Even in those circumstances, the binomial lattice model can provide a useful tool to validate the results of a BSM model and better highlight the effect of the correlation between the credit profile of the company and the value of the underlying stock on bond valuation. Also, the binomial lattice model can be helpful in addressing situations where preferred shareholders may have the power to control the timing of exit and change the allocation of value between debt holders and equity holders and between the senior and junior classes of equity, thereby affecting the bond's ultimate payoff.

VALUATION OF BRIDGE NOTES: "AS IF CONVERTED" METHOD

In an ESE, most convertible note issues occur in the form of bridge notes, in anticipation of a new round of equity financing. Bridge loans typically have a short time to maturity, and are convertible in preferred stock at the time of the new round. Also, they often provide investors with favorable conversion terms, such as a discount relative to the issue price of the forthcoming round, typically in the range of 10–25%. PIK interest is typically added to the principal value at the time of conversion. For these securities, most of the value resides in the conversion feature (the option component) while the "straight" bond component reflects an implied yield, which is consistent with venture capital rate of returns. In light of their short term to maturity and imminent conversion, convertible bridge loans are typically valued on an "as if converted" basis, using the transaction price of the new round to estimate the value of the shares that the reference bridge loan is entitled to upon conversion, and discounting the result to present value as of the measurement date.

For instance, going back to Convertible Note B, and given a weighted average price for series B preferred shares of \$0.90 per share, the valuation of Convertible Note B would consist of the following three steps.

Step 1: Estimate the Value of the Note at the Conversion Date

As of the conversion date (April 1 of Year 2), Convertible Note B is convertible into 12,750,000 shares of Series B preferred. Assuming a price of $0.90 per unit as determined in Exhibit 11.16, the value of the note at conversion is $11,475,000.

Step 2: Subtract the Value of Accrued Interest

In order to estimate the current value of the note, the accrued interest between the current measurement date and the projected date of the Series B round needs to be excluded from the note's value as the interest has not yet been earned at the measurement date. As of the conversion date, 250,000 shares are attributable to the conversion of par value due to interest accrual, calculated as:

$$\text{Number of shares upon conversion of accrued interest component}$$

$$= \text{Accrued Interest/Conversion ratio} = \$200,000/0.8 = 250,000$$

The shares attributable to the conversion of par value due to interest accrual have a value of $225,000 $(250,000 \times \$0.90)$. The value of the note net of the interest accrual component is therefore:

$$\text{Value of note net of interest component} = \$11,475,000 - \$225,000 = \$11,250,000$$

Step 3: Discount the Future Value of the Note Before Interest Accrual to Present Value

Assuming a YTM of 16%, the present value of the bridge loan is $10,840,238 calculated as:

$$\text{Present value of bridge loan} = \$11,250,000/(1.16^{0.25}) = \$10,840,238$$

VALUATION OF BRIDGE NOTES WITH WARRANTS

Valuation at Issuance

In some cases, the issuance of a convertible note may be accompanied by the issuance of warrants in anticipation of a future round of financing where the note and the warrants will be converted/exercised in the newly issued class/series of shares. In this case, the investor will have to allocate the purchase price of the combined instruments between the note and the warrants, based on their respective estimated fair values as a percentage of total purchase price, and track their fair value separately at subsequent measurement periods.

Exhibit 11.21 presents an example of a Bridge Note (Convertible Note D) with Warrants that is issued in anticipation of a "qualified" Series B preferred stock financing.

Convertible Note D has a par value of $10 million and accrues PIK interest at a rate of 8.0% per year. The note has a term to maturity of one year, at which point it is expected to either convert in the new round of Series B preferred stock with a 20% discount to the

Bond Instrument	Principal	PIK Interest	Maturity	Conversion	Conv Features
Convertible Note D (Bridge)	$ 10,000,000	8.00%	1 year	Scenario 1: Qualified Series B Preferred Financing	20% discount to next round and warrants at 15% of par
				Scenario 2: Conversion into Series A	$1 per share of Series A preferred. Warrants expire worthless.

EXHIBIT 11.21 Convertible Note D – Key Features

issue price of the new round (Scenario 1 – 40% probability), or to convert into Series A shares based on par value including accrued interest (Scenario 2 – 60% probability). The note carries warrants in the amount of 15% of its par value, which can be exercised into Series B shares within 1.5 years from the date the Qualified Series B financing at a 1× exercise ratio (1 warrant unit = 1 share of Series B preferred stock). For purpose of the warrant dilution adjustment, the company expects to have 20,000,000 units of common-stock equivalent shares on a fully converted basis before warrant exercise after the Qualified Series B financing (21,500,000 including shares issued upon warrant exercise). Under Scenario 2, the warrants expire worthless.

Exhibit 11.22 shows the breakout of the purchase price between the warrant and Convertible Note D at issuance.

The breakout of the purchase price into the note and the warrant components involves four steps.

Step 1: Note Value at Conversion As a first step, we need to determine the value of the note at conversion (the maturity date). Under Scenario 1 (new round of Qualified Series B preferred financing), the value of the note at conversion is $13.5 million, calculated as the sum of three components:

1. The original principal value of $10 million.
2. The PIK accrued interest. This amount is calculated by multiplying the PIK interest rate of 8% by the par value and by the term of the accrual expressed in years (1 year in our example).
3. The conversion discount value. This is the value of the discount from the issue price of Series B preferred stock that is granted to the note holders based on the note indenture. In our example, the discount is 20% of par at maturity, including accrued interest.

Assuming an issue price of Series B preferred stock of $1 per share, the value of Convertible Note D at conversion under Scenario 1 is calculated as:

Scenario 1 – Note value at conversion = $(\$10,000,000 \times 1.08)/(1 - 20\%) = \$10.8$ million/0.8 = $13.5 million

Convertible Note D - Note Value at Conversion:	Scenario 1	Scenario 2	Weighted Average
Probability	40%	60%	
Principal	$ 10,000,000	$ 10,000,000	
PIK Interest	$ 800,000	$ 800,000	
Conversion discount at 20%	$ 2,700,000		
Note value (1 year from issue date)	$ 13,500,000	$ 10,800,000	$ 11,880,000

Value of Warrants at Note Conversion	Scenario 1	Scenario 2	Weighted Average
Probability	40%	60%	
Underlying price (1 year forward)	$ 1,500,000	n/a	
Exercise price	$ 1,500,000	n/a	
Risk-free rate	1.75%	n/a	
Term to exercise (1 year forward)	1.50	n/a	
Volatility of preferred stock	70.00%	n/a	
Warrant Value (1 year from issue date)	$ 462,701	$ -	$ 185,080

Allocation of Value			
Value of the note + warrants – 1 year from issue date			$ 12,065,080
Issue price of note + warrants			$ 10,000,000
Implied IRR			20.6508%
PV of warrant			$ 153,401
PV of note			$ 9,846,599
PV of note + warrants			$ 10,000,000

EXHIBIT 11.22   Convertible Note D – Allocation of Purchase Price – Scenario Analysis

Under Scenario 2, the note value at conversion excludes the Series B shares conversion discount (no new round takes place). Accordingly, under Scenario 2 the value of Convertible Note B at conversion is $10.8 million (par value including accrued interest).

A probability-weighted average of the note values under the two scenarios results in an estimated value at maturity of $11,880,000 calculated as:

Convertible Note D Value at Conversion = 40% × 13,500,000 + 60% × $10,800,000

= $5,400,000 + $6,480,000 = $11,880,000

Step 2: Value of the Warrant at Note Conversion   In Step 2 we estimate the value of the warrant at the time of the Note conversion using the BSM call option model with dilution adjustment and the following inputs:

- Underlying asset value: This is the amount of value of the shares in which the warrants may convert. It is a contractual amount that is defined under the terms of the bridge note issuance as 15% of the note principal par value (15% of 10 million = $1,500,000).
- Exercise price: This is equal to the underlying asset value of the warrant (the warrant is "at the money"), or $1,500,000.

- The risk-free rate: We assume it is 1.75% to match the term of the warrant.
- Term to exit: The term is 1.5 years from the conversion date which in turn, is 1 year from the issue date.
- Volatility of Series B preferred stock (new round of shares): We estimate the volatility at 70%. This value is typically lower than the volatility of the company's equity, since preferred stock is less volatile than the overall equity.

In order to calculate the warrant dilution adjustment we also need:

- Number of Series B preferred stock shares in which the warrant may convert = 1,500,000.
- Number of shares outstanding before warrant conversion after the Series B preferred round: 20,000,000.

Under Scenario 1, the BSM resolves for a warrant value of $462,701. Under Scenario 2, the warrants expire worthless. The probability-weighted average of the warrant values under the two Scenarios is $185,080.

Step 3: Future Value of the Combined Transaction   We can now calculate the value of the combined transaction by summing the value of the note and of the warrant, for a total of $12,065,080. It's important to note that the value of the combined instrument is a future value at a point in time which corresponds to the conversion date of the note (the maturity date), one year from the issue date. We can obtain the implied Internal Rate of Return for the investment in the combined instruments by dividing the future value of $12,065,080 by the original issue price of $10 million:

Implied IRR

= Value of the Combined Instrument at one year from issue date/Original Issue Price

= $12,065,080/$10,000,000 = 20.6508% = 20.65%

Step 4: Discount to Present Value   Using the implied IRR as the discount rate, we can now calculate the present value (fair value) of the warrant and the note principal separately as follows:

Fair value of warrant at the issue date = $185,080/(1 + 0.206508) = $153,401

Fair value of note principal at the issue date = 11,800,000/(1 + 0.206508) = $9,846,599

The sum of the fair value of the warrant and the note principal reconciles to the issue price of the combined instruments of $10 million.

Valuation at Subsequent Measurement

Six months have passed from the initial transaction date. We can now calibrate the model that we have developed at the time of the initial transaction to value the warrant and the convertible note at the current measurement date. We estimate that the probability of a qualified Series B preferred financing (Scenario 1) has increased to 60%. The risk-free rate has increased to 2.0%, the estimated volatility of Series B stock has decreased to 60%, and the implied IRR

Value of Note		Scenario 1		Scenario 2		Weighted Average
Probability			60%		40%	
Principal	$	10,000,000	$	10,000,000		
PIK interest	$	800,000	$	800,000		
Conversion discount at 20%	$	2,700,000				
Note value at conversion (0.5 year from measurement date)	$	13,500,000	$	10,800,000	$	12,420,000
Estimated IRR (annualized)						20.6508%
PV of note					$	11,307,237
Value of Warrants		**Scenario 1**		**Scenario 2**		**Weighted Average**
Probability			60%		40%	
Underlying price (1 year forward)	$	1,500,000		n/a		
Exercise price	$	1,500,000		n/a		
Risk-free rate			2.00%		n/a	
Term to exercise (0.5 year forward)			1.50		n/a	
Volatility of preferred stock			60.00%		n/a	
Warrant value – BSM 0.5 year from measurement date	$	396,514	$	-	$	237,908
Estimated IRR (annualized)						20.6508%
PV of warrant					$	216,593
Value of Note + Warrants					$	11,523,830

EXHIBIT 11.23   Convertible Note D – Calibration at Subsequent Measurement

is unchanged at an annualized rate of 20.6508%. Under these assumptions, the warrant has value of $216,593 (after dilution adjustment) and the straight note component has a value of $11,307,237, with a resulting combined value of $11,523,830 at the measurement date as shown in Exhibit 11.23.

VALUATION USING BROKER QUOTES

The use of broker quotes is a common method for valuing corporate debt for publicly traded companies. For a public company with a significant market in its corporate debt, broker quotes that represent a commitment to trade or an actual trade as of the measurement date are often used as indicators for the fair value of the reference instrument. In an ESE setting, however, actionable broker quotes are rarely available. In those rare instances when value indications may be obtained from brokers, it is critical that we ask ourselves what these broker quotes really represent. To what extent is the broker willing to actually stand behind its quote and purchase the security from us at that price? Is the quote just meant to be indicative or does it provide an actual trading point for valuation? To the extent the quote reflects an actual trade that happened on or around the measurement date, does it reflect an orderly market? Does it reflect a transaction that was in the ordinary course of business or does a distressed transaction that was performed under duress? What is the trading volume in our debt instrument? Can we perhaps get other quotes to put together a model for matrix pricing? Matrix pricing can provide a more reliable indication of fair value than a single quote.

In the recently issued revised Auditing Standard 2501, the Public Accounting Oversight Board has noted that

> *When a fair value measurement is based on a quote from a broker or dealer ("broker quote"), the relevance and reliability of the evidence provided by the broker quote depend on whether: a. The broker or dealer is free of relationships with the company by which company management can directly or indirectly control or significantly influence the broker or dealer; b. The broker or dealer making the quote is a market maker that transacts in the same type of financial instrument; c. The broker quote reflects market conditions as of the financial statement date; d. The broker quote is binding on the broker or dealer; and e. There are any restrictions, limitations, or disclaimers in the broker quote and, if so, their nature.[. . .] Broker quotes generally provide more relevant and reliable evidence when they are timely, binding quotes, without any restrictions, limitations, or disclaimers, from unaffiliated market makers transacting in the same type of financial instrument.*[11]

In cases when no recent transactions have occurred either for the financial instrument being valued or for similar financial instruments, and only indicative quotes can be obtained, additional procedures should be performed to evaluate the appropriateness of the valuation method and the reasonableness of observable and unobservable inputs used by the pricing service. For a venture capital firm, this may involve developing its own model-based valuation and comparing it to the broker-dealer quotes as part of its valuation process.

One question that often arises concerning the use of broker quotes to value portfolio investments is whether it would be most appropriate to use the bid (low), ask (high), midpoint, or some other point in fair value measurement. The AICPA PE/VC Valuation Guide indicates that a fund should use its best estimate of the point in the range that is most representative of fair value.[12] The fund should have a valuation policy in place on this matter and apply it consistently, unless a change in circumstances makes a change in policy appropriate.

VALUATION OF DEBT FOR THE PURPOSE OF VALUING EQUITY

Let's now shift our perspective to that of the holder of an equity interest in an ESE, for instance, a venture capital fund. In order to value its equity interest, the venture capital fund

---

[11]PCAOB AS 2501: Auditing Accounting Estimates, Including Fair Value Measurements (as Amended for FEE 12/15/2020 and After). A9: "Using Pricing Information from a Broker or Dealer." From an audit perspective, PCAOB AS 2501. A9 indicates that "if the broker quote does not provide sufficient appropriate evidence, the auditor should perform procedures to obtain relevant and reliable pricing information from another pricing source [. . .]. "The auditor should take into account the results of the procedures performed under AS 2410 in determining whether the broker or dealer has a relationship with the company by which management has the ability to directly or indirectly control or significantly influence the broker or dealer.

[12]AICPA PE/VC Valuation Guide, Q&A 14.13: Bid/Ask Spread Considerations.

will have to subtract the value of the debt to arrive to the value of the overall equity of the firm, and then move on to the next step, which is the allocation of the firm's equity value to the various classes/series of equity securities in the firm's capital structure. How can we estimate the value of debt to subtract from enterprise value for purpose of equity valuation?

The AICPA PE/VC Guide defines the value of debt for the purpose of valuing equity as

> *the value of the liability that market participants transaction in the equity interests would subtract from the total enterprise value to establish a price for the equity interests in an orderly transaction at the measurement date.*[13]

One approach to value debt for the purpose of valuing equity is to use the estimated fair value of debt for this purpose. For instance, the investor may estimate the value of debt using a YTM methodology. A backsolve OPM, which effectively incorporates debt in the company's capital structure (and any PIK accrued interest at exit) based on its liquidation rights can also be used. The fair value of debt provides an upper bound on the value of equity, as the equity holders and the company would have to pay a price that is at least equal to that value if they were to buy back the debt in a negotiated transaction or redeem the debt before maturity.

Another possibility is to use the payoff amount of the debt. This can be a suitable approach when debt is prepayable and carries an above-market coupon, for instance, because the company's credit quality has improved or market yields have declined since the note issuance. It can also be suitable if there is a reasonable expectation that holders of the debt may demand a repayment at a change of control, and that a change of control is imminent. The equity value measured based on the enterprise value less the payoff amount provides a lower bound on the value of equity, because the equity holders could redeem the debt for this price. Alternatively, an equity investor may want to use the face value of the debt if, for instance, it is determined that it is not in a market participant's best interest to sell the company in a merger that would trigger a change in control provision and the prepayment penalty.

The book value of debt is also often used. This approach can be very attractive for its simplicity and may be suitable if the credit quality of the company has not changed significantly since the debt issuance while credit markets have been reasonably stable. When the credit quality of the company has declined or market yields have increased significantly, on the other hand, the value of debt for the purpose of valuing equity under the fair value standards may be significantly below its book value.

The value of debt of the purpose of valuing equity may be different from the fair value of debt on a stand-alone basis, due to a different set of market participants (equity holders often with greater insight into the company's operations), and a different principal market (the equity versus debt market). In other situations, equity investors may be able to negotiate conditions that lead to a value of debt that does not coincide with any of the metrics discussed earlier. For instance, they may negotiate directly with debt holders to repay the debt at an

---

[13] AICPA PE/VC Valuation Guide 6.03. On the valuation of debt for the purpose of valuing equity, see especially AICPA PE/VC Valuation Guide 6.19-6.31, Q&A 14.46: "Valuing Debt for the Purpose of Valuing Equity Using the Book Value or Face Value," IPEV Guidelines, 2.4: "Determining the value of debt to be deducted."

amount lower than the contractual payoff but higher than the fair value they would otherwise realize. In some cases, debt holders may be able to negotiate more favorable conditions at a price above fair value to give their consent for a corporate restructuring.

CONCLUSION

In this chapter, we have explored some of the most common valuation methodologies for debt instruments, with a focus on the valuation of convertible debt as the most frequently issued type of debt in an ESE. The binomial lattice model may provide a robust tool in convertible note valuation, especially when more complex features are present and when market participants may execute transactions at terms that differ from the contractual terms of the reference note. In most cases, however, methodologies based on the more simple BSM model can be used effectively to obtain an adequate representation of the note's fair value. A common methodology involves bifurcating of the optionality embedded in a convertible note from its "straight" debt component. A bifurcation process may also be used when convertible notes are issued together with other securities, such as warrants, in a single transaction, and where fair value at issuance needs to be allocated to the individual transaction components. Broker-dealer quotes for ESE debt securities are rarely available, and when they are available, they typically represent indicative quotes rather than quotes coming from actual trades or that reflect an actual intention to transact. Given these circumstances, their relevance as evidence of fair value for ESE debt is limited. As in the case of ESE equity, the best market evidence in the valuation of ESE debt is likely to come from transaction between the company and its investors or between investors in the secondary market that can be used to backsolve to the value of other interests in the firm.

CHAPTER 12

Valuation of Contingent Consideration

In the prior chapters, we have considered a sale of a business enterprise as a transaction that has the effect of a full "exit" event for the investor: the investor ceases to have an economic interest in the enterprise in exchange for a certain quantity of cash or noncash consideration at closing. In most early stage enterprise (ESE) sales, however, the seller's exposure to the enterprise's business does not end at closing. In fact, a significant component of the sale price often consists of proceeds that are contingent upon the company's achievement of certain performance or other targets after the closing has taken place under an "earnout" or "contingent consideration" provision in the sale agreement. In some cases, the seller may have the obligation to return part of the proceeds from the sale if specified conditions are met under the terms of a "clawback" provision.[1]

Earnout and clawback provisions in a sale agreement may help bridge a price gap during negotiations and provide an incentive for the seller to support the transition of ownership. An earnout provision may serve as a tax deferral tool, by spreading the cash proceeds from a transaction over multiple fiscal years. It may also provide a financing tool, by deferring certain cash payments to future periods. Earnout provisions are especially common in ESE sale transactions that involve significant postacquisition uncertainty for circumstances that may have a material impact on the company's operations. A venture capital fund may also be exposed to contingent consideration indirectly, by acquiring an interest in a portfolio company that has

---

[1]FASB ASC 805-10-20 Glossary defines contingent consideration as "usually an obligation of the acquirer to transfer additional assets or equity interests to the former owners of the acquired as part of the exchange for control of the acquired if specified future events occur or conditions are met. However, contingent consideration may also give the acquirer the right to the return of previously transferred consideration if specific conditions are met." FASB ASC 805-30-25-5 states that "the consideration the acquirer transfers in exchange for the acquire includes any asset or liability resulting from a contingent consideration arrangement. The acquirer shall recognize the acquisition-date fair value of the contingent consideration as part of the consideration transferred in exchange for the acquired." From the point of view of the seller in a business combination, most contingent consideration arrangements fall into the asset category.

been the buyer or the seller in a prior acquisition and that may have an earnout or a clawback on its own balance sheet. In this case, a valuation of the fund's equity interest in the portfolio company has to consider the impact of the cash-flows related to the earnout, in addition to those resulting from the portfolio company's own operations.

A venture capital fund that exits from an investment and receives contingent consideration as part of a sale transaction will generally have to include earnouts and clawbacks in its assets or liabilities and carry them at fair value until the contingency has been resolved.[2] An earnout at fair value will take the place of the prior portfolio company's holding and will typically be reported as a Level 3 asset in the fund's financial statements. From the perspective of the buyer, under FASB ASC 805, contingent consideration must be measured at fair value and included in the transaction's purchase price as of the acquisition date. It must then be remeasured at each subsequent reporting date until resolution of the contingency, with changes in fair value recognized in earnings. A portfolio manager will also have to assess the value of contingent consideration to estimate the proceeds at exit and investment returns.

This chapter discusses the methods generally used to value contingent consideration under the fair value standard of ASC 820/IFRS 13, with a focus on earnouts from the perspective of a venture capital fund investor that engages in a sale transaction. Most earnouts are complex and unique to the transaction and using a market approach is not appropriate as transaction prices for identical or similar liabilities do not exist.[3]

Most recently, the Appraisal Foundation has issued a valuation advisory that provides guidance on best practices in the valuation of contingent consideration (VFR #4).[4] The AICPA PE/VC Valuation Guide contains several examples of how to value contingent consideration from the perspective of a venture capital fund.[5] These documents are an important step toward establishing common industry practices for the valuation of contingent consideration, which continues to represent one of the most challenging areas in ESE valuation.

TYPES OF EARNOUTS

Earnouts are generally classified based on the type of milestone that triggers the payment, the structure, or payoff of the earnout, and the means by which an earnout is ultimately settled.

---

[2] On the financial reporting requirements concerning contingent consideration for venture capital funds, see also AICPA PE/VC Valuation Guide Q&A 14.24: Valuation of Contingent Consideration. Q: If my portfolio company is acquired and my fund becomes contractually entitled to a future payout contingent on the portfolio company's performance over the next few years, am I supposed to record a value for this contingent asset? A: Yes. In this fact pattern, the contingent consideration is a contractual right to a future payment or series of payments, and therefore is an asset that the fund should record at fair value" See also AICPA PE/VC Valuation Guide 13.83-87: Contractual Rights (Contingent Consideration).
[3] The valuation analyst may also want to consider that the earnout asset/liability is also a liability/asset, respectively for another market participant.
[4] Appraisal Foundation, VFR Valuation Advisory #4: Valuation of Contingent Consideration, 2019.
[5] AICPA PE/VC Valuation Guide 5.92–94: Milestone-Driven Valuations; 13.83–13.87: Contractual Rights (Contingent Consideration), Q&A 14.24: Valuation of Contingent Consideration, Case Study 10, Biotech Investment with a Complex Capital Structure, Multiple Investors' Perspective, C.09.80–92; Case Study 12, Clean-tech Start-up with Significant Exposure to Regulatory Factors, C12.34–40.

Milestone Metrics and Events

There are two broad classes of milestones that may trigger earnout payments:

1. Financial metrics. An earnout payment may be triggered upon the company's reaching a preestablished level in a metric that represents a company's financial or business performance. For an ESE, financial metrics for earnout payments are typically expressed in terms of revenue, revenue margin, units sold, number of customers, market share, etc. In companies that are further along in their development, metrics tied to EBITDA and measures of profitability such as EBITDA margins and net income are often used. A basic earnout structure for an ESE may consist of a payment that is expressed as a percentage of revenue above a certain threshold (say 20% of revenue above $1 million over a period of five years from the sale date). Financial metrics tend to be correlated to overall market returns. From the perspective of modern portfolio theory in the Capital Asset Pricing Model (CAPM), earnouts based on financial metrics such as revenue or EBITDA expose the holder of the earnout to a "systematic" risk related to the performance of the "market," which cannot be diversified away and that needs to be reflected in the discount rate. It is important to note that the contractual definition of the relevant financial metric may be different from the standard definition under generally accepted accounting principles (GAAP). For example, a revenue-based earnout may define "revenue" as the revenue associated only with a certain geographical area or a certain product, or might have its own idiosyncratic definition of "revenue."

2. Nonfinancial milestones: These consist of company-specific events that are deemed to have low or no correlation with the market overall performance. For an ESE, they may include regulatory approvals, the execution of certain commercial contracts, and key technical milestones such as a product launch, the hiring of a key officers, a key patent approval, etc. The risk of a nonfinancial milestone is typically company-specific, has little or no correlation with broad market conditions, and qualifies as a diversifiable risk in a CAPM analytical framework.

Some of the payments identified as "contingent payments" in a sale agreement may be related to employee or owner retention targets. For instance, a payment in the sale of a software company may be linked to the company's ability to retain at least 60% of the software developer's workforce at the end of Year 3 from the date of sale. Under FASB ASC 805, payments that are related to employee retention are postcombination expenses and are excluded from the contingent consideration component of the purchase price.[6]

Earnout Payoffs

Earnouts may have a variety of payoff structures.[7] Some of the most of common payoff structures in ESE sales are:

---

[6]FASB ASC 805-10-55-24,25 and related examples. See also Appraisal Foundation VFR Valuation Advisory #4, 202–206 and 324–328.

[7]On the payoff structure of contingent consideration arrangements, see especially Appraisal Foundation VFR Valuation Advisory #4, 3.2.1: Common Contingent Consideration Payoff Structures.

Fixed Payoff In its most basic form, an earnout may consist of a single payment of a fixed amount upon the company's reaching a target milestone. This is often the case for payments related to developmental and regulatory milestones. For instance, for a pharmaceutical company, an earnout may consist of a $1 million payment upon the company reaching a Phase 2 regulatory approval for a key product in the R&D process. Alternatively, a fixed payment may be due upon the company's achieving a contractual revenue target.

Linear Payoff In a linear payoff structure, payments are defined as a percentage of a specified financial metric, possibly subject to a cap (no additional payment after a certain threshold has been reached) and/or a floor (no payment below a certain threshold). Exhibit 12.1 shows an example of a simple linear payment of 20% of revenue with no cap and/or floor.

Exhibits 12.2–12.4 show examples of the same earnout at 20% of revenue, but with a cap at $4 million of revenue (Exhibit 12.2), a floor at $2 million of revenue (Exhibit 12.3), and a combined cap of $4 million and floor of $2 million of revenue. (Exhibit 12.4).

In Exhibit 12.2, the cap limits the upside potential of the earnout. Once the cap of $4 million in revenue is reached (for an earnout payoff of $800,000 = $4 million × 0.20), no more payments under the earnout are due.

In a payout with a floor as presented in Exhibit 12.3, no payment is due until revenues reach the contractual threshold of $2 million in this example. The holder of the earnout will then earn 20% of revenue above the threshold, with unlimited upside potential.

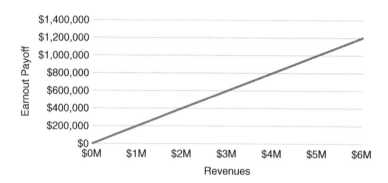

EXHIBIT 12.1 Earnout – Linear Payoff

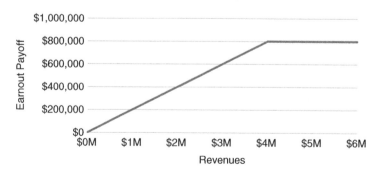

EXHIBIT 12.2 Linear Payoff with Cap

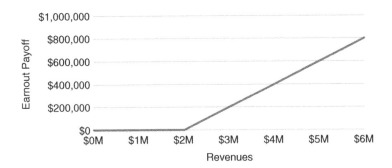

EXHIBIT 12.3   Linear Payoff with Floor

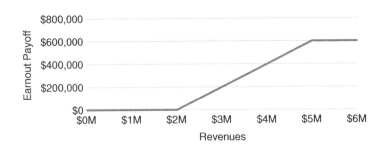

EXHIBIT 12.4   Linear Payoff with Cap and Floor

In Exhibit 12.4 the $2 million revenue floor and the $4 million revenue cap are combined so that the earnout is only payable on revenue that falls within the $2–$4 million range. For instance, for revenue of $3.0 million, the earnout payoff will be calculated as:

$$\text{Earnout payoff} = (\$3,000,000 - \text{Floor}) \times 20\%$$

$$= (\$3,000,000 - \$2,000,000) \times 20\% = \$200,000$$

Path-Dependent Payoff   In a path-dependent payoff, the proceeds received are dependent not only on the company's reaching certain contractual milestones, but also on the order and timing in which the milestones are reached. For instance, an earnout may provide for a payoff of 20% of revenue in excess of a $1 million threshold in Year 1 with a cap of $400,000 and a 20% of revenue in excess of a $1.3 million revenue threshold in Year 2, with a cap of $400,000 in Year 2. If the payment cap in Year 1 is not reached, any shortfall relative to the first-year payment cap will be added to the payment cap in the second year as a catch-up feature. In this example, the payoff in Year 2 will depend on the results of Year 1. Path-dependent payoff structures can be quite complex to model, and generally require the use of more advanced statistical techniques for valuation such as Monte Carlo Simulation.

Payoff Based on Multiple and/or Correlated Metrics   In some cases, a company earnout may depend on the company reaching multiple performance targets. For instance, an earnout may consist of a payment due upon the achievement of both an annual $10 million revenue target in Country A (the company's current market) *and* an annual $5 million revenue target in Country B (a new market). Alternatively, an earnout may consist of a payment upon the company reaching a revenue target of $10 million *and* a positive EBITDA. Earnouts that have a payoff based on multiple and/or correlated metrics are also generally valued using more advanced statistical techniques.

Earnout Settlement

Earnout payments may consist of cash or noncash consideration.[8] Generally, noncash consideration is in the form of shares of the acquiring company, which may add another layer of complexity to the valuation, particularly if the acquirer is also a private company and the acquirer's equity needs to be valued as well to estimate the value of the earnout. Cash payments tend to prevail in the sale of ESE interests. In some cases, earnout cash payments are disbursed out of an escrow account that has been set up as part of the sale closing process. To the extent the release of the escrow payment is contingent upon whether certain specified future events occur or conditions are met, the escrow payment may be considered contingent consideration. On the other hand, if the release of the escrow payment is contingent on verifying conditions that were already extant at the date of sale, the escrow payment would not be considered contingent considerations and would quality rather as a deferred fixed payment.[9]

EARNOUT VALUATION

Valuation Methodologies

The valuation of contingent consideration is typically performed using the income approach in combination with a methodology that considers the probability distribution of possible outcomes from the contingency. As noted by the Appraisal Foundation:

> *A key concept for valuing earnouts is to recognize that, except for linear payoff structures, the expected cash flows for the contingent consideration are usually not equal to the payoff associated with the expected value of the metric.*[10]

Exhibit 12.5 shows an earnout with a payoff equal to the excess of future revenue over 100, under various scenarios with related probabilities of occurrence.[11]

In the example of Exhibit 12.5, revenue has a probability-weighted expected value of $100, which is calculated by multiplying the expected revenue value under each scenario by the probability of occurrence and adding the results. Under each scenario, the earnout payoff is calculated as Max (Revenue − 100, 0). The earnout value associated with the most likely revenue outcome of 100 (which is also the expected revenue amount) is zero, calculated as

---

[8]Appraisal Foundation VFR Valuation Advisory #4, 3.3: Settlement Types for Contingent Consideration.
[9]Appraisal Foundation VFR Valuation Advisory #4, 215–222.
[10]Appraisal Foundation VFR Valuation Advisory #4, 533–536.
[11]The example in Exhibit 12.5 is a variant of Table 1 in Appraisal Foundation VFR Valuation Advisory #4 p. 22.

Scenario	Probability	Revenue	Earnout Payoff
1	5.00%	$ 200	$ 100
2	10.00%	$ 150	$ 50
3	20.00%	$ 120	$ 20
4	25.00%	$ 100	$ –
5	20.00%	$ 70	$ –
6	15.00%	$ 65	$ –
7	5.00%	$ 45	$ –
Expected Value	100.00%	$ 100	$ 14

EXHIBIT 12.5   Expected Value of Revenue and Earnout Payoff

Max (100–100, 0). However, the expected earnout payoff based on the probability distribution in Exhibit 12.5, on the other hand, is $14. As Exhibit 12.5 demonstrates, the distribution of outcomes may significantly affect the expected earnout payoff. [12]

Depending on the type of contingency and the associated payoff structure, the following valuation methods may be used in valuation:

Scenario-Based Method (SBM)   The Scenario-Based method (SBM) uses scenario analysis to identify a number of discrete outcomes for the contingency metric or event. A probability value is then assigned to each outcome and the proceeds related to each outcome are estimated and discounted to present value using a rate that reflects the riskiness of the associated cash flows from a market participant perspective. The fair value of the earnout is then calculated as the probability-weighted average of the discounted proceeds under the various scenarios.

Option-Pricing Method (OPM)   An option-pricing method (OPM) can be used when the earnout payoff is structurally similar to the payoff from an option position, as in the case of the linear structure with cap and floors that we have described in Exhibits 12.2–12.4. In an OPM, the analyst estimates the fair value of an earnout using formulas that have been developed for option valuation. The OPM relies on some fundamental associations that may limit its suitability in an earnout valuation context. Among others, the OPM assumes that the nonsystematic risk related to the earnout proceeds can be diversified away. In the examples that follow we discuss when and how the OPM may be used given these limiting assumptions.

Enhancement Techniques: Monte Carlo Simulation   Both the SBM and the OPM can be enhanced by the use of Monte Carlo Simulation, particularly when the earnout reference metrics are correlated and/or the distribution of outcomes is path-dependent. We illustrate an application of Monte Carlo Simulation in some details later in this chapter.

Discount Rates

The discount rate applicable to the earnout cash flows is a key estimate in an earnout valuation model.[13] The discount rate should reflect the specific risk profile of the payoff, based on the

---

[12] Appraisal Foundation VRF Valuation Advisory #4, 548–549.
[13] See Appraisal Foundation, VFR Valuation Advisory #4, 5.2.2: Discount Rate and Market Risk Considerations.

earnout characteristics. The discount rate for an earnout payoff typically consists of three components:

1. Risk-free rate (RFR). The RFR compensates the holder of the earnout for the time value of money. The RFR needs to be consistent with the time horizon of the earnout and with the period from the measurement date to the expected time of payment. The time horizon through the actual settlement of the earnout payment is generally longer than the time horizon through the date in which the contingency is deemed resolved. For instance, the sale agreement may establish that the settlement of the earnout must take place 90 days after the date in which the amount of the proceeds is determined. The time horizon for the RFR assessment should cover the time horizon through the end of the 90-day period under such circumstances.

2. Counterparty credit risk (CCR). To the extent the performance of the earnout payment is tied to the counterparty's ability and willingness to pay, the discount rate of the earnout must include a component that compensates its holder for CCR. The counterparty for an earnout is the entity that buys control of the ESE, which is often a larger and more established player in the market than the target ESE. In some cases, the buyer may have debt obligations in the market that can provide a framework to estimate the CCR. Alternatively, the analyst may obtain information directly from the buyer and from a review of the buyer's capital structure and yield on outstanding debt. The analyst may want to also consider mechanisms whereby CCR is either partially or fully mitigated, for instance, by depositing cash in an escrow account, obtaining a guarantee from a bank or another external party, and structuring the earnout as a note issued by the buyer, with adequate collateralization.[14] To the extent there are provisions that mitigate counterparty risk, the CCR will decline accordingly.

3. Metric-Specific Risk Premium (MSRP). While the RFR and the CCR component of the discount rate apply to all types of earnouts, the inclusion of an MSRP only applies to earnouts that have a systematic risk component in their payoff structure, namely, in cases where the risk metric is sensitive to the variability of returns in the overall market ("systematic" risk under modern portfolio theory). This is the case, for instance, of earnouts that are calculated as a percentage of revenue, a variable that is expected to have at least some level of correlation with the overall market, as represented by the return of a broad market index. It is not typically a factor in regulatory driven milestones (for instance an FDA approval), which are deemed to have little or no correlation with market returns.

Earnout Volatility

For earnouts that are valued using an option pricing model, the volatility of the underlying metric (typically revenue or net sales for an ESE) is one of the key inputs in the model. For earnouts that are based on revenue, the volatility of revenue over the time horizon of the

---

[14]Appraisal Foundation, VFR #4, 1865–1871.

earnout has to be estimated in order for an OPM analysis to be performed. The methods to estimate volatility for an earnout metric include:[15]

1. Historical Variability method. This method uses historical information to estimate the volatility of the earnout metric. The historical method tends to produce best results in situations where the metric is relatively stable and history can indeed provide a suitable way to predict future performance. This is hardly the case for ESEs, which are still in the process of developing their business model and where growth rates are likely to vary significantly over the period of the earnout. Also, the volatility of the target metric may be significantly affected by the fact of the acquisition itself, which involves a change of control for the company.[16]
2. Management Assessment method. This method relies on management's estimates and is frequently used in the valuation of earnouts of ESEs. For instance, an analyst may use management's estimate of volatility in a high case and a low case scenario, and calculate an implied volatility based on this assessment.
3. Deleveraging Equity Volatility method. In this method, the metric volatility is assessed based on the equity volatility of the company, after adjusting for both financial and operational leverage.

Checking for Biases

Given the complexity of earnout valuation, it is critical to make sure that consistency is maintained throughout the analysis and that the estimates and inputs used make sense in terms of the overall assessment of enterprise value. For instance, one may look also at equity volatility as a "cap" for the volatility of the earnout metrics (we can expect the volatility of the earnout to be lower than that of the equity value of the enterprise as a whole).

The analyst should also be aware of biases that may affect management's estimated cash flows and probabilities associated with an earnout scenario. One widely documented form of systematic bias that influences predictions by management is "anchoring," or choosing forecasts that are too close (anchored) to some easily observable prior or arbitrary point of departure. The "anchoring bias" may result in forecasts that underweight new information and can thus give rise to predictable forecast errors.[17]

Also, management's estimates may be subject to the "overconfidence bias," which highlights management's inclination to fail to consider a wide enough range of potential future outcomes. An especially critical bias for an ESE is management's tendency to develop hidden assumptions, most notably to disregard the possibility of competitive reactions to a new

---

[15]On the estimate of earnout metric volatility, see especially Appraisal Foundation, VRF Valuation Advisory #4, Section 5.2.4.

[16]The Appraisal Foundation, VFR Valuation Advisory #4 Note 84, p.57.

[17]The "anchoring bias" was described in Amos Tversky and Daniel Kahneman, "Judgment under Uncertainty: Heuristics and Biases," *Science* 185 (1974): 1124–1131.

technology or a new product introduction. Also aside from overconfidence, management cash flows forecasts are often thought to be biased toward optimism. Changes in the competitive landscape may be especially hard to conceive and to include in a quantitative forecast. However, such changes also can be a critical factor in the ability of the enterprise to meet its performance targets.

Overall, the projections used for the earnout valuation should be consistent with the projections used for the company as a whole, after allowing for any differences due to buyer-specific synergies or to different definitions of the earnout metric. In an earnout valuation, buyer-specific synergies that would affect the payoff outcome of the earnout metric are typically included in the earnout value.[18]

CASE STUDIES

Let's now review some case studies in earnout valuation that illustrate some of the considerations and methodologies that we have discussed so far. In our simplified examples where the option pricing model is applied with revenue as the earnout base (Examples 3–6 and 8), we have used the full period convention. Under the full period convention, revenue is considered crystallized at the end of the contractual term of the earnout. Alternatively, the mid-period convention may be used, which models revenue as earned over the period rather than at a single point at the end of the period and adjusts the discount term accordingly.[19] Given the very high discount rates typically applied in earnout valuation, the period convention applied when discounting (full period versus mid-period) may have a significant impact on valuation. In these examples, we use continuous compounding in the calculation of the discount factors.

Example 1: Technical Milestone with Binary Outcome – FDA Approval

Strawberry Pharma Inc., a hypothetical biotechnology company, has been acquired by a large pharmaceutical conglomerate. As part of the proceeds from the sale, the shareholders of Strawberry will receive a contingent payment of $1 million in cash upon Strawberry's obtaining FDA approval to initiate a Phase 2 clinical trial of a new drug for treating a coronavirus infection. Management estimates that Strawberry's product will receive FDA approval in two years with 70% probability. The milestone payment of $1 million is to

---

[18]Appraisal Foundation VFR Valuation Advisory #4, 972–977: "Because the earnout is valued from the perspective of a market participant buying or selling the standalone earnout posttransaction (with the relevant business under the new ownership of the actual buyer), the financial projections developed for valuing an earnout often include buyer-specific synergies. In contrast, the financial projections developed for valuing an acquired business typically include only market participant synergies, excluding synergies that are unique to the buyer and not available to other market participants."
[19]For examples of mid-period convention in the valuation of contingent consideration using option pricing models, see Appraisal Foundation VFR Valuation Advisory #4, Section 9, Case Studies. Most of the Case Studies in this section have been developed based on the examples in Appraisal Foundation VFR #4.

Scenario	Probability	Earnout Payoff	PW Proceeds
Yes	70.00%	$ 1,000,000	$ 700,000
No	30.00%	-	$ –
[1] Expected future value of earnout			$ 700,000

Discount Factor	Rate	Time	Factor
[2] Risk-free rate	2.50%	2	$0.9512 = \text{EXP}(-2.5\% \times 2)$
[3] Counterparty credit risk	3.00%	2	$0.9418 = \text{EXP}(-3.0\% \times 2)$
[4] Cumulative discount factor			$0.8958 = [2] \times [3]$
[5] PV of earnout			$ 627,084 = [1] \times [4]$

EXHIBIT 12.6 Technical Milestone with Binary Outcome: Present Value of Earnout – At Fair Value

be paid immediately upon receiving FDA approval. Assuming a RFR of 2.5% over the contingency period and a CCR of the acquirer company of 3.0%, the earnout value is calculated as shown in Exhibit 12.6.

In this example, a binary scenario analysis with a yes/no outcome has been used. Since the FDA approval milestone is not subject to market (systematic) risk, the appropriate discount rate is the RFR, plus an estimate of counterparty risk that is specific to the term and seniority of the earnout obligation. In our example, the estimated credit spread of the acquirer is 300 basis points.

Example 2: Simple Linear Payoff Structure

Assume the same set of facts as in Example 1, except that the earnout consists instead of 20% of the cumulative revenue earned by Strawberry over the two-year period subsequent to the acquisition date. The proceeds are due three months after the end of the two-year period. The RFR is 2.5%. The CCR is 3.0%. In this case, the discount rate must also include an MSRP for the market (systematic) risk of the target company's revenue, since revenue is exposed to market volatility. In our example, the MSRP is estimated at 17.5%

As in the prior example, we are using the scenario-based method with a high case and a low case scenario. In the high case scenario, the company is expected to generate $5 million in cumulative revenue, with an expected payoff of $1 million. In the low case scenario, the company will go out of business, with no value associated with the earnout. The probability adjusted cash flows of each scenario discounted to the valuation date are summarized in Exhibit 12.7.

The time horizon of the MSRP is two years, which reflects a risk exposure from the acquisition (valuation) date to the date in which the contingency is expected to be resolved while the RFR and the CCR are applied to a time horizon of 2.25 years, which covers the period through the expected date of the cash settlement (90 days after the contingency resolution date). In this case, the present value of the earnout is $435,864.

Scenario	Probability	Earnout Payoff	PW Proceeds
Yes	70.00%	$ 1,000,000	$ 700,000
No	30.00%	-	$ –
[1] Expected earnout at settlement			$ 700,000

Discount Factor	Rate	Time	Factor	
[2] Risk-free rate	2.50%	2.25	0.9453	=EXP(–2.5% × 2.25)
[3] Counterparty credit risk	3.00%	2.25	0.9347	=EXP(–3.0% × 2.25)
[4] Metric-specific risk premium	17.50%	2	0.7047	=EXP(–17.50% × 2)
[5] Cumulative discount factor			0.6227	= [2] × [3] × [4]
[6] PV of earnout			$ 435,864	= [1] × [5]

EXHIBIT 12.7   Simple Linear Payoff Structure with SBM: Present Value of Earnout – At Fair Value

Example 3: Simple Linear Payoff with Floor

Assume the same set of facts in Example 2, except that the earnout proceeds have now a floor at $4 million in revenue while maintaining unlimited upside potential. The payoff structure of an earnout with a floor has a similar profile to that of a long position in a call option. The holder of the earnout has a claim on the company's revenue that is analogous to that of an option holder with a strike price of $4 million (the revenue floor). To the extent the company's cumulative revenue over the period Year 1 + Year 2 is below $4 million, the earnout generates no proceeds. If cumulative revenue at the end of Year 2 exceeds $4 million, the holder of the earnout will receive proceeds equal to 20% of the cumulative revenue above the threshold.

In a linear payoff structure with a floor, the value of the earnout is typically modeled using the BSM call option formula. The BSM expression in this case is:

$$Call\ Option = S_0 N(d_1) - Ke^{-rT} N(d_2)$$

$$d_1 = \frac{\ln(S_0/K) + (r + 0.5\sigma^2) \times T}{\sigma\sqrt{T}}$$

and:

$$d_2 = d_1 - \sigma\sqrt{T}$$

and where

$N(.)$: standard normal cumulative distribution function

S_0 = present value of revenue (the underlying)

K = strike price

σ = volatility of the underlying

T = term to expiration

r = risk-free rate

The valuation process consists of three steps:

1. Estimate the present value of the underlying: in our case, the underlying is the expected cumulative revenue at the end of the earnout term.
2. Calculate the expected earnout payoff at the end of the earnout term.
3. Calculate the present value of the earnout.

Step 1: Present Value of Underlying   As a first step, the analyst needs to estimate the present value of the underlying, which in our case is equal to the present value of the expected cumulative revenue at the end of Year 2. Strawberry's management projects a total of $5 million over the two-year period.

Exhibit 12.8 illustrates the calculation of the present value of the Year 1 + Year 2 cumulative revenue, which is the underlying base for the calculation of the earnout payoff amount.

Notice that the time to expiration of the option corresponds to the time to the resolution of the contingency under the terms of the contractual earnout provision (two years in our example). Also, the discount rate in this step consists of the RFR and the MSRP.

Step 2: Expected Earnout Payoff at End of Term   We can now calculate the expected earnout payoff at the end of Year 2, using the BSM call option formula with the inputs in Exhibit 12.9.

With the exception of SDV and S_0, which are based on estimates, all other inputs are observable: K and T reflect the earnout contract terms, and the RFR is a market-based input. In our example, the BSM formula resolves for a call option value of $1,314,868.

Step 3. Present Value of the Earnout   The present value of the earnout is then calculated as illustrated in Exhibit 12.10.

Let's walk through the steps of the earnout value calculation in Exhibit 12.10. First, the estimated value of the call option (the expected future revenue) is multiplied by the earnout

	Rate	Time	Factor	
[1] Estimated cumulative revenue over 2-year period			$ 5,000,000	
[2] Risk-free rate	2.50%	2	0.9512	=EXP (−2.5% × 2)
[3] Metric-specific risk premium	17.50%	2	0.7047	=EXP(−17.5% × 2)
[4] Discount factor			0.6703	=[2] × [3]
[5] PV of cumulative revenue			$ 3,351,600	=[1] × [4]

EXHIBIT 12.8   Simple Linear Payoff with Floor – Present Value of Cumulative Revenue Year 1 + Year 2

$S0$ = Underlying value (PV of cumulative revenue)	$ 3,351,600
K = Exercise value (floor)	$ 4,000,000
r = RFR over contractual term	2.50%
T = Term to expiration (contingency resolution)	2
SDV = Volatility of underlying (cumulative revenue)	80%

EXHIBIT 12.9   Simple Linear Payoff with Floor: BSM Inputs

[1] PV of call option	$ 1,314,868	from BSM Formula
[2] Earnout percentage	20.00%	contractual
[3] PV of earnout – risk-neutral framework	$ 262,974	= [1] × [2]
[4] Premium factor	1.0513	= exp (2.50% × 2)
[5] Expected earnout cash flow	$ 276,464	= [3] × [4]
[6] Discount factor	0.8836	= exp [–(3.00% + 2.50%) × 2.25]
[7] Value of earnout	$ 244,284	= [5] × [6]

EXHIBIT 12.10 Simple Linear Payoff with Floor: Present Value of Earnout – at Fair Value

percentage as defined in the purchase agreement (20% in our case). The resulting value of $262,974 represents the present value of the earnout in a risk neutral framework, with the RFR included in the BSM formula and assuming the proceeds are paid at the expiration of the option (two years from the acquisition date, which is the time input in the BSM formula).

We now need to adjust our initial estimated value to account for counterparty credit risk and for the time lag between the date in which the earnout reference revenue is crystallized and the date of the earnout settlement. In Steps [4]–[5], we project the earnout value to the date in which the contingency is resolved (two years from the acquisition date) using the RFR of 2.5% in the multiplier. The resulting value of $276,464 in Step [5] represents the expected earnout cash flows based on cumulative revenue at the contingency resolution date (time horizon = 2 years from the acquisition date) but paid at settlement (time horizon = 2.25 years from the acquisition date). As a final step, we discount the expected earnout cash flows back to present value Steps [6]–[7], using a discount factor that now reflects both counterparty risk and the RFR, as well as the time horizon through the date of settlement (2.25 years), obtaining the estimated fair value of the earnout of $244,284.

Example 4: Linear Payoff with Floor and Cap

In Example 4, let's assume the same set of facts as Example 3, but with the difference that now the earnout has also a cap when cumulative revenue (Year 1 + Year 2) reaches a $7 million threshold. Also in this case, the earnout payoff profile can be analyzed in terms of option pricing theory, as a combination of a long position in a call option with a strike price of $4 million (the revenue "floor") and a short position in a call option with a strike price of $7 million (the revenue "cap"). To the extent the company's cumulative revenue is below $4 million, the earnout receives no proceeds. If cumulative revenue as of the end of Year 2 is between $4 million and $7 million, the holder of the earnout will receive proceeds equal to 20% of revenue above the threshold. Above $7 million in revenue, the earnout will receive no additional proceeds.

The inputs in the BSM formula for our example are shown in Exhibit 12.11.

These inputs are consistent with the BSM inputs discussed in Example 3. The BSM formula resolves for a long call option value of $1,314,868 and a short call option value of $818,472. The earnout value is then calculated as illustrated in Exhibit 12.12.

In Step [3] of Exhibit 12.12, we calculate the net present value of the net option position as the present value of the long call option less the present value of the short call option. We then multiply the net present value of the option position by the earnout percentage to obtain the present value of the earnout under a risk neutral framework. Steps [6] through [9] are analogous to Steps [4] through [7] in Exhibit 12.10 of the prior example, and have

	Long Call	Short Call
S0 = Underlying value	$ 3,351,600	$ 3,351,600
K = Exercise value	$ 4,000,000	$ 7,000,000
RFR = Risk-free rate	2.50%	2.50%
T = Time to contingency resolution	2	2
SDV = Volatility of underlying	80%	80%

EXHIBIT 12.11   Linear Payoff with Cap and Floor: BSM Inputs

[1] PV of long call option	$ 1,314,868	from BSM Formula
[2] PV of short call option	$ 818,472	from BSM Formula
[3] Net PV of option position	$ 496,396	= [1] − [2]
[4] Earnout percentage	20.00%	per contract
[5] PV of earnout – risk-neutral framework	$ 99,279	= [3] × [4]
[6] Premium factor	1.0513	=exp (2.50% × 2)
[7] Expected earnout cash flow	$ 104,372	= [6] × [7]
[8] Discount factor	0.8836	= exp [−(3.00% + 2.50%) × 2.25]
[9] Value of earnout	$ 92,223	= [7] × [8]

EXHIBIT 12.12   Linear Payout with Cap and Floor: Present Value of Earnout – At Fair Value

the purpose of adjusting the PV in the risk neutral framework to a value that considers also the effect of counterparty risk on the discount rate and of the extended time horizon to the settlement date versus the date in which the notional amount for the earnout calculation is crystallized. Our calculation results in a fair value for the earnout of $92,223. The difference with the value in Example 3 is due to the presence of the cap, which limits the earnout upside potential.

The OPM techniques that we have discussed so far can be extended to more complex situations when, for instance, a tiered payoff structure is present (ex: 10% of revenue in Year 1 for revenue in excess of $2 million and 20% of revenues in Year 1 for revenue above $5 million), or a structure with a series of non-path-dependent capped options (for instance, 30% of revenue in Year 1 for revenue in excess of $2 million with a cap at $3 million in revenue and 30% of revenue in Year 2 for revenue in excess of $3 million with a cap of $4 million). Earnouts may involve a variety of option-like payoff combinations, and OPM techniques can provide a very effective tool to break out a complex earnout structure into its component pieces, which can be valued separately and then aggregated to come to the earnout overall value.

Example 5: Systematic Binary Structure – Option Pricing Model

So far, we have considered an option-like linear payoff structure in which the earnout is defined as a percentage of revenue. Example 5 considers a situation where the earnout still depends on revenues hitting a certain target (a cumulative revenue target of $4 million in our case), but the payoff is expressed as a fixed amount ($1 million in our example) rather than as an amount that is linearly dependent on the underlying revenue stream. This type of payout can be analyzed using a digital/binary call option formula as follows:

$$\text{Digital/Binary Call Option} = P\,N(d_2)\,e^{-rT}$$

where:

$$d_2 = \frac{ln(S_0/K) + (r - 0.5\sigma^2) \times T}{\sigma\sqrt{T}}$$

and where

P = earnout payment due upon the underlying reaching the strike price

The inputs in the BSM formula are illustrated in Exhibit 12.13.

The BSM formula in Exhibit 12.13 results in an estimated value for the digital call option (the present value of the earnout in a "risk-neutral" world) of $236,804. As in the previous example, the present value of the earnout in a risk-free framework needs to be adjusted to consider the effect of counterparty risk on the discount rate and of the extended time horizon to the settlement date. Exhibit 12.14 presents the adjusted earnout value calculation.

In Exhibit 12.14, the present value of the earnout in a risk-neutral framework (value of the digital call option) [1] is multiplied by a premium factor that includes the effect of the RFR to obtain the expected value of the earnout as of the contractual date in which the contingency is resolved (two years from the valuation date). The expected earnout proceeds are then discounted back to present value, this time using a discount factor that includes a risk component for the RFR and CCR, and that considers the time period back from the settlement date (2.25 years from the acquisition date). The procedure in Exhibit 12.14 results in a present value for the earnout of $219,968.

Inputs of Binary Option Model	
[1] So = Expected PV of forecasted cumulative revenue	$ 3,351,600
[2] T = Term to expiration (contingency resolution)	2
[3] K = Exercise value (floor)	$ 4,000,000
[4] r = Risk-free rate	2.50%
[5] SDV = Volatility of underlying	80%
[6] P = Contractual earnout amount	$ 1,000,000

EXHIBIT 12.13   Systematic Binary Structure – Option Pricing Model: BSM Inputs

[1] Digital call option	$ 236,804	BSM formula
[2] Premium factor	1.0513	=exp (2.50% × 2)
[3] Expected future earnout cash flows	$ 248,946	=[1] × [2]
[4] Discount factor	0.8836	=exp [–(3.0% + 2.5%) × 2.25]
[5] Value of earnout	$ 219,968	[3] × [4]

EXHIBIT 12.14   Systematic Binary Structure – Option Pricing Model: Present Value of Earnout – At Fair Value

Example 6: Path-Dependent Payoff with Monte Carlo Simulation

Example 6 brings us into a more complex environment, which requires the application of more sophisticated analytical tools. In Example 6, we relax some of the assumptions that we have maintained so far: we allow for an earnout payout structure where the payoffs at various stages in the earnout time horizon are path-dependent.

In our example, let's assume that Blueberry Technology Inc., a software company, has been acquired by a strategic investor. As part of the acquisition the shareholders of the company have negotiated an earnout of $50 million at the end of the first year of the five-year period starting from the acquisition date in which the company will reach revenues of $150 million. The earnout is path-dependent in that the payout in one year depends on whether the $150 million threshold has been reached in any of the preceding years. In this example, Monte Carlo Simulation is used to simulate future revenue levels for the company for each of the annual periods in the model, and to forecast the resulting earnout value for each trial.[20] Our model utilizes the following assumptions:

- Base Year revenues are $7 million.
- The RFR for Year 1 is 2.2%, the counterparty risk rate is 2.9%, and the MSRP is 18.0%. The RFR and the CCR rate are set to increase by 0.2% and 0.1% annually, respectively, over the five-year period, reaching 3.0% and 3.3%, respectively, for Year 5. This reflects an increase in the perceived riskiness of the counterparty and in the cost of default-free capital as the time horizon increases.
- The company's management projects revenues (in million) over the five-year time horizon of the earnout of $20 (Year 1), $50 (Year 2), $90 (Year 3), $135 (Year 4), and $190 (Year 5).
- The volatility of revenues is estimated at 80% .
- The present value of annual revenue is calculated using the mid-year convention (annual revenue is assumed to be earned at mid-point during the year). For instance, in Year 2, revenue is discounted using a time factor of 1.5 instead of 2 as applicable under a full-year convention. Exhibit 12.15 shows one iteration of Monte Carlo Simulation given the earlier assumptions.

---

[20]Monte Carlo Simulation is also appropriate when the variables in the model show a statistically significant correlation. For an introduction to Monte Carlo Simulation, see Nicholas Metropolis and Stanley Ulman, "The Monte Carlo Method," *Journal of the American Statistical Association* 44, no. 247 (1949): 335–341; David Dufendach and Jason A. Andrews, "Advanced Workshop on Monte Carlo Simulations", Webinar Handbook, Business Valuation Resources, LLC, March 8, 2012. Neil Beaton and John Sawyer, "Use of Monte Carlo Simulations in Valuation," *AIRA Journal* 32, no. 2 (2019): 16–19; Erica L. Wilson and A. Vincent Biermans, "Earnouts and the Monte Carlo Method: Practice Tips for Implementation," *Business Valuation Update* 24, no. 5 (May 2018): 1–7. A variety of Statistical software packages are available to implement Monte Carlo Simulation. The Oracle software package "Crystal Ball" is a common tool that can integrate Excel formulas with Monte Carlo Simulation and that can be used to resolve a great variety of situations in an earnout calculation. Other tools include a variety of Excel plug-ins and more comprehensive software such as SAS and Stata. For guidance on financial modeling with Crystal Ball, see John Charnes, *Financial Modeling with Oracle Crystal Ball and Excel* (Wiley, 2012).

	Year 1	Year 2	Year 3	Year 4	Year 5	Notes
Simulating Future Revenue:						
[1] Calculation period (years)	1	2	3	4	5	Contractual – Periods at which payments are calculated
[2] Payment period	1.25	2.25	3.25	4.25	5.25	Contractual – periods at which earnout payments are made
[3] Midperiod	0.5	1.5	2.5	3.5	4.5	Mid-period of calculation period
[4] Time step for simulation	0.5	1.0	1.5	2.0	2.5	Simulation period consistent with mid-period assumption
[5] RFR	2.20%	2.40%	2.60%	2.80%	3.00%	Input – Assumption
[6] CCR	2.90%	3.00%	3.10%	3.20%	3.30%	Input – Assumption
[7] MSRP	18.00%	18.00%	18.00%	18.00%	18.00%	Input – Assumption
[8] Volatility estimate	80.00%	80.00%	80.00%	80.00%	80.00%	Input – Assumption
[9] Forecast/expected revenue ($)	20	50	90	135	190	Input – Assumption
[10] Revenue discount factor	0.9039	0.7364	0.5975	0.4829	0.3887	= exp $(([5] + [7]) \times [3])$
[11] Annual revenue growth rate	104.98%	91.63%	58.78%	40.55%	34.17%	= LN (Revenue T / Revenue T−1)
[12] Expected PV of revenue ($)	18.08	36.82	53.78	65.19	73.85	= $[9] \times [10]$
[13] Random Normal (0,1)	0.9510	0.6340	0.4350	0.8200	0.6200	NORM.INV(RAND(),0,1)
[14] Geometric Brownian Motion	1.4755	1.8224	1.7957	2.5322	2.6868	= $[14]t-1 \times$ EXP $((([5] - 1/2 \times [8] \wedge 2) \times [4]$ + sqrt $([4]) \times [8] \times[13])$. For Year 1, $[14]t-1 = 1$
[15] Risk-neutral Random Revenue ($)	26.67	67.10	96.56	165.07	198.42	= $[12] \times [14]$
Calculating the Present Value of the Earnout Payment:						
[16] Minimum Sales Threshold ($)	150.00	150.00	150.00	150.00	150.00	Contractual
[17] Earnout Payment before adjustment ($)	–	–	–	50.00	50.00	= IF([15]>[16],50,0)
[18] Earnout Payment after adjustment ($)	–	–	–	50.00	–	Earnout payment after excluding duplication
[19] Discount Factor for credit risk and time value	0.9382	0.8856	0.8309	0.7749	0.7184	= exp $(-([5]+[6])*[2])$
[20] PV of earnout payment ($)	–	–	–	38.75	–	= $[18] \times [19]$
[21] PV of one iteration ($)	38.75	–	–	–	–	= sum [20] for each year

EXHIBIT 12.15 Path-Dependent Payoff – Monte Carlo Simulation: Sample Iteration ($ in million)

Let's walk through the model in Exhibit 12.15 in some detail. Items [1]–[9] represent our inputs based on our risk assumptions, the contractual features of the earnout, and management's revenue estimates over the earnout time horizon. The Monte Carlo Simulation process for this sample iteration consists of four steps:

Step 1: Items [10]–[12]: Calculation of the Expected Present Value of Revenue   In this step, the expected present value of revenue is calculated by discounting to present value the revenue as forecasted by management over each of the five annual periods. The discount rate is a risk-adjusted discount rate that reflects the Risk-free Rate and the Metric-Specific Risk Premium associated with the company's revenue.

For instance, for Year 5, the management's forecasted revenue of $190 is discounted to present value at a rate of 21.0%, which is the sum of the RFR (3.0%) and the MSRP (18%) using the midperiod term of 4.5 years. The present value of revenue is calculated as:

$$\text{Expected PV of revenue} = \$190 \times \exp\left[-(3.0\% + 18.0\%) \times 4.5\right] = \$73.85 \text{ million}$$

Step 2: Items [13]–[15]: Generation of Risk-Neutral Random Revenue   The Monte Carlo Simulation software generates a revenue value as of the mid-period of each of the earnout annual periods. The model uses Geometric Brownian Motion to project the present value of revenue through the mid-period of the relevant year. For instance, in Year 2, the expected present value of revenue ($36.82 million) is multiplied by the geometric Brownian motion factor of 1.8224 to obtain the estimated value of revenue in Year 2 of $67.10 million, and so on for each of the other years in the model.

Step 3: Items [16]–[18]. Assessment of Earnout Payment   In Step 3, the earnout payment is determined by comparing the minimum threshold amount of $150 million in [16] to the randomly generated value of revenue in [15]. Based on the earnout's contractual features, a payment is due in the first year in which revenue exceeds the $150 million threshold. In this particular model iteration, the condition is fulfilled in Year 4.

Step 4: Items [19]–[20]: Calculation of Present Value of Annual Earnout Payments   In this step, the earnout payments for each annual period are discounted to present value using a discount rate that consists of the RFR and the CCR component. Note that the MSRP is not included in the discount rate in this calculation, as the cash flows from the earnout are already defined at this point and their risk profile is now similar to that of a fixed debt obligation of the acquirer. In our iteration, the earnout consists of a single payment of 50 million in Year 4, which is the year in which the earnout condition is fulfilled. The payment is discounted to present value using a discount factor calculated as:

$$\text{Discount factor for Year 4} = \exp\left[-(\text{RFR} + \text{CCR}) \times T\right]$$
$$= \exp\left[-(2.8\% + 3.2\%) \times 4.5\right] = 0.7749$$

The present value of the earnout payment in Year 4 is:

$$\text{PV of Earnout (Year 4)} = \$50 \text{ million} \times 0.7749 = \$38.75 \text{ million}$$

Percentiles:	Forecast Values
0%	0.00
10%	0.00
20%	0.00
30%	0.00
40%	0.00
50%	0.00
60%	0.00
70%	0.00
80%	0.00
90%	38.75
100%	44.28

EXHIBIT 12.16   Path-Dependent Payoff – Monte Carlo Simulation: Forecast Table ($ in million)

Step 5: Item [21]: Calculation of Earnout Value for the Iteration   The value of the earnout in this particular iteration is $38.75 million, which is calculated as the sum of the present value of the earnout payments under each annual period (all zero, except for Year 4).

In a Monte Carlo Simulation, the five steps are run for several thousand iterations. The Monte Carlo software will generate a set of random numbers for each iteration as an input in [13] assuming a standard normal distribution with mean of zero and standard deviation of 1. Given all other inputs and formulas, each random set will generate a single point estimate of value for the earnout. The individual estimates are then grouped based on probability of occurrence, and a set of summary statistical metrics for the resulting population is generated. In our sample run of 30,000 trials, the Monte Carlo Simulation results in the forecast value table in Exhibit 12.16.

Exhibit 12.16 points out that there is only less than a 20% probability that the earnout will have any value given our assumptions. The most likely value of this earnout based on the results of our sample run is in zero (the mode of the earnout distribution in our Monte Carlo Simulation run).

Example 7: Clawback

Clawback clauses provide for a refund of a portion of the purchase price received by the seller in a corporate acquisition transaction in case the acquired company fails to meet certain event milestones or financial performance targets. Like earnouts, clawback clauses find their source in the purchase agreement between buyer and seller in a corporate acquisition. Clawbacks are similar to put options in that their value increases as the company's performance deteriorates. The credit risk in clawbacks is the risk that the seller may not fulfill its obligation of refunding money to the buyer; thus, the credit risk of the seller is reflected in the discount rates, rather than that of the buyer for an earnout. Clawbacks are less common than earnout provisions, but when they are present, they may significantly affect the overall purchase price. Example 7 illustrates the valuation of a clawback for a sample company, Raspberry Communications Inc., which has recently been acquired by one of its competitors. As part of the sale transaction, Raspberry has an obligation to refund to the acquirer 20% of the purchase price in case the cumulative revenue generated over the two years following the acquisition is at or below $4 million. The clawback payment, if any, is due three months after the end of the two-year term. Raspberry's venture capital investors need to value the clawback as a liability in their portfolio. This clawback can be valued using the BSM put option formula:

$$Put\ Option = K \times N\left(-d_2\right) \times e^{-rT} - S_0 \times N\left(-d_1\right)$$

where:

$$d_1 = \frac{ln\left(\frac{S_0}{K}\right) + \left(r + 0.5\sigma^2\right) \times T}{\sigma\sqrt{T}}$$

$$d_2 = \frac{ln\left(\frac{S_0}{K}\right) + \left(r - 0.5\sigma^2\right) \times T}{\sigma\sqrt{T}}$$

$N(.)$: standard normal cumulative distribution function

$S_0 =$ present value of underlying

$K =$ strike price

$\sigma =$ volatility of the underlying

$T =$ term of the option

$r =$ risk-free rate

In our example, the inputs in the BSM formula are as shown in Exhibit 12.17.

In our example, the BSM formula resolves for a put option value of \$1,890,493. Assuming a CCR of 5.0%, the clawback value can be calculated as illustrated in Exhibit 12.18.

BSM Inputs	
$S0$ = Base revenue	\$ 3,000,000
K = Revenue threshold	\$ 4,000,000
r = Risk-free rate (RFR)	2.50%
SDV = Volatility of underlying	80%
T = Term to expiration	2

EXHIBIT 12.17   Clawback Valuation: BSM Inputs

[1] PV of put option	\$ 1,890,493	from BSM Formula
[2] Clawback percentage	20.00%	Contractual
[3] PV of clawback – risk-neutral framework	\$ 378,099	= [1] × [2]
[4] Premium factor	1.05127	= exp (2.50% × 2)
[5] Expected clawback cash flow	\$ 397,484	= [3] × [4]
[6] Discount factor	0.8447	= exp [–(5.00% + 2.50%) × 2.25]
[7] Value of clawback	\$ 335,763	= [5] × [6]

EXHIBIT 12.18   Clawback Valuation: Present Value of Clawback – At Fair Value

The steps of the clawback value calculation in Exhibit 12.18 are analogous to those described for the earnout value calculation in Exhibit 12.10 earlier in this chapter. In this case, we start from the present value of the option calculated using the BSM formula for a put option. The present value of the option is then multiplied by the clawback percentage (20% based on the purchase agreement) to calculate the present value of the clawback in a risk neutral framework in [3]. The PV of the clawback is then projected to the date in which the earnout reference revenue is crystallized using the RFR of 2.50% over the term of the option (two years). The resulting amount of $397,484 represents the expected future cash flows from the clawback, which will be paid on the settlement date 2.25 years from the valuation date. That amount is then discounted to present value, using a discount rate that includes the RFR of 2.5% and the (seller) counterparty risk rate, which is estimated at 5.0%, to obtain a fair value estimate of the value of the clawback of $335,763.

CONCLUSION

In this chapter, we have seen how option pricing theory, scenario analysis, and Monte Carlo Simulation can be used to value contingent consideration in one of the most challenging areas of early stage enterprise valuation. Here are some summary considerations as a result of our analysis:

- The valuation of contingent consideration should start from a careful review of the contractual provisions of the earnout/clawback as described in a company's purchase agreement. In particular, it is important to understand the payoff structure of the earnout, whether it is path-dependent, whether the earnout drivers are correlated and how any caps and floors factor into the payout. In most cases, the date of settlement is subsequent to the date in which the contingency is resolved, which will affect the time horizon of the earnout calculation. Also, there may be differences in the way a financial metric (for instance, revenue or net sales) is defined in the purchase agreement versus its GAAP definition.
- The discount rate for an earnout calculation may include a systematic component that reflects the sensitivity of the metric to market risk. In some cases, the WACC can be used as a proxy for the discount rate, but this is not always the case, particularly when the company has a high degree of fixed versus variable costs (operating leverage). In such cases, the volatility of the target metric (revenue/net sales) may be significantly lower than that of the free cash flows to the firm that are at the basis of the WACC calculation.
- The valuation of contingent consideration can be facilitated by breaking down the prediction analysis into smaller steps (decomposition) and by using aggregate industry information, such as the average length of time to receive regulatory approval from the FDA (cross check), to validate assumptions that rely significantly on judgment.
- Given the very high discount rates typically applied in earnout valuation, the period convention applied when discounting (full period or midperiod) may have a significant impact on valuation.
- Among the methods that are available for earnout valuation, scenario analysis is typically most suitable when the risk of the underlying metric is diversifiable (only RFR and CCR components are relevant), for instance, in a situation when the risk is driven by the achievement of a regulatory milestone. The OPM is generally used when the payoff structure of an earnout approximates that of an option or a combination of options in

the presence of caps and floors. In cases where there is path-dependency or statistically significant correlation among key variables in the model, a Monte Carlo Simulation is typically used. All of these methods fall under the income approach for fair value assessment. Given the nature of contingent consideration and the lack of an active trading market, the market approach is rarely used in valuing contingent consideration. The cost approach based on replacement cost is also typically not appropriate.

Finally, a note of warning: the reliability of the results of a Monte Carlo Simulation is strictly dependent on the quality of its inputs and assumptions. This method can be used to generate attractive summary statistics and graphs with the support of easily accessible software and powerful computer calculation tools, but ultimately it is critical for the analyst to make sure that the additional complexity of a Monte Carlo model is warranted in light of the specific characteristics of the earnout to be valued, and that the assumptions in the model are reasonable and consistent with management's estimates and other areas in the company's valuation. To the extent possible, a search for simplicity with a careful selection that highlights the key assumptions in the model and their probability distributions can help strengthen the robustness of the model and its predictive power.

References

This reference list includes a selection of the materials that we have consulted in our research for this book and that can be useful for further investigation. There is a vast literature on early stage valuation from a fair value perspective and this list is not meant to be comprehensive.

STANDARDS

Financial Accounting Standards Board, Accounting Standards Codification, Topic 350, *Intangibles – Goodwill and Other*. Available at: https://asc.fasb.org

Financial Accounting Standards Board, Accounting Standards Codification, Topic 718, *Compensation – Stock Compensation*. Available at: https://asc.fasb.org

Financial Accounting Standards Board, Accounting Standards Codification, Topic 805, *Business Combinations. Available* at: https://asc.fasb.org

Financial Accounting Standards Board, Accounting Standards Codification, Topic 820, *Fair Value Measurement*. Available at: https://asc.fasb.org

Financial Accounting Standards Board, Accounting Standards Codification, Topic 946, *Financial Services – Investment Companies*. Available at: https://asc.fasb.org

International Accounting Standards Board, International Financial Reporting Standards 13, *Fair Value Measurement*. Available at: https://www.iasplus.com

Public Company Accounting Oversight Board Auditing Standard 2501, *Auditing Accounting Estimates, including Fair Value Measurements*, July 2019. Available at: https://pcaobus.org

INDUSTRY GUIDANCE

Alternative Investment Management Association. AIMA's Guide to Sound Practices in the Valuation of Investments (latest edition: 2018).

American Institute of Certified Public Accountants. Accounting and Valuation Guide: Valuation of Portfolio Company Investments of Venture Capital and Private Equity Funds and Other Investment Companies (2019).

American Institute of Certified Public Accountants. Financial Instruments Performance Framework for the Certified in the Valuation of Financial Instruments Credential (2018).

American Institute of Certified Public Accountants. Guide: Prospective Financial Information (2017).

American Institute of Certified Public Accountants. Accounting and Valuation Guide: Valuation of Privately-Held Company Securities Issued as Compensation (2013).

American Institute of Certified Public Accountants. Statement on Standards for Valuation Services, VS Section 100: Valuation of a Business, Business Ownership Interest, Security or Intangible Asset (2007).

American Institute of Certified Public Accountants, Business Valuation Committee. Best Practices in Intangible Asset Valuation – Cost Approach Methods and Procedures (in progress).

American Institute of Certified Public Accountants. Accounting and Valuation Guide: Assets Acquired to Be Used in Research and Development Activities (2013).

American Institute of Certified Public Accountants. Financial Instruments Performance Framework for the Certified in the Valuation of Financial Instruments Credential (2018).

Appraisal Foundation. VFR Valuation Advisory #1: Identification of Contributory Assets and Calculation of Economic Rent (with Toolkit) (2010).

Appraisal Foundation. VFR Valuation Advisory #2: The Valuation of Customer-Related Assets. International Private Equity and Venture Capital Valuation Guidelines. (Latest edition: 2018).

Appraisal Foundation. VFR Valuation Advisory #4: Valuation of Contingent Consideration (2019).

Corporate and Intangibles Valuation Organization, LLC. Mandatory Performance Framework for the Certified in Entity and Intangible Valuations (CEIV) Credential and Application of the Mandatory Performance Framework for the CEIV Credential. (First edition: 2017).

Houlihan Lokey 2017 Purchase Price Allocation Study (2017).

Institutional Limited Partners Association (ILPA). Subscription Lines of Credit and Alignment of Interest (June 2017).

International Private Equity and Venture Capital Valuation Board. International Private Equity and Venture Capital Valuation Guidelines. (Latest edition: 2018).

International Valuation Standards Council. International Valuation Standards (2019).

National Venture Capital Association, Model Amended and Restated Certificate of Incorporation (January 2018).

National Venture Capital Association, Model Investor Rights Agreement (January 2018).

National Venture Capital Association, Model Management Rights Letter (June 2013).

National Venture Capital Association, Model Rights of First Refusal and Co-Sale Agreement (January 2018).

National Venture Capital Association, Model Stock Purchase Agreement (January 2018).

National Venture Capital Association, Model Term Sheet (January 2019).

National Venture Capital Association, Model Voting Rights Agreement (January 2018).

INDUSTRY REPORTS

Alternative Investment Management Association and Cayman Alternative Investment Summit. From Niche to Mainstream: Responsible Investment and Hedge Funds, 2018.

Angel Resource Institute. HALO Annual Report on Angel Investments. Angel Resource Institute: various years.

Biotechnology Innovation Organization, Clinical Development Success Rate 2006–2015. BIO: 2016.

Cambridge Associates LLC. US Venture Capital: Index and Selected Benchmark Statistics, various quarters.

Everett, Craig. 2019 Private Capital Markets Report. Pepperdine University: 2019.

Houlihan Lockey, 2017 Purchase Price Allocation Study.

National Venture Capital Association, The NVCA Yearbooks, various years.

PitchBook Data Inc. and National Venture Capital Association, PitchBook-NVCA Venture Capital Monitor, various quarters.

PitchBook Data Inc. PitchBook 2019 Unicorn Report, 2019.

PitchBook Data Inc. US VC Valuation Report, various periods.

PitchBook Data Inc. Venture Capital Outlook, various quarters.

Preqin. Private Capital Performance Update, various quarters.

Preqin and First Republic. Preqin and First Republic Update: U.S. Venture Capital in H1 2019.

Preqin and Vertex. Global Venture Capital Perspectives: A Preqin & Vertex Study, 2019.

Swiss Sustainable Finance, *Handbook on Sustainable Investments*. Swiss Sustainable Finance: 2017.

University of Oxford and Arabesque Partners: From the Stockholder to the Stakeholder: How Sustainability Can Drive Financial Outperformance, 2015.

U.S. SECURITIES AND EXCHANGE COMMISSION FILINGS

10X Genomics Inc. Amendment N.2 to Form S-1 Registration Statement under The Securities Act of 1933, Registration 333-233361, filed on September 10, 2019.

Cloudfare Inc. Amendment N.2 to Form S-1 Registration Statement under The Securities Act of 1933, Registration 333-233296, filed on September 11, 2019.

Crowdstrike Holdings Inc. Amendment N.2 to Form S-1 Registration Statement under The Securities Act of 1933, Registration 333-231461, filed on June 6, 2019.

Lyft Inc. Amendment N.2 to Form S-1 Registration Statement under The Securities Act of 1933, Registration 333-229996, filed on March 27, 2019.

Pinterest Inc. Amendment N.2 to Form S-1 Registration Statement under The Securities Act of 1933, Registration 333-230458, filed on April 8, 2019.

Slack Technologies Inc. Amendment N.3 to Form S-1 Registration Statement under The Securities Act of 1933, Registration 333-231041, filed on May 31, 2019.

Uber Technologies Inc. Amendment N.1 to Form S-1 Registration Statement under The Securities Act of 1933, Registration N. 333-230812 filed on April 26, 2019.

BOOKS, ARTICLES, AND WEBINAR TRANSCRIPTS

Amis, David, and Howard Stevenson. "Winning Angels: The Seven Fundamentals of Early Stage Investing." FT Press, 2001.

Aquinas, Thomas. *Summa Theologiae*. The Aquinas Institute ed. Emmaus Academic: 2012 (Latin and English translation).

Arzac, Enrique R. *Valuations for Merges, Buyouts and Retructurings*. Wiley, 2005.

Bagley, Consance, and Craig Dauchy. *The Entrepreneur's Guide to Law and Strategy*. Cengage Learning: 2018.

Baldwin, John W. "The Medieval Theories of the Just Price: Romanists, Canonists and Theologians in the Twelfth and Thirteenth Centuries." *Transactions of the American Philosophical Society* 49, no. 4 (1959): 8–40.

Beaton, Neil. *Valuing Early Stage and Venture-Backed Companies*. Wiley, 2010.

Beaton, Neil, Andreas Dal Santo, and Antonella Puca. "Calibration with OPM in Early Stage Enterprises: A Fair Value *Update*." *Business Valuation Update* 25 no. 3 (2019): 1–8.

Beaton, Neil, and James Herr. "Allocation of Enterprise Value Using the Option-Pricing Method: Treatment of Derivates on Common Stock." *Business Valuation Update*, October 2007. Also included in Beaton, Neil, *Valuing Early Stage and Venture-Backed Companies*. Wiley, 2010.

Beaton, Neil, Stillian Ghaidarov, and William Brigida. "Volatility in the Option-Pricing Model." *Valuation Strategies*, November 2009. Also included in Beaton, Neil, *Valuing Early Stage and Venture-Backed Companies*. Wiley, 2010.

Berkus, Dave. *After 20 Years: Updating the Berkus Method of Valuation*. Available at www.berkonomics.com

Black, Ervin L., and Mark Zyla. *Accounting for Goodwill and Other Intangible Assets*. Wiley, 2018.

Black, Fisher, and Myron Scholes. "The Pricing Options and Corporate Liabilities." *Journal of Political Economy* 81 (1973): 637–654.

Black, Keith, Donald Chambers, and Nelson Lacey. *Alternative Investments: A Primer for Investment Professionals*. CFA Institute Research Foundation and CAIA Association, 2018.

Burke, Brendan, and Darren Klees. "The Golden Mean of Corporate Venture Capital." 2Q 2019 *PitchBook Analyst Note*. PitchBook Data Inc., May 16, 2019.

Carson, Rich, and Jill Shaw. *Portfolio Benchmarking: Best Practices for Private Investments*. Cambridge Associates LLC, May 2018. Available at: www.cambridgeassociates.com

Carver, Lorenzo. *Venture Capital Valuation*. Wiley, 2011.

Catty, James P. "The First Chicago Method." Corporate Valuation Services Limited, 2008. Available at: http://corporatevaluation.ca/resources

CFA Institute. Comment Letter to European Financial Reporting Advisory Group on Equity Instruments – Research on Measurement questionnaire, dated July 29, 2019.

CFA Institute. *Environmental Markets: A New Asset Class.* CFA Institute, 2014.

CFA Institute. *Environmental, Social and Governance Factors at Listed Companies: A Manual for Investors.* CFA Institute, 2008.

CFA Institute. *Investor Uses, Expectations, and Concerns on Non-GAAP Financial Measures,* "Detailed Investor Perspectives on Specific NGFM Adjustments," pp. 37–59. CFA Institute, 2016.

Chandra, Shilpa, Andreas Dal Santo, and Antonella Puca. "Discounted Cash Flows Models in Early Stage Valuation." *Webinar Handbook, Business Valuation Resources.* LLC: October 2, 2019.

Chaplinsky, Susan, "Valuing the Early Stage Company." Darden Business Publishing UVA-F-1471, 2009.

Charnes, John. *Financial Modeling with Crystal Ball and Excel + Website.* Wiley, 2012.

Condra, Paul. "Slack in the Box: An Analysis of Slack's Competitive Positioning and Longer-Term Growth." *PitchBook 2Q 2019 Analyst Note.* PitchBook Data Inc., June 10, 2019.

Cox, John C., Stephen A. Ross, and Mark Rubinstein. "Option Pricing: A Simplified Approach." *Journal of Financial Economics* 7 (1979): 229–263.

Dal Santo, Andreas, and Antonella Puca. "The Valuation of Early-Stage Enterprises: A Fair Value Update." Webinar Handbook. Business Valuation Resources, LLC, December 18, 2018.

Dal Santo, Andreas, and Antonella Puca. "The Valuation of Private Debt Investments: A Fair Value Update." Webinar Handbook. Business Valuation Resources, LLC, February 12, 2019.

Dal Santo, Andreas, Antonella Puca, and Greg Siegel. "Effective ESG Investing: An Interview with Andrew Parry." *Enterprising Investor.* CFA Institute, June 15, 2018. Available at: https://blogs.cfainstitute.org/investor

Dal Santo, Andreas, Adam Kindreich, and Antonella Puca. "Valuation of Technology Companies: A Fair Value Update." Webinar Handbook. Business Valuation Resources, LLC, May 16, 2019.

Damoradan, Aswath. *The Dark Side of Valuation: Valuing Young, Distressed and Complex Businesses* 3rd ed. Wiley, 2018.

Damodaran, Aswath. "Valuing Young, Start-Up and Growth Companies: Estimation Issues and Valuation Challenges." *SSRN Electronic Journal,* June 2009.

Damodaran, Aswath. "The Dark Side of Valuation: Firms with No Earnings, No History and No Comparables. Can Amazon Be Valued?" *NYU Working Paper* No. FIN-99-022, March 2000.

Damodaran, Aswath. "The Small-Cap Premium: Where Is the Beef?" *Musings on Markets,* April 11, 2015.

Damodaran, Aswath, "User/Subscriber Economics: An Alternative View of Uber's Value." *June 28,* 2017. Available at: https://aswathdamodaran.blogspot.com/2017/06/usersubscriber-economics-alternative.html

Damodaran, Aswath, "Uber's Coming Out Party: Personal Mobility Pioneer or Car Service on Steroids?" April 15, 2019. Available at: https://aswathdamodaran.blogspot.com/2019/04/ubers-coming-out-party-personal.html

Davie, Alexander, and Casey W. Riggs. "Guide to Negotiating a Venture Capital Round, 2014–2017." Available at: https://www.strictlybusinesslawblog.com

DeCovny, Sherree. "Assessing Value in the Digital Economy." *Enterprising Investor,* CFA Institute, April 18, 2018. Available at https:/blog.cfainstitute.org/investor

Deloitte. "A Roadmap to Non-GAAP Financial Measures." 2019.

De Roover, Raymond. "The Concept of Just Price: Theory and Economic Policy." *Journal of Economic History* 18 (1958): 418–438.

Dhingra, Gautam, and Christopher Olson. "Franchise Quality Score: A Metric for Intangibles." *Enterprising Investor.* CFA Institute, August 27, 2018. Available at: https://blogs.cfainstitute.org/investor

DiMasi, Joseph A., Henry G. Grabowski, and Ronald W. Hansen. "Innovation in the Pharmaceutical Industry: New Estimates of R&D Costs." *Journal of Health Economics* **47** (2016): 20–33.

Di Natale, Nathan, and Mark Zyla. *Case Studies in Purchase Price Allocation*. Business Valuation Resources, LLC, 2016.

Dufendach, David and Jason A. Andrews, "Advanced Workshop on Monte Carlo Simulations", Workshop Handbook, Business Valuation Resources LLC: March 8, 2018.

Dufendach, David, Jason Andrews, John Savoyer and Tommy Tu, "Early Stage Companies: Mastering Valuation from Start-up to Success", Webinar Handbook, Business Valuation Resources, LLC. 2014.

Fabozzi, Frank. *Bond Markets, Analysis and Strategies* (9th ed.). Pearson, 2015.

Fabozzi, Frank, and Steven V. Mann. *Introduction to Fixed Income Analytics: Relative Value Analysis, Risk Measures and Valuation*. Wiley, 2010.

Fama, Eugene F., and Kenneth R. French. "A Five-Factor Asset Pricing Model." *CFA Digest* 45, no,. 4 (April 2015).

Feld, Brad, and Jason Mendelson. *Venture Deals: Be Smarter than Your Lawyer and Venture Capitalist*. Wiley, 2016.

Feng, Gu, and Baruch Lev. "Time to Change your Investment Model." *Financial Analyst Journal* 73, n. 4 (2017): 23–33.

Feng, Gu, and Baruch Lev. *The End of Accounting and the Path Forward for Investors and Managers*. Wiley, 2016.

Fernyhough, Wylie. "Sovereign Wealth Funds Overview." *3Q 2019 PitchBook Analyst Note*. PitchBook Data Inc., August 9, 2019.

Fisher, Irving. *The Theory of Interest*. Martino Fine Books: 2012 reprint of 1930 edition.

Fishman, Jay. *Standards of Value: Theory and Applications*. Wiley, 2013.

Frederick, Alex, and Jordan Beck. "Venture Capital in China." *PitchBook 1Q 2019 Analyst Note*. PitchBook Data Inc., March 18, 2019.

Frederick, Alex, and Zane Carmean. "The Emergence of Pre-Seed." *PitchBook 3Q 2019 Analyst Note*. Pitchbook Data Inc., September 13, 2019.

Friede, Gunnar, Timo Bush, and Alexander Bassen, "ESG and Financial Performance: Aggregate Evidence from More than 2000 Empirical Studies." *Journal of Sustainable Finance and Investment 5*, no. **4** (2015): 210–233.

Friedman, Milton. "The Social Responsibility of Business is to Increase its Profits." *New York Times Magazine*, September **13**, 1970.

Gornall, Will, and Ilya Strebulaev. "Squaring Venture Capital Valuations with Reality." *NBER Working Paper* No. w23895, 2017.

Hamada, Robert. "The Effect of the Firm's Capital Structure on the Systematic Risk of Common Stocks." *Journal of Finance* **27** (1972): 435–452.

Hartman, Harleigh. Fair Value: *The Meaning and Application of the Term "Fair Valuation" as Used by Utility Commissions*. Boston: Mifflin Company, 1920.

Hellman, Thomas, "A Note on Valuation of Venture Capital Deals." *Stanford Graduate School of Business*, E-95, 2001.

Hitchner, James. *Financial Valuation*. Wiley, 2011.

Hull, John. *Options, Futures, and Other Derivatives*. 10th ed. Pearson, 2017.

Hussain, Asad, and Jordan Beck. "Ridesharing Gears Up to Go Public: A Near $150 billion IPO Primer." *Pitchbook 1Q 2019 Analyst Note*. PitchBook Data Inc., February 26, 2019.

International Institute of Business Valuers. *The Black Scholes Option Model*. IIBV, 2018.

Kauppi, Dave. *Selling Your Software Company*, 2019.

Keeley, Robert H., Sanjeev Punjabi, and Lassaad Turki. "Valuation of Early-Stage Ventures: Option Valuation Models vs. Traditional Approaches." *Journal of Entrepreneurial and Small Business Finance* 5, no. 2 (1996): 115–138. Available at: https://digitalcommons.pepperdine.edu/jef/vol5/iss2/3

Keynes, John Maynard. "Alfred Marshall 1842–1924." *Economic Journal* 34 (1924): 311–372.

Kirshner, Julius, and Kimberly Lo Prete. "Olivi's Treatise on Contracts of Sale, Usury and Restitution. Minorite Economies or Minor Works?" *Quaderni Fiorentini per la Storia del Pensiero Giuridico Moderno* 13 (1984): 233–286.

Knaup, Amy E. "Survival and Longevity in the Business Employment Dynamics Data." *Monthly Labor Review*, May 2005: 50–56.

Knaup, Amy E., and Merissa C. Piazza. "Business Employment Dynamics Data: Survival and Longevity." *Monthly Labor Review*, September 2007: 3–10.

Kupor, Scott. *Secrets of Sand Hill Road.* Wiley: 2019.

Johnson, Robert. "Early-Stage Companies and Financing Valuations: The Venture Capital Method." *IESE Business School* IES375. April 2004 (revised March 2012).

Jordan, Jeff, Anu Hariharan, Frank Chen, and Preethu Kasireddy. "16 Startup Metrics." *August* 21, 2015. Available at: https://a16z.com/2015/08/21/16-metrics/

Jordan, Jeff, Anu Hariharan, and Frank Chen. "16 More Startup Metrics," *September* 23, 2015b. Available at: https://a16z.com/2015/09/23/16-more-metrics/

Laro, David, and Shannon Pratt. *Business Valuation and Federal Taxes: Procedure,* Law and Perspectives. Wiley, 2011.

Lee, Aileen. "Welcome to the Unicorn Club Learning from Billion Dollar Start-Ups." *TechCrunch, November* 2, 2013. Available at: www.techcrunch.com

Lerner, Josh. "A Note on Valuation in Private Equity Setting." *Harvard Business School,* 9-297-050, pp. 7–9, 2001.

Lipper, George. *"Is Valuation a Key Issue in Funding Startups?"* In *Valuing Pre-Revenue Companies, 11–13.* Ewing Marion Kauffman Foundation, 2007. https://angelcapitalassociation.org/data/Documents/Resources/AngelCapitalEducation/ACEF_-_Valuing_Pre-revenue_Companies.pdf

Long, Michael, and Thomas Bryant. *Valuing the Closely Held Firm.* Oxford University Press, 2008.

Lord, Hableton, and Christopher Mirabile. *Fundamentals of Angel Investing.* Wiley, 2016.

Lukas, Elmar, Jeffery Reuer, and Andreas Welling. "Earnouts in Merger and Acquisitions: A Game Theoretic Option Pricing Approach." *European Journal of Operational Research.* Elsevier, 2012.

Mard, Michael J., James R. Hitchner, and Steven D. Hyden. *Valuation for Financial Reporting.* Wiley, 2002.

Margolin, Brett A., and Samuel J. Kursh. "The Economics of Delaware Fair Value." *Delaware Journal of Corporate Law* (2005): 413–435.

Marshall, Alfred. *Industry and Trade.* University Press of the Pacific, 2003.

Marshall, Alfred. *Principles of Economics.* Digireads.com, 2012.

Marshall, Alfred. "Review of Jevons' Theory of Political Economy." In *Memorials of Alfred Marshall,* edited by Arthur Cecil Pigou, pp. 93–99. Macmillan: London, 1925.

Matthews, Gilbert E. "Statutory Fair Value in Dissenting Shareholder Cases: Part I." *Business Valuation Review* (2017): 15–31.

McKeon, Jessica. "Long-Term Trends in Non-GAAP Disclosures: A Three-Year Overview." Audit Analytics: October 10, 2018. Available at: https://blogs.auditanalytics.com

McKinsey & Company, Tim Koller, Marc Goedhart, and David Wessels. *Valuation: Measuring and Managing the Value of Companies* 6th ed. Wiley, 2015.

Mellen, Chris M. *Valuation for M&A: Building and Measuring Private Company Value.* Wiley, 2018.

Merton, Robert C. "Theory of Rational Option Pricing." *Bell Journal of Economics and Management Science* 4 (1973): 141–183.

Merton, Robert. "On the Pricing of Corporate Debt: The Risk Structure of Interest Rates." *Journal of Finance* 29, no. 2 (1974): 449–470.

Metrick, Andrew, and Ayako Yasuda. *Venture Capital and the Finance of Innovation* 2nd ed. Wiley, 2011.

Metrick, Andrew, and Ayako Yasuda. *Venture Capital and Other Private Equity: A Survey.* NBER Working Paper No. 16652, 2010.

Metropolis, Nicholas, and Stanley Ulman. "The Monte Carlo Method." *Journal of the American Statistical Association* **44**, no. 247 (September 1949): 335–341.

Mooradian, Peter, Andrea Auerbach, Caryn Slotsky, and Jacob Gilfix. *Growth Equity: Turns Out it is all about the Growth*. Cambridge Associates LLC, January 2019. Available at: www .cambridgeassociates.com

Murphy, Maria and Mark O' Smith, "How to Audit Fair Value Measurements: A New Framework for Valuation Professionals Can Help Practitioners in this Challenging Area," Journal of Accountancy, 224 (2017): 32.

Nesbitt, Stephen. Private Debt: Opportunities in Corporate Direct Lending. Wiley: 2019.

Norton, Rorie A. "Distorting Alpha: How Fund Management Practices Affect IRR Figures." *Private Equity Law Report*, September 10, 2019 (Part I), September 17, 2019 (Part II), September 24, 2019 (Part III).

Orbe, William Q., and Scott C. Budlong. "An Examination of Exit Rights for Hedge Funds Making Non-Controlling Private Equity Investments." *Hedge Fund Law Report, July* **18**, 2013.

Orbe, William Q., Thao H.V. Do, and Catherine Rossow, "Convertible Preferred Stock: How Preferred Is It." *Hedge Fund Law Report*, Part One: December 19, 2013, Part Two: January 9, 2014.

Pakes, Ariel. "Patents as Options: Some Estimates of the Value of Holding European Patent Stocks." *Econometrica* **54** (1986): 755–784.

Parr, Russell. *Intellectual Property: Valuation, Exploitation and Infringement Damages.*

Payne, William. "The Definitive Guide to Raising Money from Angels." Payne: 2006 (revised 2011).

Payne, William. "Payne Scorecard Valuation Methodology." *The Gust Blog. October* **19**, 2011.

Payne, William. "The Risk Factor Summation Model." *The Gust Blog. September* **14**, 2011.

Pearl, Joshua, and Joshua Rosenbaum. *Investment Banking*. Wiley, 2018.

Pellegrino, Michael. *BVR Guide to Intellectual Property Valuation* (2nd ed.). Business Valuation Resources, LLC, 2012.

Peters, Sandy. "Berkshire's Bottom Line: More Relevant than Ever Before." *Market Integrity Insights,* CFA Institute: December **21**, 2018. Available at: www.blogs.cfainstitute.org/marketintegrity

Pinto, Jerald, Elaine Henry, Thomas Robinson, and John Stowe. "Free Cash Flows Valuation." In *Equity*, CFA Program Curriculum 2017 Level II vol. 4, pp. 267–332. CFA Institute, 2014.

Pinto, Jerald, Elaine Henry, Thomas Robinson, and John Stowe. *Equity Asset Valuation Workbook* (3rd ed.). CFA Institute, 2015.

Poovery, Mary. "Can Numbers Ensure Honesty? Unrealistic Expectations and the U.S. Accounting Scandal." *Notices of the American Mathematical Society*, January 2003, pp. 27–35.

Pratt, Shannon, and Roger J. Grabowski. *Cost of Capital: Applications and Examples 4th ed*. Wiley, 2014.

PricewaterhouseCoopers LLP. Fair Value Measurements: Global Edition (2015).

Puca, Antonella. "Growing Trends in Private Equity: Secondary Market Investing." *Enterprising Investor*. CFA Institute, May 10, 2018. Available at: www.blog.cfainstitute.org/investor. Interview with Brett Hickey, *Star Mountain Capital LLC.*

Puca, Antonella. "Metriche di Performance per gli Investimenti ESG." Chapter 4 of *Investimenti ESG.* CFA Society Italy and AP Advisor Private, September 2018, pp. 50–61.

Puca, Antonella. "Private Equity e Venture Capital." Chapter 2 of *Alternative Investments: Le principali tipologie*. CFA Society Italy and AP Advisor Private, 2019, pp. 40–77.

Puca, Antonella. "Private Equity Funds: Leverage and Performance Evaluation." *Enterprising Investor*. CFA Institute, July 16, 2018. Available at: www.blogs.cfainstitute.org/investor

Puca, Antonella. "Investing for Retirement: Beware the Unicorn IPO Stampede." *Enterprising Investor*. CFA Institute, March 26, 2019; Available at: www.blogs.cfainstitute.org/investor

Puca, Antonella, and Mark Zyla. "The Intangible Valuation Renaissance: Five Methods." *Enterprising Investor*. CFA Institute, January 11, 2019. Available at: www.blogs.cfainstitute.org/investor

Puca, Antonella, and Mark Zyla. "Valuing Intangible Assets under the Mandatory Performance Framework: A Fair Value Update." *Business Valuation Review* 38, Winter (2019): 103–116.

Ramsinghani, Mahendra. *The Business of Venture Capital: Insights from Leading Practitioners on the Art of Raising a Fund, Deal Structuring, Value Creation and Exit Strategies*. Wiley, 2014.

Rath, Raymond. "Advancing the Quality of Valuations." *Business Valuation Review* vol. 36 n. 2 (2017): 48–53.

Rath, Raymond. "Private Company Valuation." *Equity*, CFA Program Curriculum 2017 Level II vol. 4, pp. 517:568. CFA Institute, 2014.

Razgaitis, Richard. *Dealmaking Using Real Options and Monte Carlo Analysis*. Wiley, 2003.

Razgaitis, Richard. *Valuation and Dealmaking of Technology Based Intellectual Property*. Wiley, 2009.

Reilly, Robert. "What Lawyers Need to Know about the Asset-Based Approach to Business Valuation." *The Practical Lawyer* Part I, April 2017: 40–64; Part 2, *June* **2017**: 49–52.

Reilly, Robert. "Applying the Asset-Based Approach? How to Value the Intangibles in a Business or Professional Practice." *Webinar Handbook, Business Valuation Resources*. LLC, November 2, 2017.

Reilly, Robert. "Valuing Intangible Assets: Cost Approach Methods and Procedures." *Journal of Multistate Taxation and Incentives*, August 2012.

Reilly, Robert. "Cost Approach Procedures in the Intangible Asset Appraisal." *Business Appraisal Practice*, Q3 2012.

Reilly, Robert. "Challenges in Measuring the Fair Value of Intangible Assets." *Webinar Handbook*. Business Valuation Resources, LLC, March 4, 2014.

Reilly, Robert. "The Asset-Based Business Valuation Approach: Advanced Applications" (Part 1). *Practical Tax Strategies*, July 2018: 4–15.

Reilly, Robert, and Robert P. Schweihs. *Guide to Intangible Assets Valuation*. AICPA and Wiley, 2014.

Reinfeld, Patrick. "Start-Up Valuation: Solving the Valuation Puzzle of New Business Ventures." Master's thesis, HEC Paris, 2018. http://www.vernimmen.net/ftp/Start_up_Valuation_Reinfeld_vF.pdf

Rose, David. *Angel Investing: The Gust Guide to Making Money and Having Fun Investing in Startups*. Wiley, 2018.

Sahlman, William. "A Method For Valuing High-Risk, Long-Term Investments; the 'Venture Capital Method.'" Harvard Business School 9-288-006. Revised October 1, 2009.

Sohl, Jeffrey. "The Angel Market in 2018: More Angels Investing in More Deals at Lower Valuations." Center for Venture Research, May 9, 2019.

Stanfill, Cameron. "The Only Time Slacking Off Could Pay Off." *PitchBook 2Q 2019 Analyst Note*. PitchBook Data Inc., April 30, 2019.

Stanfill, Cameron, and Jordan Beck. "Searching for Validation." *PitchBook 1Q 2019 Analyst Note*. PitchBook Data Inc., March 21, 2019.

Stanfill, Cameron, and Bryan Hanson. "VC Returns by Series: Part I." *PitchBook 3Q 2019 Analyst Note*. PitchBook Data Inc., September 27, 2019.

Stanford, Kyle. "Alternative Sources of Funding for Startups." *PitchBook 1Q 2020 Analyst Note*. PitchBook Data Inc., February 11, 2020.

Stanford, Kyle, and Darren Klees. "Venture Debt Overview." *PitchBook 4Q 2019 Analyst Note*. PitchBook Data Inc., October 11, 2019.

Stanford, Kyle and Van Le. "Non-traditional Investors in VC are Here to Stay," PitchBook 4Q 2019 Analyst Note. PitchBook Data Inc., December 6, 2019.

Stanford, Kyle and Van Le. "The Vision Fund's Only Competitor is Itself," PitchBook Q2 2020 Analyst Note, PitchBook Data Inc.: April 6, 2020.

Todeschini, Giacomo ed. Un trattato di economia politica francescana: Il De emptionibus et venditionibus, de usuris, de restitutionibus di Piero di Giovanni Olivi. Istituto Storico Italiano per il Medio Evo, Roma: 1980.

Trugman, Gary. *Understanding Business Valuation: A Practical Guide to Valuing Small and Medium Sized Businesses*. AICPA, 2017.

U.S. Securities and Exchange Commission. "Be Cautious of SAFEs in Crowdfunding." *Investor Bulletin*, May 9, 2017. Available at www.investor.gov.

Usvyatsky, Olga. "Pros and Cons of Using Non-GAAP Metrics for Executive Compensation, Including ESG Considerations." *June* 11, 2019. Available at https://blog.auditanalytics.com/category/non-gaap/

Villalabos, Luis. *Valuation Divergence. Kauffman EVenturing*: 2007, pp. 21–22.

Wiltbank, Robert, and Warren Boeker. "Returns to Angel Investors in Groups." *SSRN Electronic Journal*, November 14, 2007. https://doi.org/10.2139/ssrn.1028592

Y Combinator. "Quick Start Guide [to SAFEs]." Available at: www.ycombinator.com

Zyla, Mark. Accounting for Goodwill and Other Intangible Assets. Wiley: 2019.

Zyla, Mark. *Fair Value Measurement*. 3rd ed. Wiley, 2020.

Zyla, Mark. "Social Media: Who Owns It and What Is It Worth?" Webinar Handbook, BVR, February 23, 2017.

Index

Printed and bound by CPI Group (UK) Ltd, Croydon, CR0 4YY

16/04/2025

14658374-0001